THE CAMBRIDGE COMPANION TO N

Narrative theory is essential to everything from
novels to the latest Hollywood blockbuster. Na
stories work and how we make them work. This Companion is both an introduction and a contribution to the field. It presents narrative theory as an
approach to understanding all kinds of cultural production: from literary texts
to historiography, from film and videogames to philosophical discourse. It takes
the long historical view, outlines essential concepts, and reflects on the way
narrative forms connect with and rework social forms. The volume analyzes
central premises, identifies narrative theory's feminist foundations, and elaborates its significance to queer theory and issues of race. The specially commis-
sioned essays are exciting to read, uniting accessibility and rigor, traditional
concerns with a renovated sense of the field as a whole, and analytical clarity
with stylistic dash. Topical and substantial, *The Cambridge Companion to
Narrative Theory* is an engaging resource on a key contemporary concept.

Matthew Garrett is Associate Professor of English and American Studies at
Wesleyan University, where he directs the Certificate in Social, Cultural, and
Critical Theory. He is the author of *Episodic Poetics: Politics and Literary Form
after the Constitution* (2014) as well as essays in *American Literary History,
American Quarterly, Critical Inquiry, ELH,* the *Journal of Cultural Economy,*
and *Radical History Review,* among other journals.

A complete list of books in the series is at the back of this book.

THE CAMBRIDGE COMPANION TO

NARRATIVE THEORY

EDITED BY

MATTHEW GARRETT

Wesleyan University

CAMBRIDGE
UNIVERSITY PRESS

CAMBRIDGE
UNIVERSITY PRESS

University Printing House, Cambridge CB2 8BS, United Kingdom

One Liberty Plaza, 20th Floor, New York, NY 10006, USA

477 Williamstown Road, Port Melbourne, VIC 3207, Australia

314-321, 3rd Floor, Plot 3, Splendor Forum, Jasola District Centre, New Delhi - 110025, India

79 Anson Road, #06-04/06, Singapore 079906

Cambridge University Press is part of the University of Cambridge.

It furthers the University's mission by disseminating knowledge in the pursuit of education, learning and research at the highest international levels of excellence.

www.cambridge.org
Information on this title: www.cambridge.org/9781108428477
DOI: 10.1017/9781108639149

First published 2018

A catalogue record for this publication is available from the British Library

Library of Congress Cataloging in Publication data
NAMES: Garrett, Matthew editor.
TITLE: The Cambridge companion to narrative theory / edited by Matthew Garrett, Wesleyan University.
DESCRIPTION: Cambridge ; New York : Cambridge University Press, [2018] | Includes bibliographical references and index.
IDENTIFIERS: LCCN 2017061452| ISBN 9781108428477 (hardcover) | ISBN 9781108449724 (softcover)
SUBJECTS: LCSH: Narration (Rhetoric)
CLASSIFICATION: LCC PN212 .C365 2018 | DDC 808–dc23
LC record available at https://lccn.loc.gov/2017061452

ISBN 978-1-108-42847-7 Hardback
ISBN 978-1-108-44972-4 Paperback

For Alex Woloch

CONTENTS

CONTENTS

FIGURES AND TABLE

Figures

Table

CONTRIBUTORS

MARGARET COHEN is Andrew B. Hammond Professor of French Language, Literature, and Civilization and Professor of English at Stanford University. Her book *The Novel and the Sea* (2010) was awarded the Louis R. Gottschalk Prize from the American Society for Eighteenth-Century Studies and the George and Barbara Perkins Prize from the International Society for the Study of the Narrative. She is also the author of *Profane Illumination: Walter Benjamin and the Paris of Surrealist Revolution* (1993) and *The Sentimental Education of the Novel* (1999), which received the Modern Language Association's Aldo and Jeanne Scaglione Prize in French and Francophone literature. She has coedited two collections of scholarship on the European novel: *The Literary Channel: The Inter-National Invention of the Novel* (2002), with Carolyn Dever, and *Spectacles of Realism: Body, Gender, Genre* (1995), with Christopher Prendergast. Cohen has edited and translated Sophie Cottin's best-selling novel of 1799, *Claire d'Albe* (2003), and has also edited a critical edition of Gustave Flaubert's *Madame Bovary* (2004). She is currently completing a book showing how the modern imagination of the ocean depths has been shaped by science and technology that enables people to view a hitherto inaccessible realm and to represent oceanic conditions on land.

JONATHAN CULLER is the Class of 1916 Professor of English at Cornell University. His *Structuralist Poetics: Structuralism, Linguistics, and the Study of Literature* (1975) won the Lowell Prize of the Modern Language Association and established his reputation as analyst and expositor of critical theory. Now known especially for *On Deconstruction* (1982) and *Literary Theory: A Very Short Introduction* (1997), which has been translated into some 26 languages, he has most recently published *Theory of the Lyric* (2015). Culler has been president of the American Comparative Literature Association and was elected to the American Academy of Arts and Sciences in 2001 and to the American Philosophical Society in 2006.

MARK CURRIE is Professor of Contemporary Literature at Queen Mary University of London. He is the author of *Metafiction* (1995), *Postmodern Narrative Theory* (1998), *Difference* (2004), *The Invention of Deconstruction* (2013), *About Time*

(2007), and *The Unexpected* (2013). He is currently writing a book entitled *Absolute Uncertainty*, which aims to explore concepts of uncertainty in the physical and social sciences in relation to questions about novelty and value in literature.

HANNAH FREED-THALL is Assistant Professor of French Literature, Thought and Culture at New York University. She is the author of *Spoiled Distinctions: Aesthetics and the Ordinary in French Modernism* (2015), which was awarded the Aldo and Jeanne Scaglione Prize for French and Francophone Studies and the Modernist Studies Association Prize for a First Book.

JOHN FROW is Professor of English at the University of Sydney. He works at the boundary between literary studies and cultural studies, and his books include *Marxism and Literary History* (1986), *Cultural Studies and Cultural Value* (1995), *Time and Commodity Culture* (1997), *Accounting for Tastes: Australian Everyday Cultures* (with Tony Bennett and Mike Emmison, 1999), *Genre* (2006, revised 2015), *The Practice of Value* (2013), and *Character and Person* (2014). His latest book, *On Interpretive Conflict*, is forthcoming from the University of Chicago Press.

MATTHEW GARRETT is Associate Professor of English and American Studies at Wesleyan University, where he directs the Certificate in Social, Cultural, and Critical Theory. He is the author of *Episodic Poetics: Politics and Literary Form after the Constitution* (2014) as well as essays in *American Literary History*, *American Quarterly*, *Critical Inquiry*, *ELH*, the *Journal of Cultural Economy*, and *Radical History Review*, among other journals.

PATRICK JAGODA is Associate Professor of English and Cinema and Media Studies at the University of Chicago. He is the author of *Network Aesthetics* (2016) and, with Michael Maizels, *The Game Worlds of Jason Rohrer* (2016), as well as coeditor of special issues of *Critical Inquiry* ("Comics & Media," with Hillary Chute, in 2014) and *American Literature* ("New Media and American Literature," with Wendy Chun and Tara McPherson, in 2013). Jagoda is the cofounder of the Game Changer Chicago Design Lab and a coeditor of *Critical Inquiry*.

ILYA KALININ is Associate Professor in the Department of Liberal Arts and Sciences at Saint Petersburg State University and at the National Research University Higher School of Economics. His research focuses on Russian Formalism and early Soviet Russian intellectual and cultural history. He is editor in chief of the Moscow-based intellectual journal *Emergency Rations: Debates on Politics and Culture* (*Neprikosnovennyj Zapas: Debaty o politike i culture*), and his book, *History as Art of Articulation: Russian Formalists and Revolution*, is forthcoming from New Literary Observer Publishing House (Moscow).

DAVID KURNICK is Associate Professor of English at Rutgers University, where he teaches the nineteenth- and twentieth-century novel. He is the author of *Empty Houses: Theatrical Failure and the Novel* (2012) and translator of Julio Cortázar's 1975 novella *Fantomas versus the Multinational Vampires* (2014).

YOON SUN LEE is Professor of English at Wellesley College and the author of *Modern Minority: Asian American Literature and Everyday Life* (2013), *Nationalism and Irony: Burke, Scott, Carlyle* (2004), and numerous articles. She is currently working on a study of plot, experience, and experiment in the English realist novel.

KENT PUCKETT is Professor of English at the University of California, Berkeley. He is the author of *Bad Form: Social Mistakes and the Novel* (2008); *Narrative Theory: A Critical Introduction* (2016); *War Pictures: Cinema, Violence, and Style in Britain, 1939–1945* (2017); and, with Derek Nystrom, *Against Bosses, Against Oligarchies: A Conversation with Richard Rorty* (1998).

VALERIE ROHY is Professor of English at the University of Vermont. She is the author of *Lost Causes: Narrative, Etiology, and Queer Theory* (2015), *Anachronism and Its Others: Sexuality, Race, Temporality* (2009), and *Impossible Women: Lesbian Figures and American Literature* (2000), as well as coeditor, with Elizabeth Ammons, of *American Local Color Writing, 1880–1920* (1998).

JUDITH ROOF is Professor and William Shakespeare Chair in English at Rice University. She is the author of many books, including *The Comic Event: Comedic Performance from the 1950s to the Present* (2018); *What Gender Is, What Gender Does* (2016); *The Poetics of DNA* (2007); *All about Thelma and Eve: Side-Kicks and Third Wheels* (2002); *Reproductions of Reproduction: Imaging Symbolic Change* (1996); *Come as You Are: Narrative and Sexuality* (1996), which was awarded the George and Barbara Perkins Prize from the International Society for the Study of the Narrative; and *A Lure of Knowledge: Lesbian Sexuality and Theory* (1991).

GARRETT STEWART is the James O. Freedman Professor of Letters at the University of Iowa. Stewart is the author of many books, including *Framed Time: Toward a Postfilmic Cinema* (2007); *Novel Violence: A Narratography of Victorian Fiction* (2009), which was awarded the Perkins Prize from the International Society for the Study of Narrative; *Bookwork: Medium to Object to Concept to Art* (2011); *Closed Circuits: Screening Narrative Surveillance* (2015); *The Deed of Reading: Literature • Writing • Language • Philosophy* (2015); and *Transmedium: Conceptualism 2.0 and the New Object Art* (2017). Stewart was elected in 2010 to the American Academy of Arts and Sciences.

AMY C. TANG is Associate Professor of American Studies and English at Wesleyan University. She is the author of *Repetition and Race: Asian American Literature after Multiculturalism* (2016) and is currently working on a project that explores posthuman aesthetics in Asian American literature.

DAVID WITTENBERG is Associate Professor of English, Comparative Literature, and Cinematic Arts at the University of Iowa. He is the author of *Time Travel: The Popular Philosophy of Narrative* (2013) and *Philosophy, Revision, Critique: Rereading Practices in Heidegger, Nietzsche, and Emerson* (2001), and the coeditor of *Scale in Literature and Culture* (2017). Currently he is writing a book about the meaning of very large objects, tentatively entitled "Big Culture: Toward an Aesthetics of Magnitude."

ACKNOWLEDGMENTS

Many thanks to Ray Ryan at Cambridge University Press for the invitation to edit this volume, for his enthusiasm and intelligence throughout, and for enabling me to assemble an extraordinary group of contributors. Thanks, especially, to those contributors for the seriousness and savvy with which they approached their essays. Jim Phelan's criticisms and suggestions at the earliest stage helped me understand how a project like this one could work, and they made the book better. Joseph Fitzpatrick, Ruth Nisse, Joe Shapiro, Amy Tang, and above all Margot Weiss have been generous with their counsel. Greatest thanks to the students in my narrative theory seminars at Wesleyan University over the years, and in particular to the members of the spring 2017 seminar in the Wesleyan Center for Prison Education at Cheshire Correctional Institution, who helped me think (and think again) about the book's form and purpose in its final stage, and about the limits and the promise of narrative theory.

One Hundred Works of Twentieth-Century Narrative Theory

Dates are for publication in original language (of volume 1 for multivolume works); titles are given in English for translated works.

1899   Sigmund Freud, *The Interpretation of Dreams*
1905   Sigmund Freud, *Three Essays on the Theory of Sexuality*
1907   Henry James, New York Edition
1915   Ferdinand de Saussure, *Course in General Linguistics*
1916   Georg Lukács, *The Theory of the Novel*
1920   Sigmund Freud, *Beyond the Pleasure Principle*
1923   Georg Lukács, *History and Class Consciousness*
1925   Viktor Shklovsky, *Theory of Prose* (expanded edition, 1929)
1926   Boris Eichenbaum, "The Theory of the Formal Method"
1927   E. M. Forster, *Aspects of the Novel*
1928   Vladimir Propp, *Morphology of the Folktale*
1928   Mikhail Bakhtin/P. N. Medvedev, *The Formal Method in Literary Scholarship*
1929   Virginia Woolf, *A Room of One's Own*
1929   Mikhail Bakhtin, *Problems in Dostoevsky's Poetics*
1929   V. N. Voloshinov, *Marxism and the Philosophy of Language*
1929   André Jolles, *Simple Forms*
1936   Georg Lukács, "Narrate or Describe?"
1943   Louis Hjelmslev, *Prolegomena to a Theory of Language*
1946   Erich Auerbach, *Mimesis*
1949   Simone de Beauvoir, *The Second Sex*
1949   Sergei Eisenstein, *Film Form*
1952   Founding of the journal *Screen*
1955   Georg Lukács, *The Historical Novel*
1955   Claude Lévi-Strauss, *Tristes tropiques*

1976   Leo Bersani, *A Future for Astyanax*
1977   Luce Irigaray, *This Sex Which Is Not One*
1978   Dorrit Cohn, *Transparent Minds*
1978   Seymour Chatman, *Story and Discourse*
1979   Founding of the journal *Poetics Today*
1979   Paul de Man, *Allegories of Reading*
1981   Fredric Jameson, *The Political Unconscious*
1981   D. A. Miller, *Narrative and Its Discontents*
1982   Ann Banfield, *Unspeakable Sentences*
1982   Jonathan Culler, *On Deconstruction*
1982   Founding of *Subaltern Studies*
1983   Franco Moretti, *Signs Taken for Wonders*
1983   Paul Ricoeur, *Time and Narrative*
1984   Peter Brooks, *Reading for the Plot*
1984   Teresa de Lauretis, *Alice Doesn't*
1984   Janice Radway, *Reading the Romance*
1985   Mieke Bal, *Narratology*
1985   Eve Kosofsky Sedgwick, *Between Men*
1986   Leo Bersani, *The Freudian Body*
1986   Susan S. Lanser, "Toward a Feminist Narratology"
1986   Franco Moretti, *The Way of the World*
1987   Gloria Anzaldúa, *Borderlands/La Frontera*
1987   Nancy Armstrong, *Desire and Domestic Fiction*
1988   Henry Louis Gates, Jr., *The Signifying Monkey*
1988   D. A. Miller, *The Novel and the Police*
1989   James Phelan, *Reading People, Reading Plots*
1990   Rámon Saldívar, *Chicano Narrative*
1990   Garrett Stewart, *Reading Voices*
1991   Marie-Laure Ryan, *Possible Worlds, Artificial Intelligence, and Narrative Theory*
1993   Founding of the journal *Narrative*
1993   Ann duCille, *The Coupling Convention*
1994   Homi K. Bhabha, *The Location of Culture*
1996   Monika Fludernik, *Towards a "Natural" Narratology*
1996   Lisa Lowe, *Immigrant Acts*
1996   Judith Roof, *Come as You Are*
1997   Saidiya V. Hartman, *Scenes of Subjection*
1998   Susan Stanford Friedman, *Mappings*
2000   Marie-Laure Ryan, *Narrative as Virtual Reality*

MATTHEW GARRETT

Introduction

A book like this one should be companionable, and *The Cambridge Companion to Narrative Theory* wishes to be a true friend to the reader: in many ways a guide or introduction, yes, but also a challenge. Trustworthy but engaging. Dog and cat combined, let's say. If these essays inspire the reader to write, we will have done our job, which is to produce and also to stimulate exciting writing about narrative. For all along narrative theory – that is, the theory of how stories work and of how we make them work – has been a practice of critical writing. Its technical achievement in establishing a whole language for understanding stories is clear enough, and that achievement makes narrative theory essential to every aspect of the human sciences (and indeed to science itself, precisely at the point at which we begin to *make sense* of what we study, to give narrative shape to the non- or pre-narrative yield of research). But if we need a narrative *theory* because we really cannot help but *live* in narrative, then our theory, like life itself, deserves the pleasure and the challenge of a writing that takes the telling as seriously as the tale.

So *The Cambridge Companion to Narrative Theory* does not approach its topic as an academic discipline exactly, but rather as a critical practice of writing that cuts across – and therefore also unites – a number of different fields. If the contributors here are fundamentally literary critics more than anything else (despite, or maybe because of, the range of their work), then this is in part because narrative theory remains fastened, for better or for worse, to the literary text. But it is also because literary criticism is among the most promiscuous and eclectic of disciplines, and literary critics have tended to be especially attuned to both the texture and the infrastructure of stories across media, forms, and formats – as these essays attest, in their reach from, say, novel theory to lyric, from videogames to surveillance cameras.

Nor will the reader find here a technician's handbook. Indeed, the word "narratology" itself is mostly absent, at least as an organizing term, and it therefore may be worth stating explicitly that this volume conceives of narrative theory less as a scientific method than as a varied set of techniques –

the authors here might even say the best techniques – for dialectically approaching the relationship between stories and their social and historical ground.[1] As a result, the reader will find narrative theory in some unexpected places, a narrative theory that eagerly courts the messiness of the countless narratives of the world. And the reader will find a narrative theory that attends to the moments when systems break down and when the smooth functioning of a narrative or narrative-theoretical apparatus jams.

Our attraction to such moments is not an allergy to system-building or totalizing thinking (although not all chapters share their editor's enthusiasm for both); on the contrary, the essays assembled here produce or imply ambitious systemic thought. Indeed, *The Cambridge Companion to Narrative Theory* sees narrative itself as a constant and active process of building up and breaking down structures and order: in these essays, narrative is best conceived, following Roland Barthes, as a *structuration* rather than a structure.[2]

This book's order, its structuration, is part of its argument. Part I, "Foundations," articulates the stakes of narrative theory as a *critical* theory, expanding its intellectual range and historical imagination. Gathering up the lessons of this first section, Part II, on "Motifs," turns inward to the smaller scale of concentration on three concepts – character, time, and pleasure – as threshold categories that mark the dialectical relationship between what appear to be the inside and the outside of narratives. Part III, "Coordinates," is the site of narrative theorizing, bringing together questions of form and history. Literary historians have long understood genre to be the meeting of form and history; Part III verifies and revises this lesson, arguing that race and sexuality are perhaps even more significant locations for grasping the way narrative forms connect with and rework social forms.

The volume's program is announced in Part I in Kent Puckett's treatment of key figures in what might be called the prehistory of narrative theory but which we prefer to consider simply part of its history understood at the scale of the long duration. Aristotle, Hegel, Marx, Nietzsche, and Freud, among others, are taken by Puckett to be preeminently concerned with the relationship between story and discourse – between, that is, *what* stories tell and *how* they are told. One virtue of this opening chapter is that it suitably miniaturizes the achievements of narrative theory since its proper emergence in the 1960s, even if this is the period of codification and cross-disciplinary formation.[3] But another, positive virtue is at least as important: namely, a generous opening of the house of narrative theory, a letting-in of air and history, so that students and scholars alike can approach reading and writing about narratives with a more capacious and dialectical imagination than the oxygen-depleting terms "narratology" and "narrative theory" too often invite.

From a question of historical scope, Chapter 2 turns to questions of narrative scale, in Yoon Sun Lee's significant reflections on the perennial matter of the part and the whole. Lee's essay is, among other things, an ambitious synthesis of several high points of what is often somewhat curiously called "classical" narrative theory, from Russian Formalism to structuralism, reaching to more recent considerations on description, explanation, interpretation, and narrative scale. In our time, when questions of scale have returned with force through digital methods for studying narratives en masse (in addition to more intrinsic methodological developments), Lee's essay opens a path for further critical practice, not least by showing how formative the question of scale has been.

Chapter 3 turns from questions of the scale of the whole to ways of thinking about plot as a matter of the body. Ilya Kalinin's bold reading of Viktor Shklovsky's foundational work on the conceptualization and analysis of plot dwells on the great critic's engagement with the embodied performing arts: dance, circus acts, cinema, folk buffoonery, and avant-garde theater. Kalinin presents Shklovsky's narrative theory in a freshly utopian (and newly political) light, showing how plot itself may be understood as a kind of physical labor, both dependent on and transcendent of the everyday reflexes of body and mind alike.

In Chapter 4, Hannah Freed-Thall takes two classic works of narrative theory, Roland Barthes's *S/Z* and Gérard Genette's *Narrative Discourse*, as the occasion for rethinking the whole practice of reading for narrative structure, seeing in Barthes and Genette superlative performances that set the standard for the "adventure" of critical reading itself. Freed-Thall installs Barthes and Genette in their roles as major orientation points for *The Cambridge Companion to Narrative Theory*. Indeed, *S/Z* and *Narrative Discourse* are cited more than any other texts in this volume, and the reader will notice how varying their importance is for each of the critics who works with them. Our hope is that this return to touchstone texts will reopen the reader's sense of what is possible in the analysis of narratives, as an insistence upon that "freedom," as Barthes put it, of *rereading*. Those "who fail to reread are," as he wrote, "obliged to read the same story everywhere."[4]

Critical rereading nevertheless turns out, in the bright light of Judith Roof's intervention on "The Feminist Foundations of Narrative Theory" (Chapter 5), to be determined again and again by the patriarchal politics of sexual division. Roof traces a feminist narrative-theoretical lineage, originating in an explicitly feminist path deriving from Virginia Woolf and

Simone de Beauvoir, as well as in the work of early and mid-twentieth-century students of narrative structure like Vladimir Propp and Claude Lévi-Strauss. Joining these lines of descent with the feminist theories of the late twentieth and early twenty-first centuries, Roof delivers a decisive watchword for this volume as a whole: *"narrative theorizing is a feminist act."*

That watchword informs Chapter 6, my essay on philosophies of history, which examines the narrative theory of historical writing through three moments: structural accounts of plot formation and periodization, the thematic organization of historiographical texts, and the radical interruption of alternative histories "from below." One task of Chapter 6 is to engage with the question of historical narrative as a problem of writing, and to appreciate some formative examples of the variety of historiographical modes while retaining a strong sense of the political stakes of historiographical decisions – decisions about writing that are inseparable from the historical ground itself. The essay takes the view that effective formalisms are those thorough enough to touch that historical ground, to identify the forms already immanent within history's raw materials, and to produce a writing open to and dialectically shaped by its relation to those forms.

Together, the chapters of Part I reanimate the sources of narrative theory, taking Marx, Nietzsche, Freud, Woolf, and de Beauvoir, among others, as major figures in narrative theory's formation. Those chapters also give a sharper sense of the base of narrative theory, recentering it on questions of history, feminism, writing, and the practical dynamics of scale; as a result, narrative theory is framed as a *critical theory of meaning making*, connected with the larger enterprise of what we now think of as "theory" *tout court.*[5]

Part II, "Motifs," is an interlude or entr'acte that revisits the heart of narrative theory through the three major concepts or categories of character, time, and pleasure. Doubtless the reader will conjure other motifs that could appear in a section like this, so why have we chosen these? In short, because each sits on the threshold between what traditional criticism would call "intrinsic" and "extrinsic" approaches to a text.

Character is situated between language and implied person and, as John Frow shows in his lyrical and suggestive essay (Chapter 7), that relationship draws on (and itself shapes) the dense weave of collective social life. For Frow, the task of a theory of character is not simply to account for the linguistic or formal side of representation, holding constant the reference to the implied person. Instead, a theory of character requires analysis of social personhood, of naming, and of the body, all of which are entwined with narrative figuration.

Time is both indispensable to narrative (part of its definitional core) and a category that enfolds questions about the duration of reading and the structure of temporal change *into* the representation of time within narrative. David Wittenberg's stirring essay (Chapter 8) instructs us in the time travel, and the truth travel, involved in all narrative acts. As Wittenberg shows, every narrative discourse, every *telling*, promises a certain kind of veracity or authenticity in its reference to a real or fictional *tale* that precedes the telling. But every narrative discourse, in and through its very truth-form, also opens itself to lying. *Formally* speaking, as Wittenberg eloquently explains, narrative's game with time erases the difference between a true and a false story.

For its part, *pleasure* entwines *what* keeps readers reading with questions about *why* they read in the first place, and perhaps what interrupts reading. Centered on Henry James, but shifting nimbly from *The Bostonians* to Roland Barthes, and from *The Wings of the Dove* to hardcore pornography, David Kurnick's essay (Chapter 9) links the pleasures in and of narrative with a certain kind of historical emergence, in the appearance of responses and bodily moods that are as resistant to straightforward representation as they are powerfully felt. In so doing, the chapter also sets an agenda for the engagement with narrative pleasure.

Thus our three "motifs" are a cross-sectioning of narrative theory along three of its constitutive thresholds. They also bridge the foundational concerns of the first section and the constellation of concerns that occupy Part III, "Coordinates," in which much of the real intrinsic territory of narrative theory comes into view.

Part III treats a set of topics that have sometimes been taken as miscellaneous or thematic adjuncts but which this *Companion* understands as integral to narrative theory and vital to its principal theoretical shape. Key here is the binding together of essays on race and sexuality with pieces on specific genres and media. The argument of Part III, and therefore of the *Companion* as a whole, is that the division between social "content" and narrative "form" needs to be rethought so that aspects of the social "raw materials" may themselves be understood as formal problems. Our insistence on this revision of the content/form relationship should encourage the reader to see the essays as interanimated *by* social and generic forms. So, for example, the lyric or the game may be read with and against the question of narrativity and normativity, and the poetics of race understood as a necessary articulation of the poetics of the novel or film narrative.

Amy C. Tang's authoritative essay (Chapter 10) surveys the relationship between race and narrative poetics and synthesizes a critical tradition across three narrative categories – break, border, and utopia – without subordinating the question of race to some putatively prior narratological framework.

Moving dialectically from the historical ruptures underlying *breaks* to the problematic of the present foregrounded in the spatial concerns of *borders*, and finally to the question of ethnic literary studies' conception of the future in the figure of *utopia*, Tang recenters narrative theory.

In a consonant rhetorical mode, Valerie Rohy's lapidary contribution (Chapter 11) confirms that it is impossible to think of narrative without thinking of sexuality and, more particularly, without the intelligence of a queer analytical registration of the normative and normalizing gravity of narrative itself. Rohy's essay implies the possibility of a position against narrative itself, perhaps resisting the very order and integration of part and whole that is narrative's signature function. But it also shows that queer theory cannot abandon its engagement with narrative form: narrative is too important, and too prone to reversion to normative violence, to be responsibly let go.

Garrett Stewart's tour de force on "screenarration" (Chapter 12) – on image-repertoires old and new – constitutes both a genuine extension of current work on the narrative-film image and an introduction to the narrative analysis of images *tout court*. The essay also exemplifies the writerly ethos of the *The Cambridge Companion to Narrative Theory*, expressing its critical positionality at the level of prose style. That style is fitted to a chapter that turns from the filmic character of nineteenth-century narrative to a sampling of contemporary digital filmmaking. Stewart's essay is noteworthy both for its deployment of longstanding narrative-theoretical and film-studies categories and its lively attention to film-narrative mutations that demand fresh thinking and writing alike.

From the flickering and pixeled movement of the image, Chapter 13 turns to the present moment of lyric. Jonathan Culler's essay establishes, with characteristic measure and lucidity, a benchmark for grasping the narrativity of the lyric, which is no longer adequately understood as the static pendant to narrative kinetics. Culler's argument turns finally on the claim that lyric differs from narrative in that it is less a mimesis or imitation of past events than itself an event in our world. As Culler argues, lyrics include plenty of room for narrative effects, but that narrativity is framed or enclosed by an intervention *in* the world, without the mediation that seems to be so central to narrative. Culler's theory of lyric assumes a certain direct relevance for the study of poetry today, when narrativizing approaches sometimes threaten to subsume all forms of representation.

Matters of form concern every sentence of *The Cambridge Companion to Narrative Theory*, but Mark Currie's sharp-eyed essay (Chapter 14) takes formalist methods as its subject, assessing traditional lines of narrative-theoretical work and dwelling in depth on recent cognitive and deconstructionist approaches that help us rethink matters of temporality and reference. At the same time, Currie chronicles formalism since the 1960s, considering several of its iterations under the rubric of T. J. Clark's comment that Modernism constitutes our antiquity, and thereby asking what might constitute our "post-classical" inheritance. Among other things, Currie's chapter engages valuably with Paul Ricoeur's work on time and narrative, particularly Ricoeur's revision of the classical concept of mimesis (or imitation), with some aspects of cognitive formalism, and with the impact of Jacques Derrida (and possible misreadings of Derrida) on theories of narrative.

Formalisms of all kinds require some strong sense of form itself, and Patrick Jagoda (Chapter 15) helps us loosen and recalibrate our hold on form in his essay on narrative theory and digital games. Tacking from the analysis of playing ("ludology") to the analysis of narrative ("narratology"), Jagoda appraises the wide field of digital games as both an object of and a challenge to narrative theory. His essay invites readers to contribute to the next phase in the narrative analysis of games, even as gaming deepens its own reworking of our assumptions about the ways narratives shape and are shaped by our interactions with them.

That narrative forms are themselves energized by their potential transformations is one of the guiding lessons of Margaret Cohen's luminous essay "Narrative Theory and Novel Theory" (Chapter 16), which stands too as the valedictory moment in *The Cambridge Companion to Narrative Theory*. Cohen instructs us in the long intimacy of narrative theory and the novel, and her piece is one final and consummate example of how to read narrative and narrative theory together with history, and of how to integrate an account of theory and criticism within that larger chronicle of the interrelation between form and history.

For some of us, that nexus – of form and history – is the constant goal or object of narrative theory, and it has been part of the tradition from the beginning. Certainly, as Kent Puckett shows in his essay, the split between the two realms is both asserted and tendentiously overcome even by Aristotle's *Poetics* (to say nothing of Marx), in the parallel tracks of what Jean-Pierre Vernant called the "time of men and the time of the gods." But even so aestheticist or purportedly antihistorical a thinker as the great Russian Formalist Viktor Shklovsky taught that "plot is almost always based on a real conflict that has been resolved in different ways at different times," pointing the way to a problem of form that is also (by its nature) a historical problem: both of the historical source of that "real conflict" and of the historical path of its "resolutions" in a series or sequence of different plots.[6] And indeed Shklovsky's epoch-making concept of estrangement too is bound up with the historicity of the aesthetic object. Literary devices, for Shklovsky, slow things down, forcing the reader to work – that is, to work harder than is required by that normal or everyday language that passes unnoticed in its clear neutrality, like water or air: the "device of art makes perception long and 'laborious.'"[7] In so doing, for Shklovsky, art makes a break *with* its contemporary life-world; and that very break should be seen as a historical marker, a new object of attention for the critic (the narrative theorist), emerging out of what had appeared to be the least historical site, the sphere of the literary or the aesthetic.

And so with *The Cambridge Companion to Narrative Theory*. Concerned above all, and in diverse ways, with the conjunction of history and narrative forms, this volume too is of its moment. For as odd as it may be to think of Shklovsky as a historian, it is just as weird – on the face of it – to go to narrative theory to get a grip on history. One moral of this volume, stated and enacted in different registers across these essays, is that narrative theory tries to slow down over – to make laborious – that seemingly easy conflation of tales and their tellings. Paradoxically, when the world brims with more narrative (and more uses of the term "narrative") than ever before, it has become harder than ever to get hold of a substantial narrative of where we are, and of where we are going. Too many stories at the small scale counterpointed by an absence of plot at the largest scale: here is a dilemma that seems to be addressed by every essay in this volume, and that marks *The Cambridge Companion to Narrative Theory* as a product of its times. For if it is natural to tell stories, as we are told, there is nonetheless nothing natural about the particular stories we tell. The gap between those two facts is the space of narrative theory.

Notes

1. In any case, although it has generally been assumed that Tzvetan Todorov was playing it straight when he invented the term in his *Decameron* book, "narratology" may be better thought of as a put-on – a provisional, and therefore provisionally useful, name that also functions as a joke about the scientistic pretentions of the emerging field in the 1960s. Such a combination of playfulness and real thought announces itself outright in the work of Roland Barthes, in (for example) the wonderful word "arthrology," Barthes's coinage for a "science of apportionment" at the methodological core of semiology's science of meaning. In both cases, as so often in the heyday of structuralism and semiotics, the words appear as portmanteau terms with a whimsical gesture – a wit that retains the rigor of the terminology without fully settling into the closure of a system. See Todorov, *Grammaire du Décaméron* (The Hague: Mouton, 1969), 10; and Barthes,

Elements of Semiology, trans. Annette Lavers and Colin Smith (New York, NY: Hill and Wang, 1967), 57.

2. Roland Barthes, *S/Z: An Essay*, trans. Richard Miller (New York, NY: Hill and Wang, 1974), 5.

3. Compare Fredric Jameson's recent notes on Ezra Pound's lesson for an imperialist US culture: "if you're going to rule the world, he seemed to be telling us, then at least do it right and inherit world culture, indeed construct a world culture in which your best moments [...] take their place modestly enough alongside China, Greece, the Renaissance, and modern revolution" ("Remarks on Henry James," *Henry James Review* 36 [2015]: 296).

4. Barthes, *S/Z*, 16.

5. Insofar as "theory" emerged in contradistinction to the field of philosophy, including within itself a dialectical grasp of its own historical and linguistic limits, narrative theory is in some ways an exemplary case. See Andrew Cole, *The Birth of Theory* (Princeton, NJ: Princeton University Press, 2014).

6. Viktor Shklovsky, *Energy of Delusion: A Book on Plot*, trans. Shushan Avagyan (Champaign, IL: Dalkey Archive Press, 2007), 116.

7. Viktor Shklovsky, "Art as Device," in *Theory of Prose*, trans. Benjamin Sher (Normal, IL: Dalkey Archive Press, 1990), 6.

PART I

Foundations

I

KENT PUCKETT

Narrative Theory's *Longue Durée*

In 1958 – roughly the same time that *narratology* began to emerge as a coherent intellectual project in France – the historian Fernand Braudel offered a broad account of what he called the *longue durée*, a scale of historical reckoning that exceeded the historian's traditional focus on the "short span" and the singular event: "For the historian, accepting the *longue durée* entails a readiness to change his style, his attitudes, a whole reversal in his thinking, a whole new way of conceiving of social affairs."[1] Where, in other words, the glamor of the moment, the evidentiary illusion of cause and effect, and the blunt but deceptive force of the singular event had distracted historians from the deep rules and patterns that underwrote social experience over a definite if definitely protracted span of time ("its delusive smoke fills the mind of its contemporaries"), looking to the *longue durée*, to temporal intervals that exceed both the pull of the passing crisis and the seductive, speaking example of the individual life, could allow the historian to grasp unconscious patterns and tacit rules that really limit and condition social experience.[2] The point is not to deny the existence or the significance of the single event: Braudel's argument is rather that looking at the same stuff – a political revolution, a certain style of painting, apparently sudden shifts in the price of grain or coats or mobile phones – from the perspectives of very different but ultimately related temporal scales gives us a better sense of what those events and their contexts might at last mean: "For nothing," he writes, "is more important, nothing comes closer to the crux of social reality than this living, intimate, infinitely repeated opposition between the instant of time and that time which flows only slowly."[3]

Seen in this light, Braudel's argument for the *longue durée* is itself a theory of narrative, an effort to understand how different moments, people, and events come together both for the individual historian and for entire societies to form intelligible – which is to say *narratable* – wholes. Braudel's effort to draw our attention to the methodological as well as the ideological importance of scale is thus also an effort to call our attention to the different, the

As I am attempting.

This is true of Levy [handwritten marginal note]

more or less accurate, and the sometimes incommensurate narrative techniques with which the historian, the political leader, or the ordinary citizen can make the matter, the facts, the stuff of history *mean* something; it makes us aware, in other words, that different and seemingly opposed aspects of the same events can be revealed when we consider those events from different narrative perspectives, when we differently order and accentuate events in relation to other events as well as to apparently whole, if wholly different, stories.[4] In order to understand the immanent and essential complexity of history, we need thus to acknowledge the historical and conceptual specificity of the tools, the methods, and the narrative perspectives we bring to bear on that history. We need to reflect on *how* we narrate the *what* of what really happened.

Although there's a lot more to say about Braudel's influential account of historiographic method as a potent if implicit theory of narrative, I'm more interested here in what it might mean to use Braudel's terms to see narrative theory from the point of view of different but related historical scales – to see it, on the one hand, as a "short-span" institutional event and, on the other, as an embedded and eloquent expression of rules and unconscious assumptions that quietly structure the *longue durée* out of which it emerges. I'm interested, in other words, in seeing narrative theory not only as a way to analyze the work of historians but also as a historical event in and of itself. Narrative theory is thus both a more or less transhistorical method that helps us understand how discrete events, both real and imaginary, can be brought together to create significance in almost any narrative from almost any period of time (as an analytical method, it seems somehow to float *above* history) as well as an embedded historical set of practices that can themselves be understood as events that are differently significant at different levels of scalar abstraction. Seen from this other, longer perspective, what narrative theory ultimately *means* will depend on how we choose to manage its relation to other events and other histories. As with any historical event, narrative theory exists simultaneously at the level of the short span and the *longue durée*. What should that mean for what we can and can't say about narrative theory? What, in other words, are the different scales at which narrative theory – seen both as a methodological innovation and as an institutional event – might make different kinds of sense?

Taking the short view, most critics trace the mid-century emergence of narrative theory as a more or less coherent discipline to technical innovations derived from a pair of earlier intellectual movements: Russian Formalism and structuralism. On the one hand, in an effort to delimit that which was specifically *literary* about literary narratives, the Russian Formalists put forward a distinction between the *what* and *how* of a given narrative, referring to them as *fabula* and *sjuzhet* (others use the analogous pair *story* and *discourse*). Distinguishing between the real or imagined events that make up a given narrative and the particular way in which those events are arranged by that narrative allowed writers like Viktor Shklovsky, Boris Eichenbaum, Boris Tomashevsky, and others to *defamiliarize* the aesthetic strategies and conventions that make a particular narrative association of event and representation or story and discourse possible. On the other hand, the Swiss linguist Ferdinand de Saussure's founding distinction between the two necessary aspects of the linguistic *sign*, between the *signified* and the *signifier* (private concepts and the public forms those concepts take when linguistically expressed), provided early narrative theorists with a rigorous and seemingly timeless semiotic architecture with which to articulate, advance, and ground their analyses of particular narratives as well as narrative structure in general. If the individual sign could be better understood when seen heuristically as a relation between private concepts and their public expression, perhaps narratives could also be better understood when seen heuristically as a relation between real or imagined events and their material expression – as, once again, *story* and *discourse*.

As a result of this specific twentieth-century synthesis of formalism and structuralism, early and later theorists of narrative could develop and consolidate what remains one of narrative theory's necessary postulates: that narrative is a specific relation between story and discourse; it is, in other words, a specific relation between the real or imagined events that a narrative represents and the particular ways in which particular narratives in fact represent those real or imagined events. Narrative theorists have again and again recognized the rough centrality of this formula: Gérard Genette writes that "if one agrees, following convention, to confine oneself to the domain of literary expression, one will define narrative without difficulty as the representation of an event or sequence of events, real or fictitious by means of language and, more particularly, by means of written language."[5] Marie-Laure Ryan notes that "most narratologists agree that narrative consists of material signs, the discourse, which convey a certain meaning (or content), the story, and fulfil a certain social function."[6] For Jonathan Culler, "there is considerable variety among these traditions, and of course each theorist has concepts or categories of his own, but if these theorists agree on anything it is this: that the theory of narrative requires a distinction between what I shall call 'story' – a sequence of actions or events, conceived as independent of their manifestation in discourse – and what I shall call 'discourse,' the discursive presentation or narration of events."[7] And Monika Fludernik acknowledges that "the story vs. discourse distinction perhaps constitutes the most basic of all narratological axioms."[8]

Seen from this perspective, narrative theory is perhaps best understood as an enormously powerful and professionally situated analytic technique, as a set of descriptive terms and tools that allow us to break narratives down into their component parts in order to see how they fit together in ways that follow and sometimes transgress norms that generally govern the association of story and discourse. What, though, if we accept this indisputable short-span account of narrative theory while supplementing it with a somewhat longer view? What would it mean to see narrative theory within the context of another, more capacious and perhaps speculative historical frame? What would it mean to look past the short span to narrative theory's *longue durée*?

I want to make two claims for narrative theory's *longue durée*. First, we can perhaps see narrative theory taken in its local and technical sense (it is the systematic analysis of the relation between story and discourse) as one evocative expression of a longer intellectual history that in turn depends on an embedded conceptual infrastructure that both conditions and limits the terms of our varied relations to our own *longue durée*. More to the point, I want to make the case that, seen not as a merely technical distinction between narrative levels but rather as a broadly philosophical effort to understand why events come to mean what they do, narrative theory is an important expression of an older and deeper but ultimately still contingent endeavor to understand the nature and the production of social values – a contested and often political endeavor that reaches back at least to Aristotle and could include figures such as St. Augustine, Geoffrey Chaucer, Miguel de Cervantes, Jane Austen, Hegel, George Eliot, Marx, Nietzsche, Freud, Henry James, Max Weber, Hannah Arendt, and others. Starting with narrative theory and its effort to understand how discrete or "raw" events find significance in narrative discourse, we might be able to see better how a similar question – what allows an isolated fact to take on the status of a shared value, what allows the raw stuff of life to appear to us and to others as something significant – links together a number of other signal moments in a broad but still discrete intellectual history. What's more, seeing narrative theory in the context of an expansive but nonetheless historically limited *longue durée* might help us at once understand its powerful and seemingly universal methodological appeal and at least imagine the historical and political limits of that appeal. After all, and among other things, looking to the *longue durée* helps us understand how ideas that feel necessary at one level of abstraction can reveal themselves as wholly contingent at another.

The second claim is about narrative theory as opposed, or rather in addition, to its various historical contexts. Turning back from narrative theory's *longue durée* to narrative theory itself, we will see that, in addition to its considerable technical power, there is perhaps a quiet political force, a desire, and even a pathos to narrative theory that is sometimes obscured by its rightful status as a formidable and efficient approach toward the structural analysis of story and discourse. Turning back from the *longue durée* to the practice of narrative theory, we might, in other words, ask *why* individuals try at different moments in time to understand narrative; we might also ask *why* it seems at some times more than others urgent to understand how stories work. Some of the most potent expressions of narrative theory are also efforts to confront what stories can and can't do for us. Some of our most powerful theories of narrative are theories of the historical and practical limits of narrative's capacity to account for things as they are. Because it would be impossible in so short a space as this essay to tell so long a tale, I will instead look at just a few of its scenes in order both to broaden our sense of what might count – in a strong sense – as narrative theory and, perhaps, to gesture toward some of the unconscious beliefs or rules that tacitly structure narrative theory and a lot more.[9]

[handwritten margin note: Because of fake news.]

We might begin by looking all the way back to one of the first systematic works of literary analysis, Aristotle's *Poetics*. Although it addresses a number of different aspects of specifically tragic narratives, the *Poetics* is at bottom a theory of plot, which Aristotle takes as the structural and affective heart of any successful tragedy: "the first essential, the life and soul, so to speak, of tragedy is the plot."[10] For Aristotle a plot is not simply what happens in a given tragedy; it is the particular way in which the events of that tragedy – the riddle of the Sphinx, the blinding of Oedipus, Antigone's burial of her disgraced brother, Polyneices – are ordered, arranged, and accentuated. A tragic plot is, in other words, a generically specific configuration of real or imagined events and the representation of those events (it is both *story* and *discourse*), and the *Poetics* is an early – maybe the earliest – example of a systematic narrative theory. Aristotle offers a technical and deceptively muted definition of tragic plots:

> We have laid it down that a tragedy is an imitation of an action that is complete in itself, as a whole of some magnitude; for a whole may be of no magnitude to speak of. Now a whole is that which has beginning, middle, and end. A beginning is that which is not itself necessarily after anything else, and which has naturally something else after it; an end is that which is naturally after something itself, either as its necessary or usual consequent, and with nothing else after it; and a middle, that which is by nature after one thing and has also another after it. A well-constructed plot, therefore, cannot either begin or end at any point one likes; beginning and end in it must be of the forms just described.[11]

Aristotle's focus on a tragedy as an ordered imitation of a whole action is notable for a few reasons. First and most immediately, his understanding of a plot as an ordered mimetic representation once again anticipates the distinction between the *what* and the *how* of a given narrative. Second, because he acknowledges what is more or less "well-constructed" about a particular plot, he calls tacit attention not only to the shaping intention of the author but also to the possible and perhaps inevitable existence of other, differently constructed versions of the same plot. This would have been especially clear to Aristotle because the tragedies he considered were almost always specific and, as it were, competing discursive representations of a few familiar legends. Because audiences seeing Sophocles' tragedies would already have been familiar with the basic "facts" of Oedipus' case, they and Aristotle would have been acutely aware that the value of any single performance was as much about the *how* as about the *what* of a given version. And because an audience member would already have known the story, he or she would have been free to attend comparatively to the discourse – or, rather, to the specific relation between story and discourse that structures a given tragedy.

Third, as becomes clear in the *Poetics*, the importance of construction wasn't only a matter of aesthetic design for Aristotle; to order real, fictional, or legendary events in one as opposed to another manner was tacitly to argue about the *meaning* of those events: "The plot in fact should be so framed that, even without seeing the things take place, he who simply hears the account of them shall be filled with horror and pity at the incidents; which is just the effect that the mere recital of the story in Oedipus would have on one."[12] The point is that the whole plot should have at least as much of an effect on an audience as the events that the plot contains. It is the arrangement of real or imagined events – once again, discourse as opposed to story – that allows tragic narrative to do the work it does so well.

Seen as an account of story and discourse, Aristotle's *Poetics* is thus not only a narrative theory *avant la lettre* but also a narrative theory that makes clear the difficult relation between the nuts and bolts of narrative technique – the discursive representation of real or imagined events – and the question of value in a broader and perhaps more critical sense. To confront Sophocles' unique discursive rendering of Oedipus' well-known story was not only to see a master technician at work; it was also – and this is of course the point of Athenian tragedy – to confront essential questions about the essential and informing mystery of things. The great classicist Jean-Pierre Vernant argues that Athenian tragedy addresses the simultaneous and only apparently incoherent social experience of two different orders of time: "The drama brought to the stage unfolds both at the level of everyday existence, in a human, opaque time made up of successive and limited present moments, and also beyond this earthly life, in a divine, omnipresent time that at every instant encompasses the totality of events, sometimes to conceal them and sometimes to make them plain but always so that nothing escapes or is lost in oblivion."[13] For Vernant, this tension between what he calls "the time of men and the time of the gods" is what gives tragedy its capacity to reflect deeply on questions of fate and free will. What feels and indeed is contingent from any situated human perspective must also and at the same time seem fated to the gods. For Hannah Arendt, "This paradox, that greatness was understood in terms of permanence while human greatness was seen in precisely the most futile and least lasting activities of men, has haunted Greek poetry and historiography as it has perturbed the quiet of the philosophers."[14] It is the necessary difference between those nonetheless necessary aspects of one and the same narrative that gives tragedy its emotional and explanatory force.

Vernant goes on to relate this essential aspect of tragic form to a disorienting moment within Athenian political history, a moment at which, increasingly, secular legal innovations existed uncomfortably alongside older beliefs in the direct presence and legislative power of the gods. Tragic forms thus "reveal disagreement within legal thought itself and also betray its conflicts with a religious tradition and moral thought from which the law is already distinct but whose domains are still not clearly differentiated from its own."[15] Put differently, the narrative relation between story and discourse, between individual events and what those events might mean when seen as differently related from one or another perspective, might be taken as a structural expression of a more fundamental question: From what perspective or in terms of what narrative can or will the things that happen to us be made to make sense? Why is this political situation, this society, this world one way and not another? Beginning with Aristotle, we see that the narrative relation between story and discourse might be seen as part of something larger: a culturally embedded and historically specific effort to understand why things happen and what they might come to mean over time.

We could then turn to another, later figure less often associated with but no less important to the development of narrative theory, the philosopher Georg Wilhelm Friedrich Hegel. Although it might seem rash to skip over so many years and so many important and intervening figures – St. Augustine, Chaucer, Dante, Corneille, Racine, Shakespeare, Cervantes, Herder, Defoe, Rousseau, Austen, and so on – turning to Hegel makes sense both because his work stands as one influential answer to Aristotle's tragic theory of plot and conflict in the *Poetics* and also because that work turns on and expands the consequence of a specifically narrative distinction between discrete historical events and what those events might mean when considered from the point of view of some larger and more coherent discursive arrangement. Hegel's theory of history, which extended from the very smallest to the very largest events that history contained, depends on what we might see as a perspectival difference – Hegel might say a *dialectical* relation – between individual events and what sense those events might make when seen as part of a whole discursive arrangement. Put in our terms, to understand history and our place in it, one needed a theory of narrative, which is to say an account of the meaning-making relation between story and discourse. Hegel's early turn to narrative (or, rather, to a comparative theory of narrative) should be seen partly as a result of historical events – the French Revolution, the rise of European nationalism, the emergence of Romantic ethnography – that made it necessary to think differently and seriously about the fact that other people, other nations, other social classes can and do make different, competing, and nonetheless coherent narratives out of one and the same set of events. To understand how the same events, the same story, could be differently represented in different discursive arrangements required a narrative theory. It was, as I will suggest, partly Hegel's deep commitment to narrative that made it possible and even obvious for subsequent critics to look to narrative as an autonomous object of study as well as a potent way to understand life, history, and ourselves.

What was it about the French Revolution that encouraged Hegel to develop and to rely on a prescient theory of narrative? The French Revolution had an effect on Hegel in part because of how it began and ended – because, in other words, of how it seemed to succeed or fail as a whole and, as it were, Aristotelian plot. The early enthusiasm of the French Revolution, its overthrow of a seemingly intractable *ancien régime*, and its initial promise of universal *liberté, égalité*, and *fraternité* seemed to Hegel and many others not only to inaugurate a set of specific political and democratic improvements but also to embody an Enlightenment ideal of radical human freedom that could transcend specific political oppression and, more broadly, natural necessity. If, however, the Revolution began in hope, it quickly collapsed into what Hegel took as the disappointment of the Terror, the late period of the Revolution during which thousands died under the guillotine. This period of violence ended Hegel's hopes for the Revolution and, indeed, hastened the collapse of the revolutionary government and the concomitant rise of Napoleon as the emperor of France and, for a time, much of the world. A question thus emerged: Was it possible to save or to recuperate the promise of the Revolution's beginning in spite of its end? Would it be possible to see the failed narrative of revolutionary promise as, in fact, just one part of a much larger and longer narrative of progress and hope? What would it do to see the Revolution not only as an isolated if enormously consequential event but also as an expression of an order that Braudel would later call the *longue durée?*

The point is that, where the Revolution seemed to begin in 1789 as an event that would make sense of much that had come before, its collapse in 1793 threw the ultimate significance of that event into question. Where the Revolution had seemed at its beginning like an organic part of a shared and unfolding Enlightenment plot, it seemed at its end like a repudiation of order and, perhaps, of narrative itself. The apparent failure of revolutionary promise thus led Hegel to a kind of crossroads: Did one give up on a whole sense of history, on its immanent significance, or did one instead look for terms in which or, rather, a perspective *from* which to account for what seemed unaccountable? Was it possible, as Georg Lukács put it in *The Historical Novel*, "to demonstrate the necessity of the French Revolution, to show that revolution and historical development are not opposed to one another"?[16] Was there, in other words, a way to see the Terror not as an exceptional failure but more as an event that would, in time, be revealed as an important if bloody part of a larger narrative of human liberation? Philosophy thus appeared for Hegel as a possible narrative response to a time that had been put out of joint. Rebecca Comay writes that "This is why the French Revolution will remain the burning center of Hegel's philosophy: the event crystallizes the untimeliness of historical experience. The task of philosophy is to explicate this untimeliness."[17] Or, as Fredric Jameson puts it, "The experience of defeat of the various revolutionary movements in this period has a paradoxical consequence: it does not discourage its followers theoretically, but rather intensifies their attempts to conceptualize that mysterious historical moment which is the passage from one system to another."[18] The question Is it possible to resolve the local contradictions of the past and the present in terms of some larger process or narrative? provides one important and influential basis of Hegel's project and its reliance on a particular and broadly influential theory of narrative. On the one hand, to see history as the unfolding and inexorable resolution of conflicts and contradictions that made the past is a theory of history and, perhaps, a kind of faith. On the other hand, to see different scales of history (the short, the long, the longest) as perspectives from which exactly the same events will look entirely different – as, in other words, levels of discursive abstraction capable of fundamentally *revaluing* those same events – is a narrative theory in a rigorous and technical sense.

We could, then, perhaps look forward to three later figures, each of whom was responding to Hegel's narrative turn and who also had a direct influence on early theorists of narrative such as Julia Kristeva, Roland Barthes, and Gérard Genette. Where, however, Hegel looked to narrative as a way of ultimately and hopefully resolving the apparent disconnect between discrete and sometimes tragic events and history as a rational and progressive whole, Karl Marx, Friedrich Nietzsche, and Sigmund Freud all call attention to the limits as well as the strengths of a narrative approach toward history and life. In *Freud and Philosophy*, Paul Ricoeur famously cast Marx, Nietzsche, and Freud as an unwitting but more-or-less coherent "school of suspicion."[19] Suspicion takes different forms in each of the three. For instance, Marx's account of history as a history of class struggle depends on the idea that different classes have different stories to tell about the way things are, and that the goal of criticism is to strip those ideologically driven stories down until we reach something like a base. Hayden White writes that "the relation between the form and the content of any social phenomenon in any specific historical situation, Marx argues [...], is a product of a conflict between specific class interests as they are envisaged and lived by a given class."[20] And Jameson writes as follows:

> The most influential lesson of Marx – the one which ranges him alongside Freud and Nietzsche as one of the great negative diagnosticians of contemporary culture and social life – has, of course, rightly been taken to be the lesson of false consciousness, of class bias and ideological programming, the lesson of structural limits of the values and attitudes of particular social classes, or in other words of the constitutive relationship between the praxis of such groups and what they conceptualize as value or desire and project in the form of culture.[21]

Put differently, particular classes will arrange the materials of life into narratives that more or less reflect or support their interests insofar as those interests are defined against those of other, competing classes; they will of necessity order the same events, the same story, into discursive arrangements that support and further their interests as a class. Criticism, in that case, is the effort not only to compare those narratives but also to understand the total conditions and relations – the particular "mode of production" – that made them possible in the first place (the young Marx famously called for "a ruthless criticism of everything existing"). Criticism is to see past the different narratives that classes use to make events make sense for them and, perhaps, to see, once and for all, the events themselves. As Marx and Engels put it in *The Communist Manifesto*, "All that is solid melts into air, all that is holy is profaned, and man is at last compelled to face with sober senses his real conditions of life, and his relations with his kind."[22]

Like Marx, Nietzsche looks to narrative both as a source of delusion and as a way critically to resist bad ideas about things as they are. For instance, in his "On the Use and Abuse of History for Life," Nietzsche offers an account of history and historiography as a context between different attitudes toward both narrative and life. As opposed to the two main schools of historical reckoning – a "monumental history" that preserves the past and distorts life in the service of a status quo and an "antiquarian history" that values the past over the present and thus chooses death over life – Nietzsche offers "critical history" as the kind of history that can best deal with life as it really is: "In order to live, [the critical historian] must possess, and from time to time employ, the strength to shatter and dissolve a past; he accomplishes this by bringing this past before a tribunal, painstakingly interrogating it, and finally condemning it. But every past is worthy of being condemned – for this is simply how it is with human affairs: human violence and weakness have always played a powerful role in them."[23] To live is not to obscure the past and the present in exchange for the comforts of one or another narrative; it is to see both that we cannot narrate away what is tragic or painful about life and that, even so, we cannot live without narrative. As opposed to Marx, who broke narratives down in order to see events as they really are, Nietzsche both recognizes our limited, "human, all too human" reliance on narrative and celebrates the paradoxical freedom of this forked condition: if we have to narrate the stuff of life to understand life and if we know that those narratives will always be *more or less* untrue, we can at least recognize that fact and choose what narratives we will. Jacques Derrida characterizes this position as "the joyous affirmation of the freeplay of the world and without truth, without origin, offered to an active interpretation."[24] This tragic tension between the will to narrate and narrative's necessary limits is the critical knowledge or, as Nietzsche puts it in *The Birth of Tragedy*, the Dionysian wisdom required in order to be able truly to live.

Like Hegel, Marx, and Nietzsche, Sigmund Freud built a theory of great complexity around a basic human need to narrate, a need to put life's events into order. Freud's lifelong project, psychoanalysis, is in its way also a historical project, the effort to understand how the past, present, and future of an individual life might add up to something significant and thus legible. Patients traveled to Freud's office in late nineteenth- and early twentieth-century Vienna when it seemed that their lives no longer held together – when they could not understand their pasts, manage their relations with others, or parse how their incomplete understanding of self and desire appeared in the at-times-debilitating form of neurotic symptoms. In response to this inability to make sense, Freud encouraged his patients to talk, to free-associate, to cast their feelings, experiences, and anxieties in linguistic or, we might say, textual forms. This is why one of Freud's earliest patients referred to psycho-analysis as a "talking cure"; if it worked, it worked because it encouraged both analyst and patient to narrate, to read, and perhaps to revise the memory of past events in relation to the present and future. This therapeutic and critical reliance on talk, on stories, on narrative is one that stretches from the beginning to the end of Freud's work, from his first efforts to encourage his patients to make sense of their lives and problems by talking about them to his late reflections on the relation among beginnings, middles, and ends that drove his wildest and most disturbing reflections on the interminable and essential conflict between the forces of life and death. Indeed, many of Freud's most important concepts rely on an implicit theory of narrative form: the idea that a child must pass more-or-less "successfully" through oral, anal, phallic, and genital stages of development; that the Oedipal scene is a threshold or narrative middle that everyone needs somehow to cross; that the story of psychosexual development is only meaningful because its infantile beginning is separated from its mature end by the middle barrier of what he calls the "latency period"; that an obscurely narratable process allows the ego to emerge out of the chaos of raw biological instinct; and that there is an idiosyncratic path that we all must follow, in our own way, on the way from life to death. In each of these cases, Freud imagines human life as a partial and inherently fraught process of arranging the latent events of individual and collective human lives in a more or less significant and manifest discursive form.

Given world enough and time, we could look to many other figures who would both fit into and cast light on what I'm imagining as narrative theory's *longue durée*. We could look to St. Augustine, who writes in the eleventh book of the *Confessions* that "when a true narrative of the past is related, the memory produces not the actual events which have passed away but words conceived from images of them, which they fixed in the mind like imprints as they passed through the senses."[25] Or to Chaucer's reflections on the structure of tragedy in the prologue to "The Monk's Tale." Or to Cervantes's embedded reflections on the comparative power and limits of romance as opposed to realism in *Don Quixote*. Or to Jane Austen's thoughts on the narrative efficacy and sufficiency of "3 or 4 Families in a Country Village."[26] Or to Henry James's many reflections on the narrative relation between life and form in the prefaces to the New York edition of his novels: "Really, universally, relations stop nowhere, and the exquisite problem of the artist is eternally but to draw, by a geometry of his own, the circle within which they shall happily *appear* to do so."[27] Or to the sociologist Max Weber, who sought to define culture as an informing and fragile relation between a society's facts and the shared and tenuous values that a community might derive from and impose on those facts: "The concept of culture is a value-concept. Empirical reality becomes 'culture' to us because and insofar as we relate it to value ideas. It includes those segments and only those segments which have become significant to us because of this relation to value."[28] It is, in other words, only when we agree to see empirical social facts within a shared and informing discursive frame – a narrative – that those facts can take on value, significance, meaning.

This last example is especially useful because Weber makes clear something I take as implicit in all the figures I've discussed: the idea that the relation between things and what things might mean, between facts and values, cannot – when seen from the perspective of the *longue durée* – be taken as given. Indeed, Weber claims, in "Science as a Vocation," that the conditions of our "disenchanted" modernity (secularization, technological advance, the tyranny of exchange, and so on) have undone our old ability to agree on shared discursive frames in which to understand even the basic facts of existence; this is what he and other figures important to this story – Georg Simmel, Georg Lukács, Walter Benjamin – took as the "tragedy of culture." Weber goes on to suggest that even death, that most obviously meaningful of events, seems to have lost its immanent narrative value; we now catch "only the most minute part of what the life of the spirit brings forth ever anew, and what [we] seize is always something provisional and not definitive, and therefore death is for [us] a meaningless occurrence. And because death is meaningless, civilized life as such is meaningless; by its very 'progressiveness' it gives death the imprint of meaninglessness."[29] Weber bases his thinking about the changing narrative status of death in a discussion of Tolstoy's novels. And, indeed, his idea about the modern dissolution of the specifically narrative significance of life and death returns again and again in more and less technical terms in later discussions of narrative and the novel: in, for instance, Lukács, Benjamin, Kristeva, Barthes, and Genette. In Benjamin's great essay "The Storyteller," he writes,

> Yet, characteristically, it is not only a man's knowledge or wisdom, but above all his real life – and this is the stuff that stories are made of – which first assumes transmissible form at the moment of his death. Just as a sequence of images is set in motion inside a man as his life comes to an end – unfolding the views of himself in which he has encountered himself without being aware of it – suddenly in his expressions and looks the unforgettable emerges and imparts to everything that concerned him that authority which even the poorest wretch in dying possesses for the living around him. This authority is at the very origin of the story.[30]

And, in Genette's *Narrative Discourse*, a work that more or less set the terms for narrative theory as we now know it, he dwells on the exceptional, almost anti-narrative status of Proust's representation of the death of

Marcel's grandmother and the mourning that followed: "Above all it is not characterized, and it will remain not characterized: we will never, even retrospectively, know anything of what the hero's life has been during these few months. This is perhaps the most opaque silence in the entire *Recherche*, and, if we remember that the death of the grandmother is to a great extent a transposition of the death of the author's mother, this reticence is undoubtedly not devoid of significance."[31] Garrett Stewart makes a similar point in explicitly narrative-theoretical terms: "This is the narratological hold death has over any text. The idea of death, otherwise known as the sense of an ending, becomes the inevitable incarnation of plot in the world of sheer story, the imposition of discourse on the course of random account, of form on the amorphousness not of death but of life without it."[32] Put differently, for a certain kind of culture and for the narratives that give that culture meaning, death served to give individual lives and life in general what Frank Kermode calls "the sense of an ending," a discursive form that helped retroactively to shape the raw stuff of story into something significant.

In these terms, death is not only a social and biological fact but also proof of a symbolic order that for a long time seemed successfully to underwrite and to inform culture; it was one of the structures or rules that allowed life to make sense. For Weber, Benjamin, Genette, and others (Hegel, Tolstoy, Lukács, and so on), modern life and its various disenchantments seemed to undermine death's narrative capacity to impose discursive order onto the stuff, the facts, the raw story of life. We should, in these terms, see death as an evocative example of what can happen to ideas that structure a *longue durée*. Braudel writes, "Some structures, because of their long life, become stable elements for an infinite number of generations: they get in the way of history, hinder its flow, and in hindering it shape it. Others wear themselves out more quickly."[33] Weber and the others were, I think, trying to capture a moment at which an idea that had been necessary to the larger structure of the *longue durée* had begun to "wear itself out." I want to suggest – and I can't do much more than that – that these various figures, all of whom look like narrative theorists from the perspective of narrative theory's *longue durée*, begin to theorize narrative, which is to say the relation between story and discourse, when its status as a self-evidently preeminent social form is under threat. If death can wear itself out, then why not story and discourse? If, in other words, Weber and others imagine that death can lose or has lost its ability to order life, to shape story into discourse, that is proof less of death's reduced place in a given cultural imaginary than of limits that were always already immanent to both it and the narratives it helped shape. All of that is simply to say that, seen from the perspective of the *longue durée*, narrative theory is not only a descriptive account of how narratives work; it is also, at its best, a confrontation with the historical limits of narrative to order experience, to make facts into values, to turn story into discourse. And all of that is, in turn, to say that when we begin to see narrative theory as deeply historical, as an event that reflects, however obscurely, the immanent logic of one and not another *longue durée*, we see not only that its terms and explanatory reach have their own limits but also that narrative theory is at its best when it is able to address those limits, when it is able to see what narrative can't do, when it is able, however quietly, to see or to imagine a time or a world that would look beyond story and discourse for its significance. A critical theory is a theory capable of reflecting on limits necessary to its basic assumptions about how things work; seen from the perspective of the *longue durée*, narrative theory is, indeed and at its best, a critical theory.

Notes

1. Fernand Braudel, *On History*, trans. Sarah Matthews (Chicago, IL: University of Chicago Press, 1980), 33. Although the structural analysis of narrative had been going on for a decade or more, the term "narratology" first appeared in Tzvetan Todorov, *Grammaire du Décaméron* (The Hague: Mouton, 1969).
2. Braudel, *On History*, 27.
3. Ibid., 26
4. For a classic account of how the expectations that come along with different narrative genres affect the telling of history, see Hayden White, *Metahistory: The Historical Imagination in Nineteenth-Century Europe*, new ed. (Baltimore, MD: Johns Hopkins University Press, 2014).
5. Gérard Genette, "Frontiers of Narrative," in *Figures of Literary Discourse*, trans. Alan Sheridan (New York, NY: Columbia University Press, 1982), 127.
6. Marie-Laure Ryan, "Toward a Definition of Narrative," in *The Cambridge Companion to Narrative*, ed. David Herman (Cambridge: Cambridge University Press, 2007), 24.
7. Jonathan Culler, *The Pursuit of Signs: Semiotics, Literature, Deconstruction* (Ithaca, NY: Cornell University Press, 2002), 169–170.
8. Monika Fludernik, *Towards a "Natural" Narratology* (London: Routledge, 1996), 333.
9. Some of what follows is adapted from arguments I make in Puckett, *Narrative Theory: A Critical Introduction* (Cambridge: Cambridge University Press, 2016).
10. Aristotle, *Poetics*, in *The Complete Works of Aristotle: The Revised Oxford Translation*, ed. Jonathan Barnes, 2 vols. (Princeton, NJ: Princeton University Press, 1984), 2: 2321 (1450b).
11. Ibid., 2: 2321–2322.
12. Ibid., 2: 2326
13. Jean-Pierre Vernant, *Myth and Tragedy in Ancient Greece*, trans. Janet Lloyd (New York, NY: Zone Books, 1988), 43.
14. Hannah Arendt, *Between Past and Future* (London: Penguin, 2006), 45–46.

15. Ibid., 25.
16. Georg Lukács, *The Historical Novel*, trans. Hannah Mitchell and Stanley Mitchell (Lincoln: University of Nebraska Press, 1983), 28.
17. Rebecca Comay, *Mourning Sickness: Hegel and the French Revolution* (Stanford, CA: Stanford University Press, 2011), 5.
18. Fredric Jameson, "In Hyperspace," *London Review of Books* 37, no. 17 (September 10, 2015): 17–22.
19. See Paul Ricoeur, *Freud and Philosophy: An Essay on Interpretation*, trans. Denis Savage (New Haven, CT: Yale University Press, 1970).
20. Hayden White, "The Problem of Style in Realistic Representation: Marx and Flaubert," in *The Fiction of Narrative: Essays on History, Literature, and Theory, 1957–2007*, ed. Robert Doran (Baltimore, MD: Johns Hopkins University Press, 2010), 180.
21. Fredric Jameson, *The Political Unconscious: Narrative as a Socially Symbolic Act* (Ithaca, NY: Cornell University Press, 1981), 281–282.
22. Karl Marx and Frederick Engels, *Manifesto of the Communist Party*, in *Collected Works*, 50 vols. (New York, NY: International Publishers, 1976–2004), 6: 496.
23. Friedrich Nietzsche, *The Complete Works of Friedrich Nietzsche, Volume 2: Unfashionable Observations*, trans. Richard T. Gray (Stanford, CA: Stanford University Press, 1995), 106–107.
24. Jacques Derrida, *Writing and Difference*, trans. Alan Bass (New York, NY: Routledge, 1995), 292.
25. Saint Augustine, *The Confessions*, trans. Henry Chadwick (Oxford: Oxford University Press, 1998), 234.
26. *Jane Austen's Letters*, ed. Deirdre Le Faye (Oxford: Oxford University Press, 2011), 287.
27. Henry James, *The Art of the Novel: Critical Prefaces* (New York, NY: Scribner's, 1937), 5–6.
28. Weber, quoted in Gillian Rose, *Hegel Contra Sociology* (London: Humanities Press, 1981), 18.
29. Max Weber, *From Max Weber: Essays in Sociology*, ed. H. H. Gerth and C. Wright Mills (London: Routledge, 1970), 140.
30. Walter Benjamin, "The Storyteller," in *Selected Writings*, vol. 3., ed. Howard Eiland and Michael W. Jennings (Cambridge, MA: Harvard University Press, 2006), 151.
31. Gérard Genette, *Narrative Discourse: An Essay in Method*, trans. Jane E. Lewin (Ithaca, NY: Cornell University Press, 1980), 108.
32. Garrett Stewart, *Death Sentences: Styles of Dying in British Fiction* (Cambridge, MA: Harvard University Press, 1984), 194–195.
33. Braudel, *On History*, 31.

2

YOON SUN LEE

Questions of Scale: Narrative Theory and Literary History

Narrative theory is distinguished by its ambitious scope – to examine the numberless narratives of the world – and questions of scale are at the heart of its critical practice. Yet it reveals that scale is not a matter of *ready-made* units that can be seen or counted. Rather, narrative scale is inseparable from questions of structure, relation, and critical method. What we consider the proper scale of analysis or description depends on how we model narrative's dimensions, levels, or axes. To apprehend scale, we need to see narrative as a distinctive form of expression in general. We need to consider concretely how our critical methods may reveal that general form while sustaining our sense of specific individual narratives. Within narrative theory at its best, scale is not treated as a property already possessed by things, whether material or mental, singular or aggregate. Instead, it emerges in the course of building models of narrative shape, meaning, and context.[1]

Functions, Scale, and Morphology: The Work of Vladimir Propp

As it grew out of formalist and structuralist movements, narrative theory was preoccupied with the question of how to determine the units of narrative in general.[2] For theorists such as Roland Barthes, the answer to this question was the key that would open up all narratives. That is, in searching for the fundamental units of narrative, theorists may appear to have founded their own project as itself a *scalable* enterprise. As described by the anthropologist Anna Lowenhaupt Tsing, scalability is an aspect of capitalist production, including the production of knowledge within capitalism. It is "the ability of a project to change scales smoothly without any change in project frames." As such, scalability "requires that project elements be oblivious to the indeterminacies of encounter."[3] Aimed at expansion, scalable projects create identical units that can simply be added to each other. Such blindness to the relationship between contingency and structure might seem consonant with early narrative theory's search for fundamental units. But in fact the ways in which formalist theorists have described actual narrative forms and their component units are often the opposite of scalable, offering instead a dialectical sense of the unique, whole form and its constituent parts, as well as a vivid sense of historical change. At its most successful, narrative theory holds in tension the determinisms of scalability and what Tsing calls the indeterminacies of encounter.

The work of Vladimir Propp, whose 1928 study *The Morphology of the Folktale* may be seen as the modern genesis of narrative theory, is instructive in this regard. Propp's situation was not unlike that of literary scholars today, who are confronted by an extraordinary trove of accessible data. By the 1920s, major collections of folktales had been completed, and even larger archives were available for study. Faced with thousands of tales, folklorists' attempts at classification according to theme or content had, in Propp's view, created only chaos, since the selection of those features seemed to proceed on an arbitrary basis. "What matters," he wrote, "is not the amount of material, but the methods of investigation." Propp shifted the investigation to what he called "formal, structural features."[4] He insisted that the study of these narratives had not only to attend to parts, but more importantly to consider how they are put together into a distinctive totality. He arrives thus at the narrative unit only by considering the form of the whole tale – indeed, only by considering the tale as an entire form. Propp proposed what he calls the function as the fundamental unit of the tale: "*Function is understood as an act of a character, defined from the point of view of its significance for the course of the action.*" In this definition, the final term, "action," refers to the plot of the tale as a whole. Individual plot functions are given names such as interdiction, violation, villainy, mediation, provision of the magical agent, struggle, return, and flight. They "modify a state of affairs by making a difference."[5]

Propp's functions are "the fundamental components of the tale," and they "*serve as stable, constant elements [...] independent of how and by whom they are fulfilled.*" Famously, he concludes, "*The number of functions known to the fairy tale is limited.*"[6] There are exactly thirty-one. This composite account of plot applies to the genre; it is not the case that each tale contains all of these functions in the same guise. The functions actually occur through a wide variety of concrete situations and a diverse range of dramatis personae – human and nonhuman, animate and inanimate, whole, partial, even invisible – who carry them out. But the functions are always the same, Propp insists, and they occur, when present, in the same sequence. This sequence of functions is fixed partly through the laws of logic (an interdiction cannot be violated before it is given, for instance), but also because of the form of the genre. This leads Propp to conclude that "[a]ll fairy tales are of one type in regard to their structure."[7]

For Propp, as for Aristotle in *The Poetics*, the plot is what lends shape, coherence, and identity to a narrative. Plot, understood as a sequence of functions, also becomes the scale at which the genre of the tale achieves its identity by means of certain critical operations. So while Propp identifies five categories that define the tale as a whole, we may say that only the sequence of functions is required for what we can term *plot*. Among other things, these functions are necessary to any *summary* of a tale that conveys only the essentials.[8]

It is important to notice that Propp aims to establish a standard of measure, as he remarks after laying out the thirty-one functions schematically: "What does the given scheme represent *in relation to the tales*? [...] The scheme is a *measuring unit* for individual tales. Just as cloth can be measured with a yardstick to determine its length, tales may be measured by the scheme and thereby defined. The application of the given scheme to various tales can also define the relationships of tales among themselves."[9]

But for Propp, measuring must begin with the construction of a model of the total internal structure of the form. He suggests that to measure the tale, or the varieties of tales, is to consider not only the concrete features that they might share but also the completeness of their form. Classification and counting cannot proceed on the basis of arbitrarily selected features. Narrative *morphology*, then, the study of narrative *form*, needs to be involved in any consideration of narrative scale, and morphology requires us to look beyond the level of words. It relies on criteria of completeness and examines the relations between parts and the whole. Such relations can be felt aesthetically as well as measured.

From Narrative Function to Narrative Volume: Roland Barthes's Trajectory

While Propp does not aim to encompass more than the genre of the folktale, his approach was extended by other theorists. One of the most important developments of his ideas can be found in Roland Barthes's essay "Introduction to the Structural Analysis of Narratives" (1966). Barthes radically opens up the idea of narrative scale, taking the concept of the function as his point of departure. His essay argues that narratives are constituted by a principle of expansion, of prising apart, filling in, linking up and out. Barthes doubles down on the Proppian commitment to structural modeling; he explicates the units, levels, and operations through which narratives achieve their distinctive type of scale. He begins by remarking on

31

the "infinity of materials" confronted by the theorist of narrative, and ends by suggesting that infinity resides *within* a narrative as well. Paradoxically, Barthes's essay implies that narrative theorists can best explore the largest dimensions of scale by focusing on a single narrative text, as his future work demonstrates.

How Barthes defines the basic unit of narrative is key: "the first task is to divide up narrative and [...] to define the smallest narrative units."[10] Significantly, he stresses that "these segments will not coincide with the forms traditionally attached to the various parts of narrative discourse (actions, scenes, paragraphs, dialogues, inner monologues, etc.)." Nor will they reflect or even acknowledge the units of linguistic analysis: sometimes the units will be larger than a sentence, and sometimes even smaller than a word.[11] He chooses to define this fundamental unit as "any segment of the story which can be seen as the term of a correlation."[12] Barthes draws this notion from the work of the structural linguist Émile Benveniste. Referring to the linguistic concept of "levels of description," Barthes states, "A unit belonging to a particular level only takes on meaning if it can be integrated in a higher level."[13] A phoneme (or sound unit), for instance, has meaning when it is integrated into a word. Building on an analogy between narrative discourse and the grammatical sentence, Barthes posits the existence of multiple levels at which such narrative units can take on meaning: either by "referring to a complementary and consequential act" at the level of plot or by referring to "a more or less diffuse concept which is nevertheless necessary to the meaning of the story."[14] The latter may be concepts that have to do with "the major articulations of praxis (desire, communication, struggle)" or with the act of narration itself.[15] What is remarkable is that the unit has no fixed form or size. Barthes stresses that the smallest unit, which he also calls a function, cannot be identified through its form. It is "not the way it is made, which constitutes it as a functional unit"; rather, it is "a content unit," and that content comes from its correlation to something else in or connected to the narrative. Barthes gives the example of a partial sentence from Ian Fleming's *Goldfinger* in which Bond "picked up one of the four [telephone] receivers"; Bond's action is connected to other complementary actions and events in the plot, but the single word "four," Barthes argues, is itself a functional unit referring "to a concept which is necessary to the story (that of a highly developed bureaucratic technology)."[16]

How, then, can this smallest unit, the function, be used to determine the scalar properties of a narrative? Barthes suggests that this happens through what he calls "a simple relation of implication."[17] Some plot-related functions are already logically implied by other, more structurally decisive functions that he calls "cardinal functions" or "nuclei." Barthes's analysis of what he calls narrative syntax rests on the *sequence* of functions: "the sequence opens when one of its terms has no solidary antecedent and closes when another of its terms has no consequent."[18] This definition echoes Aristotle's description of a plot as having a beginning, middle, and end, but it differs in important respects. The sequence is only a subunit of a plot, nearly microscopic in some of the examples that Barthes gives. Moreover, what matters in the sequence even more than the *connection* between the beginning and end points are the distance and the uncertainty that lie between them – or in other words, their potential *unconnectedness*, whose negation signals the end of a sequence. Functions are correlated or completed (either in the plot or at a broader level of signification), *but only at a certain remove*.

It is easiest to see how sequences work to create scale when we consider plot. Suspense is a familiar instance of the phenomenon, and Barthes's essay allows us to imagine suspense as something that could perhaps be measured. Through delay, distortion, digression, and expansion, narratives acquire their dimensions. Sequences are juxtaposed in a contrapuntal manner, with new sequences beginning before others close. But more elusively and globally, a narrative acquires dimensionality through a retroactive sense of the distance and difficulty that mark the perception of *any* correlation, including those that have to do with the "vertical" integration of a function into a higher level of sense. This is true even of those functions unrelated to plot or to the "horizontal" unfolding of the narrative. Functions that elaborate atmosphere, character, or narration must also bear a distinctive, though invisible mark of incompletion – a sense, as it were, of waiting for the other shoe to drop. Barthes distinguishes, for example, between a type of function he calls "informants," which are simply "pure data with immediate signification," and a type he calls "indices," which require "an activity of deciphering."[19] Functions, then, through their palpable incompleteness, signal their position as part of a sequence. The sequence is the most important unit of narrative, if not the smallest.

When a function has encountered its counterpart at the level of plot, or its correlative at a higher level of signification, there arises, I would argue, a sense of qualitative completeness. This sense of completeness, which is far more likely to be relative than total, refers us back to Propp's definition of the function as "an act of a character, defined from the point of view of its significance for the course of the action." But Barthes also adds another set of dimensions to the text that give it a "vertical" quality – those "more or less diffuse concept[s] [...] nonetheless necessary to the story" but that extend obviously far beyond the narrative as given on the page: concepts such as "a highly technical bureaucracy," for instance.

Are such meanings part of the narrative's own dimensionality? In his essay "Categories of Narrative" (1966), Tzvetan Todorov addresses this problem by distinguishing between what he calls the sense and the interpretation of a literary element. Drawing on the philosopher Gottlob Frege's distinction between sense and reference, Todorov argues that "the sense (or function) of an element of the work is its potential to enter into correlation with other elements of the work and with the entire work," while "interpretation of an element differs according to the personality of the critic, his [sic] ideological positions, or [...] era."[20] Todorov emphasizes a difference between sense, which is immanent to the narrative as a delimited form, and a broader meaning contingent on the reader's experience and beliefs. But Barthes views both sense and reference, in Frege's terms, or both sense and interpretation, in Todorov's, as crucial to the dimensionality or scale of the text. He demonstrates this most dramatically in his study *S/Z* (1970).

In this work, Barthes divides Honoré de Balzac's novella "Sarrasine" into ninety-three segments, which Barthes calls "lexias" or "zones of reading." He defines a lexia as "the wrapping of a semantic volume."[21] Barthes justifies his performance by insisting that meaning is produced through the operation of larger systems "whose perspective ends neither at the text nor at the 'I': in operational terms, the meanings I find are established not by 'me' nor by others, but by their *systematic* mark."[22] Barthes names five of these "codes" that traverse the narrative. Cutting the text into units that appear of arbitrary size, Barthes explains the codes that appear and reappear in each unit – or, to use his earlier language, the codes into which the unit can be variously and multiply integrated in order to produce meaning:

> This cutting up [...] will be arbitrary in the extreme; it will imply no methodological responsibility, since it will bear on the signifier, whereas the proposed analysis bears solely on the signified. The lexia will include sometimes a few words, sometimes several sentences; it will be a matter of convenience: it will suffice that the lexia be the best possible space in which we can observe meanings; its dimension, empirically determined, estimated, will depend on the density of connotations, variable according to the moments of the text: all we require is that each lexia should have at most three or four meanings to be enumerated.[23]

S/Z moves beyond the structural analysis of narrative in several important ways: through its attention to the smallest details of the discourse, through its aim to describe as well as analyze the text, and, most importantly, through its ontological assumptions about narrative. Barthes repudiates any positivist method that establishes the existence of shared features of narrative, or even distinctive ones that mark a single narrative as a unique whole. Rather, for

Barthes, narrative is now pure difference, "articulated upon the infinity of texts, of languages, of systems": "the one text is not an (inductive) access to a Model, but entrance into a network with a thousand entrances."[24] That network is constituted by the absolute plurality of meaning, produced by codes that extend far beyond any literary corpus. But the issue of scale does not disappear. Taking the measure of narrative entails taking into account the elusive phenomenon of semantic volume. This is an operation the reader has to perform, cautiously or exuberantly unpacking the connotations offered by what Barthes calls the readerly text.[25]

Narrative as Immanent Scale-Making: Genette

Narratives are not simply objects to be measured but themselves agents that produce scale in a subtle and innovative fashion. Gérard Genette has offered perhaps the most influential account of narrative's scale-making operations. The distinction between the material of a story and the way that narrative discourse reshapes it had been discussed by Viktor Shklovsky, Boris Tomashevsky, and other Russian Formalists.[26] Genette, however, fully develops the way that narratives both invite and defy mensuration through their discursive presentation of story. In *Narrative Discourse* (1972), a study of Proust subtitled "An Essay in Method," scale is an emergent, dynamic, and dialectical aspect of any narrative.[27] Rather than trying to determine a fundamental narrative unit, Genette elaborates how the perceived incongruity between story and discourse gives rise to a dynamic sense of scale. What takes the place of Barthes's codes in Genette's approach generally is a strong sense of counterfactual narrative situations. In this context, meaning often requires grasping the particularity of a narrative element within a horizon of other possibilities. There are three major areas in which Genette's narrative theory illuminates phenomena of narrative scale: time or temporal deformation, focalization or perspective, and narrative levels or embedding.

Temporal scale, like other dimensions of narrative scale, arises from the relation between the events of the story and the way in which they are told. Story events are inherently possessed of a temporal dimension; it is impossible to conceive of a story event that does not encompass some interval of time, even if that interval departs from normal human experience. (The exception would lie in the structuralist approach that understands the deep level of story as consisting in arrangements of opposed conceptual pairs, as in the anthropologist Claude Lévi-Strauss's well-known explication of the Oedipus myth. Those oppositions and relations exist outside of time, though they are expressed in the temporal form of narrative.)[28] The relations between the time of a story event and its telling possess quantitative and qualitative dimensions. Most simply, the amount of chronological or clock time that a story event takes can be compared to the amount of discourse devoted to relating it. As Genette remarks, it is a matter of convention to assume that a scenic representation, in which speech is directly quoted, approximates a one-to-one ratio between story-time and discourse-time, while in a summary, longer stretches of time in the story can be packed into a small amount of discourse. Ellipsis is proposed by Genette as a category in which story events are not told at all. By contrast, in a descriptive pause, the time of the story is suspended while the narrator describes something: "the narrator, forsaking the course of the story [. . .] makes it his business [. . .] to describe a scene that at this point in the story no one, strictly speaking, is looking at."[29] The discourse can thus be imagined as having a speed that can be, and often is, highly variable both between works and within a single work. In Proust, the tempo ranges from "a page for one minute to a page for one century."[30] Narratives make us aware of such variations of speed as a relation between the eventfulness of the story and the amplitude of the discourse.

But in addition to quantitative duration, narratives invoke and manipulate a range of temporal *intensity*. In his discussion of frequency, Genette notes that an event in the story need not be told only one time. In the singulative mode, an event that happens once is told once (or *n* occurrences are told *n* times). But in the iterative mode, an event that happens *n* times is told only once in the discourse. The repetitive mode tells an event that happens once *n* times, over and over.[31] By manipulating duration and frequency, narrative discourse arranges a story's events on a scale of significance and intensity. In the case of duration, it is often the case that discourse slows down and lingers on events or moments of greater significance, moving forward more quickly when the story's chronology cools, as it were. But manipulations of scale can also be subtle and counterintuitive, particularly where frequency is concerned. We might assume the singulative frequency to be normative for narrative. This is more likely to be the case when narrative exposition is clearly marked off from the plot.[32] Genette argues that in classical narrative, the iterative serves as a background against which the singular event emerges. But the iterative mode can become a means of communicating a deeper temporal intensity, as well as a different affective experience of time. Thus, temporal scale results from the inherent tension between a story and the discourse that gives it verbal form. To some extent we must think of pure story as occurring within or against the background of a time that elapses at a more or less regular pace, even if it is not the empty, homogeneous clock time of modernity. The discourse that we read, however, is stretching, expanding, compressing, pausing, or eliding the time of the story, as well as endowing events of all types with variable frequencies. Narrative temporality has the qualities not only of speed – fast or slow – but also of volume: thick or thin, resonant or dull.

All of these aspects of narrative scale are themselves dependent on what may be the most fundamental feature of narrative: the fact that it is mediated. Genette approaches mediation as a matter of what he terms focalization, or narrative mood. Unlike dramatic mimesis, narrative has to be told, and, as Genette remarks, "one can tell *more* or tell *less* what one tells, and can tell it *according to one point of view or another.*"[33] This variability can be extremely pronounced in any given narrative. Though much ink has been spilled by narrative theorists over the optimal application of the term, we can agree that focalization has to do with the highly variable *quantity of information* about the story itself that can be conveyed by a narrative. This quantity is modulated as the discourse adopts various positions relative to the fictional world, as well as various positions within it. The narrator may be all-knowing or may be a character with restricted knowledge. Sometimes the discourse takes the viewpoint of one character or another within the story, using them as focalizers. Depending on the position taken, the quantity of information changes. Some things will be known, others surmised, and still other things, events, and characters left completely opaque. The quantity and quality of *affirmation* will change as well, as Genette reminds us.[34]

Narrative discourse can be thought of as incessantly measuring the distance between characters, or between narrator and characters, in large part through focalization. Here, distance is understood not primarily in terms of Cartesian space, but rather as something deeply intersubjective, socially saturated, and ideologically fraught. Thus the narrative theorist Shlomith Rimmon-Kenan has argued that focalization encompasses not only phenomena of perception and knowledge but also of emotion and ideology.[35] The relation between a narrator and a given character at any moment can be distant, diffident, neglectful, frustrated, disapproving, sympathetic, curious, intimate, or omniscient; the relations between characters as shown in their focalizations of each other show a similar range. A single or simple hierarchy cannot encompass the range of relations and values thus evoked. Sometimes the intimate knowability of a character raises its value, but not always: distance and opacity can also confer prestige or incite desire.

Thinking about focalization therefore reveals that questions of scale must consider far more than simply whether a unit is small or large. Opacity and transparency, closeness and distance may in fact be more important scales to examine, particularly whenever the production of knowledge is concerned – as indeed it always is in narrative. Such an examination reminds us that scale depends on the location and position of the perceiver, not to mention the narrator. Nor can questions of access and authority, whether real or fictive, be dismissed.

The act of narration itself has dimensions of time and significance, as Genette reminds us. Telling a story takes time, takes place somewhere, and presumably embodies some intention. This fact is emphasized when narratives embed narratives within themselves – a phenomenon studied in terms of narrative levels. Thinking about narrative levels can productively disrupt common models of scale. The relation between the discourse we encounter first (the "outer" or "frame" narrative) and that which we encounter only afterward (the "inner" or "embedded" story) is inherently difficult to characterize. As Genette remarks, "It is a fact that the embedded narrative is narratively subordinate to the embedding narrative, since the former owes its existence to the latter and is based on it. [... W]e must [...] accept this contradiction between unquestioned narrative subordination and possible thematic precedence."[36] That is, the enclosed, embedded, or subordinated narrative may be more important than the one that contains it. The outer frame or embedding narrative may simply serve as the occasion for the all-important tale. But this embedding narrative is by definition more capacious as well as prior in reading sequence: more inclusive, capable of containing other discourses, sometimes many of them. How, then, can their relative sizes or importance be established? More recently, Genette hesitates to endorse his earlier terminology, which relied on spatial imagery. Discussing the relations between narratives nonhierarchically is difficult but necessary: "if it is true that the second narrative depends on the first narrative, it does so, rather, in the sense of resting on it, as the second story of a building or the second stage of a rocket depends on the first."[37] We can see here the point at which spatial thinking about scale reaches its limits.

Narrative Theory, Comparison, and the Scale of History: Formalism and Structuralism Revisited

Though both Genette's *Narrative Discourse* and Barthes's *S/Z* focus on the example of a single text, they develop concepts of great analytical power and breadth. Narrative theory at its best maintains its awareness of the sheer size of its object of study, and of narrative's cultural and historical ubiquity. But can it measure or account for the historical dimensions of narrative? At what scale of analysis should the work of comparing and classifying narratives proceed? In the work of the Russian Formalists, the group of important Soviet critics and theorists whose major work appeared in the 1920s, we find that genres need not be the starting point for the investigation of either form or historical change. In Propp's work, the genre of the folktale does provide a point of departure, but its nature only appears dialectically on the basis of the functions that are discovered. Propp's contemporaries Boris Tomashevsky and Boris Eichenbaum show other ways in which the examination of small narrative units can ground historical and comparative investigations. Tzvetan Todorov's later work on narrative transformations also offers a framework that can productively be applied to the study of narrative across languages and historical periods.

"The unique claim of the Russian Formalists is," as Fredric Jameson put it in his classic study, "their stubborn attachment to the intrinsically literary, their stubborn refusal to be diverted from the 'literary fact' to some other form of theorization."[38] Yet in Boris Tomashevsky's *Theory of Literature* (1925), the formalist investigation of narrative's internal structure actually leads to questions about the rate and mode of historical change within the realm of literature. Tomashevsky begins by subordinating the story-discourse distinction to the notion of a "theme": "The theme (what is being said in a work) unites the separate elements of a work."[39] The theme is the substance to be subdivided, and Tomashevsky takes what appears to be a rather casual approach to the now-familiar question of the smallest unit of narrative: "After reducing a work to its thematic elements, we come to parts that are irreducible, the smallest particles of thematic material: 'evening comes,' 'Raskolnikov kills the old woman,' 'the hero dies,' 'the letter is received,' and so on. The theme of an irreducible part of a work is called the *motif*."[40] This loose definition of the motif, however, allows Tomashevsky to focus on what he calls motivation, or the strategies (devices) through which the inclusion of any motif must be justified. His principle of "compositional motivation" is often cited: "Not a single property [i.e., object] may remain unused in the telling, and no episode may be without influence on the situation."[41] What receives less attention, though, is how the discussion of motivation allows Tomashevsky to move naturally to the level of genre. Detective novels, for example, are characterized by "misleading motivation: props and episodes may be used to distract the reader's attention from the real situation."[42] A genre even dearer to Tomashevsky, and many other formalists, is that of parody: "the play upon generally known literary rules [of compositional motivation] [...] is indispensable for parody."[43] Although his observations are less rigorous or sustained than Barthes's or Genette's, Tomashevsky's discussion of the various principles of motivation is striking for its attentiveness to the continuities and discontinuities of literary history. He suggests that generic conventions and established styles depend on the way that attitudes toward motivation strategies shift over time. For example, in his discussion of his colleague Viktor Shklovsky's important concept of "defamiliarization" – the process by which art "makes perception long and 'laborious'" – Tomashevsky suggests that, as a conscious artistic strategy, defamiliarization has to contend with the forces of literary history:

> Devices are perceptible for perhaps two reasons: their excessive age or their excessive newness. Abandoned, old, archaic devices are felt as intrusive remnants, as having lost their own vitality and enduring by a strong inertial force [. . .N]ew devices strike their own peculiar, unaccustomed note if they are taken from a previously forbidden repertory [. . .]. We must keep our appreciation of perceptible and imperceptible devices in a historical perspective.[44]

Tomashevsky's analysis illustrates an important contention made by Boris Eichenbaum about the Formalist project. Eichenbaum noted that, for these critics, "the problem of literary evolution" arose organically out of an attention to formal concerns:

> [T]he original attempt of the Formalists to take a particular structural device and to establish its identity in diverse materials became an attempt to differentiate, to understand, the function of a device in a given case. This notion of functional significance was gradually pushed toward the foreground. [. . .] The theory itself demanded that we turn to history.[45]

By focusing on the "specific functions of this or that device," the Formalists, Eichenbaum argues, were enabled to write a more empirically grounded literary history, one that moved beyond "somewhat vague notions such as 'realism' and 'romanticism,'" and beyond biographical criticism. The small functional device gave them an effective weapon against non- or anti-historicist methods and showed them a workable scale of literary history.[46]

The Formalists demarcated literature and literary history quite sharply from their social surroundings. But within that delimited history, they achieved results that continue to generate significant work. The productivity of such an approach can be seen in more-recent studies that delineate a motif or device and trace its functional significance over time. In his influential and important *Graphs, Maps, Trees*, as well as his earlier essay, "The Slaughterhouse of Literature," Franco Moretti traces the device of the clue in detective fiction. As he points out, the clue ranges in size from a sentence to "not even a full word," yet it enables a broad view of how the genre acquired its formal characteristics.[47] Tracing such a device reveals literary history as a series of divergences and convergences.[48] In another example, Monika Fludernik focuses on a device that arose to handle "how [. . .] narratives manage to get from one set of characters in one location to another set of characters in a different location."[49] When shifting the scene, medieval and early modern narratives often used a particular verbal formula such as "now leave we/now turn we."[50] Tracing this device from medieval to modernist narratives, Fludernik finds that "a formula that used to be employed to shift between plot strands ends up at chapter beginnings coinciding with scene shifts, and later on acquires an analeptic, metaleptic, and metafictional function."[51] Once the convention of chapter breaks led readers to expect a change in setting, the original function of the device was no longer necessary; thus it "could be refunctionalized for ironic purposes."[52] Fludernik's and Moretti's analyses show how focusing on the function of the small narrative unit can help produce a supple, well-focused, and cross-cultural literary history.

The devices analyzed by Tomashevsky exist for the most part at the level of story, of what happens. In other words, they can be paraphrased and described. Tomashevsky, for instance, names as two motifs "the rescue of the hero always occurs five minutes before his seemingly inevitable death" and "all the characters turn out to be close relatives."[53] This feature raises a question that can be put more explicitly: For the large-scale analysis of narrative, is it more productive to look (or measure) at the level of language or of meaning? Can we be justified in looking beyond or beneath the discourse, the words on the page? In his remarkable essay "Narrative Transformations" (1969), Todorov notes these "two tendencies in the analysis of narrative: one, a propositional or semic analysis, elaborates its units; the other, a lexical analysis, finds them ready-made in the text."[54] (Barthes's example in *S/Z*, of course, shows that even a lexical analysis has to construct its units.) Todorov demonstrates how much can be gained by attending to the inner structure of narrative in terms of *propositions that are related in a certain way*.

Doing so requires a radical abstraction or reduction. Todorov begins by noting that Propp's functions are not quite the right size, nor are they uniformly related: some can be further broken down, while others seem to be identical. "A prohibition is imposed on the hero," Propp's second function, consists of two actions: there is "the immediate action of prohibition," in addition to the possible but unrealized action of the hero's violating that command.[55] Conversely, Propp's fourth and fifth functions – "The aggressor seeks to gain information" and "The aggressor receives information about his victim" – state the same action, the first time as intention and the second time "as a fait accompli."[56] This insight leads Todorov to propose that the basic structure of narrative relies on what he calls transformation, based on the linguistic concept of that name: "Two propositions may be said to be in a relation of transformation when one predicate remains identical on both sides."[57] For example, the proposition "*x* works" can be transformed into propositions such as "*x* decides to work," "*x* begins to work," or "*x* succeeds in his work." Complex transformations include a second action that depends on the first, such as "*x* pretends that *x* works," or "*y* learns/reveals/suspects that *x* works." Todorov uses this relationship of transformation, as well as the typology of transformations (both simple and complex), to do several things. He suggests that groups of narratives can be classified according to the type of transformation that predominates. He also offers an intriguing account of narrative sequence. Todorov argues that we know instinctively when a narrative sequence has been completed when a transformation occurs: for example, a prediction is given and then realized, or a riddle is posed and then solved.[58]

What Todorov's notion of narrative transformation allows us to see, in a way very different from Genette's, is that a key to the inner structural scale of story may lie in *repetition*. In an earlier essay, "Categories of Narrative," Todorov stresses the critical role played by repetition at the level of discourse and of story: antithesis, gradation, and parallelism are all forms of repetition, though only some are verbally present.[59] The repetition involved in narrative transformations is deeper, but it reminds us that, even at this level of story, scale is, in a sense, another word for the effects of repetition.

Narratives consistently and constitutively engage in the work of scale-making. Durations, distances, positions, and relations are created, measured, and manipulated within narratives and between them. In narrative theory, scale can be seen to be an activity, more like a performance than an objective quality possessed by objects. But the production of scale relies on making certain moves: noting repetitions, marking certain motifs, waiting for events, waiting for completion, following paths and networks of connotative meaning, feeling time stretch or thicken in the course of a narrative. Such moves occur within historically changing and culturally variable circumstances. What makes narrative theory useful is the attention that it gives to functions, the thought that it gives to the delineation of units, and its commitment to producing instruments that allow us to commensurate the ways in which different narratives extend, contort, and measure themselves into being.

Notes

1. See Mark Algee-Hewitt, Ryan Heuser, and Franco Moretti, "On Paragraphs, Scale, Themes, and Narrative Form," Stanford Literary Lab Pamphlet Series 10 (2015), on the "conjunction of very small units and a very large outcome" (4). See also the special issue of *Modern Language Quarterly* (77 [2016]) on "Scale and Value: New and Digital Approaches to Literary History," and in particular the introduction by James English and Ted Underwood, which considers the dramatic explosion in the scale of literary analysis that resulted from the digital availability of large archives and the expansion in methods used to study this material; the

essay by Hoyt Long and Richard Jean So, "Turbulent Flow: A Computational Model of World Literature," which aims to describe the system of world literature by looking at the global diffusion across languages of the modernist form of "stream of consciousness"; and the essay by Mark McGurl, "Everything and Less: Fiction in the Age of Amazon," which offers a "practical theorization of the literary field" in relation to the changing conceptualization and consumption of genre fiction (450).

2. In "Defining Narrative Units," Jonathan Culler provides a helpful overview and critique of how different narrative theories have gone about this task. He notes that "[e]ach theory, constrained to define for itself the basic units of narrative, becomes a coherent and self-contained system [...] and consequently, they are difficult to compare" (in *Style and Structure in Literature*, ed. Roger Fowler [Ithaca, NY: Cornell University Press, 1975], 125). Culler goes on to suggest that "competing theories of plot structure can only be evaluated by their success in serving as models of a particular aspect of literary competence: readers' abilities to recognize and summarize plots, to group together similar plots, etc." (127).

3. Anna Lowenhaupt Tsing, *The Mushroom at the End of the World: On the Possibility of Life in Capitalist Ruins* (Princeton, NJ: Princeton University Press, 2015), 38.

4. Vladimir Propp, *The Morphology of the Folktale*, 2nd ed., trans. Laurence Scott, ed. Louis A. Wagner (Austin: University of Texas Press, 1968), 4, 6.

5. Ibid., 21.

6. Ibid.

7. Ibid., 23.

8. The five categories that define the tale as a whole are functions, conjunctive elements, motivations, the forms of characters' appearances, and characters' attributive elements or accessories (ibid., 96).

9. Ibid., 65. This standard of measure works in both directions since, as Propp notes, the application of the scheme to a particular tale "can only be resolved by an analysis of the texts" (ibid.).

10. Roland Barthes, "Introduction to the Structural Analysis of Narratives," in *Image-Music-Text*, trans. Stephen Heath (New York, NY: Noonday-Farrar, Strauss and Giroux, 1977), 88.

11. Ibid., 91.

12. Ibid., 89.

13. Ibid., 86.

14. Ibid., 92.

15. Ibid., 107.

16. Ibid., 91. For an interesting reading of Barthes's choice of example as reflecting a Cold War context, see Kent Puckett, *Narrative Theory: A Critical Introduction* (Cambridge: Cambridge University Press, 2016), 240–242.

17. Barthes, "Introduction," 98.

18. Ibid., 101.

19. Ibid., 96.

20. Tzvetan Todorov, "Categories of Narrative," trans. Joseph Kestner, *Papers on Language and Literature* 16 (1980): 382.

21. Roland Barthes, *S/Z: An Essay*, trans. Richard Miller (New York, NY: Hill and Wang, 1974), 14.

22. Ibid., 10–11.

23. Ibid., 13–14.

24. Ibid., 3, 12.

25. Connotation, as Barthes defines it, is the actual amount of plurality that we are able to see in any narrative (as opposed to the transcendent plurality he imagines as the ground of narrative). His discussion of connotation as occurring in "a sequential space" and "an agglomerative space" still recalls the model of narrative offered in his earlier essay (ibid., 6–11). But his more explicit emphasis on readerly activity in *S/Z* marks an important departure from structuralism.

26. See the important essays in *Russian Formalist Criticism*, ed. and trans. Lee T. Lemon and Marion J. Reis, 2nd ed. (Lincoln: University of Nebraska Press, 2012); Viktor Shklovsky, *Theory of Prose*, trans. Benjamin Sher (Elmwood Park, IL: Dalkey Archive Press, 1990), a collection of essays by a key figure in Russian Formalism; and Seymour Chatman, *Story and Discourse* (Ithaca, NY: Cornell University Press, 1978), a foundational work of American narratology.

27. Genette's study was originally published in French as part of *Figures III* (Paris: Éditions du Seuil, 1972); it appeared in English as *Narrative Discourse: An Essay in Method*, trans. Jane E. Lewin (Ithaca, NY: Cornell University Press, 1980).

28. See Claude Lévi-Strauss, "The Structural Study of Myth," in *Structural Anthropology*, 2 vols., trans. Claire Jacobson and Brooke Grunfest Schoepf (New York, NY: Basic Books, 1963–1976), 1: 206–232.

29. Genette, *Narrative Discourse*, 100.

30. Gérard Genette, *Narrative Discourse Revisited*, trans. Jane E. Lewin (Ithaca, NY: Cornell University Press, 1990), 35. In this work, Genette responds to his critics and revises some of his original ideas.

31. Genette, *Narrative Discourse*, 113–117.

32. See Meir Sternberg, *Expositional Modes and Temporal Ordering in Fiction* (Baltimore, MD: Johns Hopkins University Press, 1978).

33. Genette, *Narrative Discourse*, 161–162.

34. Ibid., 161.

35. Shlomith Rimmon-Kenan, *Narrative Fiction: Contemporary Poetics* (London: Methuen, 1983), 80–84.

36. Genette, *Narrative Discourse Revisited*, 90.

37. Ibid., 91.

38. Fredric Jameson, *The Prison-House of Language: A Critical Account of Structuralism and Russian Formalism* (Princeton, NJ: Princeton University Press, 1972), 43.

39. Boris Tomashevsky, "Thematics," in *Russian Formalist Criticism*, 63.

40. Ibid., 67.

41. Ibid., 79.

42. Ibid., 80.

43. Ibid.

44. Viktor Shklovsky, "Art as Device," *Theory of Prose*, trans. Benjamin Sher (Elmwood Park, IL: Dalkey Archive, 1990), 6; Tomashevsky, "Thematics," 93.

45. Boris Eichenbaum, "The Theory of the 'Formal Method,'" in *Russian Formalist Criticism*, 132.

46. Ibid., 133. Nevertheless, the Formalists were embroiled in arguments over the relationship between form and history. For two authoritative accounts, see Jameson, *Prison-House*, 43–98, and Caryl Emerson, "Literary Theory in the 1920s: Four Options and a Practicum," in *A History of Russian Literary Theory and Criticism: The Soviet Age and Beyond*, ed. Evgeny Dobrenko and Galin Tihanov (Pittsburgh, PA: University of Pittsburgh Press, 2011), 64–89.
47. Franco Moretti, *Graphs, Maps, Trees* (London: Verso, 2005), 76. See also Moretti, "The Slaughterhouse of Literature," *Modern Language Quarterly* 61 (2000): 207–227. Moretti is more interested than the Formalists in the question of literary diffusion in space as well as time, and argues for "the dependence of morphological novelty on spatial discontinuity" as well as on historical change (*Graphs*, 90).
48. Moretti, *Graphs*, 78–81.
49. Monika Fludernik, "The Diachronization of Narratology," *Narrative* 11 (2003): 334.
50. Ibid., 336.
51. Ibid., 334.
52. Ibid., 342.
53. Tomashevsky, "Thematics," 81.
54. Todorov, "Narrative Transformations," in *The Poetics of Prose*, trans. Richard Howard (Ithaca, NY: Cornell University Press, 1977), 230.
55. Ibid., 221.
56. Ibid., 222.
57. Ibid., 224.
58. Ibid., 232. Todorov cites these examples from Shklovsky's essay "The Construction of the Story and of the Novel," in the latter's *Theory of Prose*.
59. Todorov, "Categories," 385–386.

Structure in terms of CNF ?
Difference ?

3

ILYA KALININ

The Body of Plot: Viktor Shklovsky's Theory of Narrative

> From the standpoint of plot, there is no need for the concept of "content" in our analysis of a work of art.
> —Viktor Shklovsky, *Theory of Prose*

The Russian Formalists' opposition between story ("a phenomenon relating to the material") and plot ("a phenomenon of style") presents the latter as the aspect of the work that not only organizes "the totality of events," but also organizes them intentionally in order to increase readerly tension. The recombination of story events into a plot (with its interruptions, retardations, and decoys) makes possible the emancipation of the narrator and the reader, and even the author, from "what happened in actuality." This division between "the material of life" and its "artistic deformation and decomposition" is the basis for the Formalist theory of narrative.[1]

What is now known as Russian Formalism developed within the Society for the Study of Poetic Language (OPOIaZ), whose most famous member, Viktor Shklovsky, formulated the principles for the application of the theory of poetics to narrative theory. Generally speaking, for Shklovsky the laws of literary narrative are autonomous from the laws of logic, psychology, common sense, and social routines that hold sway beyond the bounds of literature; furthermore, the basic mode through which story elements (or motifs) are combined into a plot is montage, which (like montage or editing in film) establishes dynamic relationships of disequilibrium, surprise, reordering, transposition, repetition, and so on.[2] This dynamism is essential to what the Formalists took to be the central aesthetic effect: *form made difficult*, that complication of form that makes art what it is, emancipating human beings from the automatized perception characteristic of everyday life.[3] Yet emancipation from automatization does not constitute a retreat into the autonomy of the aesthetic. Rather, it accomplishes the opposite: a return to life and its immediate sensory perception. "And so," as Shklovsky put it, "in order to return sensations to our limbs, in order to make us feel objects, to make a stone feel stony, man has been given the tool of art."[4]

46

In this treatment of the Formalists' theory of plot, I endeavor to discover, in the configuration of metaphors that constitutes its conceptual apparatus ("impedance," "retardation," "delay," "linkage," "threading," "repetition," "transposition," "deviation," "deceleration," "shift," "stepwise construction," and so on), a relatively persistent parallelism with the bodily and plastic modality of the performing arts: dance, circus acts, cinema, folk buffoonery, and avant-garde theater. Focusing on this tropological aspect of the metalanguage of Russian Formalist narrative theory will make it possible to grasp its relationship with aspects of Modernist thought that are more typically overlooked when Formalism is seen simply as a precursor of structuralism. Formalism, and Shklovsky's thought in particular, attributed far-reaching utopian potential to art, potential that arose from commonalities with the plastic bodily movement that underwrites art's capacity to return humanity to the sensation of the real – to the stoniness of the stone.[5]

A shift of attention from the purely semantic or meaning-making aspects of language (including poetic language) to the mechanisms of sound utterance was a typical move in the early twentieth century, both in academic studies and in the language studies of those Russian symbolists interested in literary scholarship. The "movement of articulation" and the "sonic gesture" became authoritative concepts in the expression of knowledge about language.[6] Such bodily, plastic analogies gained broader currency in the artistic practices of the avant-garde, especially in the artistic experiments of the Futurists. Further, we are dealing here not merely with structural analogies establishing a correspondence between sound, word, and gesture, but rather with a paradigm shift, signaling that the hope for the renewal both of art and of what Shklovsky called the "faded perception of the world" was now placed precisely on the kinetic possibilities of the body, in opposition to the word in its purely semantic dimension. Consider, for instance, a fragment from a manifesto by one of the leaders of the Russian avant-garde, Mikhail Matiushin: "The gesture – rapid, like all our contemporary reality – is already taking the place of the faded word. [...] The new art discovers the possibility of understanding the world via a simple, immediate act of motion of the body itself, via facial movements, via gesture."[7]

Such a stance reflected a perception (general for the avant-garde, central for Futurism) of the referential rigidity and semantic hollowness of the word as such, which urgently demanded compensation by means of a transfer of attention to the external, sonic aspect of the *poetic* word, understood as a special form of phonetic gesture. Note too that the solution for this problem was not thought to be that some forms of art (in this case the temporal forms of literature and music) must give way before others (the spatial forms of painting, the plastic arts, and so on). Rather, resolution of the problem of the new art's emergence was to be found in the reorientation of poetry itself toward the production of visual and plastic representations. In Futurist poetics, the word did not die off, to be replaced by the gesture; rather, the mechanism of poetic meaning production began to be conceived as an "expressive-gestural act."[8]

Dance was perhaps the most polyvalent form of plastic art, and for this reason it frequently served as a model, indicating how other forms of non-bodily and nonplastic art (both spatial and temporal, both painting and poetry) could compensate for their limited expressive and cognitive possibilities. In the words of Russian art historian Ekaterina Bobrinskaia, "The movements of dance, in which the human body becomes simultaneously instrument, material and work of art in itself, in which the psychic and the bodily are fused, became for the Russian avant-gardists a frequent internal metaphor and prototype for their own experiments in visual art and poetry."[9] One of Shklovsky's teachers, the artist and art theorist Nikolai Kul'bin, called for a "dancification of all life." At the end of the 1910s, yet another representative of the Russian avant-garde, Igor' Terent'ev, described the dialectical development of sound into gesture and of gesture into dance as follows: "When one is at a loss for words, when sound loses its force – this is when gesticulation, delirious flight, leaping, and thrashing about on the ground begins. Dance is the last thing that remains after you have tried everything else."[10] More examples could easily be adduced, demonstrating that gesture – both calculated and free, ecstatic movement – not only accompanies the poetic word, but is conceived as a persistent artistic motif, a conceptual metaphor for art as the most adequate means for representing the world and for human self-expression, as well as for the reestablishment of an organic linkage between world and individual.

Shklovsky expressed his own thinking about dance as the highest form of poetic expression, with his typical laconic radicalism, in the 1916 essay "On Poetry and Trans-Sense Language": "It may even be that in general the greater part of the pleasure in poetry is to be found in the articulation, in the original dance of the speech organs."[11] In this comparison of the movements of the organs of articulation with those of a dancing body, we may discern the shift of attention toward the physical, sonic aspect of poetic speech, related to its pronunciation, that was characteristic of Formalist theory. Yet we must also note the less obvious connection, equally characteristic of these thinkers, between the evocation of aesthetic emotion and the dance-like movement of articulation. Across Shklovsky's works we find similar conceptions concerning dance (as well as other plastic and visual forms of art), in relation not just to poetry and the articulatory "organs of speech," but also to narration and the "devices of plot construction" that organize it. In Shklovsky's narratological formulations we find an underlying sense of the body in movement as the generator of meaning.

Traditionally, Russian Formalism has been understood as the theoretical background to structuralism, rooted in the emphatic rejection of any motivating factors external to the text (relating to everyday life, psychology, and "content" in general), in deference to a focus on the internal laws of language itself and the poetic laws of the artistic text. As early as his first essay devoted to the formulation of new theoretical problems in the study of plot from 1919 ("The Relationship between Devices of Plot Construction and General Devices of Style"), Shklovsky critiques the attempt to explain a coincidence of plot motifs across cultures as a reflection of cultural contacts and borrowings or comparable historical circumstances that ostensibly led to the similar expressive structures observed in various national literatures. Shklovsky's position was based on his proposal that neither a comparative historical nor a social ethnographic method could offer an adequate account of "plot similarities in the folk tales of various peoples." Instead, it was necessary to seek an explanation in the "laws governing of plot formation" and in the laws governing poetic language in general, in light of which, to Shklovsky's mind, it was obvious that coincidences in motif were founded not on historical or psychological similarities "but rather on pure rhythmic repetition."[12] This theoretical emphasis on the immanence of linguistic and poetic laws has made it possible to view Formalism as the direct predecessor of structuralist semiotics, which explicitly and systematically adopted a linguistic model as the basis for its theoretical constructions, affirming the "identity of language and literature," and linking the production of artistic meaning to mechanisms of semiosis rather than reference.[13] Furthermore, although Shklovsky polemicizes with Alexander Veselovsky, he also follows his lead in turning to folklore and to early forms of narrative, which provide optimal material for a demonstration of the compositional articulation of motifs in the plot.[14] In this regard one may also observe the theoretical focus, characteristic for structuralism as a whole, on "cooled-off structures" – iterative folklore structures, or rigid generic structures that have lost their original flexibility – the exposed schematism of which makes it possible to effectively apply methods of analysis typical for this school of theory.

Structuralism postulated the same homology between the laws of language and the laws governing the unfolding of literary texts, yet with an orientation on the narrower field of the theory of plot: "In the current state of research, it seems reasonable that the structural analyses of narrative be given linguistics itself as founding model," affirmed Barthes.[15] Shklovsky's works might seem to offer a similar identification of the linguistic and the narrative-discursive. Aage Hansen-Löve, for instance, writes that "Shklovsky postulates both a methodological and a structural analogy between the constructive techniques for linguistic (stylistic) devices ('parallelism,' 'repetition,' 'shift') and plot devices."[16] In fact, however, it is impossible to establish an identity in Shklovsky's thought between the "linguistic" and the "stylistic" – that is to say between the grammar of language and the rhetoric of the text.

On the one hand, within the framework of early Formalism, the immanence of plot or stylistic devices is the converse of the rejection of historical, psychological, or social motivations – which is to say, of "external" (in Shklovsky's terms) or "extralinguistic" (in Paul Ricoeur's terms) motivations.[17] On the other hand, in the case of early Formalism, the concept of literary immanence, as opposed to the "external," was by no means a consequence of the idea of the closure of a linguistic structure as Ricoeur defines it. To the contrary, the immanence of the literary (notwithstanding purely polemical, heated denunciations of the positivist theory of reflection) was imagined as an emancipation from the closure characteristic of practical language, which had lost not only its intentional but also its emotional linkages with reality – linkages that art was called upon to reestablish. Thus with Formalism we are dealing rather with a manifestation of the autonomy of the artistic text from the automatized grammar of everyday language. The rejection of external causation was founded on a rejection of the normativity, automatization, and lack of consciousness underlying "extrapoetic" reality and reinforced in the laws of practical language (for instance, in the law of "economy of psychic effort," affirmed by positivism).

Shklovsky's theory of plot aligns methodologically less with linguistics than with poetics and rhetoric – with the work of poetic language, organized according to unpredictable compositional shifts and semantic displacements (and remaining functional only insofar as this unpredictability is maintained), rather than with the work of language as such (that is to say, with practical, "prosaic" language), organized by means of the orderly and persistent system of juxtapositions and oppositions.[18] It was precisely for this reason that all of Shklovsky's efforts to create typologies and classificatory systems of devices (whether relating to style or plot) were so reminiscent of Borges's Chinese encyclopedia of animals: afflicted by obvious contradictions, the absence of general foundations, and juvenile pretensions to "scientific" status. The reason for these "failures" was simple: the system of literature, as conceived by Shklovsky, was open, so that each new text selected for analysis demanded a whole new typology, for each violated previous norms and articulated new shifts.

At the start of his discussion of the principles of plot construction, Shklovsky rejects the obvious analogy with grammar, proposing that the plot in literature is not related to the unfolding of a normal sentence (as Barthes would affirm[19]) but rather "may be defined as an unfolding parallel. Parallelism is akin to so-called figurativeness."[20] In this manner, Shklovsky describes plot not in terms of a syntagmatic linear development, but instead in terms of the paradigmatic equivalency of parallelism. It might seem that the accent on the paradigmatic, as opposed to the syntagmatic, could serve as an additional confirmation of the superiority of structuralism over Shklovsky's conceptions. Indeed, structuralist narratology (Greimas, Brémond, Todorov) focused precisely on this aspect of the problem in building on and pushing off from the work of Vladimir Propp[21] (who, to tell the truth, either could not or did not want to claim the mantle of "forefather of Structuralism"). But as we know, the devil is in the details. For the structuralists, the paradigmatic matrix, which gives rise to the linearity of the plot, was founded on either a logical model (as in the case of Bremond, who sought to create a complete "syntax of human actions"[22]) or a linguistic one (as in the case of Lévi-Strauss, Roland Barthes, and Greimas, who constructed their system of functional oppositions between narrative elements).[23] For Shklovsky, in contrast, conceptions of the paradigmatic character of artistic narrative were based on the metaphorical structure of figurative parallelism and the poetic model of the violation of norms, false expectations, and "form made difficult." According to Shklovsky, parallelism (figurative, psychological, or plot-related), giving rise to "a sense of non-coincidence coupled with similarity," works not by means of the establishment of persistent structural relationships between distinct semantic planes, but, to the contrary, leads to a shift in perception, one of the basic devices for realization of the principle of defamiliarization.[24]

The meaning of the organization of material in plot is founded, therefore, not on the expression of the internal laws of language or of a logical syntax, but on the creation of challenges related to the violation of the norm – for instance, the retardation of plot development by means of the introduction of novel material, alien to the action itself. Shklovsky explains at length the functional identity of narrative devices with organizational devices of the lyric text: "moments of delay and deceleration, which slow down the development of the action and introduce into the plot the difficulty that underlies the 'aesthetic' experience of a certain suspense in the adventure novel and in cinema, play the same role as, for example, parallelisms, sound orchestration, and so on in a poem."[25]

So understood, the laws of plot construction, common to narrative texts and cinema, are based on a paradigmatic structure that takes as its goal the creation of form that has been made difficult – form of the sort that distinguishes the work of art from objects that are not perceived in an aesthetic manner. Plot is a violation of the logic of story, a violation that should be unexpected for the reader and demand the expenditure of additional effort in its reception in order to overcome this unexpected quality. Form made difficult evokes the additional effort necessary for the comprehension of the nonlinear plot construction, but it also offers emancipation from the restrictive order dictated by the story reality of events, history, human life, or psychology. This emancipation exceeds the "narrative freedom" denied by structuralism. In Shklovsky's description, the immanent laws of plot construction liberate us from the automatizing effects of everyday life and other limitations.

Perhaps the most vivid example of such a narrative emancipation may be found in Soviet psychologist Lev Vygotsky's classical analysis in the middle 1920s of Ivan Bunin's novella *Light Breathing*. Although Vygotsky criticized the Formal method for its expressed anti-psychologism, he based his work on the opposition of plot and story, so foundational for Formalist narratology, showing how Bunin's recombination in the plot of the fatal order of the story allowed him to eliminate the natural and, it would seem, inevitably tragic qualities of the described situation. Death, the foundational element of the novella's story, is conquered by the "light breathing" of the plot, which recombines fragments of narrative material in a manner that emphasizes the freedom of the poetic imagination from everyday considerations of necessity and possibility.[26]

Victory over the hopelessness of life is in fact the victory of plot over story, presided over by the muse of narrative, Scheherazade. Shklovsky insistently returns to consideration of narrative devices that he conceptualizes as a reaction against the negative pragmatics of the narrative environment (the situation in which the narrator is located). For instance, the so-called framing device constitutes "the type of storytelling where the principal characters tell their stories in succession ad infinitum until the first story is completely forgotten." The tragic situation of narrators and listeners constitutes the motivation for this device of threading plots together, but the simple fact of the tale's extension ensures the possibility of a continued balancing between life and death.[27]

The *1,001 Nights* is important for Shklovsky not with regard to psychological realism (or its absence), but for its demonstration of the existential potential of the art of narration, which can emancipate the individual from lived circumstances. Shklovsky was himself a master of this art. At one point in his autobiographical novel *Sentimental Journey* (1923), the author describes with characteristic narcissism and flamboyance how he avoided arrest when he was serving as a fighter for the Socialist-Revolutionary underground: "The [Cheka[28]] interrogator suggested that I give some testimony about myself. I told him about Persia. He listened, his assistant listened, and so did another prisoner who had been brought in for questioning. They let me go. I'm a professional raconteur."[29]

In this perspective, we may also offer an alternative (non-protostructuralist) account for Shklovsky's persistent interest in folklore and early forms of narrative. They were significant not merely for their schematism, which exposed the structure of plot composition, but also because folklore balances on the boundary between art and life, constituting a realm of immediacy that recalls archaic ritual practices and interdependence with the real.[30] Emphasis on precisely this type of material (folktale, Greek novel, medieval epic, Renaissance narrative collections, and picaresque and chivalric novels, as well as their parodic deformation in the novels of Cervantes and Sterne) made it possible for Shklovsky to broaden the bounds of narratology, linking it both to the anthropological function of storytelling and to the existential problematic of death and freedom from lived routine.

In this manner, the artistic logic that the OPOIaZ group insisted upon was not founded on a closed formal logic of thought, "in itself and for itself," and not even on the structural logic of language. It derived its "structure" and explanatory power from another source: from the contrapuntal constructive laws of works of music and from the plastic laws of dance, hand-to-hand combat, and circus acts that generate dramatic visualizations of music. "Let me make a comparison," writes Shklovsky:

> The methods and devices of plot construction are similar to and in principle identical with the devices of, for instance, musical orchestration. Works of literature represent a web of sounds, movements and ideas. In a literary work an idea may take a form analogous to the pronunciatory and sonar aspects of a morpheme or else the form of heterogeneous element.[31]

So the narrative logic of the plot relies on the very same devices as the phonetic "logic" of composition in a lyric poem: thought and sound turn out to be inseparable from articulatory movements, and the devices of plot construction are in principle identical with the devices of sound orchestration.

Early Formalism, to be sure, eliminated most historical, extra-artistic motivations from its description of literary production, turning attention instead to the formal relationships that organize the material and arise as a result of the work of literary devices. However, this rejection of historical and psychological motivation is related only to the level of the material (the content) of the unfolding narrative. At the same time, in their deeper nature, those dialectical relationships that, according to the Formalists, interlinked the story and the plot extended beyond the bounds of artistic form and were rooted in the relationships of the author, narrator, and reader with the world itself. The compositional freedom of the plot, realized in various deformations of story order, achieves in Shklovsky's description an anthropological and even existential dimension. The plot is a path to emancipation from the normative logic (and ethics) of human deeds, from the biological predetermination of human life, from the laws of common sense, founded in habits of the everyday, and so forth. Form, rendered difficult by means of plot, may be compared with the efforts expended by a dancer, gymnast, or acrobat in order to achieve professional formal possibilities that create a "superstructure" above the usual physical capabilities of the body (above the normal "structure" of life), and in this sense offer a liberation from them – or to be precise, a liberation from the limitations of a normal, untrained body.

Frequently (especially in analysis of early or, in some sense, pure forms of plot construction), Shklovsky describes the articulation of the plot and the compositional linkage between its distinct elements as a realization of the principles of pure movement. This is motion that establishes a certain rhythm, the inertia of which (and with it the violation of expectations evoked by this inertia) constitutes well nigh the only actual compositional motivation for the development of the plot. Shklovsky goes so far as to introduce into his analysis the figure of a storyteller whose very image is built around an acrobatic device that undergirds the development of the plot and the mechanics of the combination of its elements. This narrator-acrobat and his situation, which is "made difficult" and "lacks verisimilitude" from the point of view of normal bodily mechanics, lays bare the absence of any need for an extra-compositional (logical or psychological) motivation.

> If, for compositional reasons, an author decided to connect two fragments, then this need not necessarily imply a causal relationship. [...] In one of Oriental tales a story is told by a hero carrying a spinning wheel on his head. This thoroughly untrue-to-life situation did not in any way embarrass or confuse the compiler of the story because the parts of this work are not necessary linked to each other, nor are they depended upon each other in accordance with any non-compositional laws.[32]

The motif of the wheel spinning on the head of the narrator is in fact completely adequate for resolution of the compositional goal of linking two elements of a plot. Shklovsky emphasizes this purely mechanical form of connection via the figure of the circus stunt or the pre-cinematic device of the magic lantern, which in a "miraculous manner" transforms static images into a moving presentation, projected on the surface of a screen. The interrelationship of distinct components of the narration is limited to the simple fact of their adjacency, which may be founded on no other logic than that of simple accumulation, of the threading together of components along a common compositional axis or the turning of the wheel of a kaleidoscope, replacing one constellation of elements with another. Hence, the movement of the plot corresponds not to the laws of psychology (the achievement of some goal) or formal logic (dependence on a cause), but rather to the dynamic laws of movement per se: rhythm, inertia and the overcoming of inertia, the mechanics of the circular motion of a wheel.

The dialectic of story and plot, in which the material of the story content is transcended in the compositional form of the plot, is analogous to the opposition of "everyday," "practical," "prosaic" movements against the "poetic" laws of dance, which are a sublation (an abolishment but also a preservation, or Aufhebung in Hegelian term) of everyday physical laws based on the economy of effort. The distinction introduced by the Formalists between story and plot may be reinterpreted, beyond Shklovsky's own conceptual metaphors, in terms of the distinction between walk and dance – or any plastic movement founded on the operations of false expectations, defamiliarization, form made difficult, and so on.

For Shklovsky, poetic language poses a basic question: "Why walk on a tightrope? And as if that were not enough, why squat every four steps?"[33] The answer is obvious: the whole acrobatic performance returns sensation to the act of walking. In general, the plot is built like a system of "transpositions" of motifs, "deviations" from direct chronological sequence, recombinations of the material of experience, repetitions of leitmotivs, retardations – in short, as a transcendence of the extra-aesthetic story, with its tendency toward economy of psychological effort in reception. In other words, the plot is constructed as a rejection of an automatized, everyday mode of walking, like a dance that simultaneously establishes and violates rhythmic repetitions. Or, in Shklovsky's own definition of the complicated "choreography" of art: "Art is not a march set to music, but rather a waking dance to be experienced."[34]

For this reason, when Shklovsky writes about a "well-constructed plot," a "forceful plot intrigue," "plot tension," "the spring of the plot," and so forth, we comprehend these conceptual, terminological metaphors as more than mere expressions of the scholar's vivid imagination. Indeed, these metaphors are founded on a persistent "figurative parallelism" that establishes a functional correlation between the narrative movement of the plot and artistic gesture – movement itself – acting as a condensation point for a panoply of avant-garde (and generally Modernist) scientific, artistic, and philosophical conceptions (from Friedrich Nietzsche to Isadora Duncan), rehabilitating plasticity as opposed to semantics, the body as opposed to pure abstract and formal logic comprehension of sense.[35]

Yet let us return to the Formalist theory of the plot, and to one of the most significant illustrations of its application and development: Shklovsky's classic analysis of *Tristram Shandy*, the parodic structure of which he conceived as a prototypical model for the genre of the novel as such.[36] Shklovsky focuses attention on the bodily-spatial dynamic that, in his view, underlies the unfolding of the plot. He presents Laurence Sterne's *Tristram Shandy* as a novel in which plot construction transcends story material exclusively as a result of the internal energy of its own unfolding, realized primarily thanks to a particular bodily plasticity. This novel demonstrates pure plot motion, pure aesthetic form: "presented without any motivation whatsoever, simply as is."[37]

Shklovsky presents practically every example of defamiliarization of the natural story flow by means of description of the strange poses and situations in which the characters find themselves at moments when Sterne demonstrates, over and over again, the devices of plot development (retardation, digression, repetition, step-wise composition, and so on). Shklovsky notes in particular that "Sterne was the first writer to introduce description of poses into the novel. They're always depicted by him in a strange manner, or rather they are estranged."[38] In Shklovsky's analysis, the plot of Sterne's novel (like the novelistic plot in general) is transformed into a sophisticated and extraordinarily energetic "original dance of the speech organs."[39] Every plot retardation or digression is rendered in dance steps that practically rise to the level of yoga, elaborated in order to defamiliarize the action of the corresponding plot device, rendering it up to the senses. In fact, these defamiliarized poses and movements are presented as the sole motivations for plot developments. In consequence, the form of the plot achieves a perceptible, sensed character thanks to the plastic capacity of the characters. Consider one of Shklovsky's examples:

> The palm of his right hand, as he fell upon the bed, receiving his forehead, and covering the greatest part of both his eyes, gently sunk down with his head (his elbow giving way backwards) till his nose touch'd the quilt; – his left arm hung insensible over the side of the bed, his knuckles reclining upon the handle of the chamber pot, which peep'd out beyond the valance, – his right leg (his left being drawn up towards his body) hung half over the side of the bed, the edge of it pressing upon his shin-bone.[40]

Tristram's father is destined to remain in this pose for the next fifty pages – occupied by yet another novelistic digression motivated solely by the inaction of the character – heroically frozen in this strange attitude, after which he "began to play upon the floor with the toe of that foot which hung over the bed-side."[41]

Or consider an example of repetition that "knits together" plot fragments that lack any connection or mutual causation. Tristram's father and his uncle Toby are in discussion, leaping from topic to topic, and so introduce new material that makes it possible for the plot to advance, in spite of the absolute immobility of the story's action. At this moment Tristram's mother, walking past the door of the room where the conversation is taking place, and moved only by feminine curiosity, leans down and brings her ear to the keyhole. And there she stands, eavesdropping in the dark corridor – as Sterne, "concerned for the compositional unity" of the novel, informs us every twenty or thirty pages. In fact, from Shklovsky's point of view, the immobility of this pose and the regular repetitions within the plot reminding the reader of the eavesdropping character's motionlessness form the basis both for the plot development of this portion of the novel and for the baring of the device of plot development. As Shklovsky notes, "by reminding us of the fact that his [Tristram's] mother has been left standing bent over, Sterne fulfills the device and compels us to experience it."[42] The challenging position of this character, serving to defamiliarize a plot device, can perhaps be taken as the emblem of art's orientation toward the difficulty of form and the law of expenditure of excess effort in the realm of aesthetic perception. The elevated difficulty of form is laid bare here in the elevated difficulty of poses, which seem to participate in a mechanical ballet of figures who speak, listen, act, and observe the development of the plot intrigue. In some sense, the difficulties of Tristram's mother, the excess effort that she is prepared to make in order to satisfy her curiosity, the pose in which she has frozen – all of this is a precise bodily allegory of the difficulty that the reader of this novel (and of literary texts in general) must overcome.

In sum, the autonomy of the laws of narrative from the laws of psychological motivation or logical thought, continuously proclaimed by Shklovsky and other Formalists, cannot be described as aesthetic escapism or a retreat to a Kantian disinterested pleasure and pure judgment of taste.[43] The Formalist theory of narrative reproduced the same economy of form made difficult that constituted the basis for the OPOIaZ theory of poetic language. Narrative difficulty was to produce the dialectical effect of emancipation from the limitations of the physical, psychological, and logical determinism of everyday life. International modernism's utopian and mystical investment in the specially organized movement of the human body, which was thought to make possible a transcendence of the alienation of the individual from the self and the world, underwrote those properly conceptual plastic and kinetic metaphors that made it possible to see in the dance-made-difficult of the movement of the plot a means for overcoming both the unconscious and the automatized stride of direct story action – that is, of the lived material that art is called upon to estrange.

Notes

1. Boris Tomashevsky, *Teoriia literatury. Poetika* (Moscow: Gosizdat, 1925), 137.
2. See Gérard Genette, *Figures II* (Paris: Éditions du Seuil, 1969), 195–197; and Tzvetan Todorov, "Some Approaches to Russian Formalism," in *Russian Formalism*, ed. Stephen Bann and John Bowlt (New York, NY: Barnes and Noble, 1973), 6–19.
3. Viktor Shklovsky, "Art as Device," in *Theory of Prose*, trans. Benjamin Sher (Normal, IL: Dalkey Archive Press, 1990), 4–7.
4. Ibid., 6.
5. On the performative political potential of the principal of estrangement see Galin Tihanov, "The Politics of Estrangement: The Case of Viktor Shklovsky," *Poetics Today* 26 (2005): 665–696; and Cristina Vatulescu, "The Politics of Estrangement: Tracking Shklovsky's Device through Literary and Policing Practices," *Poetics Today* 27 (2006): 35–66.
6. "Because the sounds of speech cannot arise without articulation, we may conclude that their central feature is precisely articulation – movement in the mouth and the face – and therefore that sound constitutes a mimetic, expressive gesture" (Wilhelm Wundt, *Elements of Folk Psychology*, trans. E. L. Schaub [London: Allen, 1916], 121); or "Language is the audible result of the proper actions of muscles and nerves" (Jan Niecisław Baudouin de Courtenay, "Nekotorye obshchie zamechaniia o iazykovedenii i iazyke," in *Izbrannye trudy po iazykoznaniiu* [Moscow: Nauka, 1963], 1: 77). See also Andrej Belyi, *Glossolalia. Poema o zvuke.* (Berlin: Epokha, 1922); Andrej Belyi, *Masterstvo Gogolia* (Moscow: GIKhL, 1934); Evgenij Polivanov, "Po povodu zvukovykh zhestov iaponskogo iazyka," in *Sborniki po teorii stikhotvornogo iazyka* (Petrograd: 1916), 1: 31.
7. Mikhail Matiushin, "Lecture about Theater, the Poster, and Cinema" (unpublished), cited in Ekaterina Bobrinskaia, "Zhest v poetike rannego russkogo avangarda," in *Russkii avangard: istoki i metamorfozy* (Moscow: Piataia strana, 2003), 203.
8. Igor' Smirnov, "Khudozhestvennyi smysl i evoliutsiia poeticheskikh sistem," in *Smysl kak takovoi* (St. Petersburg: Akademichskii proekt, 2001), 107.
9. Bobrinskaia, "Zhest v poetike rannego russkogo avangarda," 215.
10. Cited in Tatjana Nikol'skaia, "Igor' Terent'ev v Tiflise, in *L'avanguardia a Tiflis*, ed. Luigi Magarotto, Marzio Marzaduri, and Giovanni P. Cesa (Venice: Comune di Venezia, 1982), 197.
11. Viktor Shklovsky, "On Poetry and Trans-Sense Language," trans. Gerald Janecek and Peter Mayer, *October* 34 (1985): 20.

12. Shklovsky, "The Relationship between Devices of Plot Construction and General Devices of Style," 18, 22.
13. Roland Barthes, "Introduction to the Structural Analysis of Narratives," in *Image–Music–Text*, trans. and ed. Stephen Heath (London: Fontana Press, 1977), 85.
14. Aage Hansen-Löve, *Der russische Formalismus. Methodologische Rekonstruktionen seiner Entwicklung aus dem Prinzip der Verfremdung* (Wien: Österreichische Akademie der Wissenschaften, 1978), 239.
15. Roland Barthes, "Introduction to the Structural Analysis of Narratives," 82.
16. Aage Hansen-Löve, *Der russische Formalismus*, 243.
17. Paul Ricoeur brilliantly described the interrelationship of immanence and closure in structuralist narratology: "Structure may be defined as the closed multiplicity of internal relationships between a finite number of individual elements. The immanence of relationships, that is to say the indifference of the system to extra-linguistic reality, is an important consequence of the rule of closure, characteristic of structure." Here immanence is recognized as an effect of closure and, as a result of the finite number of elements, provides for a "closed" (that is, potentially finite) multiplicity of relationships. Paul Ricoeur, *Time and Narrative*, 3 vols., trans. Kathleen McLaughlin and David Pellauer (Chicago, IL: University of Chicago Press, 1984–1988), 2: 38.
18. Whereas in structuralism even the "unforeseeable expansions" of the narration were interpreted not as expressions of narrative freedom, but rather in light of the conviction that in fact "the nature of the narrative is precisely to include these 'deviations' ["unforeseeable expansions"] within its language" (Roland Barthes, "Introduction to the Structural Analysis of Narratives," 117).
19. "A narrative is a long sentence, just as every constative sentence is in a way the rough outline of a short narrative" (ibid., 84).
20. Viktor Shklovsky, *Literature and Cinematography*, trans. Irina Masinovsky (Champaign, IL: Dalkey Archive Press, 2008), 39.
21. This point of view was expressed in its most concise form by Claude Lévi-Strauss: "The chronological succession will come to be absorbed into an atemporal matrix structure whose form is indeed constant" (Claude Lévi-Strauss, "Structure and Form: Reflections on a Work by Vladimir Propp" [1958], in *Structural Anthropology*, vol. 2, trans. Monique Leyton (Chicago, IL: University of Chicago Press, 1976), 184).
22. See Claude Brémond, "La logique des possibles narratifs," *Communications* 8 (1966): 6–76.
23. See Algirdas J. Greimas, "Un problème de semiotique narrative: les objets de valeurs," *Langages* 31 (1973): 13–35; and *Introduction à la sémiotique narrative et discursive* (Paris: Hachette, 1976).
24. "The purpose of parallelism is the same as that of imagery in general, that is, the transfer of an object from its customary sphere of perception to a new one; we are dealing here with a distinct semantic change" (Shklovsky, "Art as Device," 12).
25. Shklovsky, *Literature and Cinematography*, 45.
26. Lev S. Vygotsky, *The Psychology of Art* (Cambridge, MA: MIT Press, 1971), ch. 7.
27. Shklovsky, "The Relationship between Devices of Plot Construction and General Devices of Style," 42.

28. The Cheka (*Chrezvychaynaya komissiya*, Emergency Committee) was the first of the Soviet state security organizations. It was created on December 20, 1917.

29. Viktor Shklovsky, *A Sentimental Journey: Memoirs, 1917–1922*, trans. Richard Sheldon (Champaign, IL: Dalkey Archive Press, 2004), 141.

30. On the significance of folklore and of Veselovsky's cultural-historical school for Shklovsky's narrative theory, see Jessica E. Merrill, "The Role of Folklore Study in the Rise of Russian Formalist and Czech Structuralist Literary Theory" (PhD Dissertation, University of California, Berkeley, 2012), 14–61.

31. Shklovsky, "The Relationship between Devices of Plot Construction and General Devices of Style," 45.

32. Ibid., 42.

33. Ibid., 15. Shklovsky takes this line from Russian writer Saltykov-Shchedrin's well-known but apocryphal pronouncement concerning poetry.

34. Ibid., 22.

35. In this connection, see Irina Sirotkina and Roger Smith, *The Sixth Sense of the Avant-Garde: Dance, Kinaesthesia and the Arts in Revolutionary Russia* (London: Bloomsbury, 2017).

36. See: Emily Finer, *Turning into Sterne: Viktor Shklovsky and Literary Reception* (London: Legenda, 2010).

37. Shklovsky, "The Novel as Parody: Sterne's *Tristram Shandy*," in *Theory of Prose*, 147.

38. Ibid., 152.

39. Viktor Shklovsky, "On Poetry and Trans-Sense Language," 20.

40. Laurence Sterne, Quoted in Shklovsky, "The Novel as Parody," 152.

41. Ibid.

42. Ibid., 154.

43. For another Formalist example, see Boris Eichenbaum's famous essay, "How Gogol's Overcoat Is Made" [1919], in *Gogol from the Twentieth Century: Eleven Essays*, ed. Robert A. Maguire (Princeton, NJ: Princeton University Press, 1995), 267–293.

4

HANNAH FREED-THALL

Adventures in Structuralism: Reading with Barthes and Genette

To the twenty-first-century reader, free to choose among (and creatively combine) any number of critical paradigms, the phrase "structuralist narrative theory" might not sound particularly enticing. It likely conjures up a dusty and somewhat technical set of terms – devices, coordinates, levels, functions, codes, semiotic squares – enabling a highly rule-bound practice of textual analysis. And yet structuralism gave rise to some of the most inspired and virtuosic literary criticism ever written, including two key works that this chapter takes as case studies: Gérard Genette's *Narrative Discourse: An Essay on Method* (originally published as "Discours du récit" in *Figures III*, 1972; English translation 1980) and Roland Barthes's *S/Z* (1970; English translation 1974). Both of these now-classic works represent the culmination of structuralist narratology and its breaking point. Both stand at the boundary between structuralism and poststructuralism, between rigorous analysis of categories, devices, and forms, and a more open-ended and playful attention to semiotic gaps and ambiguities. In dazzling displays of what Genette calls "methodological giddiness," these works draw on extant categories but also venture beyond the edges of what has been named.[1] This unusual conjunction of analytical precision and imagination is why structuralist narrative theory remains so compelling today.

Although structuralism encompasses many different styles of analysis, the basic premises shared by all of them can be traced back to one foundational text: Swiss linguist Ferdinand de Saussure's treatise on structural linguistics, *Cours de linguistique générale* (1916). In this compilation of late lectures given at the University of Geneva, reconstituted and posthumously published on the basis of his students' notes, Saussure invents modern linguistics. Moving away from his previous work in historical linguistics (he had written on etymology and linguistic change), Saussure here focuses on the distinction between language as a general system (*la langue*) and language-in-use (*la parole*). According to this influential division, any particular utterance – and any particular speaker's motivations and intentions – only become intelligible in the context of the larger, impersonal linguistic system that shapes the possibilities of our thought. Language speaks us, in other words. At the same time, however, its value is not intrinsic; it only becomes valuable when it is used. In this regard, words are like coins: lacking innate significance, they acquire meaning when exchanged. Moreover, words are not naturally bound to the things they designate. Instead, linguistic structures are made up of signs, which can in turn be broken down into two parts: the signifying concept, or "signifier" (*signifiant*), and the signified concept, or "signified" (*signifié*). Although speakers might imagine that words and things are innately linked, Saussure demonstrates that the relationship between the two elements of the sign is entirely arbitrary. Saussure's analysis also troubles familiar assumptions about language as the spontaneous expression of a speaker's interiority. Instead, he demonstrates that *difference* produces meaning in all sign systems. As Saussure himself puts it, "the distinguishing characteristic of the sign – but the one that is least apparent at first sight – is that in some way it always eludes the individual or social will."[2]

One of the most important implications of this theory is that both the order and the underlying arbitrariness that constitute language can be extended to *all* sign systems. Saussure offers a partial list of such systems, which include "symbolic rites, polite formulas, military signals, etc."[3] Language, reimagined as a system made up of *langue* and *parole*, signifiers and signifieds, can now be enshrined as the model for a new science, which Saussure names "semiology."

Thus Saussure both denaturalizes language and decenters the individual speaker. His insights about the relational basis of meaning were key to the mid-century French structuralist movement, which took hold in disciplines ranging from anthropology and sociology to psychoanalysis and film studies. Theorists as different as psychoanalyst Jacques Lacan, anthropologist Claude Lévi-Strauss, and sociologist Pierre Bourdieu were inspired by Saussurean semiology when they mobilized their de-essentializing structuralist analyses of a variety of phenomena, such as the unconscious, South American mythology, and bourgeois aesthetic taste. Literary scholars likewise drew on the linguistic model in readings of both canonical and popular literary texts. Structuralism raised literary studies to a new level of rigor and complexity even as it overturned traditional ideas about canons, masterpieces, and the author's authority. (For example, demonstrating that all texts are interesting from a structural point of view, Barthes's seminal 1966 essay, "Introduction to the Structural Analysis of Narratives," investigates the codes at work in Ian Fleming's *James Bond* novels.) The linguistic model enabled structuralists to replace substantialist with relational thinking and thus to expose the techniques, codes, and functions at work in those cultural phenomena that seem the most natural and the least constructed. As Fredric Jameson puts it, structuralism sees reality itself as "a series of interlocking systems [...] of signs."[4]

Although structuralism laid the analytical foundation for the many theoretical movements that followed, from deconstruction to queer theory, it is not uncommon for critics to dismiss its methods as reductively static, unable to contend with time and contingency.[5] As the work of the most creative structuralist critics demonstrates, however, engaging narrative with an eye to its "functions" does not impoverish the act of reading. On the contrary, a critical approach that underscores function is simply downplaying *product* in favor of *process* – the present-tense, active work of reading or untangling a text. When the author's authority is bracketed, and textual personhood is reimagined as nothing but an "impersonal network of symbols" configured around a proper name, reading becomes more active and participatory than ever before.[6] For Barthes, especially, attention to structure (rather than authorial intention) liberates the reader from the oppressive shadow of the capital-A Author.[7] As Jonathan Culler has pointed out, structuralism provides no single fixed method. Instead, it activates a certain mode of attention, a desire to "name the various languages with and among which the text plays."[8] The structuralist's task is not to uncover some underlying authorial master plan, but rather to learn to listen to the text's interplay of voices; to linger in the interstices between narrative levels; to explore the experimental realms of tone, mood, and atmosphere; and to examine how meaning is produced by the friction among these and other elements.

S/Z

Barthes's *S/Z*, published in 1970 and based on a seminar given in 1968 and 1969 at the École Pratique des Hautes Études, brings about a shift of emphasis within structuralist literary criticism. While structuralism had previously focused on general theory rather than particular texts, *S/Z* sets the stage for a new kind of critical performance: the virtuosic close reading. In *S/Z*, Barthes remains attentive to the idiosyncrasies of the text at hand – here, Balzac's 1830 novella, *Sarrasine* – while developing a method of analysis with wide-ranging consequences for literary study. As Robert Scholes suggests, *S/Z* stretches the concept of "structure," devising a new critical language in order to examine the codes determining even the most apparently marginal details of the text, which Barthes terms the "capillaries of meaning."[9]

Barthes's objectives in *S/Z* are twofold: first, to "appreciate what *plural* constitutes the classic text," and second, "to make the reader no longer a consumer, but a producer of the text."[10] Inspired in part by his student Julia Kristeva's theory of "intertextuality," in *S/Z* Barthes explores the uncontainable multiplicity inherent in even the most seemingly restrained text.[11] He also underscores the innovative and productive force of critical reading, now elevated to the level of literary creation itself.

S/Z is an experiment: how does a text appear once the idea of the "Author" (as God, father, or proprietor of the work) is set aside? Such an experiment is especially meaningful in the case of a text like Balzac's *Sarrasine*, which is strongly associated with a paternalistic, bourgeois author function. Barthes selects *Sarrasine* as the object of his analysis precisely because this work appears at first blush to close and contain rather than open up meaning. In fact, as his analysis will reveal, *Sarrasine* is a "limit-text" – a work less legible and more "modern" than one might assume.

Barthes opens *S/Z* by dividing all texts into two camps: "classic" (or "readerly") versus "modern" (or "writerly"). For Barthes, the ideal text – the writerly – is one that transforms the reader from passive "customer" to participant in the production of meaning. By contrast, the readerly, realist text – of which *Sarrasine* is an example – would seem to exclude the reader from the pleasure of writing. A mere consumer of the work, the reader of the classic text is able only to accept or reject what is offered.[12] The modern, or writerly, is thus initially invoked as a sort of phantom haunting the work of critique: a utopian, undecipherable other against which to measure the more staid symmetries and codes of the classic work. Yet over the course of Barthes's analysis, this readerly/writerly division becomes less and less decisive. One could say that Barthes's objective in *S/Z* is to uncover the writerly within the readerly, to bring out the experimental forces at work in the most classic text. Despite the microscopic intensity of Barthes's analysis, *S/Z* illustrates that no reading is ever final or totalizing: even as he attempts to account for all of the codes at work in *Sarrasine*, Barthes demonstrates that the text is ultimately unconquerable. Instead of insisting on his own critical mastery of the work, he underscores the "blanks" and "looseness" of his own analysis ("like footprints marking the escape of the text").[13]

If one of Barthes's goals is to transform the classic text into a playground for a newly liberated reader, he also wants to denaturalize realism by exposing the artificiality and conventionality of the codes that compose it. He does this by rigorously fragmenting the novella, attacking it sentence by sentence and subjecting it to what D. A. Miller terms "discursive pulverizations."[14] Each fragment is shown to correspond to a critical code, and each grouping of fragments is in turn cut by a critical digression on a topic such as voice, beauty, the portrait, or the proper name.

Much of Barthes's reading here is local and specific to *Sarrasine*, and yet his elaboration of five overlapping codes has broad implications for the study of narrative. These codes include the *hermeneutic* (relating to the positing and resolution of an enigma – including "snares," detours, and the cultivation of suspense); the *semantic* (relating to hints and flickers of meaning, or the hazy field of "connotations," which Barthes describes as "static" in the text's communicative system);[15] the *symbolic* (similar to the semantic, but bigger in scale, dealing with repetitions, patterns, binaries); the *proairetic* (relating to actions; along with the hermeneutic code, the proairetic code engages the dynamics of plot, with its deferrals and ultimate resolution); and the *cultural* (relating to what Barthes sometimes calls "doxa," or shared knowledge about the world, including, in the case of *Sarrasine*, bourgeois commonplaces). None of these five levels of meaning dominates the others; instead, they form a fugal counterpoint of equally weighted voices.

This focus on the codification of the text is not as systematic as it might appear. One of the lessons of *S/Z* is that even in their most "classic" guise, texts always exceed the codes that shape them. Barthesian structuralism seeks out these instances of flight. It bears witness to the multiplicity of codes, but also to the tears and rips in their texture, to those moments when they fail to contain their object. The point of identifying a set of codes is not that the reader should absorb and rigorously apply them. Rather, we should add to Barthes's list and approach texts as cultural objects buzzing and humming with contradictory meanings. Indeed, although the cut is a key trope in *S/Z*, Barthes is attuned to what in a text does not lend itself to clear delineation. Hence he foregrounds the importance of textual enigma: one of the defining features of the "classic" text is that it perpetually holds out and defers meaning. And although he assiduously carves *Sarrasine* into precisely 561 fragments, or "lexias," and interprets these textual bits through the framework of his five codes, Barthes admits that this particular fragmentation of the work is "arbitrary in the extreme." This arbitrariness is powerful, however: in order to undo the apparent "naturalness" of the text (its "ideology of totality"), the critic must work to "break" and "interrupt" its seemingly organic divisions.[16]

Although he proceeds through the text chronologically, "step-by-step" or page-by-page, Barthes wants to highlight the "reversibility of the structures from which the text is woven." He also refers to his method as a "systematic use of digression." Because structuralism embraces methods of dissection and decodification that are transferrable across all texts, it is often seen as a critical turn toward a more impartial, scientific mode of analysis. It is important to recognize, however, how self-consciously unscientific Barthes's method really is in *S/Z*. Making clear from the outset that he is departing from the pseudo-clinical tone he took in his earlier "Introduction to the Structural Analysis of Narratives," Barthes likens the critic to a "soothsayer" reading the textual sky: "drawing on it with the tip of his staff an imaginary rectangle wherein to consult, according to certain principles, the flight of birds, the commentator traces through the text certain zones of reading, in order to observe therein the migration of meanings, the outcropping of codes, the passage of citations."[17]

Published in the wake of the massive student and worker protests of May '68, *S/Z* launches an attack on bourgeois ideology itself, with its emphasis on closure and totality, individuality, authorship, money, and heteronormativity.[18] *S/Z* destabilizes conventional ideas about personhood, foregrounding the polymorphous force of *desire* (slippery, mobile, grounded in absence) and *voice* (plural, sourceless, fugal) in lieu of any stable notion of identity. Hence Barthes's refrain in the book is "qui parle?" ("who is speaking?"). The act of granting power to "voice" instead of "person" – and of insisting on vocal plurality and polymodality – is meaningful: it implies a democratic, anti-bourgeois, difference-multiplying, potentially queer (or at least gender-denaturalizing) destabilization of univocal authority.

In this regard, a particularly telling moment in *S/Z* occurs when Barthes insists that the function of writing is to "annul the power (the intimidation) of one language over another, to dissolve any metalanguage as soon as it is constituted."[19] This pushback against "arrogance" – a mode of resistance powerfully on display in *S/Z* – is a key feature of everything Barthes wrote. Indeed, although *S/Z* is in some regards Barthes's most swashbucklingly ambitious critical enterprise, it is also at its core an homage to slow, patient, "gradual" interpretation.[20] Barthes suggests that this slowed-down unraveling of the text is a mode of contestation, a resistance to consumer culture with its instantaneous gratification and its throwaway ethos. By insisting on the value of close reading (and rereading), *S/Z* offers a critique of the capitalist logic of built-in-obsolescence and of literature-as-commodity. But to accentuate the value of slowness is not to deny the pleasures of reading. For Barthes, if critical reading frees the text from its commoditization, it is precisely because it transforms consumption into play.[21] *Play* is a key concept in *S/Z*. In fact, according to Barthes, not only is reading analogous to playing, but the text itself is in a perpetual state of play, made up of "a constant interplay of potentials, whose 'falls' impart 'tone' or energy to the narrative."[22]

Another key concept in *S/Z* is indeterminacy. Along with its dethroning of authorial power, *S/Z* undermines essentialist ideas about sexual difference. Balzac's novella explores the desire and anxiety aroused by a castrato (at once a "Superlative Woman" and a cross-dressed urchin) named La Zambinella. The feminine is the mobile signifier at the center of the text's snares and equivocations: woman is not where she seems to be. In his analysis of Balzac, Barthes engages the central trope of castration in order to transform a conventional (naturalizing) conception of masculinity and femininity into a structural one. Instead of understanding "man" and "woman" as fixed identities, Barthes invites us to think in terms of a mobile and reversible set of oppositions: active versus passive, castrating versus castrated. Men and women can occupy either pole, or even swing between them, as does the novella's gender-bending star.

Despite the apparent precision of his various codes and lexias, Barthes grants readers a great deal of freedom and flexibility. Piling analogy on top of analogy, he expands and stretches our sense of what a text is and what literary criticism can be. In *S/Z*, a text is a medium of exchange, or "merchandise"; it's a "braid" of slackly woven threads, a tangle or dense weave of codes and significations; it's a "piece of Valenciennes lace created before us under the lacemaker's fingers"; it's alternately a "sky" or a "tree" of expanding, outwardly branching discourse, its growth propelled and fed by desire. At one moment, the text is cinematic in its "dissolves"; at the next, it's theatrical, made of utterances accompanied by "off-stage voices" (the codes). Or rather, it's an acoustic space, polyphonic, "stereographic," fugue-like. Even here, Barthes splits the metaphor into different lines: either the text is a "cacography" – the "writing of noise," like a "telephone network gone haywire," its reception "broken, refracted, caught up in a system of interferences" – or it's a more orderly acoustic composition, a classical music score.[23] In teaching us both to read that score and to hear the text as a crisscrossing, noisy, polymodal network, *S/Z* offers a master class in close listening.

Narrative Discourse

If *S/Z* represents the high point of late structuralist bravado, Genette's *Narrative Discourse* is a less flashy but equally inspired critical performance. Indeed, as Scholes notes, Genette's book has arguably aged better than most literary analyses of the era. Perhaps this is because it is exclusively focused on the mechanical or musical structure of the text, and brackets both the ideology critique and the Lacanian tropes that were in vogue in the early 1970s. For Genette as for Barthes, the ideal reader is a listener. And like *S/Z*, *Narrative Discourse* attunes us to the particularities of one exemplary work – in this case,

Proust's *In Search of Lost Time.* At the same time, however, Genette devises a methodology applicable to any narrative text. The reader of *Narrative Discourse* comes away with an understanding of the Proustian text (and, by extension, all narrative) as a complex mechanism with multiple moving parts.[24]

One of the remarkable things about *Narrative Discourse* is the way Genette builds on and complicates the narrative analysis Vladimir Propp offers in his classic formalist work, *Morphology of the Folktale.* While Propp revolutionizes literary analysis by demonstrating that folktales are made up of a set "grammar" of actions, Genette combines Propp's analytical distance with attention to *how* this grammar works in action. As in *S/Z,* the invention and application of a set of categories is key to Genette's critical practice in *Narrative Discourse.* Genette approaches his reading of Proust through a set of five different methodological frames: order, frequency, duration, mood, and voice. For the structuralist, *what happens* in a narrative is far less consequential than *how* it happens – in what tempo, in what voice, through whose point of view, and so on. Genette is alert not just to the order and combination of various functions, but also to the layered effects of perspective, or "focalization," and to the quasi-acoustic phenomenon of textual "rhythm."[25] Indeed, an analogy between literature and music echoes throughout *Narrative Discourse.* Genette describes narrative "duration" in terms of "tempo" and expands on the musical metaphor in the "mood" chapter, suggesting that the many-voiced quality of Proust's text is akin to Stravinsky's polymodal system in *The Rite of Spring.*[26] As we have seen, Barthes also develops a musical analogy in *S/Z,* likening the literary text to a score and the development of its central enigma to the "retards, ambiguities, and diversions" of a fugue.[27]

One might wonder why Genette chose Proust's massive, seven-volume novel, *In Search of Lost Time,* as the object of his narratological inquiry: he could hardly have selected a more unwieldy text, especially given that some of the *Search* was published posthumously and editors have debated which variants to include. But the contingency that underlies the work's publication history is part of its appeal for Genette. *In Search of Lost Time* is often misread as an autobiography or confession, and thus as an organic narrative form, the unmediated expression of a singular authorial subject. Genette is keen to identify the many artificial and arbitrary devices that structure Proust's narrative, from its editorial framing to its zigzagging temporality, ellipses, syncopation, and destabilized point of view. As he puts it, "vision can also be a matter of style and of technique."[28]

A virtuosic taxonomist, Genette nonetheless underscores ambiguity: his vision, like Proust's, is oriented toward outliers and deviations. Warning against hypostatizing the terms he generates, he demonstrates in each of his chapters how Proust's novel breaks or stretches the imposed concepts, mixing and combining expected modes of narration. His vision, like Proust's, is oriented toward outliers and deviations. As Kent Puckett notes, Genette is less interested in "normal" narrative functioning than in all the ways in which Proustian narrative form "breaks down" or "fails."[29] *Narrative Discourse* is thus a book about blurred lines, contaminated categories: transgressions of temporal order, distortions of speed, and crossings of narrative boundaries.

For example, in the chapter on "order," Genette establishes the opposition of analepsis (backtrack) and prolepsis (fast-forward), and then examines occasions in which the distinction is blurred (in the temporal "seesawing" of analeptic prolepses and proleptic analepses, or fast-forwards that contain backtracks within them, and vice versa).[30] In his chapter on "frequency," he establishes the generative opposition of the "singulative" (events that only occur once) and the "iterative" (repeating or habitual scenes) only to explore the "contaminating" of the former by the latter, which creates the "disconcerting" impression of temporal "floating."[31] In his discussion of narrative "mood," Genette examines direct and indirect speech, and then turns to that most ambiguous mode of narrative utterance, free indirect discourse: "gradual or subtle blends of indirect style and narrated speech."[32] Here the critic is also interested in moments of speech that occur at the threshold between sleep and waking. He terms such nonsense "infralinguistic hodgepodge," a "transitory and borderline misunderstanding" that represents the "gulf" between the logic of alert consciousness and that of dream.[33] Finally, in the "voice" section, Genette's discussion of narrative "levels" leads to an exploration of their transgression via the technique of "metalepsis," the "intrusion by the extradiegetic narrator or narratee into the diegetic universe," or the inverse.[34] In metalepsis, the narrative plays a game with the boundary that circumscribes and defines it. (What's "disturbing" about this, Genette compellingly suggests, is that it implies that we too might "belong to some narrative.")[35] Throughout the book, Genette highlights what in Proust appears incoherent, including "the process of the disintegration of character"; "the paradoxical coexistence of the greatest mimetic intensity and the presence of a narrator"; the "height of dialogic mimesis" coinciding with "the height of literary gratuitousness"; and the "concurrence of theoretically incompatible focalizations."[36]

Ultimately, Genette and Barthes share a fascination with how texts work to "emancipate" speech "from all narrative patronage."[37] Both authors emphasize the reader's liberation from conceptions of authorial intentionality and mastery. Their sense of narrative as a horizontal network of signs – a loose braid or weave of language, not the sacred expression of an Author-God – is structuralism's gift to all subsequent literary theory. By treating narrative as a mechanism to be disassembled and artfully explored, these critics raise the stakes of literary analysis. We are free to "rewrite" the work, Genette argues, noting that the true author is not only the narrator but also the narratee – the one to whom the text's crisscrossing tangle of messages is addressed. In both Barthes and Genette, then, what begins as a rigorous investigation of a text's codes, lexias, levels, and functions becomes a "vertiginous" adventure in listening and reading.[38]

Notes

1. Gérard Genette, *Narrative Discourse: An Essay in Method*, trans. Jane Lewin (Ithaca, NY: Cornell University Press, 1980), 23.
2. Ferdinand de Saussure, *Course in General Linguistics*, trans. Wade Baskin (New York, NY: Columbia University Press, 2011), 17.
3. Saussure, *Course in General Linguistics*, 16.
4. Fredric Jameson, *The Prison-House of Language: A Critical Account of Structuralism and Russian Formalism* (Princeton, NJ: Princeton University Press, 1974), 33.
5. Jameson offers a helpful critique of structuralism's ahistorical bent – its rigorous exclusion of contingency and preference for the static "syntagmatic" pole of meaning over the dynamic "paradigmatic" one. But Jameson also praises structuralism as one of the first attempts to "work out a philosophy of models," i.e., to demonstrate that "all conscious thought takes place within the limits of a given model and is in that sense determined by it" (*The Prison-House of Language*, 101).
6. Barthes, *S/Z: An Essay*, trans. Richard Miller (New York, NY: Farrar, Straus and Giroux, 1974), 94.
7. On this phenomenon, see Barthes's "The Death of the Author" in *Image-Music-Text*, trans. Stephen Heath (New York, NY: Noonday-Farrar, Straus and Giroux, 1977), 142–148. *S/Z* is in many ways an expansion of the argument made in "The Death of the Author."
8. Jonathan D. Culler, *Structuralist Poetics: Structuralism, Linguistics, and the Study of Literature* (London: Routledge, 2002), 302.
9. The seminar that would form the basis for *S/Z* was interrupted by the protests of May '68, and the egalitarian, authority-destabilizing tenor of the book should be read in light of those events. On the importance of May '68 for Barthes, see Andrew Stafford, "S/Z: événement(s), ébranlement, écriture," in *Barthes, au lieu du roman*, ed. M. Macé and A. Gefen (Paris: Edition Desjonquères, 2002), 47–51. For a more ambivalent account, see Tiphaine Samoyault, *Roland Barthes: Biographie* (Paris: Éditions du Seuil, 2015), 429–476.

10. Barthes, *S/Z*, 19. Some critics contend that Barthes's reading is weakened by its extreme "closeness" to the particularities of Balzac's novella. According to Scholes, "there is something too arbitrary, too personal, and too idiosyncratic about this method. The system operating here is not systematic enough to be applied easily by other analysts to other texts" (*Structuralism in Literature: An Introduction* [New Haven, CT: Yale University Press, 1974], 155).

11. *S/Z*, 5, 4.

12. Kristeva, newly arrived from Bulgaria, attended Barthes's seminars in the late 1960s. On her influence on the theory of textual plurality that Barthes develops in *S/Z*, see François Dosse, *History of Structuralism, Volume 2: The Sign Sets, 1967–Present*, trans. Deborah Glassman (Minneapolis: University of Minnesota Press, 1997), 54–65.

13. *S/Z*, 5–6.

14. Ibid., 20.

15. D. A. Miller, *Bringing Out Roland Barthes* (Berkeley: University of California Press, 1992), 47.

16. *S/Z*, 9.

17. Ibid., 13, 15.

18. Ibid., 13–14.

19. Ibid., 98.

20. Ibid., 12.

21. Ibid., 15–16.

22. Ibid., 270.

23. Ibid., 152, 145, 160, 14, 128–9, 42, 21, 132.

24. Scholes describes Genette as "a French critic whose work will 'travel' like the best French wine, without losing any virtues in crossing the Atlantic" (*Structuralism in Literature*, 159). While Barthes cites almost no other critic in his analysis of *Sarrasine*, "Genette gives us a structural *dialogue*, citing the other poeticians and critics, crediting, qualifying, disagreeing, always assuming response and continuation" (ibid., 160).

25. Genette, *Narrative Discourse*, 88.

26. Ibid., 210.

27. Barthes, *S/Z*, 29.

28. Genette, *Narrative Discourse*, 159. For an excellent discussion of the "defamiliarizing" effect of Genette's exposure of narrative techniques and devices, see Kent Puckett, *Narrative Theory: A Critical Introduction* (Cambridge: Cambridge University Press, 2016), ch. 6.

29. Puckett, *Narrative Theory*, 260.

30. Genette, *Narrative Discourse*, 81.

31. Ibid., 121, 151.

32. Ibid., 176.

33. Ibid., 181.

34. Ibid., 234–235.

35. Ibid., 236.

36. Ibid., 247; 210–211.

37. Ibid., 174.

38. Ibid., 261–262.

5

JUDITH ROOF

The Feminist Foundations of Narrative Theory

Feminist writers and literary scholars have pushed narrative theorists to take sexual difference into account as a foundational aspect of narrative structure. Approaching the binary practices of structuralism primarily from three perspectives – the representation of women in narrative and women's writing, feminist film theory, and the feminist critique of psychoanalysis – feminist theorists and critics have amply demonstrated that no theory of narrative has neutral terms or assumptions. From this basic premise it follows that all narrative and all theories about its structure and operations have ideological premises and functions, starting with the asymmetries of sex itself. This assessment begins in earnest as narrative structure and practice make their way into the forefront of consideration in the early twentieth century.

Morphologies

In his 1928 "Forward" to *Morphology of the Folktale*, Soviet folklorist Vladimir Propp offers the possibility of making "an examination of the forms of the tale which will be as exact as the morphology of organic formations."[1] Propp compares his version of folktale morphology (that is, the study of the *form* of the folktale) to botanical morphology, giving an analogy between the elements of folktales, taken as an exemplary class, and "the component parts of a plant, of their relationship to each other and to the whole – in other words, the study of a plant's structure."[2] Propp's study revealed the correlation between the roles and the sexes of the agents in the tale's plot. In Propp's schema, active, subject roles belong to male agents; passive object roles are the place of female characters. In exposing the sexed bases for plot and action in folk tales, Propp's *Morphology* also exposes the sexism that has systematically undergirded narrative itself.

Virginia Woolf's 1929 meditation *A Room of One's Own* fleshes out experientially what Propp's narrative binaries represent. As Woolf writes,

"It is strange what a difference a tail makes."[3] Pondering the differential relationships enjoyed by the male and female components in the cultural project of literature, Woolf elucidates the inequities that have made writing fiction difficult for women – and as an effect and cause of that, the inequities represented in literature itself, which reflect a "morphology" that would produce a baseless inequity in the first place. "I thought how unpleasant it is to be locked out; and I thought how it is worse perhaps to be locked in; and thinking of the safety and prosperity of the one sex and of the poverty and the insecurity of the other and of the effect of tradition and of the lack of tradition upon the mind of the writer, I thought at last that it was time to roll up the crumpled skin of the day."[4]

Treating broad cultural narratives about the relative values and capabilities of the sexes, Woolf's essay intervenes at the point of the production of the sexed author, showing the ways cultural myths deriving from these narratives distribute imagined capabilities for authorship between the sexes. This distribution in turn tends to characterize the narratives each sex is likely to produce, which in the end then tend to repeat the cultural myths about sex that generated the narratives in the first place. Critics, whose tastes reiterate sexed cultural values, then, value these sexed narratives. "Speaking crudely," Woolf notes, "football and sport are 'important'; the worship of fashion, the buying of clothes 'trivial.' And these values are inevitably transferred from life to fiction. This is an important book, the critic assumes, because it deals with war. This is an insignificant book because it deals with the feelings of women in a drawing-room."[5] That Woolf demonstrates the connections between the layers of literary production and reception and cultural myths about the sexes suggests that narrative itself operates on the same multiple levels and that the broadest level – cultural myths about the relative values and capabilities of the sexes – may be intrinsic to narrative insofar as its structural asymmetries delimit the creative capabilities of both women and men.

Showing that assumptions about the relative value of the sexes are themselves the product of narrative, Woolf's essay produces a map of the incipient field of narrative theory as, first of all, consisting of multiple sites – culture, literature, criticism – for the operations of narrative. Second, narrative always both produces and reflects a socio-political imaginary that shapes and delimits cultural forms and expression; and third, narrative involves, and in fact may depend upon, sexed assumptions about the very minds and temperaments – the psychologies – of both writers and subject matter. Narrative is a powerful agent that reproduces itself, but its terms can be parsed – morphologized – as a way both to envision its operations and imagine social change. This change occurs not only as an effect of the kinds of stories that circulate, but also in the ways that the relations between character and role take on new configurations – the female scholar/author, for example, as Woolf suggests.

Woolf's linking of cultural narratives to social conditions accompanies the broader academic turn to structuralism in the mid-twentieth century, which offers both the means through which the relations between sexes might be understood as binary positions in often-patriarchal kinship structures *and* a method by which narrative might be analyzed as a parsable process in a similar binary protocol. Offering, thus, a vision of the parallelism among social structures, their narratives, and narrative in general, structuralism makes apparent narrative's function as a dynamic pattern iterated throughout cultures.

In its acknowledgment of both conscious and unconscious processes, structuralism also becomes an important element of contemporaneous psychoanalysis, linking the social and psychical to structures such as myth and kinship. The encounters between structuralist thinking, feminism, and psychoanalysis that together forge a portion of feminism's contributions to narrative theory come together spectacularly in 1949 in Simone de Beauvoir's review of structuralist anthropologist Claude Lévi-Strauss's *The Elementary Structures of Kinship*, which appeared in the philosophical journal *Les Temps modernes*.[6] Writing the review at the same time that she was completing work on *The Second Sex*, de Beauvoir incorporated structuralist insights into her encyclopedic analysis of the phenomenon of the woman.[7]

"Lévi-Strauss's discovery, in de Beauvoir's eyes, is that the exchange of women transforms them from their natural and biological condition to social values capable of circulating and of producing the desire of males," Frédéric Keck observes in his review of de Beauvoir's review.[8] According to Keck, de Beauvoir was less interested in Lévi-Strauss's emphasis on avoiding incest than on the function of marriage itself in a patriarchal structure that relegates woman to the place of "other": "All marriage is social incest," de Beauvoir commented in her review, "in so far as the husband absorbs in himself a certain wellbeing instead of escaping himself towards otherness; at the very least society exists but in the breast of this egotistical act where communication might be maintained: this is why, even if the female might be something other than a sign, she is nonetheless, like a word, something which is exchanged."[9]

Just as Lévi-Strauss's 1958 *Structural Anthropology* makes his structural method even clearer and even more significant to studies of narrative, de Beauvoir's *The Second Sex* ranges through available cultural discourses – "Destiny," "History," "Myths," "The Formative Years," "Situation,"

"Justifications," and "Toward Liberation" – evincing the same structural narrative of male/self and female/other that Lévi-Strauss outlines in his anthropological studies.[10] Both Lévi-Strauss and de Beauvoir understand that with structural methods they can discern the interrelation of cultural elements as well as the relation of these elements to the whole of culture. Lévi-Strauss comments as he compares myth to structuralist understandings of language that "[t]he only method we can suggest at this stage is to proceed tentatively, by trial and error, using as a check the principles which serve as the basis for any kind of structural analysis: economy of explanation; unity of solution; and ability to reconstruct the whole from a fragment, as well as later stages from previous ones."[11] Structuralist readings of culture and narrative go one step further, linking manifest socio-cultural phenomena to unconscious structures:

> In anthropology as in linguistics, it is not comparison that supports generalization, but the other way around. If, as we believe to be the case, the unconscious activity of the mind consists in imposing forms upon content, and if these forms are fundamentally the same for all minds – ancient and modern, primitive and civilized (as the study of the symbolic function, expressed in language, so strikingly indicates) – it is necessary and sufficient to grasp the unconscious structure underlying each institution and each custom, in order to obtain a principle of interpretation valid for other institutions and other customs, provided of course that the analysis is carried far enough.[12]

De Beauvoir's *The Second Sex* indeed makes this "unconscious" structure visible as it defines broadly the relations between the sexes (and perhaps even defines the sexes as binary in the first place). And while de Beauvoir does not directly address the sexualized roles of narrative that Propp makes explicit, she does continue Woolf's exposition of sexual asymmetry and inequitable patterns both as cultural narratives (part IX, part XI) and in the work of five fiction writers – Henri de Montherlant, D. H. Lawrence, Paul Claudel, André Breton, and Stendhal (part X) – reading against their renditions of the sexes and showing the ways plot depends upon the alignment of oppositional binaries around sex. Echoing Woolf's analysis of the inequality of roles as defined by a pervasive narrative of relative value, de Beauvoir observes: "The terms *masculine* and *feminine* are used symmetrically only as a matter of form, as on legal papers. In actuality the relation of the two sexes is not quite like that of two electrical poles, for man represents both the positive and the neutral, as is indicated by the common use of *man* to designate human beings in general; whereas woman represents only the negative, defined by limiting criteria, without reciprocity."[13] Beginning her study by listing many of the cultural narratives of the contemporaneous "failure" of females – which, as she notes, might be corrected if only those females became more feminine and took on their proper roles – de Beauvoir rejects these myths, recasting the question as "What is a woman?" *The Second Sex* is a thorough examination of what "woman" is if we discard the biases of pervasive cultural narratives that confirm sexual asymmetry as a foundational fact of life.

The conception of feminism as actively trying to undo the sacrifice of one sex for the benefit of the other exists in explicit relation to narrative understood in the structuralist sense as an account that relates parts to a whole "unity" subtending social relations as well as the unconscious of both individuals and their cultures. "She is," as de Beauvoir comments at the end of the section "Dreams, Fears, Idols," "servant and companion, but he expects her also to be his audience and critic and to confirm him in his sense of being, but she opposes him with her indifference, even with her mockery and laughter. He projects upon her what he desires and what he fears, what he loves and what he hates. And if it is difficult to say anything specific about her, that is because man seeks the whole of himself in her and because she is All. She is All, that is, on the plane of the inessential; she is all the Other."[14] De Beauvoir's feminist analysis thus not only links the analysis of narrative to the political stakes of exposing the inequities of sexual difference – *narrative theorizing is a feminist act* – but also offers several narrative fronts upon which feminist analysis might be enacted: the study of narrative (and narratives) as the formal expression and proliferation of oppressive sexual ideologies; the analysis of socio-cultural myths and the practices the myths rationalize as these undergird feminist political struggle; and the study and critique of psychoanalysis as both explanation and justification of the effects of sexual difference in the psyche as the basis for understanding and critiquing representations of women in culture and the media.

Theory and Praxis I: Feminist Criticism of Narratives

Examining not only specific stories but also the narrative dynamics and ideologies that subtend them is an overtly feminist process that instigates, forges, and contributes to conceptions of narrative theory itself as formulating a dynamic shaped by the binary asymmetrical positions (or roles) of patriarchal ideology. As 1960s feminist critics and activists discerned, studying the inequities inherent to Western notions of narrative also means reproducing the narrative itself. Even if, as both Woolf and de Beauvoir argue, sexual egalitarianism would be the desired product of a narrative analysis that makes visible the sexist elements of narrative patterns, the very process of exposing narrative's undergirding sexual ideology paradoxically reproduces the same asymmetrical narrative dynamic. Thus, in analyzing what appear to be narrative's structural elements, feminist critics have often ended up pleading (albeit eminently rationally) from the perspective of the sex whom narrative praxis suggests is not able to narrate in the first place – and hence trying to overcome narrative's structural asymmetries by merely reiterating them. One counter to simple revelation is to offer corrective stories (both literary and cultural). Thus both academic critics and feminist activists have contrasted narratives by male and female writers and the ways these narratives portray and deploy female characters in order to bend narrative analysis toward a liberationist end, and to elaborate a feminist narrative theory.

Kate Millett published *Sexual Politics* twenty years after de Beauvoir's critique of male writers' renditions of women characters. A much more overtly politicized examination of "sexual politics," Millett's book, like *The Second Sex*, includes sections on both psychoanalysis and the work of male writers.[15] As Millett declares in her preface, "[t]he first part of this essay is devoted to the proposition that sex has a frequently neglected political aspect. I have attempted to illustrate this first of all by giving attention to the role which concepts of power and domination play in some contemporary literary descriptions of sexual activity itself." More overtly inclined toward "politics," as its title would suggest, Millett's study focuses explicitly on patriarchy as undergirding disparate power relations between the sexes as a matter of a pervasive ideology that aligns "sex roles" with lived disparities. Millett's work moved narrative theorizing from Woolf and de Beauvoir's more broadly socio-cultural query about women's contribution toward an act that in itself constitutes a feminist politics. Tracing the "sexual revolution" through its various "Political," "Polemical," and finally "Literary" manifestations, *Sexual Politics* envisions the "Literary" as a testament to the ongoing struggle between the sexes. The book thus positions its final "literary" analyses as "responses to the sexual revolution in the literature of the period." Millett's work divides literature into stages in which the first two – the "realistic or revolutionary" moment of reformers and the "sentimental and chivalrous school" of polite delay – occupy progressive if reluctant change in sexual relations. The third stage, dubbed "fantasy," is, according to Millett, reactionary; it "expresses the unconscious emotions of male response to what it perceives as feminine evil, namely sexuality."[16] The book's extended readings of the misogynist writings of D. H. Lawrence, Henry Miller, and Norman Mailer enact narrative analysis as a mode of political critique, and critique as a mode of narrative theory.

After *Sexual Politics*, feminist critics commenced several decades of recovery work, continuing the analysis of the ways women are represented in narrative, exploring the characteristics of women's writing, and discerning the specific practices of female-generated and female-centered narratives. Such 1970s critical projects as Patricia Meyer Spacks's *The Female Imagination* (1975), Mary Ann Ferguson's *Images of Women in Literature* (1975), Annette Kolodny's *The Lay of the Land* (1975), Sandra Gilbert and Susan Gubar's *The Madwoman in the Attic* (1979), and Josephine Donovan's *Feminist Literary Criticism* (1974), as well as the proliferation of essay collections on women's writing, images of women in literature, and critiques of patriarchal narratives, characterized the next two decades' development of a specifically feminist criticism focused on narrative practice.[17] While these tended to flesh out the ways patriarchal ideologies inflected specific narratives, contributions from such French feminist theorists as Hélène Cixous and feminist narratologists, including Susan Lanser, rendered narrative theory itself a field more attentive to its own presumptions and political effects.

In her 1975 essay "The Laugh of the Medusa," Hélène Cixous examines the relations between sex and writing as themselves both foundation and effect of a cultural unconscious steeped in a masculinity defined as neutral.[18] "Nearly the entire history of writing," Cixous declares, "is confounded with the history of reason, of which it is at once the effect, the support, and one of the privileged alibis. It has been one with phallocentric tradition." Linking the practice of writing to bodily experience both literally and metaphorically, Cixous exhorts women to write as a way to change history – and with history, narrative itself: "The new history is coming; it's not a dream, though it does extend beyond men's imagination, and for good reason. It's going to deprive them of their conceptual orthopedics." And, Cixous continues, "There is, there will be more, and more rapidly pervasive now, a fiction that produces irreducible effects of femininity."[19]

These phallocentric structures are also the object of narratology, the study of the ways narratives resolve the relations between story (the ordering of events) and discourse (the way the narrative renders events). Founded on Propp's structuralist parsing of folktales, narratology (as opposed to the broader field of narrative theory) was less directly challenged by feminist commentators, as Susan Lanser suggests, at least partly because "the technical, often neologistic, vocabulary of narratology has alienated critics with political concerns." But, Lanser continues, there are "at least three crucial issues about which feminism and narratology might differ: the role of gender in the construction of narrative theory, the status of narrative as mimesis or semiosis, and the importance of context for determining meaning in narrative." Asking, "Upon what body of texts, upon what understandings of narrative and referential universe, have the insights of narratology been based?" Lanser notes that narratological study (and by extension narrative theory itself) has an intrinsic limitation produced by its partial (i.e., male-centered) field of investigation. Noting too that "feminist thinking about narrative" is primarily mimetic (concerned representation and social reference), while narratology has been "primarily semiotic," Lanser's essay asks what might happen if feminist narrative insights revised the underlying assumptions of narratology – and by extension how a specifically feminist narratology might shift narrative theory itself.[20]

Theory and Praxis II: In Media

Taking cinema as their object, feminist film theorists also began questioning and analyzing both narrative renditions of females in film and the structural dynamics of narrative as film deployed it. But their project rapidly outstripped its medium to question the inherent binaries of structuralism, structuralist theories of narrative, and their conjoined dependence upon the asymmetries of the sexual binary. Beginning in the 1970s, such theorists as Claire Johnston, Molly Haskell, and Laura Mulvey began to link systematically the subject matter and addressees of cinema with narrative topoi and structures. Claire Johnston's "Women's Cinema as Counter-Cinema" (1973) not only returns to the function of "myth" as that which "transmits and transforms the ideology of sexism and renders it invisible," but also works against film's presentation of myth as verisimilitude to disengage story from cinematic style and thus make visible a film's underlying ideologies.[21] Molly Haskell's "The Woman's Film" (1974) not only maps the typical narrative of films addressed to female viewers, but like Propp's *Morphology* discerns a set of thematic actions that undergird the narratives of women's film, seeing them, as did Propp, akin to "grammatical models from which linguistic examples are formed."[22]

Laura Mulvey's oft-cited 1975 essay "Visual Pleasure and Narrative Cinema" examines the interrelation of image and narrative in cinema, working with concepts of narrative and psychoanalysis to demonstrate the ways female characters are passive spectacle, while male characters are active agents. "The presence of woman is an indispensable element of spectacle in normal narrative film, yet her visual presence tends to work against the development of a story-line, to freeze the flow of action in moments of erotic contemplation." The film narrative works psychologically to restage a drama of castration anxiety for male viewers, as female characters imply "a threat of castration and hence unpleasure," offering "an icon, displayed for the gaze and enjoyment of men, the active controllers of the look," but which also "threatens to evoke" the castration anxiety signaled by images of the female body. Thus, film narrative, according to Mulvey, offers the "male uncon-scious" the possibilities of either a "preoccupation with the original trauma (investigating the woman, demystifying her mystery) which is counterba-lanced by the devaluation, punishment or saving of the guilty object" or fetishizing the woman so as to endow her figure with the missing object, thus overcoming fears of castration.[23]

Feminist film theory's introduction of psychoanalysis as a discourse through which narrative itself might be interrogated not only opens narrative theorizing to a broad realm of theories and practices focused on the question of the subject (including most specifically issues of sexual difference), but also links psychoanalysis to the structuralist assumptions and methods of extant narrative theory to critique and continue the development of narrative theory itself. Most significant in crafting a theory linking sexual difference, struc-turalism, and psychoanalysis a decade later are the essays in Teresa de Lauretis's *Alice Doesn't: Feminism, Semiotics, Cinema*.[24] A crucial medita-tion on the intersection of structuralist notions of narrative, sexual differ-ence, subjectivity, and cinematic practice, de Lauretis's study enacts the ways feminist attention to the foundational role of sexual difference produces a critique of structuralism that makes apparent the sexualized shape and stakes of narrative dynamics.

Taking up, for example, the question of "Desire in Narrative," de Lauretis assesses the state of narrative theory in the early 1980s: "Today narrative theory is not longer or not primarily intent on establishing a logic, grammar, or a formal rhetoric of narrative; what it seeks to understand is the nature of the structuring and restructuring, even destructive processes at work in textual and semiotic production." Some of this "restructuring" is due to the work of feminist critics such as Cixous, whom de Lauretis cites later in the chapter in a face-off with Sigmund Freud over sex-specific responses to the figure of Medusa. Suggesting that the concerns of narrative theory in film study had been "displaced by semiotic studies," de Lauretis returns to Laura Mulvey's 1974 assertion that "sadism demands a story," linked to the possible attitudes offered by film narrative to its viewers. De Lauretis sees the connection between sadism and narrative as "constitutive of narrative and of the very work of narrativity."[25]

The connection between sadism and narrative depends upon a third term, psychoanalysis, from which issues of spectacle, fetishism, voyeurism, maso-chism, and the castrating threat of females derive. Focusing on the question of whose desire it is upon which the myths and assumptions of narrative operate, de Lauretis points to the centrality of the Oedipus myth in both psychoanalysis and narrative theory. De Lauretis turns to Freud's deploy-ment of *Oedipus Rex*, noting that just as the Sphinx's question to Oedipus becomes Oedipus' question, so "Oedipus' question then, like Freud's, generates a narrative, turns into a quest. Thus not only is a question, as [Shoshana] Felman says, always a question of desire; a story too is always a question of desire."[26] Demonstrating the connections among the Oedipal narrative's question, quest, and desire as narrative's motivating dynamics, de Lauretis analyzes the ways Propp's structural analyses ultimately reflect the shift to patriarchal cultures for which Oedipus becomes the archetypal narrative structure, focusing on the roles of the "mythical subjects" acting in this drama.

De Lauretis's chapter continues to explore the question of the evolution of narrative from Propp's account of mythical structures to semiotician Jurij Lotman's notion that "the origin of plot must be traced to a text-generating mechanism located 'at the center of the cultural *massif*' and thus coextensive with the origin of culture itself."[27] De Lauretis notes Lotman's conclusions about the reduction of myths to fewer functions – identifying the role of "immobilized characters" who operate at boundary points, condensing the primary characters to hero and antagonist, and distilling Propp's thirty-one narrative functions to what becomes a gendered duo interpreted in terms of movement through space: "entry into a closed space, and emergence from it." Pointing out the binary sexual character of the opposition of space and hero, de Lauretis's interpretation of Propp and Lotman demonstrates the inevitable relation between structural binaries and sexual difference in which the female occupies the empty space and the male the role of the hero. "Female," she notes, "is what is not susceptible to transformation, to life or death; she (it) is an element of plot-space, a topos, a resistance, matrix and matter." Her analysis of the tradition of structural narrative theory leads her to conclude that "[t]he work of narrative, then, is a mapping of differences, and specifically, first and foremost, of sexual difference into each text; and hence, by a sort of accumulation, into the universe of meaning, fiction, and history, represented by the literary-artistic tradition and all the texts of culture."[28]

The question of desire in narrative requires finally, as de Lauretis shows, the combination of narrative and psychoanalysis in analyzing the functions of the subject and sexual difference. When an Oedipal narrative defines cultural and subjective development, how could sadism not demand a story (or, as de Lauretis reverses it, "story demands sadism") insofar as female subjects occupy the extra-subjective role of topoi instead of the part of agents? As an effect of the same myths by which structuralist notions of narrative cast females as objects of exchange and as lacking the capacity to consent, rebel, or act, how can any female character undertake the kind of agency necessary to fend off sadism, to be anything other than that which is sacrificed to patriarchy generally (culturally, biologically, psychologically)? Desire in narrative is finally the desire promulgated by a "politics of the unconscious," which moves to secure narrative's uncertain and uncontrollable sense of closure by gaining "women's consent" in one way or another to acceding to "femininity" – to playing the role of the conquered and meaningless cipher to males' questions about their own meaning.[29]

Theory and Praxis III: Feminism and Psychoanalysis

De Lauretis's combination of structuralist narrative theory and psychoanalysis parallels and consolidates feminist critiques of psychoanalysis as itself a specifically narrative practice. As de Lauretis points out, "it is Freud who allows us to see, in the very process of narrativity (the movement of narrative, its dramatic necessity, its driving tension) the inscription of desire, and thus – only thus – of the subject and its representations."[30] Freud's work reveals the necessary intercalation of narrative, subjective processes, and sexual difference insofar as Freudian psychoanalysis deploys narratives (both Oedipus and the narratives of analysands) as ways of understanding developmental trajectories and of discerning individual symptoms. That sexual difference is intrinsic to both of these narrative processes is an element feminist psychoanalytic critics teased out of Freud's work. In the process, they continued the work of producing a narrative theory that envisioned the sexual and subjective stakes of narrative dynamics.

De Lauretis's focus on desire develops earlier feminist work that questioned – from the perspective of psychoanalysis itself – the very conditions in which the co-conspirators' narrative and psychoanalysis must depend upon this hierarchized, sexual dichotomy. In essays in her 1977 collection, *This Sex Which Is Not One*, Luce Irigaray (following de Beauvoir) interrogates the structuralist insight that women are the objects of exchange among men. "Are men all equally desirable?" Irigaray asks. "Do women have a tendency toward polygamy? The good anthropologist does not raise such questions. *A fortiori*: why are men not objects of exchange among women?" Why, in other words, is the story not different – or differential? "It would be interesting to know," Irigaray observes in "The Power of Discourse," "what might become of psychoanalytic notions in a culture that did not repress the feminine." "What meaning," she asks, "could the Oedipus complex have in a symbolic system other than patriarchy?"[31]

Irigaray's work demonstrates the extent to which structuralist notions of narrative and psychoanalysis are imbricated, sustaining one another around Oedipus as the signal and symptomatic artifact of patriarchy. Stimulated by French feminists' interrogations of psychoanalysis and its dependence on narrative, feminist critics of the 1980s began analyzing narrative and psycho-analysis together as two aspects of the same problem of a binary asymmetry based on an imaginary of sexual difference that pervaded all cultural and subjective experience – and that also provided the means for its self-perpetuation. Even challenging the story on its own terms reproduces the same old story. Irigaray illustrates this circular logic in "Commodities among Themselves": *"How can relationships among women be accounted for in this system of exchange?* Except by the assertion that as soon as she desires (herself), as soon as she speaks (expresses herself, to herself), a woman is a man."[32] No female can narrate herself, nor others like her. As the structural alibi of an ever-compensatory patriarchal fiction, narrative subtends and perpetuates the binary inequalities upon which it is premised.

It is thus difficult to deploy narrative to unman narrative, to push under-standings of narrative beyond their apparent binary aegis into a mode of thinking that can imagine multiples instead of a hierarchized pair, or to perceive a narrative practice that has always existed beyond the parameters of Oedipus. Narrative is not intrinsically a structuralist phenomenon; our ways of looking at narrative are. And the recognition that theory has a kind of stranglehold on the notion of story derives from the practice of feminist psychoanalytic critics who began to untangle the knotted skeins by which the two practices reinforced one another – by which narrative and psychoanalysis were virtually the same dynamics asking the same questions, but arriving at slightly different accounts.

One crucial narrative in feminist critical estimations of the collaboration of narrative and psychoanalysis is Freud's *Fragment of an Analysis of a Case of Hysteria*, or "Dora's Case."[33] Freud's analysis of his hysterical patient Dora depended upon Dora's narrative of her own circumstances and Freud's ability to interpret the inconsistencies and omissions in her accounts. The case also turned on Freud's misreading of transference, or the analysand's emotional investment in the analyst himself, when it was per-haps Freud who had invested – "counter-transferred" – in Dora. What feminist critics of Freud's published case study discerned, as collected in the anthology *In Dora's Case*, were the patriarchal and masculinist preconcep-tions at the heart of Freud's account, which made it impossible for him really to hear Dora's story.[34] Assuming, for example, that Dora's repulsion at the molesting Herr K. was really an attraction to him, Freud read Dora's cough as a repressed desire to perform fellatio. Feminist readers of Freud's narra-tive – and especially of the note Freud himself added to a later version, in which he admitted that he had mistaken the object of Dora's romantic interest, which was really Frau K. – identified the blind spot in Freud's (and perhaps much) psychoanalytic narrative as the now-visible presumption of male centrality that had less to do with some psychical reality and more to do with the narratives of psychoanalysis itself.

Other influential studies of this matrix of psychoanalysis, narrative, and sexual difference magisterially carry forward French feminists' insights about psychoanalysis's assumptions. Jane Gallop's *The Daughter's Seduction* (1982) offers elegant close readings of the symptoms of psychoanalysis's assumptions; Jacqueline Rose's *Sexuality in the Field of Vision* (1986) engages in a crucial analysis of the intersections of feminism, psychoanalysis, subjectivity, and narratives.[35] Numerous collections of essays on feminism, psychoanalysis, and literature and film appeared in the 1980s, all of which demonstrated the extent to which narrative and psychoanalysis comprise two related aspects of the same conceptual asymmetry based upon and expressed in terms of a naturalized sexual difference, reinscribed not only in narratives but also as the foundational dynamic of narrative itself.

Building on the bases offered by feminist narrative theory and criticism of the 1980s, the study of narrative and feminism continued through the 1990s as a fleshing out of the possibilities of altering the sex/gender/sexuality of structural positions and/or narrating from the point of view of various underrepresented subject positions, including work on questions of narrative and race, class, and post-colonialism.[36] In the past decade, narrative theory has begun to engage new, nonstructuralist, dynamic models of narrative derived from systems theory and a new critical focus on the psychoanalytic notion of the "drive" that suggest that the mutual reinforcement of binary asymmetries that persists in traditionally structuralist conceptions of narrative's deployment of sex/genders might finally give way to a more varied, less rigidly positional way of both narrating and understanding the narratives we create.[37]

Notes

1. Vladimir Propp, *Morphology of the Folktale*, 2nd ed., trans. Laurence Scott, ed. Louis A. Wagner (Austin: University of Texas Press, 1968), xxv.
2. Ibid.
3. Virginia Woolf, *A Room of One's Own* (New York, NY: Harcourt Brace Jovanovich, 1929), 13.
4. Ibid., 24.
5. Ibid., 77.
6. Claude Lévi-Strauss, *Les structures élémentaires de la parenté* (Paris: PUF, 1949); Simone de Beauvoir, "Les Structures élémentaires de la parenté," *Les Temps Modernes* 49 (1949), 943–949.

7. Simone de Beauvoir, *The Second Sex*, trans. H. M. Parshley (New York, NY: Bantam, 1953).

8. "La découverte de Lévi-Strauss, aux yeux de Beauvoir, c'est que l'échange des femmes les transforme, de données naturelles et biologiques, en valeurs sociales capables de circuler et de produire le désir des hommes" (Frédéric Keck, "Beauvoir lectrice de Lévi-Strauss. Les relations hommes/femmes entre existentialisme et structuralisme," *Les Temps Modernes* 647–648 [2008]: 242–255).

9. "Tout mariage est un inceste social, puisque l'époux absorbe en soi un certain bien au lieu de s'échapper vers autrui; du moins la société exige-t-elle qu'au sein de cet acte égoïste la communication soit maintenue; c'est pourquoi, bien que la femme soit autre chose encore qu'un signe, elle est cependant comme la parole quelque chose qui s'échange" (cited in Keck, "Beauvoir lectrice de Lévi-Strauss," 248).

10. Claude Lévi-Strauss, *Structural Anthropology*, trans. Claire Jacobson and Brooke Grundfest Schoepf (New York, NY: Basic Books, 1963).

11. Ibid., 211.

12. Ibid., 21.

13. Simon de Beauvoir, *The Second Sex*, xv.

14. Ibid., 185.

15. Kate Millett, *Sexual Politics* (Urbana: University of Illinois Press, 1969).

16. Ibid., xix, 127, 127–128.

17. Patricia Mayer Spacks, *The Female Imagination* (New York, NY: Knopf, 1975); Mary Anne Ferguson, *Images of Women in Literature* (Boston, MA: Houghton Mifflin, 1973); Annette Kolodny, *The Lay of the Land: Metaphor as Experience and History in American Life and Letters* (Chapel Hill: University of North Carolina Press, 1984); Sandra Gilbert and Susan Gubar, *The Madwoman in the Attic* (New Haven, CT: Yale University Press, 1984); Josephine Donovan, *Feminist Literary Criticism: Explorations in Theory* (Lexington: University of Kentucky Press, 1974).

18. Hélène Cixous, "The Laugh of the Medusa," trans. Keith Cohen and Paula Cohen, *Signs* 1 (1976): 875–893.

19. Ibid., 879, 883.

20. Susan Lanser, "Toward a Feminist Narratology," *Style* 20 (1986): 343.

21. Claire Johnston, "Women's Cinema as Counter-Cinema," in Sue Thornham, ed., *Feminist Film Theory: A Reader* (New York: New York University Press, 2006), 32.

22. Molly Haskell, "The Woman's Film," *Feminist Film Theory*, 24. The collection's excerpt is from Haskell's book, *From Reverence to Rape: The Treatment of Women in the Movies* (Chicago, IL: University of Chicago Press, 1974).

23. Laura Mulvey, "Visual Pleasure and Narrative Cinema," in *Visual and Other Pleasures* (Bloomington: Indiana University Press, 1989), 19, 21. The original essay was published in *Screen* 16, no. 3 (1975): 6–18.

24. Teresa de Lauretis, *Alice Doesn't: Feminism, Semiotics, Cinema* (Bloomington: Indiana University Press, 1984).

25. Ibid., 105, 135, 22, 109.

26. Ibid., 112. De Lauretis refers here to Shoshana Felman's essay, "Rereading Femininity," *Yale French Studies* 62 (1981): 19–44.

27. De Lauretis, *Alice Doesn't*, 116.

28. Ibid., 118, 119, 121.
29. Ibid., 134.
30. Ibid., 129.
31. Luce Irigaray, *This Sex Which Is Not One*, trans. Catherine Porter and Carolyn Burke (Ithaca, NY: Cornell University Press, 1985), 171, 73.
32. Irigaray, *This Sex*, 194.
33. Sigmund Freud, *Fragment of an Analysis of a Case of Hysteria* in *Standard Edition of the Complete Psychological Works*, vol. 7, ed. and trans. James Strachey (London: Hogarth Press, 1905), 3–122.
34. Charles Bernheimer and Claire Kahane, eds. *In Dora's Case: Freud-Hysteria-Feminism* (New York, NY: Columbia University Press, 1985). Dora's analysis was ultimately a failure.
35. Jane Gallop, *The Daughter's Seduction: Feminism and Psychoanalysis* (Ithaca, NY: Cornell University Press, 1982); Jacqueline Rose, *Sexuality in the Field of Vision* (London: Verso, 1986).
36. See for example, Hortense Spillers's collection, *Comparative American Identities: Race, Sex, and Nationality in the Modern Text* (New York, NY: Routledge, 1991); Judith Roof, *Come as You Are: Narrative and Sexuality* (New York, NY: Columbia University Press, 1996); Sangeeta Ray, *En-Gendering India: Woman and Nation in Colonial and Postcolonial Narratives* (Durham, NC: Duke University Press, 2000); Teresa de Lauretis, *Freud's Drive: Psychoanalysis, Literature and Film* (London: Palgrave Macmillan, 2010). See also the essays in the present volume by Matthew Garrett, Valerie Rohy, and Amy Tang.
37. Bruce Clarke offers a systems theory analysis of narrative in *Posthuman Metamorphosis: Narrative and Systems* (New York, NY: Fordham University Press, 2008). For a feminist take on systems and narrative, see Judith Roof, "Out of the Bind: From Structure to System in Popular Narrative," in *Narrative Unbound: Queer and Feminist Approaches*, ed. Robyn Warhol and Susan Lanser (Columbus: Ohio State University Press, 2015), 43–58.

6

MATTHEW GARRETT

Philosophies of History

> Instead of writing history, we are always beating our brains to discover
> how history ought to be written.
>
> —Hegel, *The Philosophy of History*

Perhaps the best way to conceive of narrative theory's proper relationship to
history is as a slow-motion version of Hegel's brain-beating struggle to
discover how it ought to be written. One name for this problem is "philosophy of history," by which we mean the theory of history: of the past as such,
its connection with our present and possible futures, and its representation
within and beyond professional history writing. While the historians themselves most often begin with the ambition of reconstructing what happened
(in narrative theory's terms, the *fabula* or *story*), narrative theory instead
strives to discern what the construction of the *sjuzet* or *discourse* may tell us
about both the "raw material" of history itself and our own moment of
writing it.[1] Narrative theory is in this regard an eminently *metahistorical*
enterprise, focused, as Hayden White put it, on holding together the "explanatory and the interpretative aspects" of historical narrative.[2] As we will see,
the material conditions of history are not so easily divided from historical
representation: problems of history are problems of form, and problems of
form are problems of history. This essay moves progressively from schematic
formalism toward the restoration of history's material basis through
a dynamic approach to form itself. In the first part, the basic issue of
narrativity is introduced through Hayden White's theory of historiographical emplotment, which in turn is examined in relation to the more concrete
formal question of periodization. In the second section, Roland Barthes's
analysis of the work of Jules Michelet provides a model for engaging with the
relationship between writing and history, giving a method of reading (in
terms of the connection between theme and form) and a mode of critique that
takes writing seriously as writing. In the third section, Ranajit Guha's call for
a revolutionary historiography is presented as a strong supersession of the
first two moments, retaining their lucidity on matters of form and writing
while introducing a more thoroughly materialist grounding in historical
representation.

It is already clear that narrative theory is concerned dialectically with the relationship *between* historical discourses and the stories they tell. The division between representational and pre-representational, between us and the objects of our attention, is already blurry. It is "common ground," the great historian Eric Hobsbawm wrote, "that in history 'the facts' are always selected, shaped, and perhaps distorted by the historian who observes them."[3] Matters of selection and reconstruction are not only individual and subjective; they are also more deeply ideological and collective. That is, rather than begin with an antinomy or pure opposition between the facts or events and their representation within historical narratives, we are better served recognizing that what counts as fact or event is as conditioned by our regimes of representation as those regimes are, in turn, determined by the history that stands as their fundamental ground. As Karl Marx wrote in a famous passage that will return in the course of this essay, human beings "make their own history, but they do not make it just as they please; they do not make it under circumstances chosen by themselves, but under circumstances directly encountered, given and transmitted by the past."[4] And so too do we write our history: within the constraints, but also therefore the freedoms, of both the history we are living and the past processes and events to which we try to give narrative shape. Marx's open text supplies an important reminder that freedom and determination appear together. The three sections of this essay present similarly valuable calls to attention, at a time when the possibilities for thinking historically about narrative, and in narrative terms about history, seem as stifled as ever.

Narrativity: From Emplotment to Periodization

White refers to the formal configuration of past events as "emplotment," by which he means the construction of a story: "The historian arranges the events in the chronicle [the list of dates and events] into a hierarchy of significance by assigning events different functions as story elements in such a way as to disclose the formal coherence of a whole set of events considered as a comprehensible process with a discernable beginning, middle, and end."[5] In White's first codification of his metahistory, focused on the major figures of nineteenth-century European historiography, he claimed that historians were typically limited to four modes of emplotment, corresponding to those plot structures taxonomized in Northrop Frye's important study, *Anatomy of Criticism* (1957) (romance, tragedy, comedy, and satire). White further argued that emplotments were coordinated with ideological, explanatory, and figural or tropological forms, and that the most engaging historians were those who combined incongruent modalities to produce

TABLE 6.1: *Hayden White's Historiographical Combinatory*

Mode of Emplotment	Mode of Ideological Implication	Mode of Argument	Associated Trope
Tragedy	Radical	Mechanistic	Metonymy
Comedy	Conservative	Organicist	Synecdoche
Romance	Anarchist	Formist	Metaphor
Satire	Liberal	Contextualist	Irony

Note: Arranged according to the "elective affinities" between categories.

a dynamic historical narrative, one that could register the tensions both within the material and within competing styles of representation (see Table 6.1). For our purposes, the nuances of White's argument are less significant than the very gesture of the enterprise itself; for *Metahistory* not only insisted on the priority of plot in the telling of history (thereby querying the professional historians' traditional insistence on the division between truth and fiction in historical narrative), but it also – perhaps more scandalously, at least for the attentive reader – limited the generic possibilities *for* history writing. And if historical narratives of any ambition could appear – or had hitherto appeared, according to White – in only four generic modes, then those modes themselves should require further analysis if any real grasp of history and its representation were to be possible.[6]

From the point of view of narrative theory, then, the vital contribution of White's theory of emplotment is its insistence on the narrative dimension of all historical representation: "every history, even the most 'synchronic' or 'structural' of them, will be emplotted in some way," as for instance in satirical modes of storytelling (like those of Jacob Burckhardt), since irony itself depends upon "frustrating normal expectations about the kinds of resolutions provided by stories cast in other modes."[7] White's claim here is more than definitional: it is not simply that *narrative* histories will be emplotted; the further, more radical implication is that all historical representations are *intrinsically* narrative. Narrative is thus taken to be, as Fredric Jameson puts it, "the central function or *instance* of the human mind."[8] We therefore face a substantial question: What is the relationship between our *narrativization* of the world, as a crucial cognitive operation, and the possibility of an intrinsic *narrativity* within the world? Although we may be tempted to consider this a nonsensical question, based on something like a pre-Kantian conflation of category with the noumenal thing-in-itself, we will see that the issue is inseparable from the serious consideration of the philosophy of history.

With its commitment to narrative, White's account of historical representation resonates with, even as it is superseded by, an important line of thought most effectively rendered in recent decades by Jameson and articulated programmatically in *The Political Unconscious: Narrative as a Socially Symbolic Act* (1981).[9] There, Jameson insisted upon the essential narrativity of all forms of representation and, indeed, of cognition itself. A later text articulated the problem of narrative history more specifically in terms of the delineation of historical periods: "We cannot not periodize."[10] This watchword adds both color and structural complexity to the *grisaille* of White's combinatory system, bringing under scrutiny the prior assemblage of historical materials (and the periods of history themselves) as itself a narrative or proto-narrative act. Moreover, the problematic of periodization is here understood to be unavoidable (whence its double negative): integral to a truly historical perspective, even though a whole culture of scientific and structural methods has tried to evade both the problem of narrative representation and its pendant, periodization.[11] Periodization, in Jameson's sense, is a primary means of making sense of history in narrative terms. So when one speaks of "the contemporary," "the Sixties," "ancient Greece," "medieval Japan," "the Cold War," "the Neolithic," or "postmodernity," one is establishing not merely – not even mostly – a chronological space or zone; instead, one's periodizations are means of producing workable *totalities* or *totalizations* of some materials from the past (or the present!), which may then be understood in relation both to one another and to the provisional (or more durable) totality within which they are now situated.[12]

Theme and Form: History as a Problem of Writing

Thus far, historical representation has appeared as a matter of form rather than theme: only formal analysis, one might gather, gives the theorist any handhold on history.[13] Yet there are many ways of considering the question of history – and of form too. Roland Barthes, who had more than a little to say about all of these matters, offers an idiosyncratic and generative approach in his book on the nineteenth-century French historian Jules Michelet (a book that deserves more attention in this regard than it has received). At the end of a study that examines Michelet as an "eater of history" – and considers Michelet's historical judgments as, above all, registrations of the historian's bodily moods and dispositions ("Contrary to popular opinion, Michelet's morality is not at all rhetorical; it is a morality of the body; History is judged at the tribunal of the flesh.") – Barthes expresses his method in terms not of form but of thematics, and totality: "We cannot read Michelet in a linear fashion, we must restore to the text its strata and its network of themes: Michelet's discourse is a kind of crypto-gram, we must make it into a grid, and this grid is the very structure of the work. It follows that no reading of Michelet is possible if it is not total: we must resolutely locate ourselves within the closure."[14] Here Barthes gives a program for studying a historian's oeuvre as a total textual system or structure *across* the individual historiographical works. But the program is bolder even than that. It formulates an agenda for studying historiography: not only the works of a single historian, but whole fields and patterns of representation whose reach and depth may be rigorously considered by critical readers of history through the fracturing and reconstitution of the historiographical text. These procedures provide a means of grasping the historicity *of* the historiographical text, its conditions of emergence, and the ideological determinations of its narrative form. On the one hand, in its concentration of attention on thematics, Barthes's method in *Michelet* differs from the emplotment-based approaches we have already encountered (and which might appear to be closest to narrative theory *stricto sensu*, not least in Barthes's own work on the structural analysis of narratives). On the other hand, Barthes's method of attack bridges the gap between thematic and formalist criticism, revealing, in its practice of reading, the way that motifs and thematic repetitions (including *repetition* itself) produce and condition emplotments.[15]

Take, for example, Barthes's commentary on Michelet's avowal of homo-geneity, both in nature and in history. In Michelet's work, the theme or motif is integral *to* its mobilization within the rhythms of storytelling. There is no thematics, that is, without strong determination by form:

> History grows [...] like a plant or a species, its movement is less a succession than a continuity. Are there, strictly speaking, historical facts? No; history is rather a continuity of identities, just as the plant or the species is an extension of one and the same tissue. As we have seen, moreover, Michelet advances into History like a swimmer through the water, History surrounds him like a solution. Except that the *tableau* has a visual, hence comparative, hence logical function. All the rest of history is walking, i.e., muscular existence, uneasy hence strong apprehension of a continuity.[16]

The "continuity of identities" – what Barthes elsewhere refers to as Michelet's commitment to unity, to a *"concrétion chimique"* – in which the whole loses all trace of its constituent parts (and which, for Michelet, distinguishes *unity* from mere *union*), is here punctuated by the movement of swimming or walking: the logic of the *tableau* is counterpointed by the "strong" yet "uneasy" apprehension of a continuity that must be enacted or actualized by the historian.[17]

Grasping Michelet's historical writing as a totality *through* the flow of themes (of identities and continuities) is therefore part of a recognition of the *plot* of that history. Crucially, what Barthes finds in Michelet is therefore also a strong determination *within* the historical raw materials themselves; for Barthes, it is not that Michelet's writing gives form to a shapeless past; on the contrary, Michelet's implicit argument – the argument of his writing – is that writing and history are united. Jean Genet wrote to Barthes that he had the feeling, in reading *Michelet*, of immersion not just in Michelet's "humors and blood, but the humors and blood of history" itself, and one understands that Genet was, in this sense, attuned to Barthes's sense that historicity appears in writing.[18]

That sense of unity is woven into Michelet's ethics of writing, and especially what Barthes sees as his commitment to prose:

> Prose is superior, insofar as it is the absence of individual characteristics, the product of a fusion and not of a collection. [...] Prose being the product of an erasure, we must give this erasure a moral name: it is unity. Unity has a doubly imperfect version: union. Union is an inferior state because it merely compounds positive elements which it can harmonize but not abolish. Unity is superior to it, insofar as it destroys the very memory of the constitutive individualities and elicits in their place a zone of absence, in which everything is once again possible, presented to the incubation of cordial warmth; this is freedom.[19]

For Barthes's Michelet, then, historical understanding – the theory and philosophy of history – is articulated *through* writing. As the vehicle for historiography, prose appears as a *medium* like water (Barthes will remind us that Michelet figures himself as a swimmer in history: "I swim laboriously. I am rowing vigorously through Richelieu and the Fronde"), which can, as Barthes elaborates, "support the thousand intermediary states of matter: the clear, the crystalline, the transparent, the fleeting, the gelatinous, the viscous, the whitish, the swarming, the rounded, the elastic. [... W]ater is the archetype of all links and connections."[20] Prose, then, appears as the "support" for the dynamics of material state-change; more than just the instrument of linkage, prose here is both apparatus and allegory, both the means of connection and the quintessence of relation.

Thus for Michelet prose writing gives narrative and textual shape to history; yet it does so not by *adding* to history but rather by precipitating or emulsifying the truth of history's medium through its own mediating capacities. Michelet therefore reiterates what we may call the ideology of prose: the claim that prose is inert, characterless, scientific, neutral. Barthes's point is that this very claim to neutrality is an ideology, a specific content that presents itself to us as an inert form. In medieval Europe, prose is established as *unmarked* writing: the neutral term standing against the *marked* or complex term of verse; an important part of this construction of the neutrality of prose was the accompanying claim that prose established the basis or zero level of linguistic representation. As Wlad Godzich and Jefferey Kittay write in their classic study of the historical emergence of prose,

> "I will play matter to your form" – this will be the position that prose will come to occupy with respect to other signifying practices. Here, in response to the accusation that it is amorphous, prose will find a ready reply: "I am not yet form." This may seem to be a subordinate position, an invitation that form be imposed upon it, but in fact it is a very powerful one. [. . . W]e understand that this reply functions more precisely to locate the position in which prose can stand *alone* and from which prose can claim a certain priority by virtue of a lack of secondary elaboration, rendering itself immune to the critiques addressed to [. . .] written verse as [an] inadequate [mode] of representation.[21]

For Barthes, Michelet extends and renovates this ideology of prose for the nineteenth century. More importantly for the student of narrative theory, we can see how this ideology of prose – of a perfectly representational medium that is also, for Michelet, the medium of mediums – is itself the basis for Michelet's narrative history. Michelet confronts history as "a story that develops," yes; but the story develops fundamentally by sweeping up event and detail within the story form of *repetition*.[22] Development is stasis.

The vehicle for that repetition, the historical category that is borne along by the flow of prose, is "the People," that nineteenth-century notion of "a kind of general grouping of the poor and 'underprivileged' of all kinds, from which one can recoil in revulsion, but to which one can also, as in some political populisms, nostalgically 'return' as to some telluric source of strength."[23] Myths of race and nation will of course append themselves to this category, like the rats that accompany Dracula on his travels, and soon enough we shall see how alternative configurations of history writing may combat the vampire. But Barthes is careful to notice that Michelet's "People" (on whom he published the formative historical treatment, *Le Peuple*, in 1846) is in fact a class category:

> What then is the People for Michelet? It is Herr Omnes (a phrase of Luther's, quoted by Michelet). Mr. Everyone. No one to be left out? [. . .] No sociological rigor in Michelet's definition: the People is not a collection of determined classes, it is an element defined by its double sex, its power of incubation, i.e., ultimately, its potential of warmth. [. . .] Since the People is an element and not a social group, there is no necessity to describe the ethics of each class.

> Throughout Micheletist History, there is only one mode of life, which is that of Michelet himself: all humanity lives in a petit-bourgeois setting.[24]

Mr. Everyone is, like prose, anonymous: Mr. No One. Michelet's petit bourgeois universality reduces history to the lukewarm mood of mid-nineteenth-century acquisitive stability and aspiration: all warmth and parthenogenesis. In terms of narrative emplotment, the yield is double. History goes nowhere by going everywhere: every transformation, every variation, every crisis returns to the repetition of *unity* that is history's logic and narrative form. And history is both enacted and viewed from the unmarked, prosaic, petit bourgeois standpoint. It is fitting, therefore, that Barthes ignites his study with the flash of Karl Marx's commentary:

> One must not form the narrow-minded notion that the petty bourgeoisie, on principle, wish to enforce an egoistic class interest. Rather, they believe that the *special* conditions of their emancipation are the *general* conditions within the frame of which alone modern society can be saved and the class struggle avoided. [...] What makes [the political representatives] representatives of the petty bourgeoisie is the fact that in their minds they do not get beyond the limits which the latter do not get beyond in life, that they are consequently driven, theoretically, to the same problems and solutions to which material interest and social position drive the latter, practically.[25]

Marx here is making a point about the complexity of ideology in his reckoning with the debacle of 1848. Whereas a vulgar or simple-minded approach to the question of class and representation might seek precise one-to-one correspondences, Marx instead identifies a subtler though more potent truth about ideology. Its force comes from the *limits* it establishes on thought and practice. And this is where Barthes's study of Michelet achieves its most striking effect. For as Barthes tells us, "politically, Michelet had no original views, he had only the average ideas of the petite-bourgeoisie around 1840."[26] As with prose, Michelet is both quintessence and medium of his class ideology: so supremely fitted to its mediocrity that even his alignment with it is only "average." Yet nothing about that pose of middleness would attract Barthes's (or our) attention were it not for the fact that Michelet *realizes* that class affiliation through real *writing*: "But transformed into themes, these common ideas become specific experiences. [...] Thus, the theme sustains a whole system of values; no theme is neutral, and all the substance of the world is divided up into beneficent and maleficent states."[27]

Finally, then, we can see that the contribution of Barthes's approach to historiography is twofold. Barthes produces a critique of Michelet's homogenizing and dehistoricizing historical narrative, his reduction of history to a version of the present. By implication, this critique extends beyond Michelet too, since Barthes indicates Michelet's exemplary status as a bearer of class ideology. Yet Barthes's very critique has as its basis a celebration of the ingenuity and indeed the rigor of Michelet's writing *as* writing. Michelet's work is not to be read, denounced, and dismissed; instead, it is to be read slowly, lingered over, engaged with and discarded, returned to, and so on – all as a means of registering the necessary connection between history and its fraught capture within the work of writing.

We have already seen that Barthes's thematic approach is also a treatment of narrative form; and we register the effect all the more forcefully in Barthes's inventory of Micheletist thematics. The theme in Michelet is *iterative* (that is, repeated throughout all the work); the theme is *substantial* (keyed to a bodily affect or mood); and the theme is *reducible*, each topos or motif connected to its thematic network "by relations of dependency and reduction." Repetition, affective substance, and reduction: the network of Micheletist thematics is evidently geared, again, toward the present, toward a standpoint that assimilates history to a non-narrative *moment* – but does so only *through* the detour of narrative writing itself. Readers of Michelet will recognize here that narrative is not secondary or merely instrumental to the non-narrative ambition of stasis; it is, on the contrary, as essential to this history as any narrative middle. Only here we have to do with a middle that is, as it were, properly structural, since narrative itself appears as the way station or necessary exercise between two moments (beginning and end) that are unified precisely in their positions of *rest*.

Interruption: Toward Radical Reemplotment

Homogeneity may thus turn out to have an elective affinity with a kind of bad presentism, since both will seem to have drained history of its very historicity, filling it up (as Barthes puts it in his essay on bourgeois myth) with the false but familiar. The result is history writing as distortion. Yet all history writing may be distortion insofar as there is no "outside" to ideology, and so, instead of an agon between truth and lie, we face the challenge of competing ideologies, a clash of social forces rendered in representation. But if that is the case, then the lessons from White, Jameson, Barthes, and our other theorists of historical narrative should be, at the very least, that any *evaluation* of a history must consider both its content and its form, indeed the very content *of* its form.[28]

Recent discussions by historians and theorists of history have been concerned with new modes of history writing, and some have queried White's four modes of emplotment, seeking contemporary alternatives. Yet it may be that such a quest – setting out, like the Proppian hero of a fairy tale, to compensate for a lack – misidentifies the level of abstraction at which the most significant structural invention may occur. Rather than seeking abstract plot forms, or thinking solely in terms of genres, we might instead recognize the deep structural shift that occurs when a new *politics* of historiography appears on the scene. One commanding example of that style of political reemplotment comes from the work of the great postcolonial historian Ranajit Guha, whose essay "The Small Voice of History," given as a lecture in 1993 and first published in 1995, provided a manifesto for a renovated philosophy of history. Guha's essay calls for "the overthrow of the regime of bourgeois narratology" in history writing. Specifically, Guha centers his argument around a series of historical accounts that reproduce what he calls "statist discourse" within academic and popular historiography. One key example in his essay is the conflict between two accounts of the 1946–1951 uprising of peasants and agricultural laborers in the southeast Indian region of Telangana, in what is today Andhra Pradesh. The uprising was led by the Communist Party, and its official, "monumental" account proceeds, as Guha writes, with "singularity" of purpose, toward the anticipation of the seizure of state power.[29] But a competing account, published much later – and deliberately constructed in a minor key, *against* the monumentality of the official Party history – emphasizes instead interviews with women who participated in the uprising. Their testimonies differ in *form* from the Party history:

> What was it that the women were saying in undertones of harassment and pain? They spoke, of course, of their disappointment that the movement had not lived up fully to its aim of improving the material conditions of life by making land and fair wages available [. . .]. But the disappointment specific to them as women resulted from the leadership's failure to honour the perspective of women's liberation it had inscribed in the ideology and programme of the struggle. [. . .] They saw in it the promise of emancipation from an ancient thralldom which with all the diversity of its instruments and codes of subjugation was unified by a singular exercise of authority – that is, male dominance. Such dominance was, of course, parametric to Indian parliamentary politics. That it would be so for the politics of insurrection as well was what Telangana women were soon to find out from their experience as participants.[30]

For Guha, to *hear* what these women have said is to recognize not just a fresh historical content, but in fact a different narrative *form* altogether: "Emancipation would be a process rather than an end and women its agency rather than its beneficiaries."[31] From Guha's point of view, shifting into a new mode of listening yields several historiographical benefits. But the crucial change, from the point of view of narrative theory, is an explicitly "narratological" one. The narrative representation of history would itself need to change in order to give the "small voice of history" a "hearing." That voice must

> [interrupt] the telling in the dominant version, breaking up its storyline and making a mess of its plot. For the authority of that version inheres in the structure of the narrative itself – a structure informed in post-Enlightenment historiography, as in the novel, by a certain order of coherence and linearity. It is that order which dictates what should be included in the story and what left out, how the plot should develop in a manner consistent with its eventual outcome, and how the diversities of character and event should be controlled according to the logic of the main action.[32]

None of White's four generic modes of emplotment (tragedy, comedy, romance, and satire) effectively captures Guha's altered morphological strategy. For here is a call for incoherence, disunity: a true fracturing of narrative form, such that the ruin of the official or "statist" framework remains visible on a landscape now populated by myriad small historical figures making true history.[33]

The effect, one assumes, might rather be like the truth already delivered by Marx, that human beings do indeed "make their own history, but they do not make it just as they please; they do not make it under circumstances chosen by themselves, but under circumstances directly encountered, given and transmitted by the past." At the start of this essay, I suggested that Marx's maxim held together (as in suspension) freedom and determination; under the pressure of Guha's intervention, we can see that the emphasis on freedom, on the practical activity of historical actors (which is to say, human beings), may also be understood within historiography *against* the background of those narratological frameworks and apparatuses that would stifle them, or force them to conform to a history that is no more than Michelet's specious *concrétion chimique*. Another phrase for that mode of telling has been "history from below." What Guha adds to our understanding, and what we may take into both our analyses of history writing and our better and yet-to-be-constructed philosophies of history, is the argument that until the division between the telling and the tale has been overcome in our collective life, our narrative theories must attune themselves to the radical reemplotments supplied by interruption.

Notes

1. "In general," as Perry Anderson wrote in an important *fin de siècle* assessment, "modern historians have nearly always reacted, understandably, against philosophies of history. But these have not gone away, and are unlikely to, as long as the demand for social meaning over time persists" ("The Ends of History," in *A Zone of Engagement* [London: Verso, 1992], 284–285).

2. Hayden White, "Interpretation in History," in *Tropics of Discourse: Essays in Cultural Criticism* (Baltimore, MD: Johns Hopkins University Press, 1978), 52.

3. Eric Hobsbawm, "The Revival of Narrative: Some Comments," *Past and Present* 86 (1980): 3.

4. Karl Marx, *The Eighteenth Brumaire of Louis Bonaparte*, in *The Collected Works of Karl Marx and Frederick Engels*, 50 vols. (New York, NY: International Publishers, 1976–2004), 11: 103.

5. Hayden White, *Metahistory: The Historical Imagination in Nineteenth-Century Europe* (Baltimore, MD: Johns Hopkins University Press, 1973), 7. I have discussed the relationship between narrative part and whole in terms of the formal category of the episode, which differs from the event precisely in its real or notional relation to a complete narrative. See Matthew Garrett, *Episodic Poetics: Politics and Literary Form after the Constitution* (New York, NY: Oxford University Press, 2014), 13–15 and *passim*.

6. The combinatory aspect of White's original argument, which is evident in Table 6.1, links his project with the structuralist tradition of narrative theory, reaching back to Aristotle's codification of plot forms and forward to the post-Propp tradition of plot analysis. A recent provocative and illuminating approach to the question of genre and history, one that offers much theoretical and historical nourishment to the student of narrative theory, appears in Joshua Clover, "Genres of the Dialectic," *Critical Inquiry* 43 (Winter 2017): 431–450.

7. White, *Metahistory*, 8. For valuable commentary on the influence of White's work, with accent on the major theoretical cruxes, see *Philosophy of History after Hayden White*, ed. Robert Doran (London: Bloomsbury, 2013). An indispensable supplement, still current in many of its unresolved antagonisms, is *Probing the Limits of Representation: Nazism and the "Final Solution,"* ed. Saul Friedländer (Cambridge, MA: Harvard University Press, 1992), particularly the essays by White and Perry Anderson. The reader may wish to examine the recurring attention to White's work (and to philosophy of history *tout court*) in the journal *History and Theory*. See also, in a related vein, the work of Frank Ankersmit, beginning with "Six Theses on Narrativist Philosophy of History," in *History and Tropology: The Rise and Fall of Metaphor* (Berkeley: University of California Press, 1994), 33–42.

8. Fredric Jameson, *The Political Unconscious: Narrative as a Socially Symbolic Act* (Ithaca, NY: Cornell University Press, 1981), 13. For White's ambivalent response to Jameson, see "Getting Out of History: Jameson's Redemption of Narrative," in *The Content of the Form: Narrative Discourse and Historical Representation* (Baltimore, MD: Johns Hopkins University Press, 1987), 142–169.

9. For the longer historical perspective, see Kent Puckett's contribution to the present volume.

10. Fredric Jameson, *A Singular Modernity* (London: Verso, 2002), 29.

11. On the broader question of the narrative dimension of concepts themselves, see Arthur Danto, *Narration and Knowledge* (New York, NY: Columbia University Press, 1985), which provides one relay for Jameson's argument.

12. Here the reader may wish to loop back to White's claims about generic modes of emplotment, and to consult the great treatise on the relationship between genre, history, and the representational time-space of narrative, Mikhail Bakhtin's "Forms of Time and of the Chronotope in the Novel," in *The Dialogic Imagination: Four Essays*, trans. Caryl Emerson and Michael Holquist, ed. Holquist (Austin: University of Texas Press, 1981), 84–258. What Jameson calls periodization may be thought of as the construction of historical chronotopes, which, as Bakhtin shows, determine what is representable within a particular narrative. See also David Wittenberg's contribution to the present volume.

13. By "theme" here I refer to the recurring ideas, questions, and issues that are organized within a representational form: "Whatever we talk about is only the content of speech, the themes of our words," as Vološinov put it. Or, as Tomashevsky wrote in his influential essay, the "idea expressed by the theme is the idea that *summarizes* and unifies the verbal material of the work," and the "development of a work is a process of diversification unified by a single theme." A theme is therefore typically an abstraction, whereas a "motif" is more typically understood as the concrete instantiation of the theme. So, for example, according to Roland Barthes, Michelet thematizes *unity* through the central motif of the French Revolution in 1789. See V. N. Vološinov, *Marxism and the Philosophy of Language*, trans. Ladislav Matejka and I. R. Titunik (Cambridge, MA: Harvard University Press, 1986), 115; and Boris Tomashevsky, "Thematics," in *Russian Formalist Criticism: Four Essays*, ed. and trans. Lee T. Lemon and Marion J. Reis (Lincoln: University of Nebraska Press, 1965), 65.

14. Roland Barthes, *Michelet*, trans. Richard Howard (New York, NY: Hill and Wang, 1987), 203, 206.

15. Barthes's articulation of the structural approach appears in "Introduction to the Structural Analysis of Narratives," in *Image-Music-Text*, trans. Stephen Heath (New York, NY: Hill and Wang, 1977); the reader should also consult Hannah Freed-Thall's contribution to the present volume for a lucid assessment of his later, and crucial, *S/Z*. One must keep in mind that, in any case, the source of Barthes's intellectual dynamism is his work's refusal to fall into rote procedure: "In the days when the structural analysis of narrative obsessed criticism, Barthes produced the only narratology to transcend its overall grim technicity, the only one with a discernible animus" (D. A. Miller, *Bringing Out Roland Barthes* [Berkeley: University of California Press, 1990], 46–47).

16. Barthes, *Michelet*, 35.

17. Barthes, *Oeuvres complètes* (Paris: Éditions de Seuil, 2002), 1: 310.

18. Quoted in Tiphaine Samoyault, *Roland Barthes: Biographie* (Paris: Éditions de Seuil, 2015), 278.

19. Barthes, *Michelet*, 28.

20. Ibid., 22, 33.

21. Wlad Godzich and Jeffrey Kittay, *The Emergence of Prose: An Essay in Prosaics* (Minneapolis: University of Minnesota Press, 1987), 175.

22. White, *Metahistory*, 230.
23. Jameson, *The Political Unconscious*, 189.
24. Barthes, *Michelet*, 186.
25. Marx, *The Eighteenth Brumaire of Louis Bonaparte*, quoted in Barthes, *Michelet*, 11.
26. Barthes, *Michelet*, 203.
27. Ibid. "Strip Michelet of his existential thematics, he remains no more than a petit-bourgeois" (95).
28. These points on content and form are reiterated throughout the present volume. Within the literature under consideration in this essay, the reader may find useful commentary in Jameson, *The Political Unconscious*, 99–100, 146–148, and *passim*; White, *Metahistory*, 93 and *passim*; and Barthes, "Myth Today," in *Mythologies*, trans. Annette Lavers (New York, NY: Hill and Wang, 1972). That "the content of the form" must be treated as such in its own right is something of an embattled truism, reaching back, in one way or another, to Aristotle, though the touchstone articulation of the argument appears in Louis Hjelmslev, *Prolegomena to a Theory of Language* (Madison: University of Wisconsin Press, 1961), especially section 13, "Expression and Content." More practically, and in a mode that resonates particularly with Barthes on Michelet's thematics, form is "*the repeatable element of literature*: what returns fundamentally unchanged over many cases and many years" (Franco Moretti, "The Slaughterhouse of Literature," *Distant Reading* [London: Verso, 2013], 86).
29. Ranajit Guha, "The Small Voice of History," *The Small Voice of History: Collected Essays*, ed. Partha Chatterjee (Ranikhet: Permanent Black, 2009), 312. The two histories discussed in this portion of the essay are P. Sundarayya, *Telangana People's Struggle and Its Lessons* (Calcutta: Communist Party of India-Marxist, 1972) and Vasantha Kannabiran and K. Lalitha, "That Magic Time," in *Recasting Women*, ed. Kumkum Sangari and Sudesh Vaid (New Brunswick, NJ: Rutgers University Press, 1990), 190–223.
30. Guha, "Small Voice," 313.
31. Ibid., 314.
32. Ibid., 316–317. Guha's sustained critique of Enlightenment philosophy of history as a form of colonialist knowledge, particularly in the world-historical perspective powerfully articulated by Hegel, appears in *History at the Limit of World History* (New York, NY: Columbia University Press, 2002). It is worth noting that these raids on traditional historiography make no compromise with social power of the kind resumed by Perry Anderson, surveying the fate of Guha's *Subaltern Studies* group, as "an increasing turn to discursive constructions of power and cultural rather than material determinations of consciousness or action" (*The H-Word: The Peripeteia of Hegemony* [London: Verso, 2017], 100). On the contrary, Guha saw his interventions within academic history to be a necessary corrective at the level of historical authority itself (see *History at the Limit of World History*, 1–6 and *passim*).
33. Guha's grasp of the nexus of history and form has two intellectual forebears, Antonio Gramsci and Mikhail Bakhtin. We may see the call for the interruption of generic closure (a closure that subjects the dominated classes to the airless representational regime of the ruling class) as the demand for a properly

Bakhtinian dialogization (or novelization) of historiography, and also a Gramscian lesson: namely, as Gramsci wrote, that the "history of subaltern social groups is necessarily fragmented and episodic. There undoubtedly does exist a tendency to (at least provisional stages of) unification in the historical activity of these groups, but this tendency is continually interrupted by the activity of the ruling groups; it therefore can only be demonstrated when an historical cycle is completed and this cycle culminates in a success. Subaltern groups are always subject to the activity of ruling groups, even when they rebel and rise up: only 'permanent' victory breaks their subordination, and that not immediately" (*Selections from the Prison Notebooks of Antonio Gramsci*, ed. and trans. Quintin Hoare and Geoffrey Nowell Smith [New York, NY: International Publishers, 1971], 54–55). See M. M. Bakhtin, "Discourse in the Novel," in *The Dialogic Imagination*, 259–422. Guha's debt to both is evident throughout his work, particularly in the magisterial *Dominance without Hegemony: History and Power in Colonial India* (Cambridge, MA: Harvard University Press, 1997). For discussion of Bakhtin's position within novel theory, see Margaret Cohen's contribution to the present volume.

PART II

Motifs

7

JOHN FROW

Character

We read a broken string of words at the beginning of a text, Samuel Beckett's *Worstward Ho*: we understand them, hear them, as a voice speaking; we attribute a speaker to that voice, saying, "On. Say on. Be said on."[1] The words are in the imperative mood: a voice speaks to itself or to another, urging someone, perhaps itself, to continue speaking, or to say "on," but also then, as it reconsiders, to "be said" rather than to "say": to be spoken, not to speak, or perhaps the two things are the same: to say is to be said; or, in a further correction, to "be said," to be spoken, to be given existence, is to be "missaid," to be (in George W. Bush's happy neologism) misspoken; but also: speaking ("say") substitutes for "be missaid"; the passive and the erroneous is replaced, legitimately or not, by the active positing of a world, real or imagined, said or missaid, which is yet to emerge.[2]

Whose voice is this, and speaking to whom? An answer begins to form in the third paragraph: "Say a body. Where none. No mind. Where none. That at least. A place. Where none. For the body. To be in. Move in. Out of. Back into. No. No out. No back. Only in. Stay in. On in. Still."[3] The speaking, or the being said or missaid, is hesitant, painfully groping its way forward. It posits a body, although there is none; it posits that there is no mind (or that we should not mind that there is no body); and that "that at least" can be said: words, a body, a place, but with no necessity for there to be a psychological ground, or perhaps better: with no necessity for speaking, or storytelling, to suppose anything other than a body and a place; even movement, posited as the third dimension of this emergent world, is then negated: there is no in or out of or back into this place, only a staying, a stillness that implicitly, like "saying," has duration ("On in. Still").

And from these minimal beginnings the storyworld expands. There is an "It" that "stands" ("Say it stands"); we can say "bones" and "ground" and "pain," even though there are none, and these things are linked: although there is no mind, it can be said that there is pain, and that the pain is in the bones and forces "it" to stand. And then there is (but there are no verbs of existence in these strings of words) "Another. Say another," an ancient figure, "germ of all," which in the dim light we can see standing: "That shade. Once lying. Now standing. That a body? Yes. Say that a body [. . .]." And then we see, or "missee," "an old man and child," the child holding the man's hand.[4] The two, the twain, plod back and forth, changed and unchanged, in the dim, "shade-ridden void"; and then we are aware that there is a "skull," in which "one and two gone," the man and the child again denied existence: perhaps, but perhaps not, the skull from which the narrative voice speaks, and from which it stares; and the cast is completed by the "bowed back" and the "words" of an "old woman."[5] That's it: appearance and disappearance, being and the negation of being, a voice and a gaze and the figures that this voice projects.

The sparse fictional world of this text is brought into being through four acts of invention:

    A composition of person
    A composition of place
    A composition of time
    A composition of action

These acts (which I'm modeling on the "composition of place" that under-pins Loyolan meditation)[6] yield the minimal elements of narrative: a medium of representation ("Say"); a speaking voice, or some corresponding enun-ciative moment (the composite gaze through which we view a film, for example), which activates that medium; and the movement of persons, or quasi-persons, through space and time and relationships in a represented world that may be as minimal as this landscape of Beckett's, or as fully elaborated as the early nineteenth-century Russia of *War and Peace* or the late twentieth-century Los Angeles of Robert Altman's *Short Cuts*. The persons or quasi-persons of a narrated world may be, as the speaker of these words here is, entirely implicit (unless the "body" that is "said" is that of the speaker, imagining itself, speaking itself into being, before it imagines and speaks others), or as incompletely sketched as this old man, this child, this old woman; or they may have the physical and psychological depth of the dramatis personae of *Middlemarch* or *Gone with the Wind*.

Peter Boxall, whose recent book on the novel drew my attention to this passage, writes of the way it illustrates that "[i]n making fictions, we propose bodies taking up spaces, in the full knowledge that these bodies and these spaces do not exist."[7] "Say a body. Where none. [. . .] Say a place. Where none." Fictional bodies and places are in some sense like real persons and places, and in another sense are of a quite different order of being.

Here is a passage from a novel by another Irish author, describing the portrait of a woman in a Dutch painting that the protagonist is about to steal:

> There is something in the way the woman regards me, the querulous, mute insistence of her eyes, which I can neither escape nor assuage. I squirm in the grasp of her gaze. She requires of me some great effort, some tremendous feat of scrutiny and attention, of which I do not think I am capable. It is as if she were asking me to let her live.
>
> She. There is no she, of course. There is only an organisation of shapes and colours. Yet I try to make up a life for her. She is, I will say, thirty-five, thirty-six, though people without thinking still speak of her as a girl. She lives with her father, the tobacco merchant.[8]

First we respond to a person-like figure, in a painting or a story, as though it were a person, with emotions, a biography, a life; subsequently we may or may not remind ourselves that "[t]here is no she, of course. There is only an organisation of shapes and colours." The painting has at once two dimensions (the flat plane of the picture on which paint is applied) and three (the illusion of depth that turns the paint into the likeness of a woman). This duality of response applies to stories and figural representations of any kind: a stick figure in a cartoon, a frog or a fox in a fable, the servant whose only act in a novel is to open a door, the avatar in a digital game (which may be something as elemental as the blinking cursor that represents the player in the gameworld), a vampire or a hobbit, the shade of a dead person in Vergil's *Aeneid* or Dante's *Inferno*: they come alive as we, the readers or viewers or players, imagine them into a life that is only conceivable as a form of *human* life. Usually a character is a person; it has a name; it speaks; it is embodied, unitary, and persistent over time; and it performs an action or a series of actions, on the basis of which we impute intentionality to it. But none of these minimal conditions need be met. Anything at all can be imagined to be like a person, and no story exists without being driven by the quasi-persons that we call characters.

The category of fictional character is one of the fundamental building blocks of any account of narrative texts, and theoretical models of character tend broadly to take the form of one or another pole of a dichotomy: either characters are verbal or visual constructs, pieces of text, part of the formal patterning of picture and plot; or they are like people, and can be treated as though they had lives independent of their textual existence, lives that can't be reduced to a description of text.

The first of these poles can be defined by way of a tradition that goes back to Aristotle. In tragedy, he writes,

[I]t is action that is imitated, and this action is brought about by agents who necessarily display certain distinctive qualities both of character and of thought, according to which we also define the nature of the actions. [...] The plot, then, is the first essential of tragedy, its life-blood, so to speak, and character takes the second place. [...] Tragedy is the representation of an action, and it is chiefly on account of the action that it is also a representation of persons.[9]

In the Russian and French structuralisms of the twentieth century, fictional characters are understood as bundles of plot functions that cohere around a proper name and instigate or undergo actions. The dominant tone is caught in Charles Grivel's thesis that *"le personnage (comme le nom l'indique) n'est personne"*: character is no one/is not a person.[10] Grivel's Aristotelian reduction of character to a function of plot is explicitly directed against the identification of characters with persons, and it treats character as a matter of the disturbance and restoration of compositional order. That reduction is also evident in A. J. Greimas's influential concept of the *actant*: the slot or character-class defined by a permanent group of functions and qualities and by their distribution through a narrative; the term carefully refuses to distinguish between human and nonhuman actors.[11]

This formalist mode of analysis carries through into much contemporary narratology, and it has a number of weaknesses. First, the structuralist model of the actant has no way of dealing with mental states and states of affairs. Second, it tends to have no way of dealing with the processes of affective engagement by which textual constructs acquire their hold on readers, acting on us *as though* they were real. And third, its assertion of the irreducibility of character to person rests upon an assumption that the two are quite different: it makes it ultimately impossible to think of "actual" persons as in some, very real sense "fictional," imaginary or at least imagined.

That assumption similarly informs the other pole of the dichotomy around which theoretical accounts of character tend to form, the mode of criticism that Fredric Jameson calls "ethical," by which he means an "essentially psychological or psychologizing" mode of interpretation, which deals in notions of personal identity, of the quest for self, and of the unification of the self understood as a self-contained entity.[12] The methodology of ethical analysis is, at its simplest, the discussion of the moral makeup (the *ēthos*) of characters, as though they were acquaintances whose virtues and shortcomings one were dissecting: they have faults and admirable qualities, perhaps a "fatal flaw," they do foolish and wise things, they show different sides of their personality (Mr. Darcy seems arrogant, but Elizabeth comes to understand his true nature), and we try to see deep into their hearts. Here too both character and person are thought of in terms of presence – of "real" personhood – rather than as effects of textual and cultural mediation. The ethical analysis of character is closely tied to the technologies of self-cultivation (*Bildung*) that developed in the eighteenth century, and in part through the novel from Richardson onward, to ground personal identity in "an essential core of selfhood characterized by psychological depth, or interiority,"[13] and that survive in the techniques of literary analysis that are at the heart of much of the literature syllabus in secondary schools: "supplementing the text with a moral discourse on character-type"; the derivation of universal moral imperatives from the text; and the novelistic construction of character interiorities through techniques of "character appreciation."[14]

The dichotomy of theoretical approaches to the concept of fictional character reflects something about the kind of thing it is, or rather the divided forms in which it exists. The first part of the problem we have in understanding the nature of fictional character, then, is that it's not just one kind of thing. Characters and persons are at once ontologically discontinuous (they have different manners of being) and logically interdependent. There is a tension between thinking of characters as pieces of writing or imaging, and thinking of them as person-like entities. The two ways of understanding them are difficult to hold together; and yet we do so in our every encounter with fictional character: we accept that this string of words, this collection of dialogue, this chain of images is at once a formal construction and something like a real person.

The second part of the problem is this: Why and how do we endow these sketched-in figures with a semblance of reality? Why are we moved by these ontologically hybrid beings that people the pages of novels or the space of the theater or the story line of films? What makes us imagine that these clusters of words or images are in some way like persons?

The work done by fictional character is a function of its ability to engage us affectively – to do emotional as well as representational work. Its figural pattern asks us to respond with curiosity about a destiny: What happens next; what will the fate of this character be? Because its work is that of enticing the reader's interest, it is "as much a reconstruction by the reader as it is a textual construct."[15] Conversely, you could say that, without the awakening of an interest in a figure that in some way resembles us, we won't engage fully or deeply with the process of the text.

There are various ways of thinking about that affective engagement that brings a character "to life" for us, all of which, I think, depend upon the central paradoxes of our relationships with other people – that is, the way we recognize other people as being in some sense like us, even though we cannot get inside their heads and can only assume that they are subjects of consciousness, of will, and of desire in the same way we take ourselves to be. As children we develop a "theory of mind" that allows such an imputation of subjectivity to others.[16] We learn that the word "I," which seems to designate my unique selfhood, is used interchangeably by every other speaking self, and that I myself can pass according to circumstances from being an "I" to being a "you" to being a "he" or "she." Our selfhood lies at the intersection of those multiple identifications, where I come to understand the equivalence of substance that underlies those different pronouns, and then from the distribution of pronouns understand that others might have a comparable substrate of selfhood. Similarly, the reciprocality of speaking – the way in which your speaking to me seems to be the same kind of manifestation of an inner self as my own speaking to you – underpins that intersubjectively constituted sense of kinship with other people. Even the fact that I can use language to lie or to misconceive my own emotions or interests is something that I can come to recognize in others. And finally, the unity of your body, its equivalence with who you are as a person (so that, as P. F. Strawson says, "a necessary condition of states of consciousness being ascribed at all is that they should be ascribed to the *very same things* as certain corporeal characteristics, a certain physical situation etc."),[17] acts as a mirror for the unity of self that I impute to myself and that I locate in the unity of my body and its persistence over time. (What is paradoxical about these forms of recognition, however, is that they entail not only my sameness to myself but also my otherness to myself: my self-unlikeness, my assimilation to the other.)

We could say, then, that by analogy with my recognition of other people as entities more or less like me, it is a process of recognition, structured along the same axes (those of speech and pronouns and bodies), that brings fictional characters into being. More precisely, recognition is at once an effect generated by fictional character and a process by which we activate that effect. It is only through such a process of recognition that characters become interesting to us, in the double sense that we find a frame for understanding what kind of being they are and that in some way we see ourselves in these figures and make an affective investment in them.

That affective investment is often called "identification": a term that has traditionally been central to theories of character because of its ability to mediate between character as a formal textual structure and the reader's structured investment in it, but a term that is in many ways problematic, particularly because, in assuming a general structure of relations between fictional characters and readers or spectators, it underestimates the complexity and specificity of modes of response.

Identification has two relevant and closely linked senses: identification *of* a character and identification *with* a character. Identification "of" is generated by triggers such as a name or a personal pronoun, a body, a face or a mask, or a voice, and it has to do with the separation of a character from all others in the storyworld and with the sense that the character is self-identical over time (this is the form of continuity of the self that Paul Ricoeur calls *idem*).[18] Identification "with" has to do with the filling of that initial moment of identification with an affective content. But these are not two separate moments: the act of recognition that identifies a figure in a text is at the same time a way of relating to that figure, not necessarily appreciatively, not necessarily thinking of them as being similar to me, but relating in ways that tie me emotionally to them.

When I recognize a string of words or marks inscribed or painted on a flat surface or a moving and speaking image as a fictional character, my recognition depends on my prior knowledge of the kind of thing persons are. I understand characters as quasi-persons. Both fictional characters and kinds of persons are models of an aspect of the world, schemata that generalize and simplify human being in conventional ways and make it available to understanding and action.

The category of the person is formed by a rich set of changing sociotechnical practices that distinguish human from nonhuman being and bring together religious, legal, medical, ethical, civic, and socioeconomic taxonomies in a single point. In Foucault's terms, the person is less a concept than a *dispositif*, an evolving apparatus for the shaping of social arrangements. And that apparatus endows the form of the form of the person with different affordances and relations in different cultures, meaning that there can be no general, transcultural concept of "person" with a necessary or unified form.

The codification of the person by way of the apparatus of the law into the characteristic property relations of modernity gave rise to one modality of personhood that Clifford Geertz called "the Western conception of the person as a bounded, unique, more or less integrated motivational and cognitive universe, a dynamic center of awareness, emotion, judgment, and action organized into a distinctive whole and set contrastively both against other such wholes and against its social and natural background," a conception he described as "a rather peculiar idea within the context of the world's cultures."[19] This format corresponds to what Marilyn Strathern calls "Western proprietism," according to which the person is self-possessed and self-contained, separate from the world of social others and the world of things; things have a singular value in relation to the person, and it is the external social world that gives things the plurality and diversity of their value. This assumption runs counter, however, to the supposition of many traditional societies "that persons are intrinsically plural and diverse in origin and in their acts" and that they are intimately bound up with the things with which they continuously exchange meanings and values.[20]

The category of personhood is given by the gods, by totemic ancestors, by ancestral law embedded in country, or by a more or less secular system of law. The category designates a bounded set of capacities, and it is defined in part by a set of exclusions: it is distinct from the members of other species, and from inanimate things; it is distinct from the dead and the unborn. Roberto Esposito points to the way the *dispositif* of the person works with a kind of violence to perform an act of simultaneous inclusion and exclusion by distinguishing full persons from semi-persons and nonpersons (children or the insane or slaves, for example).[21] As a positive construct, the person is bounded by the human body. It bears rights and obligations, and is the subject of will and cognition; and it is something like a place defined by a social order.

Yet each of these distinctions and capacities must be qualified. Natural persons (unlike certain kinds of legal persons, such as corporations) are, and are continuous with, animals. Their mode of relation to the world may be individual or dividual, permeable or partible; their identity may be limited to this world, may continue into an afterlife, or may pass by a process of metempsychosis into the identity of another person. Persons are never discontinuous with things, since they project their will and capacities into ritual or technological things, and their sociality is, in many ways and increasingly, a "sociality with objects."[22] The interaction of humans and machines can be understood as a mode of distributed intelligence, and the "self" as no more than "a small part of a much larger trial-and-error system which does the thinking, acting, and deciding."[23] Persons are joined in culturally various ways to the dead who gave them birth and who live in their memories, to the world of spirits, and to the unborn to whom they bequeath their genes, their name, and the world they leave behind; they occupy a transient space between nonbeing and death. The personal body may be incomplete, is subject to constant continuous and discontinuous change, and may be prosthetically extended. The will is negated in sleep, in sexual passion, in dreams, in the logic of the unconscious; cognition is driven by metaphor and desire. Rights and obligations are subject to the play of social power and the pressure of social forces. And to the extent that the person is a place defined by a social order, it is a different kind of thing in each society, differentially defined by a sociology, an anthropology, an ontology, and an eschatology.

Fictional characters are a composition of person based in norms of social personhood and elaborated according to the conventions of particular genres; they are technically fabricated quasi-persons. What is at play in the composition of person is a predication of the existence, implicit or explicitly stated, of a person-like being and of a storyworld in which actions take place. Some of the basic constituents of such quasi-persons are a name; a body; and that they are both a subject and an object of discourse, both speaking and being spoken.

I take the process of nomination, of naming, to be at once a central condition for the existence and recognition of fictional character and a central dimension of narrative structure, worked out differently in different genres. Like but unlike pronouns, names inscribe us in the social order, making us recognizable as persons or nonpersons, and we come, partly or wholly, to inhabit them – to assume that we are our name.

We can posit a number of dimensions along which names operate. First, they tie social persons to particular bodies. Second, they designate and enact kinship relations, including those that have to do with legitimacy of birth and position, with the transmission of property and status, and with continuity or discontinuity between generations. Third, they establish relations with the world of the ancestors or the spirit world, and thereby bring supernatural forces into play. Fourth, they perform relations of familiarity or formality – of solidarity and intimacy, or of social distance and deference – between speakers. And they distinguish between an identity one is born with and (in the case of nicknames or titles, for example) an emergent or achieved identity. This is to say that names enact many of the central aspects of a culture.

Crucially, names engage the body: to its complex singularity corresponds the multiplicity of relations that names evoke. As Michael Ragussis argues, the name shares with the body "the function of bringing another person into existence and assigning that person's status," and fiction makes manifest the "profound transaction between body and name."[24] Many plots are thus naming plots. A child lost or abandoned by its parents is brought up by strangers before discovering his or her true name (Oedipus, Perdita, Oliver Twist); "Don Quixote de la Mancha" is the knightly name of one Don Quixada or Quesada or Quexana, who rebaptizes himself from the sphere of the novelistic mundane into the higher sphere of the courtly romance; a nameless young woman becomes the second Mrs. de Winter; Superman disguises himself under the alias Clark Kent; the name of the Master of Go, in

Kawabata's novel, disappears into his title; the former British prime minister Adam Lang in Robert Harris's *The Ghost* bears a remarkable resemblance to Tony Blair; the characters "Robespierre" and "Lee Harvey Oswald" in Hilary Mantel's *A Place of Greater Safety* and Don DeLillo's *Libra* have much in common with Robespierre and Lee Harvey Oswald. Names are a key site of struggle in fiction: the struggle to reconcile sexual desire, gendered power, and alliance in marriage; generational struggle over inheritance; struggle to assert one social identity over another; the struggle to find or to conceal a true identity.

Bodies are named, and name themselves as an "I"; names and pronouns settle on bodies, pass from one body to another, struggle to assert themselves in relation to bodies: to be named, to name oneself, is to find or take a place within a kinship network or a social order that is, at the most basic level, an order of bodies.

While many fictional plots are naming plots, then, all fictional plots are body plots: stories about birth and death, sexual desire, pain, aging, struggle, eating, touching, excreting, blushing, speaking, seeing and being seen, feeling, becoming. Yet bodies are never just bodies: they are a component of an assemblage made up of bodily appearance and bodily habitus; of the complex status of the person within kinship networks, cultural networks, social networks; of the fantasies through which the imaginary body works out its relation to other people, other bodies, to the bodies of the dead and its own, unimaginable death; and of the temporality that governs the passage of a body through a plot or a life. My body represents me, grounds my sense of being an embodied self, myself and no other, a self relative to other selves and the world I inhabit. The scale of my body is my measure of that world and orders the language through which I speak it. Yet my body is never simply identical with me. I am and am not my body.

The symbolic ordering of the body is what I call its fantasmatic dimension. That dimension is constructed from "evanescent and fragmentary evidence derived from multiple sensory systems such as vision, proprioception and hearing";[25] and its key coordinates are the boundaries between the inside and the outside, between the self and the other, between male and female, between the clean and the polluted, and between the living and the dead. Moira Gatens describes what she calls the "imaginary body" as the effect of a "system of exchange, identification and mimesis" in which I shape my sense of myself by way of an incorporation of the bodies of others.[26] It may at times have about it "an eerie anonymity and otherness," and it allows us to be "objects, for ourselves and to ourselves: recipients of our own sadism/masochism; esteem/disdain; punishment/reward; love/hate. Our body image is a body double that can be as 'other' to us as any genuine 'other' can be."[27]

It is through this imaginary body that our fundamental fantasies about who we are and how we engage with others are shaped.

Here is a description of a fictional character:

> Samuel Spade's jaw was long and bony, his chin a jutting v under the more flexible v of his mouth. His nostrils curved back to make another, smaller, v. His yellow-grey eyes were horizontal. The v *motif* was picked up again by thickish brows rising outward from twin creases above a hooked nose, and his pale brown hair grew down – from high flat temples – in a point on his forehead. He looked rather pleasantly like a blond Satan.[28]

This character has a name, although it's deceptive: "Samuel" is a formal given name that is never used after this opening paragraph; the character is "Sam" (or, once, "Sammy") to his friends and some of his enemies, and "Spade" to the narrator and some of his other enemies. This description is a portrait: a face without a body, and a highly stylized face at that, made up of five ascending *v*'s, as though our gaze were sweeping upward from chin to head. The final sentence gives the portrait its thematic kick: Spade is a bad guy, but "blond" and "pleasantly" render him a good, even angelic kind of satanic hero. (The "horizontal" eyes, "yellow-grey" like a goat's, reinforce the satanic reference.) A spade is a digging implement, and the word belongs to a saying about plain speaking. And, although it's an unusual surname, "Spade" is an ordinary English word, and we assume that this character is ethnically Anglo-American, with all the cultural and social values that go with that ethnicity (although the word's derogatory slang sense of "black male" perhaps complicates the ethnic reference). So this brief description gives a range of information about Spade's moral qualities – qualities that are conveyed differently, in a more vividly physical way, when we encounter him in Humphrey Bogart's personation in the film adaptation of *The Maltese Falcon*. But these qualities, and the description that invokes them, are specifically aligned with the genre of detective fiction that shapes them and that they help modify at a crucial point in its evolution (that is, the moment of transition from the classic "polite" crime novel to its hard-boiled American version, and from the pulp fiction magazines in which that version was formed to more mainstream publications). Character is a function of genre, and what is plausible or moving in one genre is implausible or out of place in another.

Other descriptive elements fill out Spade's thematic role in the novel. One is his job: he is a private investigator, and in this genre that means that he is normatively tough, cynical, at loggerheads with the police, disrespectful of authority, that he follows hunches, and so on. He will display more interest in money and less interest in women than he actually feels, and he respects the law only insofar as it corresponds to his personal code of ethics. He is a creature of the city, and his ability to range across the social scale is part of the way in which the city is brought into representation in twentieth-century fiction. More generally, Spade's actions in the novel – his complicated relationship with his partner, with whose wife he has been sleeping; his pretense of being out for himself; his taunting of the gunsel Wilmer; his bantering familiarity with Effie Perine and other minor women characters; his brutal and calculated enforcement of justice against Brigid O'Shaughnessy – add up to a portrait of a character with complex moral commitments acting neither corruptly nor with an unambiguous integrity. It's an idealized portrait, of course; and it projects a world that is, again, generically specific: a corrupt urban world in which a kind of degraded knight errantry is acted out by imperfect male heroes.

The storyworlds of fictional texts, including the characters that are a crucial component of them, are at once self-contained and self-referential, and yet emblematic of the world, or the many worlds, in which we live: not (necessarily) because they strive for emblematic status, but because the very fact of the framing of fictional texts within restricted boundaries forces our attention to what lies beyond those boundaries. Every storyworld and every fictional character can thus be read – however hard the text might resist such an extrapolation – as a token of some more general type (of world, of person). These typifications are both drawn from and feed back into the social text; Leo Bersani gives the example of analysis in French schools of the Racinian monologue, which "provides useful training in the more or less official psychological language of our culture."[29] But we could also cite the various folk taxonomies on which fictional texts draw, including such forms of everyday knowledge as folk physiognomies, with their "system of strictly coded equivalences" (a hooked nose designates greed, fleshy lips designate sensuality),[30] the psychological doctrine of the ruling passion, models of gender roles, or notions of the racial or social "type." Texts also draw on models of social hierarchy and legal and religious order such as the Great Chain of Being or the social contract or the class system – and on specifically fictional character taxonomies such as those of the New Comedy or the Baroque heroic opera or cinematic space opera or television sitcoms. The character typologies on which fictional texts draw and to which they contribute thus provide a readymade model of personhood that is usable on the one hand for immediate recognition of characters in texts, and on the other for application to persons in the world.

In the case of the novel, typological abstraction works as an informal and secular operator of extrapolation through layers of "sociological" generality.

Age, gender, ethnicity, occupation, and social class are the characteristic markers that we read from the persons of the novel, and there is a continued tension between reading character as a contingent particularity and reading it as the representative of a larger class of persons. Much of the energy of the novel has gone into refusing allegorical or symbolic reference; yet to the extent that character is a structural moment of the semantic patterning of the novel, that refusal is almost impossible to achieve. Novelistic character is thus a mechanism for scaling up and down between orders of generality.

This is to say that fictional character always tends to work as a moment of "internal" compositional structure: as a way of weaving patterns through a text. T. S. Eliot highlights this function in a note to *The Waste Land*:

> Tiresias, although a mere spectator and not indeed a "character", is yet the most important personage in the poem, uniting all the rest. Just as the one-eyed merchant, seller of currants, melts into the Phoenician Sailor, and the latter is not wholly distinct from Ferdinand Prince of Naples, so all the women are one woman, and the two sexes meet in Tiresias.[31]

While Eliot's faux-scholarly notes can scarcely be taken seriously, the principle is nevertheless valid: parallels and contrasts between characters build larger textual patterns. Gender is a key organizing mechanism for many texts. Think of Mozart's *Magic Flute*, where the barely distinguished couple of Tamino and Pamina at one social level and Papageno and Papagena at another correspond to the dichotomy of Sarastro and the Queen of the Night, metonyms respectively of the sun and moon, of male and female principles, and of patriarchal and matriarchal social orders. The figure of the double similarly organizes contrastive pairs (detective and murderer, Jekyll and Hyde, Smiley and Karla) as mirror images. And Shakespeare consistently uses counterpointing plots to construct thematically significant contrasts and parallels. In *Lear*, the good daughter, Cordelia, is set against the bad daughters, Regan and Goneril, and the bastard, Edmund, against the legitimate Edgar; Kent disguised as Caius parallels Edgar disguised as Tom o'Bedlam, and the tormented Lear accompanied by his Fool parallels the blinded Gloucester accompanied by Tom.

Such patterns may extend beyond individual texts to an entire oeuvre. The narrator of Proust's *In Search of Lost Time* notes that in Hardy or Stendhal the use of a repeated leitmotif operates in the form of recurrent structural parallelisms, so that "all those novels [...] can be superimposed on one another."[32] In Dostoevsky, the "same" scene and the "same" characters may be repeated either within a single novel or from one novel to another; and Dostoevsky acts doubly as a model, first because of the essentially identical nature of his women characters and second because of the *content* of the obsessively repeated scenes: parricide, the father's rape of the mother, Smerdiakov's suicide after killing Karamazov.[33]

"Realist" texts tend to disavow but can never escape such effects of formal patterning. They can never escape them because of the ontological ambiguity of the character form, at once a more or less plausible simulacrum of a person and a moment of the formal structure of texts. The theoretical challenge is to understand that ambiguity, that hybridity, and the historically and generically specific forms in which it is manifested – and to find a language that will hold both of its moments together.

Notes

1. Samuel Beckett, *Worstward Ho*, in *Nohow On: Three Novels* (New York, NY: Grove Press, 1996), 77.
2. Ibid.
3. Ibid.
4. Ibid., 78, 79, 80.
5. Ibid., 87, 92.
6. The Spanish theologian St. Ignatius Loyola devised a set of spiritual exercises for the Jesuit order he founded; among these exercises, the "composition of place" is a method of visualization of a sacred scene in order to bring it vividly to the imagination.
7. Peter Boxall, *The Value of the Novel* (Cambridge: Cambridge University Press, 2015), 71.
8. John Banville, *The Book of Evidence* (1989; repr. London: Picador, 1998), 105.
9. Aristotle, *On the Art of Poetry*, in *Classical Literary Criticism*, trans. T. S. Dorsch (Harmondsworth: Penguin, 1965), 39–40.
10. Charles Grivel, *Production de l'intérêt romanesque* (The Hague: Mouton, 1973), 113.
11. A. J. Greimas, "Réflexions sur les modèles actantiels," in *Sémantique structurale* (Paris: Larousse, 1966).
12. Fredric Jameson, *The Political Unconscious: Narrative as a Socially Symbolic Act* (Ithaca, NY: Cornell University Press, 1981), 60.
13. Dror Wahrman, *The Making of the Modern Self: Identity and Culture in Eighteenth-Century England* (New Haven, CT: Yale University Press, 2004), xi.
14. Ian Hunter, "Reading Character," *Southern Review* 16 (1983): 231. Cf. Deidre Shauna Lynch, *The Economy of Character: Novels, Market Culture, and the Business of Inner Meaning* (Chicago, IL: University of Chicago Press, 1998), 10: "With the beginnings of the late eighteenth century's 'affective revolution' and the advent of new linkages between novel reading, moral training, and self-culture, character reading was reinvented as an occasion when readers found themselves and plumbed their own interior resources of sensibility by plumbing characters' hidden depths."

15. Philippe Hamon, "Pour un statut sémiologique du personnage," in Roland Barthes, Wolfgang Kayser, Wayne Booth, and Philippe Hamon, *Poétique du récit* (Paris: Seuil, 1977), 119.
16. Cf. Lisa Zunshine, *Why We Read Fiction: Theory of Mind and the Novel* (Columbus: Ohio State University Press, 2006).
17. P. F. Strawson, *Individuals: An Essay in Descriptive Metaphysics* (London: Methuen, 1959), 102.
18. Paul Ricoeur, *Oneself as Another*, trans. Kathleen Blamey (Chicago, IL: University of Chicago Press, 1992), 119.
19. Clifford Geertz, "From the Native's Point of View: On the Nature of Anthropological Understanding," in *Local Knowledge: Further Essays in Interpretive Anthropology* (New York, NY: Basic Books, 1983), 59.
20. Marilyn Strathern, *The Gender of the Gift: Problems with Women and Problems with Society in Melanesia* (Berkeley: University of California Press, 1988), 159.
21. Robert Esposito, "The Dispositif of the Person," *Law, Culture and the Humanities* 8 (2012): 25–26.
22. Karin Knorr Cetina, "Sociality with Objects: Social Relations in Postsocial Knowledge Societies," *Theory, Culture and Society* 14 (1997): 1–30.
23. Gregory Bateson, *Steps to an Ecology of Mind* (Chicago, IL: University of Chicago Press, 2000), 331–332.
24. Michael Ragussis, *Acts of Naming: The Family Plot in Fiction* (New York, NY: Oxford University Press, 1986), 228.
25. V. S. Ramachandran, "Consciousness and Body Image: Lessons from Phantom Limbs, Capgras Syndrome and Pain Asymbolia," *Philosophical Transactions of the Royal Society of London B* 353 (1998): 1854.
26. Moira Gatens, *Imaginary Bodies: Ethics, Power and Corporeality* (London: Routledge, 1996), 31.
27. Ibid., 35.
28. Dashiell Hammett, *The Maltese Falcon* (New York, NY: Vintage Books, 1972), 3.
29. Leo Bersani, *A Future for Astyanax: Character and Desire in Literature* (Boston, MA: Little, Brown & Co., 1976), 20.
30. Patrizia Magli, "The Face and the Soul," ed. Michael Feher, *Fragments for a History of the Human Body, Part Two* (New York, NY: Zone Books, 1989), 89.
31. T. S. Eliot, *The Waste Land*, ed. Michael North (New York, NY: W.W. Norton, 2001), 23 (note to l. 218).
32. Marcel Proust, *The Captive, In Search of Lost Time*, vol. 5, trans. C. K. Scott Moncrieff and Terence Kilmartin, rev. D. J. Enright (New York, NY: Modern Library, 2003), 507.
33. Ibid., 509, 512–513.

8

DAVID WITTENBERG

Time

That "narratives unfold in time" is a notion so obvious that narrative theorists scarcely mention it outside prefaces or introductory paragraphs. When narrative theorists do begin in earnest to deal with the problem of time, it is usually to observe the multiplicity of time in narrative texts or, in Tzvetan Todorov's words, the fact that "two temporalities are found juxtaposed"[1] in all narratives: first, a temporality belonging to the history (fictional or nonfictional) in which events take place, and second, a temporality in which those same events are reconstructed and retold in a particular plot. Such dualism, which perhaps updates the content/form distinction of more archaic literary theory, arrives accompanied by a medley of other binary oppositions both explicit and tacit. Seymour Chatman recaps the scenario in language that is frequently invoked: "I posit a *what* and a *way*. The what of narrative I call its 'story'; the way I call its 'discourse.'"[2] Some version of this story/discourse pairing underlies nearly all analyses of time in narrative theory, especially as such theory emerges out of structuralism and formalism, and even where theorists inevitably supplement and complicate the schema. H. Porter Abbott rightly identifies the story/discourse distinction, originating with the Russian Formalists' *fabula* (story) and *sjuzet* (plot) in the 1920s, as "the founding insight of the field of narratology."[3] Its prevalence tends to make the problem of narrative time less about "unfolding" (or any other species of linearity – in short, less about the "beginning, middle, and end" that Aristotle suggests form a "whole" plot)[4] than about deviations between what Chatman further calls "discourse-time – the time it takes to peruse the discourse – and story-time, the duration of the purported events of the narrative."[5] Thus, narrative theory, particularly in its more technical modes in structuralist and poststructuralist narratology, is largely occupied with developing tools to analyze precisely how story-time and discourse-time diverge and how a reader or viewer then receives such divergence within particular texts or genres.

Gérard Genette's tripartite schema of "order, duration, and frequency" is a standard rubric for analyzing temporal divergence, and Genette usefully offers an additional set of figural modes or techniques – he calls them "anachronies" – through which discourse-time can vary from story-time: prolepsis, analepsis, anisochrony, analexia, ellipsis, paralipsis, and so on.[6] The arcane Greek terms, as well as the intricate, even quasi-mathematical architectonics of plot analysis that Genette's inheritors tend to employ, suggest the extremes to which chronological story-time might be fruitfully contorted in a given plot. And one should not presume that the most radical examples of "anachrony" belong to the most experimental or avant-garde texts. Highly accessible narratives can exhibit multiple and diverse distortions, and even the plotting of an eminently consumable novel or film – for instance, the stylized fragmentation of *Pulp Fiction* or the much-admired aging montage in the Pixar/Disney film *Up*[7] – might vary from story-time in as thorough or convoluted a manner as a plot line in Proust, Woolf, or Kurosawa. Perhaps for this reason, Viktor Shklovsky teasingly describes Laurence Sterne's *Tristram Shandy*, with its myriad digressions, delays, overlappings, and interruptions – in short, its whole repertoire of "exaggerated violations of the usual plot structure" – as "the most typical novel in world literature."[8]

The fact that the basic dualism of narrative so readily gives rise to extreme complexity in actual plots suggests that readers and viewers themselves are already negotiating, perhaps just as capably as narratologists, very intricate and nuanced divergences of narrative time. In this light, I wish politely to disagree with Mieke Bal, who suggests that "the 'average' or 'natural' reader – not the analyst – does not make [...] a distinction" between the "different layers of the text."[9] It seems to me more plausible to assert that "natural" readers and viewers are continually engaged in distinguishing textual layers, albeit with greater or lesser degrees of self-consciousness, in both fictional and nonfictional narratives: Where has Holmes been this whole time, and when will I get to the part where Watson tells us? How long will it take Pip to figure out (in his own life, of course, but also in terms of pages and chapters) that Miss Havisham is not his benefactor? Is *Killing Reagan* an accurate history? How is this series going to continue without Ned Stark? What was Jason Bourne's former identity, and will he learn more about it in a prequel? Do the circumstances preceding this video of a police shooting alter its significance? When did *Lost* jump the shark? All such questions are simultaneously plot-bound and metatextual, and above all cognizant of mismatches between story-time and the (inevitably) different time(s) at which events are conveyed within the plot, text, or paratext. Presumably, no reader or viewer is ever so fully absorbed by the events of a story – barring a hallucination or con – as to lose sight of their divergence from the time of the narrative discourse, or, in short, the fact that every narrative emerges or subsists in a time other than that of the story it relates.

If we thus consider temporal dualism in narrative not so much a formal feature as a dynamic process inherent in pragmatic acts of reading or viewing, even a continual renegotiation of the nature or status of discourse, it should become clear that terms like Todorov's "juxtaposition" – or, for that matter, symmetrical renderings of discourse and story such as Mieke Bal's "double linearity" or Christian Metz's "doubly temporal sequence"[10] – are ultimately too placid to describe the restlessness or volatility of narrative time. It would be more accurate to say that the essence of the discourse/story pairing is discrepancy or disparity: a narrative plot *always* goes astray with respect to the events it communicates; plotted time always emerges in "different ratios"[11] than whatever linear "unfolding" the underlying story might exhibit, or the text might induce the reader or viewer to reconstruct. And this is the case even where discourse-time verges on a one-to-one correspondence with story-time, as in seemingly unmediated or "isochronic"[12] texts like a personal diary or a live video feed. A structurally inescapable *gap* exists between story-time and discourse-time, introduced at the very least by the relative remoteness and potential duplication of readers or viewers who receive the text; this is equally true of nonfictional or "live" texts. As J. Hillis Miller remarks, "every diegesis is secondary and presupposes in one way or another the absence of what it relates,"[13] and therefore any impression created by a text, even a patently nonfictional one, that the temporality of story events is unfiltered or unreconstructed is always subject to further criticism. A quick perusal of, say, the fraught history of courtroom video evidence should immediately reveal the consequences of the structural discordance between story, discourse, text, and paratext. No narrative event, however straightforwardly factual or real it is, ever emerges exactly in its own time, but necessarily in other or multiple times, for new audiences and contexts and under new social and political conditions.

Thus, even "the straightest narrative lines"[14] reveal convolutions or ambiguities of discourse-time that introduce potential discrepancies ("I went to the store to buy milk" – but exactly when did I go, and is exactitude important here? What other significant events occurred while I was out? Above all, why are we revisiting the story *now* – what is the narrator's motive for disclosing the "original" events in this "new" discursive moment?). At the same time, the logic of temporal dualism entails that every divergence or discordance in discourse-time is resolvable, in principle, into story-time. Narrative discourses "implicitly assume the existence of a kind of zero degree that would be a condition of perfect temporal correspondence between narrative and story."[15] In other words, while narrative discourse is inherently discrepant – always to some degree "anachronic" – it simultaneously implies the possibility of a full or true "reconstitution" of events, an idealization comparable to the eschatological presumption of fullness or *kairos* behind or beyond mundane human history.[16] But we can be more down-to-earth: there is always a "right" time in which a story took place, in which it "actually" happened, and of which the temporality of the discourse is at best an approximation or a figuration, a mere "logical time."[17] In short, narrative discourse *postulates* the "real" temporality of its story as regular, linear, true time, recoverable in principle if never fully in practice. For this reason, Genette employs the provocative term "pseudo-time" to characterize the temporality of narrative discourse; it is "a false time standing in for a true time," implying that reading or viewing a narrative is always an act of valuation and hierarchization, possibly a moral decision about the way events went or were supposed to have gone.[18] Even where plots are thoroughly indefinite or ambiguous concerning the events they communicate, whether deliberately or accidentally – "achronic," in Genette's term, or "fuzzy," in David Herman's[19] – a presumption of underlying regularity tends to abide, such that linear story-time is in principle recuperable from the merely functional, partial, or equivocal "pseudo-time" of discourse. We might say, very peculiarly, that discourse-time is more *fictional* (more "pseudo") than story-time; never mind the fact that, of course, a fictional story may be entirely "a mental construction that the reader derives from" the discourse itself.[20] The story, even in a fictional narrative, occupies the structural position of the *real* or the *true*, to which the discourse refers and to which it is reducible, and therefore proper "time," as Barthes provocatively suggests, "belongs not to discourse strictly speaking but to the referent."[21]

Of course, we would not have much in the way of interesting fiction, or even nonfiction, if "zero degree" temporality were a practical possibility rather than a hypothetical *telos* or fantasy. If the essence of narrative discourse is to go astray, to get story-time *wrong*, then the text simultaneously implies and evades the "mimetic illusion"[22] that some linear, chronological narrative is dialectically recoverable through the deviations undertaken by the text to communicate it. In this sense, the whole gamut of dilations, digressions, and shortcuts that literary and cinematic narrators employ to represent story events – all the means of "generalized distortion"[23] by which a narrative discourse, in its "pseudo-time," fails straightforwardly to repeat the linear chronology of a story – are the very essence of narrative. This would be why a number of theorists suggest that *suspense* is narrative's most primal attribute or "master force,"[24] and that narration, per se, comprises the delay or deferral of communication: it is essentially an "indeterminate shuttling or oscillation," a "dilatory structure," or "a dynamic system of gaps."[25] And even as the agreeable frustration of suspense is grounded in the anticipation of an ending that will compensate for its deferments or other liberties, narratives must always vacillate between the ideal of chronological reconstitution and the continual perversion of time – a narrative is like Freud's organism that "wishes to die" but "only in its own fashion."[26]

To briefly recap, I have described narrative as characterized not only by temporal dualism, but more pointedly by an inherent discrepancy between temporal layers, one of which, the "pseudo-time" of discourse, always tends to postulate or reduce itself to the other, the regular, linear chronology of story. Therefore, even in outright fictions, in which story and discourse are created at the same moment, narratives imply a hierarchy of temporalities such that story-time is positioned as "prior," more "real," and more "complete" than discourse-time. Most crucially, even those readers or viewers whom Bal calls "average" or "natural" are continually engaged in negotiating relations between alternately valued and hierarchical layers of time, resolving where and when to locate the *truth* of a given sequence of events, or how or to what degree to adjudicate its relative fictionality. Above all, I wish to maintain that the presumably analytical activity of distinguishing, evaluating, distilling, and synthesizing divergent levels of time in narrative is as much a routine function of all reading and viewing practice as it is a project of theoretical or philosophical analysis. It is therefore no coincidence that narrative's oscillation between the "generalized distortion" or "dilatory space" of discourse and the chronological regularity and priority of story appears to echo fundamental metaphysical distinctions – appearance and form, signifier and signified, becoming and being – that preoccupy the history of Western (and not only Western) philosophy. Phenomenological thinking, in particular, suggests that the strange games we perpetually play with time, dividing and recombining it in equivocal yet entirely common acts of storytelling, reflect an elemental narrative structuring of human perception and experience. Freud, long before he theorized the death wish, was already describing "all the complicated activity of thought" as a vast narrative detour back to a primal satisfaction from the infantile past, in effect, "the long way round to wish-fulfillment which experience has made necessary."[27] Heidegger, distinguishing the "primordial temporality" of *Dasein* from mere "clock time," describes human experience as an "ecstatic unity" of past, present, and future: "In running ahead *Dasein is* its future, in such a way that in this being-futural it comes back to its past and present."[28] In general, following Husserl's description of the "protentions" and "retentions" that structure time-consciousness, both philosophy and psychology have leaned toward characterizing all human time as inherently narrative, a continual coalescing of past and future into what

Merleau-Ponty calls "the thickness of the pre-objective present,"[29] or Heidegger, in a suitably tortuous composite, the "ahead-of-itself-in-already-being-in-a-world."[30] Paul Ricoeur, in his three-volume *Time and Narrative*, conducts the most comprehensive study of such "reciprocity": "time becomes human time to the extent that it is organized after the manner of a narrative; narrative, in turn, is meaningful to the extent that it portrays the features of temporal experience."[31] And with his grand topic of "mimesis," Ricoeur returns us from philosophy back to fiction, the "kingdom of the *as if*," by reconnecting the "followability" of any narrative discourse to its ontological roots in "emplotment," a primordial "configurating operation" that structures all human "games with time," whether experiential, literary, or historiographical.[32]

This brief jaunt through philosophy hopefully has at least the merit of reminding us that when readers or viewers play the game of reconstructing story-time through the "generalized distortion" of discourse-time in a narrative text, they retrace a dialectic fundamental to both psychology and metaphysics. It is therefore possible or even handy to consider the reader or viewer already a nascent philosopher of time, continually evaluating in situ the dialectical tensions of discourse, its simultaneous reduction and resistance to story. Reading and viewing practice are inherently judgments of the relative fictionality of discourse-time (in both fictions and nonfictions) and, in turn, of the relative "truth" of story-time – or, in brief, judgments about the specific *genre* of a narrative's reference to reality. But if I am correct that the reader or viewer plays the role of primary theorist here, we do best to turn, finally, to specific textual examples to observe narrative theory in action.

Colson Whitehead's 2010 novel, *Zone One*, begins with these words: "He always wanted to live in New York."[33] Despite the seeming straightforwardness of the narrator's simple past tense, the text already permits several interpretations of the timing of story events, if one cares to look so closely at a book's first sentence: Is the protagonist currently living in New York, as he had "always wanted to" do? Does he yearn to move to New York in the indefinite near future, leaving behind whatever less stimulating town he now inhabits? Or is he waxing nostalgic about some youthful longing, fulfilled or not, to someday get himself to the big city? Based on what immediately follows in the text, the last of these three readings looks to be the correct one, as the narrator compiles an increasingly detailed account of childhood excursions into New York from the suburbs: "his mother and father dragged him to the city for that season's agreed-upon exhibit or good-for-you Broadway smash"; "his family posed on the museum steps or beneath the brilliant marquee" for snapshots; they "stopped by Uncle Lloyd's" on

Lafayette Street, where "he drank the seltzer, he watched monster movies, he was a sentry at the window." During these visits, the boy is fascinated by the alternately modern and ramshackle stuff of city life – the "leather of the cappuccino sectional" and the "latest permutations in home entertainment" in his uncle's apartment, but also the "ancient water towers" and "tar-paper pates of tenements" outside the windows. For several pages, we read what appears to be a sentimental, perhaps slightly ambivalent, reminiscence, implying an eventual contrast between the boy's exuberance and a more resigned adult demeanor set to arrive when the reader catches up to the narrator's present moment. The simple past tense encourages the reader to identify the novel as a growing-up tale, the kind that observes both bonds and cracks between present and past, and might verge on wistful platitudes: "Time chiseled at elegant stonework"; "He remembered how things used to be"; "His uncle's apartment resembled the future, a brand of manhood waiting on the other side of the river."

And then, from one sentence to the next, almost in the form of a cinematic dissolve, both the story's temporality and its mood veer in a disturbing new direction:

> When his unit finally started sweeping beyond the wall – whenever that was – he knew he had to visit Uncle Lloyd's apartment, to sit on the sectional one last time and stare at the final, empty screen. [...] He searched for the apartment, counting metallic blue stories and looking for movement. The dark glass relinquished nothing. He hadn't seen his uncle's name on any of the survivor rolls and prayed against a reunion, the slow steps coming down the hall.

So the reader's initial assumptions about the narrative's temporality were wrong: this is no wistful chronicle of past adolescence, but rather an action-adventure plot happening very much in the present moment – moreover, a present violently severed from its past by events sufficiently calamitous to have resulted in "survivor rolls" and the stillness of whole apartment blocks. The significance of the narrator's simple past tense abruptly shifts, as well. It was not, after all, in the service of a recollection or tableau of an old New York, but was instead a free-indirect, conventionally "literary" past tense of the kind Käte Hamburger calls "epic preterite," conveying actions and sensations occurring in an indeterminately located present[34] – "whenever that was," as the narrator says. In any case, the novel's new mode is far from nostalgic: "He slung his rifle over his shoulder and parted the blinds at the end of the corridor. [...] He was fifteen floors up, in the heart of Zone One, and shapes trudged like slaves higher and higher into Midtown." The real-seeming New York of the novel's quasi-biographical opening has been twisted out of its history into something uncannily both realistic and fantasmatic; we are in the aftermath of a zombie apocalypse.

To make it through this revolution in the narrative discourse, obviously the reader must grasp that the narrator's viewpoint has shifted its location in time, so to speak. But in addition, just to continue receiving the story smoothly, the reader must infer that the narrative's abrupt new way of talking is a fully dialectical transition between modes of referencing past events, which is to say, between contrasting styles of narrative-discursive present. The transition isn't especially difficult – the narrator is neither arcane nor reticent – and of course the reader need not explicitly name the tenses involved as simple past and epic preterite. Nevertheless, in theoretical terms, it is no easy thing to account for the full nature of even the "average" or "natural" reader's accomplishment. First of all, we can observe that the pairing of divergent layers of narrative, in and of itself, provides an insufficient interpretive schema for describing this narrator's revised temporal location. Assuming that the reader comprehends the new relation between present and past spontaneously, there must be levels over and above the basic dualism of discourse-time and story-time at which such a synthetic reading can occur – a meta- or hyper-discourse, so to speak, with its own time or quasi time, or as Miller puts it, "another narration, that story all readers tell themselves as they read."[35] And because the voices of narrator and author appear to overlap or interfere at such a meta-discursive moment – we become aware that it is Whitehead himself pulling a trick or manipulating our initial expectations – we also see why narrative theorists are perpetually obliged to discover additional layers of structure, from "implied author" to "focalization" to "metanarration."

Indeed, the supplementary temporality that Chatman calls "reading-time" – or Miller, "another story" – now evinces its own considerable flexibility or multidimensionality. Even as the reader looks ahead, perhaps guessing at the future plans of both narrator and protagonist in the tale, he or she might notice for the first time (yet in the immediate past of the discourse) that the descriptions of New York had already foreshadowed a zombie story. Air-conditioning units atop buildings "hunkered and coiled [...], glistening like extruded guts"; in half-curtained windows, "pieces of citizens were on display"; renovated buildings hint that "behind the façades their insides were butchered"; and "new buildings in wave upon wave drew themselves out of the rubble." Without literally going back to read over these turns of phrase in a new discourse-time, the reader might nonetheless intuit, perhaps slightly hazily, that he or she had been alert to a queasy ambiguity in the novel's initial "growing up" story, an undercurrent of revulsion in the portrayal of New York City, implying that the boy's past was already a tenuous, unfleshed, possibly decrepit one – a mere fragment of plot set up to be sacrificed to whatever ominous events impended.

Interestingly, the novel's temporal shift is not marked by any new grammar – epic preterite alters nothing in the syntax of simple past. Instead, the shift is *entailed* through the emergence of a vocabulary of action that has the secondary effect, as it were, of updating the discourse to a war or science-fiction plot, a fully rhetorical rather than syntactical operation. And as the reader notices this new rhetoric, he or she simultaneously observes that the revision in temporality has brought along with it a wholesale transformation of genre. In theoretical terms, it is not clear which of these – temporal revision or generic transformation – underlies the other. It might be fairer to say that they mutually occasion one another, and that grasping what has happened to time in this discourse is equivalent to comprehending that a whole new category of story will also ensue. Indeed, in a slightly uncanny way, the underlying story now becomes *more* fictional – a species of antirealism or fantasy – even as the "pseudo-time" of the discourse becomes more present, or "epic."

Earlier, following clues furnished by Barthes, Genette, and Miller, I suggested that the simultaneous reduction and resistance of the "pseudo-time" of discourse to the chronology of story is a dialectical interpretation of the relative reality of story events, which is also to say, of the relative fictionality of a given discourse. As we see in *Zone One*, when the reader arrives at the *right* construal of discourse-time – or at least is compelled to revise the initial errant one – he or she also corrects the novel's type from a realist or quasi-historical account of life in recent-day New York to something more categorically imaginative. Discourse-time becomes more present than past, the protagonist becomes more fantastical than biographical, and New York City becomes more fictional than historical. The reader's experience of the text is a series of interconnected decisions about the specific reality of story-time, which is also to say, an assessment of the precise fictionality of the novel overall.

In short, the discrepant and hierarchical structure of temporal dualism in narrative intimately involves – is perhaps even tantamount to – a theorization of fictionality. The reality or factuality of any given event is less an inherent attribute of its material history than a kind of narratological deduction, arrived at through a reader's or viewer's interpretation of whatever discursive, textual, paratextual, and contextual clues are available. This makes fictionality potentially as variable and recalculable as narrative time itself. If no event in a story (or history) ever arrives outside the "pseudo-time" of a narrative discourse, then our capacity to judge the fictionality or factuality of an event, even within an ostensibly factual narrative, is subject to an ongoing and nuanced interpretation – even a continually evolving theory –

of the temporal dualism by which the event fails ever to be fully or directly *present*.

No wonder, then, that it proves rather difficult to establish what Dorrit Cohn calls "a difference in kind, not just in degree, between fiction and historiography,"[36] and why, in practice, the two so frequently and disturbingly bleed into one another. The extent to which even ironclad historical facts are subject to revisionism can be scandalous, but it is theoretically unsurprising – nor does one need to become a historical relativist or an antirealist to comprehend why. The elemental dualism of narrative – the fact that discourse-time is essentially discrepant with story-time, but nonetheless continually determining, for the reader or viewer, the specific reality or "genre" of the "past" it conveys – means that no historical event, however ineluctably true, ever emerges in its own time (perhaps not even for the firsthand witness, as theorists of trauma realize). The story never abides other than through the traces comprised by its discursive reappearance, and even the most concrete history is always at least doubled, always both past and present, and therefore every bit as dependent upon the structuring conditions of discourse-production as any fictional story. In precisely this theoretical sense, as Hayden White asserts, "history is no less a form of fiction than the novel is a form of historical representation"[37] – there is no primary story preceding the "fictionalizing" of a narrative discourse, or that evades the "pseudo-time" of re-presentation. As Barbara Herrnstein Smith observes, "it is not the events told that are fictive but the *telling* of them."[38]

Thus it becomes possible for even seemingly indubitable events of the past – the moon landing, the 9/11 attacks, Obama's Hawaiian birth, the Sandy Hook school massacre, *the Holocaust* – to emerge in revisionist narratives that impugn their authenticity or even doubt their very existence, rendering them "fictional" in the mundane sense of the word. The factuality of such histories may be unquestionable in every sense except the strictly theoretical, yet the discrepant temporal dualism of their appearance in discourse opens the door for deviations that can, regardless of their logical or ideological perversity, prove lamentably persuasive. The structure of even a patently false historiography still apes that of a true one. So, for instance, the talk-show host Alex Jones finds himself capable of expressing an entirely specious yet narratologically feasible skepticism toward what he refers to as the "packaged," "staged," or "faked" narrative of the Sandy Hook killings.[39] Narrative discourse, per se, is a "false flag," a form of hearsay that inevitably establishes a timeline divergent from the story it "purport[s]" (to use Chatman's loaded term) to convey. The ignominy of a revisionism like Jones's may be the price we pay for telling all our stories out of time, or for requiring only one temporality for history but being granted at least two.

Notes

1. Tzvetan Todorov, *Introduction to Poetics*, trans. Richard Howard (Minneapolis: University of Minnesota Press, 1981), 29.
2. Seymour Chatman, *Story and Discourse* (Ithaca, NY: Cornell University Press, 1978), 9.
3. H. Porter Abbott, "Story, Plot, and Narration," in *The Cambridge Companion to Narrative*, ed. David Herman (New York, NY: Cambridge University Press, 2007), 40.
4. Aristotle, *Poetics*, 1450b25.
5. Chatman, *Story and Discourse*, 62. This specifically temporal distinction is commonly traced to Günther Müller's 1948 dualism of *Erzählzeit* (narrating time) and *erzählte Zeit* (narrated time). See "Erzählzeit und erzählte Zeit," in Müller, *Morphologische Poetik*, ed. Elena Müller (Berlin: de Gruyter, 2014), 269–286.
6. Gérard Genette, *Narrative Discourse: An Essay in Method*, trans. Jane E. Lewin (Ithaca, NY: Cornell University Press, 1980), 35ff and *passim*.
7. *Pulp Fiction*, dir. Quentin Tarantino (Miramax, 1994); *Up*, dir. Pete Docter and Bob Peterson (Pixar/Disney, 2007).
8. Viktor Shklovsky, "Sterne's *Tristram Shandy*: Stylistic Commentary," in *Russian Formalist Criticism: Four Essays*, 2nd ed., trans. Lee T. Lemon and Marion J. Reis (Lincoln: University of Nebraska Press, 2012), 55, 57.
9. Mieke Bal, *Narratology: Introduction to the Theory of Narrative*, 3rd ed. (Toronto: University of Toronto Press, 2009), 7.
10. Bal, *Narratology*, 80; Christian Metz, *Film Language: A Semiotics of the Cinema*, trans. Michael Taylor (Chicago, IL: University of Chicago Press, 1991), 18.
11. David Herman, *Story Logic: Problems and Possibilities of Narrative* (Lincoln: University of Nebraska Press, 2004), 215.
12. Monika Fludernik, *An Introduction to Narratology*, trans. Patricia Häusler-Greenfield and Monika Fludernik (New York, NY: Routledge, 2009), 32–33.
13. J. Hillis Miller, *Reading Narrative* (Norman: University of Oklahoma Press, 1998), 48.
14. Miller, *Reading Narrative*, 48.
15. Genette, *Narrative Discourse*, 36.
16. See Frank Kermode, *The Sense of an Ending* (New York, NY: Oxford University Press, 2000), 44–48.
17. Roland Barthes, "Introduction to the Structural Analysis of Narratives," in *Image-Music-Text*, trans. Stephen Heath (New York, NY: Hill and Wang, 1977), 119.
18. Genette, *Narrative Discourse*, 34. For a further discussion of "pseudo-time," see Genette, *Narrative Discourse Revisited*, trans. Jane E. Lewin (Ithaca, NY: Cornell University Press, 1988), 22–23, 33.
19. Genette, *Narrative Discourse*, 40, 84; Herman, 212, 214ff.
20. Peter Brooks, *Reading for the Plot: Design and Intention in Narrative* (Cambridge, MA: Harvard University Press, 1992), 13.
21. Barthes, "Structural Analysis," 99.
22. Brooks, *Reading for the Plot*, 13.

23. Barthes, "Structural Analysis," 119.
24. Meir Sternberg, "Telling in Time III: Chronology, Estrangement, and Stories of Literary History," *Poetics Today* 27 (2006): 129.
25. Brooks, *Reading for the Plot*, 100; Barthes, *S/Z*, trans. Richard Miller (New York, NY: Hill and Wang, 1974), 77; Kermode, *Sense of an Ending*, 51.
26. Sigmund Freud, *Beyond the Pleasure Principle*, trans. James Strachey (New York, NY: Norton, 1961), 47.
27. Freud, *The Interpretation of Dreams*, trans. Joyce Crick (New York, NY: Oxford University Press, 2008), 397, 370.
28. Martin Heidegger, *The Concept of Time*, trans. William McNeill (New York, NY: Wiley-Blackwell, 1992), 13E. See also Heidegger, *Being and Time*, trans. Joan Stambaugh (Albany, NY: SUNY Press, 2010), 329–333, 364–366, and in general, div. 2, ch. 4, "Temporality and Everydayness." All page references to *Being and Time* are to the German edition (Tübingen: Max Niemeyer Verlag, 1953), given in the margins of most English editions.
29. Maurice Merleau-Ponty, *The Phenomenology of Perception*, trans. Colin Smith (London: Routledge Kegan and Paul), 433. See Edmund Husserl, *On the Phenomenology of the Consciousness of Internal Time (1893–1917)*, trans. John Barnett Brough (Boston, MA: Kluwer, 1991), *passim*. Mikhail Bakhtin echoes this phenomenological concept in an explicitly literary-critical context, observing that in literature, "time, as it were, thickens, takes on flesh" ("Forms of Time and of the Chronotope in the Novel," in *The Dialogic Imagination*, trans. Caryl Emerson and Michael Holquist, ed. Michael Holquist [Austin: University of Texas Press, 1981], 84). See also Mieke Bal's interesting commentary on the politics of temporal "thickness" in *Narratology*, 77–79.
30. Heidegger, *Being and Time*, 192. The original German term is *"Sich-vorweg-im-schon-sein-in-einer-Welt."*
31. Paul Ricoeur, *Time and Narrative*, vol. 1, trans. Kathleen McLaughlin and David Pellauer (Chicago, IL: University of Chicago Press, 1984), 3.
32. Ricoeur, *Time and Narrative*, vol. 1, 64, 67; *Time and Narrative*, vol. 2, trans. Kathleen McLaughlin and David Pellauer (Chicago, IL: University of Chicago Press, 1985), 157.
33. Colson Whitehead, *Zone One* (New York, NY: Anchor, 2012). All quotations of Whitehead's novel are from the first few pages.
34. See Käte Hamburger, *The Logic of Literature*, 2nd ed., trans. Marilyn J. Rose (Indianapolis: Indiana University Press, 1993), 64ff.
35. Miller, *Reading Narrative*, 47.
36. Dorrit Cohn, *The Distinction of Fiction* (Baltimore, MD: Johns Hopkins University Press, 2000), 156.
37. Hayden White, "The Fictions of Factual Representation," in *Tropics of Discourse: Essays in Cultural Criticism* (Baltimore, MD: Johns Hopkins University Press, 1986), 122.
38. Barbara Herrnstein Smith, *On the Margins of Discourse: The Relation of Literature to Language* (Chicago, IL: University of Chicago Press, 1978), 128, Herrnstein Smith's emphasis.
39. "Alex Jones' Final Statement on Sandy Hook," www.infowars.com/alex-jones-final-statement-on-sandy-hook/, accessed 1/23/2017.

9

DAVID KURNICK

Pleasure

Is it pleasure, what bluestocking Olive Chancellor offers to the charismatic, vacant Verena Tarrant on their first private meeting?

> Olive had taken her up, in the literal sense of the phrase, like a bird of the air, had spread an extraordinary pair of wings, and carried her through the dizzying void of space. Verena liked it, for the most part; liked to shoot upward without an effort of her own and look down upon all creation, upon all history, from such a height. From this first interview she felt that she was seized, and she gave herself up, only shutting her eyes a little, as we do whenever a person in whom we have perfect confidence proposes, with our assent, to subject us to some sensation.[1]

How one reads the scene will dictate whether one understands Henry James's *The Bostonians* (1885–1886) as lesbian tragedy or heterosexual comedy. Understood as a scene of pleasure, this is the moment in which Verena is introduced to the possibility of same-sex desire, and the novel that lies ahead is a grim reckoning with the scant social space permitted in the second half of the nineteenth century for such desire to take durable form. Taken as a scene of something other than pleasure, this is the moment when Verena allows herself to be "subject[ed]" to Olive's domineering need; Verena's compliant nature will keep her with Olive for most of the rest of the text, but in the end James will give Verena what she has come to feel she wants in marriage to Olive's (equally domineering, equally needy) cousin Basil Ransom. Of course, a definitive choice is impossible: James's text only names for us "some sensation," and any attempt to specify it will only reflect our own desires – our sense of what Verena should want, or of what it should be possible to avow in 1870s Massachusetts.[2]

What is undeniable is that sex is on the table. Or rather, it's in the air: *literally* in the air, if we follow James's peculiar insistence that his description is no figure of speech but an account of one woman taking another up into space "in the literal sense of the phrase." However we navigate this insistence – by deciding that James is simply confused, or by picturing Olive and Verena as Chagall lovers who have floated into a Beacon Hill drawing room – we are clearly present at a scene of rapture. Olive's impressive wingspan, her avid seizing of her prey, the godlike power indicated by the notion that the women are looking "down upon all creation" – all of this recalls nothing so much as Zeus's rape of Leda while disguised as a swan, or his abduction, in the shape of an eagle, of Ganymede: these are raptures in the double sense of being both rapes and scenes of ecstatic levitation. The indifference to gender in the classical antecedents seems obscurely connected to the ambiguous ontological status of the scene James crafts here, his quasi-magical-realist claim that this levitation is a real diegetic event. That James stages this conflation of the literal and the figural against a background of perverse eroticism is, this chapter will suggest, a significant fact for the theorization of narrative pleasure.

Henry James will be the significant thread in this chapter in part because his work constitutes a career-long analysis of the concept of pleasure – an analysis nowhere more sustained than in the novels of the 1880s that treated "responsible" sociopolitical themes of female suffrage, class revolution, and parliamentary politics. A short stretch of pages in the middle of *The Princess Casamassima* (1885–1886), for example, shows James referencing all of our most prominent conceptions of pleasure. When the socially aspirant bookbinder Hyacinth Robinson first enters an aristocratic parlor, he admires the decor with an "appreciative" eye that signals a comfortable enjoyment of the accouterments of high culture. After a few days in the vicinity of this outlandish wealth, his pleasure takes on a sharper edge, and even seems fraught with fear and a piercing physicality: "More than once he saw everything through a mist; his eyes were full of tears." While these two moments embody with uncanny exactness the two varieties of pleasure that Roland Barthes will famously map out in *The Pleasure of the Text* (1973) as enjoyment (*plaisir*) and bliss (*jouissance*), a few pages later we find Hyacinth reflecting on his new awareness that "every class has its pleasures" – a pithy anticipation of the account offered by Pierre Bourdieu and other sociologists of culture for whom the experience of aesthetic pleasure is first and foremost a barometer of social access and social distinction.[3]

I wrote that James "references" these various conceptions of pleasure, but it is more accurate to say that he narrativizes them, embodies them in fictional beings and puts them into dynamic relation to one another in an unfolding fictional sequence that lets us see both their social positioning and their tendency to fade into one another; he is, in other words, a novelist. But James is also one of the earliest and still most influential theorists of novelistic form, and the indissolubility of theory and practice will also be a hallmark of the texts we will examine. For an account of narrative pleasure, the most useful material will come in unlikely places – novelistic plots that tend toward reflection on their own procedures, seemingly random moments of intense rhetoric in books of narrative theory officially about other topics, pornographic films where the narrative presentation of pleasure is intensely literal. These texts share the taxonomic habit of mind that structures the field of narrative analysis; what sets them apart is a determination to seek out the places where the taxonomies falter or suffer some kind of meltdown.[4] We'll see that certain theorists understand the conceptual meltdown itself as pleasurable, and that they collectively suggest that this pleasure indexes a historical force that they tend to call modernity and that we can think of more loosely as historical emergence itself.

Narrative theory is infrequently accused of being a pleasurable genre, or a genre about pleasure. Many of the classic texts in the tradition that would seem to offer promising starting places for an understanding of the topic turn out on closer inspection to be about something else or to be less interested in pleasure per se than its uses and abuses. Peter Brooks's landmark *Reading for the Plot: Design and Intention in Narrative* (1984) builds a case that narrative movement mimics the pulsions of desire. But desire is not pleasure, and Brooks's metaphors of restraint, effort, and striving suggest that the former is a rather grimmer affair. Plots, he writes in one characteristic formulation, "struggle toward the end under the compulsion of imposed delay"; his words suggest that narrative desire is fueled by a mirage of pleasure but has little do with the thing itself.[5] Meanwhile, one of the best-known essays to conjoin the notions of pleasure and narrative in its title, Laura Mulvey's classic of feminist film theory, "Visual Pleasure and Narrative Cinema," is devoted not to exploring the phenomenology of pleasure but to describing the phallocentric ego-maintenance that she argues cinematic pleasure upholds. A consequence of this orientation is an overt hostility to the pleasure she delineates: "It is said that analysing pleasure, or beauty, destroys it," Mulvey writes in one famously bracing line. "That is the intention of this article."[6]

These refusals of pleasure follow from conceptual and political commitments, but the problem with talking about pleasure may be more fundamental still. Few terms are harder to fill with conceptual content. That it is strongly associated with the erotic, and with the erotically outré, is undeniable – as if the only way to be sure we are in the realm of the pleasurable is to know that our enjoyment is disapproved of by someone, somewhere. As Barthes, still our preeminent theorist of narrative pleasure, and to whom this chapter will return, put it, "Perversion, quite simply, *makes happy*."[7] This is still not quite a definition of pleasure, of course: the term designates a kind of vanishing point on the field of affective possibilities. Fredric Jameson opens his landmark 1983 essay on the topic by underlining this point: "So pleasure, we are told, like happiness or interest, can never be fixed directly by the naked eye – let alone pursued as an end, or conceptualized – but only experienced laterally, or after the fact, as something like the by-product of something else."[8] (That Jameson begins his essay with a conjunction – as if the conversation were already long under way, or had just wrapped up – is a sly syntactic nod to pleasure's elusive temporality.)

Pleasure's vexed relation to questions of time and history resembles that of narrative theory itself, whose structuralist lineage has given it a reputation for accommodating historical questions only tangentially and awkwardly – even when the history in question is literary history. As the narrative theorist Susan Lanser has recently put it, "the relationship between narratology and studies of the novel [. . .] remains something of a standoff, and nowhere more vividly than on the turf of history."[9] It is striking that Lanser's own attempt to resolve this impasse makes its case by taking up the question, precisely, of pleasure. Lanser's essay traces the centrality to the history of the novel of what she calls "sapphic dialogics," a narrative structure first arising in early modern amorous dialogues in which heterosexual plots emerge from erotic conversations between women. Lanser tracks the structure from Pietro Aretino's *Ragionamenti* (1534) to eighteenth-century fiction, establishing a centuries-long tradition of queered narrative grammar in which "[t]he arousal of women by women that happens on the level of narration thus depends on a heterosexual story, while the heterosexual story depends on the sapphic structure of its narration." The power of Lanser's argument is in no way diminished by its resemblance to the cliché that for heterosexual men the most arousing thing in the world is the imagination of two women's sex; she is fully aware that Aretino's dialogues were "doubtless written for the titillation of men."[10] Lanser in fact shows how that cliché rests on a documentable literary history (clichés, another cliché assures us, have their element of truth): from Aretino to Proust to Prince, the imagination of female same-sex eroticism has been a conventional emblem of unimaginable pleasure, and not just for men.[11]

For those who still require proof, then, Lanser handily succeeds in showing the amenability of narrative analysis to historical questions. Perhaps more important for our purposes, she makes clear how central the imagination of pleasure has been to narrative innovation – and how central the idea of perverse enjoyment is to the imagination of pleasure *tout court*. Lanser does not bring her account forward to James's moment – she shows that sapphic dialogics fade away in the buttoned-up nineteenth century – but *The Bostonians* would continue her story nicely, since here too narrative perspective is sexualized in ways that touch centrally on questions of lesbian-ism's inextricability from heterosexual structures. In James's novel, focaliza-tion alternates between the symmetrically paranoid visions of Olive and Basil as they pursue Verena and – with an energy exactly equivalent to their desire – attempt to ward off one another. The pattern of alternation is so insistent that the reader understands the outcome of the story long before its dénouement simply because that pattern has become a barometer of sexual possession. We know Basil will end up with Verena because he bears the focalization for the last third of the novel; his desiring and possessive view-point seems to guarantee it. Even thus foretold, the conclusion of *The Bostonians* is cataclysmic, and, as with Olive's earlier possession of Verena, it is far from clear whether we are meant to take the novel's final scene of rapture – in which Basil absconds with Verena as she is on the verge of making her first big appearance as a public speaker – in the orgasmic or traumatic sense.

I'll return to that ending at the close of this chapter, since it allows us to read the very slipperiness of narrative pleasure as a gauge of historical mean-ing. For now I want to note that in *The Bostonians*, formal patterning carries a remarkable amount of the story's dramatic tension, and that this is a shorthand way to describe James's pivotal role in the history of the Anglophone novel and of narrative theory: we might describe it most simply by saying that James *formalized* novelistic art – a formalization he went on to advertise in the prefaces to the New York Edition (published 1907–1909), which later became a touchstone for Anglophone theories of the novel. Where an early generation of critics described James's fiction as marking the novel's maturity, contemporary scholars are more likely to understand the conspicuous formal patterning of his work as an attempt to "elevate" novel-writing and novel-reading: creating works that demand intense intel-lectual attention, James effectively declared that only (educationally, cultu-rally, economically) credentialed readers need apply.[12] The critical accounts do not cancel each other out, of course, but they differ on their sense of whether James's texts offer any readerly pleasure at all, and what kind of pleasure it is. James himself repeatedly (wishfully?) referred to his work as providing "fun" for the reader, a proposal that would have seemed laughable to the critic James Atlas, who in 1997 confessed in the *New York Times Magazine* that he had "a question" about the Master: "Does anyone enjoy reading him?"[13] Atlas's performance of half-serious philistinism suggests that the only pleasure one can honestly take in James's writings is the one you derive by looking down your nose at everyone who won't or can't take the time to work at it.

The prefaces in which James articulated the premises of his art can indeed seem forbidding – stylistically, in the tortuous syntax and imagistic density characteristic of his late style, and conceptually, in their elaboration of a multiplicity of sometimes obscure formal categories. But it remains startling – especially for any account of James's work that insists on its difficulty and conceptual rigor – how incoherent those categories are, and how closely pleasure is associated with their conceptual decomposition. Nowhere is this clearer than in the preface to *The Ambassadors*, in which James introduces his famous distinction between "scene" and "picture" as narrative principles: he proposes the terms as if their meaning were clear, and insists that the novel "sharply divides" itself between the two methods: "everything in it that is not scene [...] is discriminated preparation, is the fusion and synthesis of picture."[14] When James goes on to congratulate himself on the "scenic" success of an early chapter in which details of Lambert Strether's past are given entirely through his conversation with a friend, his words suggest that the "scenic" is to be understood as a principle of action-centered storytelling, narration that dispenses with the expository summaries (presumably "pictorial") that so many realist texts employ in filling the reader in on characters' backstories.[15]

But in the preface's closing pages, James refers us to an exquisitely tense moment in which Strether becomes aware that the "solid stranger" standing behind him in a box at the Comédie Française is Chad Newsome, whom he'd last seen as a feckless youth in Woollet, Massachusetts. By the definition James has just intimated, these pages clearly qualify as "scenic." James's allegiance to the unfolding moment is so complete – the narrative pacing is so tightly sutured to the diegetic action – that when the narrator speaks of the "long tension of the act" we are not sure if the reference is to Strether's mental processing or to the second act of the play the characters watch.[16] So when James's preface insists that the passage is effective despite the fact that it is an "absolute attestation[...] of the *non-scenic* form," it is clear that the meaning of the terms has shifted.[17] *Scene* is now being contrasted not with summary but with something like dialogue; in this new opposition, the pictorial is aligned not with narrative exposition but with psychological interiority. Such waffling would be a small matter if James hadn't seemed to insist on the clarity and all-importance of the binary in the first place. Gérard Genette, among the most incisive of the narrative theorists who have attempted to sort through these tangles, remarks that James's analysis of *The Ambassadors* "is as vague as it is vehement."[18] The confusion spawned by this moment can stand for many similar contradictions in the prefaces, which founded a significant strain of narrative theory atop a group of distinctions that James delivers to us, as it were, pre-melted.

The metaphor is less arbitrary than it might seem. *The Ambassadors* is awash in startlingly gooey images of hard distinctions failing to hold. Paris beguiles Strether, in one famous passage, precisely because it is a place where "parts were not to be discriminated nor differences comfortably marked. It twinkled and trembled and melted together, and what seemed all surface one moment seemed all depth the next." Later, Strether admires Marie de Vionnet's gift for making brief friendships feel so developed, as if she is capable of "melting, liquefying" time itself. And at the novel's climax, in which Strether belatedly realizes the sexual nature of Marie and Chad's affair, the narrator deploys in rapid succession the very terms that litter the preface – "picture," "scene," "stage," "play" – in describing the discovery. The reader's confusion as to how these distinctions are meant is also Strether's: as he assimilates his awareness of the affair, we read that "the picture and the play seemed supremely to melt together."[19] The former term seems to refer to the traumatizing vision Strether has had of the trysting lovers in a boat, the latter to the pretense of normality Marie upholds during the awkward afternoon that follows – but James characteristically insists that the very distinctions he has been insisting on have been defeated. That the agent of that defeat is the discovery of sex is crucial to the more general issue of pleasure's relation to theorization: the lesson of the episode seems to be not only that the atmosphere of sexual pleasure can melt supposedly hard-and-fast lines but that the process of conceptual meltdown is itself productive of pleasure – a pleasure hard to distinguish from pain. This, it turns out, is perhaps the key insight offered by Roland Barthes, who spent a career erecting and decomposing distinctions in the name of pleasure.

Roland Barthes refers to Henry James only a few times in his work. The strangest of these references is in his 1971 book, *Sade, Fourier, Loyola*. The book collects essays on the Enlightenment pornographer, the utopian socialist, and the founder of the Jesuits, and proposes to analyze this unlikely trio as "devotees of the Text" – the latter defined as "the ritual that orders pleasure."[20] In Barthes's account, the three writers share a commitment to maximizing pleasure through the creation of intoxicating taxonomies of body parts, modes of prayer, moods, portions of the day, culinary flavors; the contents matter less than the modular grammar that proliferates categories, isolates sensations, savors degrees of intense response. Discussing the Spanish saint (but the logic of the book means he might be talking about any of them), Barthes writes that Loyola's monastic rituals conjure an "economy in which everything, from the accidental to the futile and trivial, must be utilized: like the novelist, the exercitant is 'someone for whom nothing is lost' (Henry James)."[21] In the movement from James's

English to Barthes's French to translator Richard Howard's English rendering of Barthes, James's famous pronouncement in his 1884 essay "The Art of Fiction" has been tellingly altered: James claimed that the novelist must be "one of those people *on* whom nothing is lost," his preposition signaling an ideal state of total cognitive alertness.[22] Barthes's version redirects James's idea from the mental to the acquisitive, with the result that the disposition invoked becomes less about registering everything than experiencing it; the world here does not impress itself *on* the subject's consciousness so much as it exists *for* her – for her use, pleasure, possession.

This is less a departure from James's dictum than an explicitation of its appetitive energies. Indeed, the account Barthes offers of the distinctive features of his three subjects would work uncannily well as descriptions of James's writing. If Loyola's devotional schemes make him sound to Barthes like James's hyperaware artist, Fourier's minutely detailed accounts of the utopian future are devoted to the notion (in Barthes's words) that "nuance [...] is a guarantee of pleasure" – clearly the same principle according to which one might describe *The Golden Bowl* as *fun*; likewise, Barthes's claim that Fourier's penchant for mad, motley lists "produces a sonorous pleasure and a logical vertigo" will be familiar to anyone negotiating the labyrinths of a Jamesian sentence. Even Sade's orgies, organized according to the principle of the "erotic combinative," in which "all functions can be interchanged," follow a choreography similar to that structuring Strether's lambent libidinal attention, which has him wavering among Maria Gostrey, Chad Newsome, Little Bilham, and Marie de Vionnet – and treated by each of them in turn as a half-serious object of flirtatious attention. For Barthes, the maximally modular narrative syntax shared by these writers is mirrored in an inexhaustibly promiscuous style: "The principle of Sadian eroticism is the saturation of every area of the body: one tries to employ (to occupy) every separate part," he writes. The frankness of the claim might seem to distance it from James's work – until Barthes clarifies that "[t]his is the same problem the sentence faces [...] for nothing (structurally) permits terminating a sentence: we can always add to it that supplement which will never be the final one."[23]

This assimilation of group sex to long sentences depends of course on Barthes's determination to corporealize the text, to read its figures and syntax as standing in for, and addressing, a literal body. This determination becomes most explicit, as we've seen, in *The Pleasure of the Text*, where it underwrites the opposition between texts of pleasure (*plaisir*) and those of bliss (*jouissance*). The metaphorical textures that do so much of the persuasive work of Barthes's writing insistently assimilate this polarity with images of a body either swaddled in the footed pajamas of Culture ("Text of pleasure: the text that contents, fills, grants euphoria; the text that comes from culture and does not break with it, is linked to a *comfortable* practice of reading") or in the throes of an orgasmic convulsion that breaks with it ("Text of bliss: the text that imposes a state of loss, the text that discomforts (perhaps to the point of a certain boredom), unsettles the reader's historical, cultural, psychological assumptions").[24] The more extreme corporealization, though, attends the latter concept, which thus seems at first glance the clearly valorized term: the book closes with a plea that the text be understood as a projectile, quasi-plastic entity, one that meets the body of the reader as a co-presence in three-dimensional space: "it granulates, it crackles, it caresses, it grates, it cuts, it comes: that is bliss."[25] This must be called the book's climax, and it seems clear that only the fainthearted would admit to preferring the armchair coziness of *plaisir* to these more rigorous ecstasies.

This hierarchy may make the *plaisir/jouissance* distinction seem merely a reformulation, or rechristening, of that between realism and modernism, convention and the avant-garde, that Barthes had been writing about for most of his career under various names (the Work vs. the Text, the readerly vs. the writerly). Even before *The Pleasure of the Text*, though, these distinctions – and the programmatic aesthetic vanguardism they supported – had been implicitly presented by Barthes as a matter of readerly disposition rather than as an ontological distinction between kinds of text; here the orientation of Barthes's entire project toward the reader becomes overt, and overtly eroticized. In the paragraph following his initial naming of the structuring dichotomy, Barthes shifts his attention from a taxonomy (and tacit hierarchy) of texts to the image of the *reader* who "keeps [. . .] in his hands the reins of pleasure and bliss," and thus enjoys the "consistency of his selfhood" even as he "seeks its loss": the distinction is now between forms of textual consumption, and it is precisely in traversing or straddling the dichotomy that a whole practice of pleasure – Barthes calls it "the erotic" – becomes visible: "Neither culture or its destruction is erotic; it is the seam between them, the fault, the flaw, which becomes so."[26]

The Pleasure of the Text thus makes particularly clear an implicit feature of all Barthes's work: that it doesn't take entirely seriously the terminological distinctions it spends so much time elaborating. In a reminiscence of Barthes, Tzvetan Todorov recalls that Barthes "was continuously joking about his own constructs when in friendly company, as if he were saying 'Signifier/signified, connotation/denotation – we're not going to really take such terms seriously, are we?'"[27] D. A. Miller puts a similar insight more pointedly, and in terms more responsive to the erotic valence of this form of conceptual irony in Barthes's work. Noting Barthes's tendency to construct elaborate theoretical paradigms and then retreat from them to immerse himself in (frequently sexualized) examples,

Miller writes that the back-and-forth can "make the whole wobbly dialectical apparatus start to look like a perverse erotic enhancer."[28] We might take Barthes's pleasurable melting of the distinctions that have fueled his career as a commentary on the taxonomically obsessed field of narratology itself, a field for which Barthes implausibly figures at once as founding father and perverse (gay) uncle.[29]

The gender and sexual dynamics condensed in Barthes's persona (and considered with varying degrees of explicitness in his work) have provoked some of the most compelling appreciations and critiques of his writing. Feminist critics like Naomi Schor have noted that Barthes's pleasured and pleasure-giving "body" is almost always unmarked by gender, a silence that for Schor signals a "denied sexual difference" that ultimately reinstates the gender schemas Barthes would seem well poised to challenge.[30] From Miller's perspective, it is just that silence – motivated, he compellingly argues, by the closet – that makes Barthes's narratology suggestive for an analysis of gay men's position in a sex-gender system structured equally by misogyny and homophobia. The palpable disagreement attests to a deeper concordance: for both critical schools the theory of narrative pleasure for which Barthes here stands is necessarily inflected by gender and sexuality, and even its blindnesses gauge the evolution of and relations between those terms. Narrative theory's account of pleasure, in other words, is historical all the way down.

Scholars of pornography have put this point less abstractly, stressing that there is a genre that takes the gendered embodiment of pleasure with determined literalness, and moreover that the genre constitutes a sustained theoretical meditation on narrative. The field of porn studies is not usually taken as central to narrative theory, but one of its now-canonical texts, Linda Williams's *Hard Core: Power, Pleasure, and the "Frenzy of the Visible"* (1999), is notable not only for how centrally it pursues questions of narrative presentation but also for its relation to some of the key texts in the narratological tradition. Discussing the porn convention of the "money shot," which dictates that male performers ejaculate externally, Williams writes that in the 1970s the trope came to be understood as "the ultimate climax – the sense of an ending – for each heterosexual act represented."[31] Williams's breezy reference to Frank Kermode's landmark *The Sense of Ending* (1966) makes that book seem euphemistic or avoidant despite its total lack of interest in the question of bodies penetrating bodies (Kermode's book concerns itself with Christian apocalypticism rather than the filmic rendering of orgasm). If Williams's joke here is tangential to Kermode's project, her provocation can be taken as directed at the tradition of narrative study more generally, which she implicitly asks how literally it wants to take the bodies and pleasures it so frequently invokes.

It is striking at first glance how little it changes to deal with hard-core material – how contiguous Williams's analysis is with the theoretical and thematic concerns of (unlikely though the connection seems) Henry James. Never cited in Williams's book, James's spirit might nonetheless be said to pervade it. The distinction between picture and scene for which he claimed so much analytic importance hovers in the background, for example, of Williams's chapter on the narrative structure of 1970s heterosexual porn. The chapter creates a typology according to how porn emplots the scenes of explicit sex that Williams argues are invested with utopian energy: where "separated utopias" cordon off hard-core "numbers" from narrative exposition, "integrated utopias" allow diegetic concerns – including plotlines about bad jobs, sexual violence, and everyday sexism – to be taken up inside the sex scenes, in a way that allows them to address "the sorry realities that created the desire for pornotopia in the first place." And in "dissolved utopias," the line between scenes of intense erotic pleasure and diegesis is utterly blurred, with the result that pornotopia is presented as "already achieved": "Dissolved utopias present worlds in which power and pleasure are at odds neither in the numbers nor in the narrative."[32]

We have seen that James too understands his work as alternating between exposition and scene, "narrative" and "number," and that the distinction is as important as it is unstable. We have also seen that that formal instability derives from moments of thematized erotic tension – when it doesn't, more weirdly, seem to *cause* an erotic agitation inside the diegesis. When in *The Wings of the Dove* Milly Theale dines at the palatial home of a nobleman who is courting her, the details of aristocratic luxury strike her as "touches in a picture and denotements in a play," and the confusion of metaphors puts her in "a state of vibration [...] almost too sharp for her comfort" – exactly as if she has eavesdropped on her creator's theoretical musings on narrative structure and received his categorical confusion as some kind of scandalous secret.[33] We recall that a similar dissolution in James's narrative categories was precipitated by Lambert Strether's meeting with Chad Newsome – whose figure the older man registers as "brown and thick and strong," whose new "smoothness" strikes him as palpably "as the taste of a sauce or the rub of a hand," and whose self-possession seems to him "marked enough to be touched by the finger." Here again, an insistently corporealized affective state is correlated to a collapse in narrative categories, as if there were something excitingly pleasurable about the confusing mode – summary, description, event? – in which these passages elapse. "[S]he bristled with discriminations," James's narrator says of Milly at yet another exciting moment, "but all categories failed her."[34] The will to discrimination, the categorical failure, the bristling that accompanies them – all might serve equally as descriptions of the late-Jamesian novel itself, which seems wholly devoted to an almost tantric ambition to refuse the difference between the excitements of event and the enveloping aura of atmosphere.

Reading these passages in the vicinity of Williams makes it clear that James's reputation as a prude cannot survive any inclination to read him with a camp inflection – to read, that is, as if the confusion of metaphorical and literal registers were in itself a pleasure. But the resonance between James's work and twentieth-century pornography is also thematic. In uncanny moments, the films discussed by Williams might be deliberately riffing on James's texts. In *The Resurrection of Eve* (1976) – exemplary of Williams's "integrated" form – the heroine is encouraged by her boyfriend to expand her sexual repertoire, and ends by outpacing his erotic imagination and stamina. After a final and (for him) traumatic orgy scene, the chastened boyfriend asks if they can go back to the "way it used to be," but (in Williams's account) "Eve says only, 'It's over, Frank,' and there the film ends."[35] The exchange closely echoes James's conclusion to *The Wings of the Dove*, where Merton Densher assumes that – despite the games he and his lover Kate Croy have been playing with other partners – they can resume their relationship just "as we were." Kate says only, "We shall never be again as we were" – and there the novel ends.[36] When, at the close of the "dissolved utopia" *Insatiable* (1980), Marilyn Chambers exclaims that she wants "more, more, more!" ("though," Williams comments, "she has already 'had' a great deal"), she might be a latter-day pupil of Lambert Strether, who counsels a young friend in experiential maximalism by famously urging him to "Live all you can; it's a mistake not to. It doesn't so much matter what you do in particular".[37] These comparisons are not entirely facetious: the late-century aestheticism that informs Strether's advice was also a defense of perverse pleasure, and James's work is no less fascinated with the sexual act than is hardcore porn. Most important, these scenes each testify to moments of a rapidly evolving social balance of sexual power marked by the assertiveness of women and an accompanying waning of traditional versions of male potency – a dissolution that produces an after-glow of ambient pleasure for those in the vicinity. That this dissolution and its accompanying pleasures become visible with the help of narrative theory points again to the utility of this tradition for historical and literary-historical understanding. Even more striking, this dissolution of previously firm categories to a significant degree *is* the narrative theory of pleasure, which has been built precisely on the will to shore up conceptual distinctions and to experience their collapse as productive of something like bliss.

The theory of narrative pleasure, I have been suggesting, is carried out most compellingly on the ground, in overtly self-conscious fictional form or in theoretical writing willing to indulge the vicissitudes of critical pleasure. If Roland Barthes is the seductive propagandist for such a critical practice, Gérard Genette is a quieter but no less effective professor of pleasure. His *Narrative Discourse: An Essay in Method* (first published in French in 1972) is one of the most technically granular books in the narratological tradition; it patiently itemizes – and invents terminology for – the narrative building blocks of Proust's *In Search of Lost Time*. But *Narrative Discourse* is notably disinclined to sacrifice pleasure either as an object of analysis or as a critical affect.[38] One of the book's most striking sections concerns Genette's identification of what he calls the "iterative," a narrative modality in which an event that is said to happen regularly at the level of story ("every Sunday," "summer mornings") is recounted once in the discourse, sometimes with a specificity that belies the ritual quality it has been explicitly assigned. In Genette's account, the iterative is at once a figure for a pleasurable blurring between the singular and the repeated narrative event and a mark of Proust's originality that Genette himself takes an obvious pleasure in identifying. The preponderance of the iterative in Proust, he writes, heralds "a very appreciable modification in temporal texture." And appreciate it Genette does, in prose that produces its own strikingly palpable textures: "the strictly narrative moments [. . .] seem to emerge from a sort of descriptive-discursive magma very remote from the usual criteria of 'scenic' temporality and even from all narrative temporality [. . .] as if [. . .] the narrative wanted, at the end, to dissolve gradually and to enact the intentionally indistinct and subtly chaotic reflection of its own disappearing." The novel that results, Genette claims, is wholly transformed by this *"intoxication with the iterative."*[39]

That Genette is himself intoxicated is clear. As the analysis progresses, it becomes evident that his enjoyment is also a way of registering Proust's world-historical innovation to novelistic form. Because the iterative makes it impossible to distinguish an account of *how things were* from an account of *what happened*, its inflation means that "the traditional alteration summary/scene is at an end" and signals Proust's "rejection pure and simple – as we watch – of the millennial opposition between *diegesis* and *mimesis*."[40] This is, of course, precisely the same categorical dissolve that so excites James's characters, James himself as he tries to taxonomize his own practice in his prefaces, and the erotic adventurers who find the world pleasurably infused with sex in "dissolved" pornographic utopias. The convergence suggests that pleasure is at once the sign and the result of the linked phenomena of literary innovation and historical change themselves.

The connection between pleasure and newness is also visible in another of Genette's signal discoveries, this one featuring Henry James's novels of the 1880s. In *Narrative Discourse Revisited* (1988), Genette identifies a change in the conventions governing the opening of novels over the course of the nineteenth century. In the firmly realist mid-century, most novels opened by clearly identifying the characters whose actions kick off the narrative (Genette labels this type of opening "A"). One mark of modernism was the adoption of a convention (Genette calls it "B") "where the character whose presence opens the action is presumed at the very start to be known" – leaving the reader in the dark (temporarily), and giving even mundane stories a nimbus of mystery. This "historical evolution," visible at the large scale over the course of the century, is present in particularly stark form in James's career, where "we find a clear transition, from a predominance of A up to *The Bostonians* to a predominance of B dating from *Casamassima* (both published 1885) and on to the end. The turning point, perhaps provisionally, is indeed, therefore, located in that zone, let us say symbolically 1885." In other words, it is *The Bostonians* that ushers James over the border into an emergent world – we can call it modernity, or, less grandiosely, the world of the modernist novel – where the predicates of being are up for grabs, where we have only "referentials without referents."[41] (Virginia Woolf's Clarissa Dalloway gives us perhaps the most efficient report from this condition when she reflects that "[s]he would not say of any one in the world now that they were this or were that": the words of course appear in a novel that pushes the mysterious "Type B" opening to its extreme.)[42]

It does not seem coincidental that it is *The Bostonians* that catalyzes James's move into this new territory, obsessed as that novel is with seismic shifts in gender roles and emergent rules of erotic engagement – both of which preoccupations take shape, as we saw in this chapter's opening, as the possibility of inventing new forms of pleasure. Nor, given the linkage we have been tracking between intense affective states and the dissolution of narratogical categories, is it surprising that the novel reaches a climax in a distended sentence that pushes James's prized perspectival clarity to the breaking point and in the process disseminates a general mood of agitation in which panic, triumph, and sheer excitement are impossible to disentangle. The scene is laid backstage at Boston's Music Hall, where Verena is about to skip out on her first large speaking engagement to elope with Basil Ransom. James places us with Basil, looking through a door into the greenroom where Verena hangs back with her friends. He is wildly confident of his imminent erotic success, and it feels like this:

What he wanted, in this light, flamed before him and challenged all his manhood, tossing his determination to a height from which not only Doctor Tarrant, and Mr. Filer, and Olive, over there, in her sightless soundless shame, but the great expectant hall as well, and the mighty multitude, in suspense, keeping quiet from minute to minute and holding the breath of its anger – from which all these things looked only small, surmountable, and of the moment only.[44]

The sentence is elaborately subordinated, as if James's contorted late manner is already bearing down. One of the effects of that style is a kind of distribution of consciousness, and the details taken in here are indeed so multifarious that the passage seems to register a rupture in Basil's psychology, as if the story has reached a frontier where the individual and its attendant narrative technology of focalization will no longer serve James's purposes.[43] That psychological dissolution is also marked by the confusion between "scene" and "picture" that we have encountered elsewhere in James: this is overtly a "moment" – in fact the most eventful one in the narrative so far – but the panoramic view James offers suggests the fixity of a tableau. And these formal oddities underscore the passage's imagistic and thematic peculiarity, in which Basil's "manhood," placed in conspicuous apposition with his "determination," appears (literally?) to rise to the rafters. Basil wishes to believe this inflation a mark of his potency; but it is also clearly a compensatory fantasy, and thus an index of how uninevitable heterosexuality has come to seem in this narrative world. This psychological undecidability points to a historical one: Is *The Bostonians* a brusque dismissal of faddish feminism or a serious registration of a new historical force?[45] The case for the latter is made in strongest terms by the very intensity of this emotional paroxysm, which if nothing else indicates that the historical energies coming to a head in this scene are forces to reckon with.

It might seem perverse to align anything that's happening here – Basil's panicked assertion of male prerogative, Verena's sorrowful resignation, least of all Olive's devastation – with pleasure. But we should recall Barthes's insistence that pleasure at its most intense can be hard to distinguish from pain, rupture, self-dissolution. We might also turn to Fredric Jameson's recent claim in *The Antinomies of Realism* (2013) that such unnamed intensities of feeling (following recent work on the emotions, he calls this "affect") signal that a new item has presented itself to the historical sensorium. Jameson's book is a contribution to narrative theory, as well as a rapprochement with James, a writer he has mostly invoked slightingly over the course of his career. Here, Jameson gives James his due as a theorist of the novel, and aligns the surge of affect with the "scenic" principle.[46] This intuition that the Jamesian scene's narrowing to the present conduces to the surge of intense emotions has been borne out by this chapter, and it suggests that the end of *The Bostonians* heralds the advent of some new social arrangement. Basil's vision is of ecstatic elevation; as such it not only recalls Olive and Verena's earlier levitation but also prefigures the ascension that will happen in a moment, when Olive transmutes her erotic despair into determination and steps onto the stage in Verena's place. The novel ends just before we learn whether Olive is hounded from the stage by the angry crowd or comes into a new eloquence that keeps them listening or ... something else entirely. It is one of the most strangely inconclusive novelistic endings in the nineteenth century. What the narrator makes clear is that Olive has been transmogrified into a "heroine," as if she's ascended to some higher plane, shortly to be recognized as a new and as-yet-unnamed historical type.[47] That we have come to recognize that type as the lesbian is a crucial part of this novel's literary historical significance, but only a part. For now, Olive is a referential without a referent.

Is it a pleasure, to be thus raptured by History? Like our opening question, this one is unanswerable, and probably nonsensical: Olive's life does not extend beyond these pages, and of course like all literary characters she has always existed on the razor's edge between the idea of a real person and a collection of words. Olive's difference might be that she seems to live that condition as an agitation that shades into fear on one side and exhilaration on the other. The narrative theory of pleasure has sometimes been stymied by this slipperiness, by the tendency of pleasure to escape our analytic attention by becoming something else, or simply vanishing before we can force it to yield up any conceptual content. But just as frequently that theory has been itself exhilarated by that elusiveness, and has taught us to read it as a sign of the dislocations of the modern. To the extent that narrative theory's will to systematicity has been accompanied by a will to dissolve that systematicity, that theory performs a mimesis of historical change, imitating the ways social structures harden and come undone in a ceaseless process. And in linking that process to a "pleasure" that by turn resembles comfort, ecstasy, and pain, narrative theory further suggests the ways history makes itself felt in the most intimate recesses of the subject. Thus does this tradition become a profound if almost accidental phenomenology of historical emergence.

Notes

1. Henry James, *The Bostonians* (1886; Oxford: Oxford University Press, 2009), 73.
2. Published serially in 1885–1886, the book is set in the mid-1870s. On the dating of the action, see R. D. Gooder's appendix 2 to James, *The Bostonians*, 439.

3. Henry James, *The Princess Casamassima* (1886; Harmondsworth: Penguin, 1986), 305, 316, 337. See Roland Barthes, *The Pleasure of the Text*, trans. Richard Miller (New York, NY: Hill and Wang, 1975), and Pierre Bourdieu, *Distinction: A Social Critique of the Judgment of Taste*, trans. Richard Nice (Cambridge, MA: Harvard University Press, 1984).

4. In this drive to stage the collapse of its own taxonomies, the most inventive narrative theory resembles psychoanalytic writing as analyzed by Leo Bersani in *The Freudian Body*. In Bersani's account, Freud's repeated positing of self-undermining binaries constitutes an exploration of "the secretive and pleasurable phenomenon of a self-destroying intelligence." Although this conception of the pleasure of collapse echoes and arguably grows out of Bersani's earlier work on narrative forms – particularly *A Future for Astyanax: Character and Desire in Literature*, where the self-derangements of desire threaten to undo the intelligible characters of nineteenth-century realism – Bersani is not generally read as a narrative theorist. This may in part be due to his tendency to understand narrative *tout court* as a repressive sense-making mechanism (as in the claim in *The Freudian Body* that "a rigorously psychoanalytic logic [...] implicitly mocks all the philosophically narrativizing procedures and distinctions of Freud the prophetic thinker." In accordance with this understanding, Bersani's later work has turned increasingly away from narrative forms to focus on visual and performative arts. That turn notwithstanding, his work has deeply informed my thinking here. See Bersani, *The Freudian Body: Psychoanalysis and Art* (New York, NY: Columbia University Press, 1986), 12, 21; and *A Future for Astyanax: Character and Desire in Literature* (New York, NY: Columbia University Press, 1976).

5. Peter Brooks, *Reading for the Plot: Design and Intention in Narrative* (New York, NY: Knopf, 1984), 107.

6. Laura Mulvey, "Visual Pleasure and Narrative Cinema," *Screen* 16, no. 3 (1975): 8.

7. Roland Barthes, *Roland Barthes*, trans. Richard Howard (Berkeley: University of California Press, 1977), 64.

8. Fredric Jameson, "Pleasure: A Political Issue," in *The Ideologies of Theory: Essays 1971–1986, Volume 2: Syntax of History* (Minneapolis: University of Minnesota Press, 1988), 62.

9. Susan S. Lanser, "Sapphic Dialogics: Historical Narratology and the Sexuality of Form," in *Postclassical Narratology: Approaches and Analyses*, ed. Jan Alber and Monika Fludernik (Columbus: Ohio State University Press, 2010), 186. Lanser points out that the received idea that formalist-narratological approaches are incompatible with historical ones has survived the critical fame of Erich Auerbach, Lucien Goldmann, Ian Watt, and Jameson, along with many others who have combined these methods.

10. Lanser, "Sapphic Dialogics," 190, 192.

11. On the philosophically productive obsession of Proust's Marcel with lesbian pleasure, see Elisabeth Ladenson, *Proust's Lesbianism* (Ithaca, NY: Cornell University Press, 2007); on the "astonishingly Proustian" qualities of Prince's 1987 track "If I Was Your Girlfriend" – whose focalizing structure falls firmly within Lanser's paradigm – see Eve Kosofsky Sedgwick, *Tendencies* (Durham, NC: Duke University Press, 1993), 172.

12. The classic statement of the former case is Percy Lubbock's *The Craft of Fiction* (1921; New York, NY: Viking, 1957); for the latter, see Mark McGurl, *The Novel Art: Elevations of American Fiction after Henry James* (Princeton, NJ: Princeton University Press, 2001).

13. James Atlas, "'Literature' Bores Me," *New York Times Magazine*, March 16, 1997: 40.

14. Henry James, *The Art of the Novel: Critical Prefaces* (New York, NY: Scribner, 1934), 323.

15. Wayne Booth understands the picture/scene distinction this way when he reads *The Ambassadors* as attempting to solve "the problem of summary." For Booth's ethically oriented criticism, the solution is only half successful, since limiting the reader's information to characters' thoughts and conversation means that "the convention of absolute reliability [of the narrative perspective] has been destroyed." See Wayne Booth, *The Rhetoric of Fiction* (1961; 2nd ed., Chicago, IL: Chicago University Press, 1983), 174–175.

16. Henry James, *The Ambassadors* (1903; Harmondsworth: Penguin, 2008), 116–117.

17. James, *The Art of the Novel*, 325; emphasis added.

18. Gérard Genette, *Narrative Discourse Revisited*, trans. Jane E. Lewin (Ithaca, NY: Cornell University Press, 1988), 111.

19. James, *The Ambassadors*, 83, 415, 416.

20. Roland Barthes, *Sade, Fourier, Loyola*, trans. Richard Howard (New York, NY: Hill and Wang, 1976), 5.

21. Ibid., 52.

22. See Henry James, "The Art of Fiction," in *Major Stories and Essays* (New York, NY: Library of America, 1999), 581. Howard accurately translates Barthes's French, which cites James's words as "quelqu'un pour qui rien n'est perdu." Barthes may have taken this phrasing (which also amends James's "one of those people" to "someone") from Michel Butor's "Intervention à Royaumont" (1959), which cited this passage of James in what appears to have been Butor's own translation. See Barthes, *Sade, Fourier, Loyola* (Paris: Éditions du Seuil, 1971), 57; Butor, *Répertoire I* (Paris: Éditions de Minuit, 1960), 272.

23. Barthes, *Sade, Fourier, Loyola*, 103, 91, 32, 30, 129.

24. Barthes, *The Pleasure of the Text*, 14.

25. Ibid., 67.

26. Ibid., 14.

27. Tzvetan Todorov, *Duties and Delights: The Life of a Go-Between: Interviews with Catherine Portevin*, trans. Gila Walker (New York, NY: Seagull, 2008), 88.

28. D. A. Miller, *Bringing Out Roland Barthes* (Berkeley: University of California Press, 1992), 27.

29. Seymour Chatman offers a representative commentary (at once appreciative and wary) on Barthes, whom he describes both as having done "much of the important work" of enumerating narrative codes and as taking "a remarkably casual and poetic attitude" toward the question of his enumeration's systematicity. See Chatman, "Styles of Narrative Codes," ed. Berel Lang, *The Concept of Style* (1979; 2nd. ed., Ithaca, NY: Cornell University Press, 1987), 236–237.

30. See Naomi Schor, "Dreaming Dissymetry: Barthes, Foucault, and Sexual Difference," in *Bad Objects: Essays Popular and Unpopular* (Durham, NC: Duke University Press, 1995), 33.

31. Linda Williams, *Hard Core: Power, Pleasure, and the "Frenzy of the Visible"* (1989; 2nd. ed., Berkeley: University of California Press, 1999), 93. Williams derives these categories from Richard Dyer's work on the structure of musicals; see Dyer, "Entertainment and Utopia," in *Genre – The Musical: A Reader*, ed. Rick Altman (London: Routledge, 1985).

32. Ibid., 170, 174, 181.

33. Henry James, *The Wings of the Dove* (1902; Harmondsworth: Penguin, 2008), 129.

34. James, *The Wings of the Dove*, 128–129, 100.

35. Williams, *Hard Core*, 168.

36. James, *The Wings of the Dove*, 533.

37. James, The Ambassadors, 176.

38. Devoted to precision, Genette makes clear that he's not going to let the taxonomic get tiresome. In *Narrative Discourse Revisited*, in which he takes up classificatory challenges to the earlier book, Genette refers to "the excess of precision as an epistemological obstacle," and confesses that "I see no reason for requiring narratology to become a catechism with a yes-or-no answer to check off for each question, when often the proper answer would be that it depends on the day, the context, and the way the wind is blowing." This sensibility consorts with his willingness to admit that he assigns value to – and derives pleasure from – narrative innovation, a confession that marks out his marginality to a fully scientific or impartial narratological science. See Genette, *Narrative Discourse Revisited*, trans. Jane E. Lewin (Ithaca, NY: Cornell University Press, 1988), 26, 74.

39. Genette, *Narrative Discourse*, 111–2, 126; emphasis in original.

40. Ibid., 167–168.

41. Genette, *Narrative Discourse Revisited*, 68–69, 70.

42. Virginia Woolf, *Mrs. Dalloway* (1925; New York, NY: Harcourt, Brace, Jovanovich, 1953), 11.

43. James, *The Bostonians*, 455.

44. Seymour Chatman's *The Late Style of Henry James* (Oxford: Blackwell, 1972) points to the disorienting effect of James's habit of making abstract mental qualities the subjects of sentences (as in this one, where "what he wanted" launches the syntactic "action"). Sharon Cameron's *Thinking in Henry James* (Chicago, IL: Chicago University Press, 1989) is the most sustained analysis of the collectivization of consciousness in James.

45. These options are considered, and the distinction between them convincingly refused, in Jennifer Fleissner, *Women, Compulsion, Modernity: The Moment of American Naturalism* (Chicago, IL: Chicago University Press, 2004), 123–160.

46. See Fredric Jameson, *The Antinomies of Realism* (London: Verso, 2013). The conceptualization of affect, which informs the entire book, is elaborated on pp. 26–44.

47. James, *The Bostonians*, 462. For an account of the centrality of such traumatic scenes of emergence-into-typicality to queer literary history, see Heather Love, *Feeling Backward: Loss and the Politics of Queer History* (Cambridge, MA: Harvard University Press, 2007).

PART III

Coordinates

10

AMY C. TANG

Breaks, Borders, Utopia: Race and Critical Narrative Poetics

If, as Paul de Man observed, the study of literature has been shaped by "the recurrent debate opposing intrinsic to extrinsic criticism," this has been especially so in the case of ethnic literary criticism.[1] A field that emerged out of the social movements of the late 1960s, ethnic studies has from its inception foregrounded its relationship to the social world. Yet the precise nature of this relationship has hardly been settled. While some cultural nationalisms may have seemed to prioritize the referential function of literature, a deep and robust tradition of literary critics has argued against the tendency – by white and ethnic critics alike – to read ethnic literature as "having *only* an ideological importance" or "not as fictive invention but as transparent historical documents."[2] Urging greater attention to ethnic texts' "internal structures as acts of language" and to "interventions at the level of form as well as content," such scholarship prioritizes the reflexive over the referential, the textual over the experiential, the aesthetic over the sociological.[3]

Of course such binarisms are only ever analytical constructions, as the decades of work on race and narrative poetics show. We might note, for instance, how critics have shown that even the overtly ideological Black Arts Movement demonstrated a serious concern with such "intrinsic" matters as readerly address (as in the criticism of protest literature aimed at white audiences), the interpolation of vernacular forms (such as jazz, blues, or gospel music), and the mixing of genres (such as poetry and drama).[4] More broadly, recent scholarship has encouraged us to view the literary cultural nationalisms of the late sixties as performative and rhetorical rather than merely referential. That is, rather than using literature to passively reflect an already defined ethnic content, ethnic writers often saw literary experimentation as a way to invent distinctive cultural sensibilities. In such writing, then, the question of racial identity is "as much a formal as a social or political one," and what the ethnic text foregrounds is the inseparability of intrinsic and extrinsic concerns.[5]

While it is certainly true that narrative theory has often presumed race to lie "outside" its bounds, focusing on canonical Western literature and neglecting the formal properties of ethnic literature, from the perspective of ethnic studies, it is often "theory" that has seemed extrinsic and even extraneous. We can see this clearly in the debates that emerged during the 1980s, when literary critics such as Robert Stepto, Houston A. Baker Jr., and Henry Louis Gates Jr. began using the insights of structuralist, poststructuralist, and other forms of literary theory to interpret African American literature. In response, scholars such as Barbara Christian and Joyce A. Joyce argued that such critical theory was "alien to and opposed to" African American literature and that "a poststructuralist methodology imposes a strategy upon Black literature from the outside."[6]

Set against what Fredric Jameson calls our postmodern "tendency toward immanence," our "flight from transcendence," the anxiety about the hegemony of "theory" expressed in these earlier criticisms may seem quaint.[7] Yet the question of cultural imposition continues to loom large when narrative theory is placed in conversation with race. As Sue J. Kim notes, even as some narrative theorists have begun to study ethnic and postcolonial texts, all too often scholars continue to presume that "white and Western theorists speak the universal, analytical voice, while the minority text is the single instantiation; the narrative theory is the langue, the minority text merely the parole."[8] The problem, Kim notes, arises from the very notion of "applicability" – a misnomer since theory arises from the close analysis of specific literary texts; while historically, this has meant canonical European and American texts, this need not always be the case. We might then ask, what does a narrative theory immanent to a non-Western literary tradition look like?

For an example, we might turn to Gates's book *The Signifying Monkey* (1988), which sought to "identify a theory of criticism that is inscribed within the black vernacular tradition," and "to allow the black tradition to speak for itself [...] rather than to read it, or analyze it, in terms of literary theories borrowed whole from other traditions."[9] Theorizing from this indigenous perspective, *The Signifying Monkey* delineated two frameworks combining race and narrative poetics whose influence continues to be felt today. First and foremost, Gates argued that the African American literary tradition is constituted through the vernacular practice of "Signifyin(g)," a self-conscious strategy of intertextual repetition and revision that marks the tradition with a legible "black difference."[10] Locating racial specificity in aesthetic form rather than content, Gates's vernacular model showed how a formalist approach could debunk ideas of racial essence even while asserting cultural particularity. At the same time, since Gates argued that African American literary texts signify upon both Western and African American antecedents, his theory also asserted the fundamental hybridity of African American literature, which he framed as an internally differentiated tradition that draws on mainstream and marginal canons.

Although Gates's vernacular model has since come under fire, as much for its interest in poststructuralist theory as for reinforcing the racial differences it sought to textualize, *The Signifying Monkey's* twin emphases on the vernacular and the hybridity of African American literature nonetheless continue to encapsulate two major formalist approaches to ethnic literature.[11] The remainder of this essay will trace these critical paradigms across a range of ethnic literary criticism. In the first section I consider the question of a culturally specific aesthetic through the concept of the narrative "break." Surveying key strands of ethnic literary criticism premised on the idea of multiple modernities, this section foregrounds ethnic literary criticism's engagement with a fundamental category of narrative theory, temporality. The second section turns to theories of hybridity, ambivalence and self-difference which I link through the concept of "borders." These theories relocate the problematic of racial difference from the level of genre to that of the subject, shifting attention from the diachronic to the synchronic, or from time to space. In the final section, I turn from the historical ruptures underlying "breaks," and the problematic of the present foregrounded in the spatial concerns of "borders," to the question of ethnic literary studies' conception of the future. While any discussion of ethnic futures must contend with the inevitable specter of the "postracial," here I reinterpret this bête noire as the narrative category of "utopia" as a way of exploring scholarship that presses on ethnic literature's representational limits. Throughout, my aim will be to draw out the ways that narrative theory has been mobilized within ethnic literary criticism and to offer a sense of how the study of ethnic literature has contributed to narrative theory. While this essay thus traces some key intersections between race and narrative poetics, no discussion of this rich and varied field encompassing so many literary and critical traditions could make any claim to comprehensiveness; indeed, I will draw many examples from my own field of Asian American literary studies – itself something of a minor minority tradition – to suggest ways in which a closer look at our literary and critical margins might shed light on the whole.

Breaks

> Invisibility, let me explain, gives one a slightly different sense of time, you're never quite on the beat. Sometimes you're ahead and sometimes behind. Instead of the swift and imperceptible flowing of time, you are aware of its nodes, those points where time stands still or from which it leaps behind. And you slip into the breaks and look around.
> —Ralph Ellison, *Invisible Man*

If Anglo-American novel theory from Henry James to the New Critics has approached literary criticism as a study of organic wholes, writers and critics principally concerned with race have tended to focus on the language of gaps, ruptures, and breaks. On the one hand, such breaks index the social and material ruptures that constitute racialized experience: in the US context, what Paul Gilroy has called "the temporal and ontological rupture of the middle passage" usually takes precedence, but such ruptures also character-ize the histories of US settler colonialism, imperialist expansion, and wars abroad, as well as experiences of immigration, exclusion, and exile.[12] On the other hand, while these ruptures no doubt constitute sites of trauma and negation, for many critics of ethnic literature, they also enable the emergence of alternative cultures, giving rise to aesthetic forms that crucially depart from dominant European and American forms. At the root of such work is the sense that capitalist modernity's uneven transformations provide the conditions for a variety of modernisms that reflect and contest those distinc-tive experiences.[13] Thus Gilroy forwards his seminal insight that the cata-strophic rupture of the middle passage also instantiates the black Atlantic as a "counterculture of modernity" such that this primal break entails not only "terror" but also dialectically generates "countercultural aspirations towards freedom, citizenship, and autonomy" that shape distinct intellectual and expressive cultures.[14] Lisa Lowe echoes this argument in discussing the very different history of Asian Americans, arguing that although a history of legislative exclusion; war-driven migration; and economic, political, and cultural marginalization continually locates Asian Americans "outside the cultural and racial boundaries of the nation," it is precisely "this distance from the national culture" that "preserves Asian American culture as an alternative site where the palimpsest of lost memories is reinvented, histories are fractured and retraced, and the unlike varieties of silence emerge into articulacy."[15]

While Gilroy locates his strongest examples of a black Atlantic counter-culture in African diasporic music (in line with a long tradition of African American criticism from W.E.B. DuBois to Amiri Baraka to Robert

O'Meally to Fred Moten), Lowe situates the notion of a "break" in an explicitly narrative context, taking the novel as her primary example of a racially inflected counterdiscourse, and the European *Bildungsroman* as the hegemonic form against which Asian American writing stages its break. For Lowe, the concept of the narrative "break" emerges at the levels of both genre and style. Beginning from the premise that the primary ideological function of the *Bildungsroman* is to model "the reconciliation of the individual with the social order," she argues that since "the historical specificities of racialization, ghettoization, violence, and labor exploitation" preclude racial subjects from such forms of national and cultural belonging, minority literatures will frequently produce "effects of dissonance, fragmentation, and irresolution."[16] For Lowe, these generic breaks take the form of narrative gaps and fissures that interrupt the realist novel's telos of resolution. Thus Lowe shows how an Asian American *Bildungsroman* such as Carlos Bulosan's *America Is in the Heart* (1943) fails to narrate the development of a protagonist from youth to maturity, portraying the hero's education as "disrupted, partial and fragmentary," his movement marked by "continual migration" rather than settlement. Highlighting, in other words, the novel's tendency toward episode over emplotment and repetition over resolution, Lowe shows how narrative breaks encode the discrepancy between American ideologies of democratic inclusion and histories of racial exploitation, and between modernity's promise of progress and the mechanical repetitions of industrial labor. Similarly, Lowe shows how Jessica Hagedorn's use of the "antinarrative and antidevelopmental" form of gossip and Fae Ng's backwards chronology work to interrupt and challenge dominant narratives of immigrant assimilation and upward mobility. In all these cases, Lowe finds Asian American writing disrupting "the orthodoxies of both historical and novelistic representation," inventing new forms for representing racial histories shaped by uneven development.[17]

As Lowe's reading of Asian American revisions of the *Bildungsroman* suggests, genre criticism has been a key locus of ethnic studies' engagement with narrative poetics, with genre functioning as a mediating category linking modernity's social and historical "breaks" to the stylistic "breaks" of the varied modernisms it generates. One important example is the rich body of feminist work detailing the ways that ethnic writers have reworked the conventions of domestic fiction to critique hegemonic social arrangements and to express alternative political desires. As Ann duCille writes in *The Coupling Convention* (1993), "making unconventional use of conventional literary forms, early black writers appropriated for their own emancipatory purposes both the genre of the novel and the structure of the marriage plot" to contest patriarchal authority and racial ideologies.[18] Similarly,

Claudia Tate tracks how black women's post-Reconstruction domestic novels refashioned "idealized domestic tropes" to express "liberational racial and sexual desire," while Rachel Lee shows how Asian American writers draw on the "heterosexual romance plot" to foreground "female interruptions to [...] national narratives of self-making, home ownership, and entrepreneurship," as well as on the "antiprogressive diegetic structure" of the Brazilian telenovela to challenge discourses of economic development and technocratic efficiency.[19] More recently, writing in the Native American context, Beth Piatote argues that writers such as S. Alice Callahan and E. Pauline Johnson "called upon the sentimental genre to make maternal love legible against cultural and legal discourses that framed Indian mothers as unfit," refurbishing familiar narrative tropes to contest policies of forced assimilation.[20] Taken together, such scholarship demonstrates how the ethnic novel, across different literary traditions, makes its ideological arguments not in lieu of but *through* literary form.

Although foregrounding ethnic literature's "breaks" or departures from dominant narrative conventions has inspired innovative readings, this strategy is not without its risks. Madhu Dubey argues, for instance, that postmodern celebrations of African American vernacular culture as "a reservoir of subversive stylistic strategies" often rely upon a primitivizing logic that locates African Americans "in pockets of sheer alterity within or outside contemporary social conditions."[21] While Dubey acknowledges that "primitivism can support sharp critiques of modernity," she observes that it can also "slide over into fetishism of racial 'others'."[22] In addition, Jinqi Ling cautions that reifying the political oppositionality of textual disruptions can lead to "ahistorical [...] celebrations of difference" that occlude the historical contexts that enable and constrain textual meanings across time, while also oversimplifying the politics of the realism such criticism sets itself against.[23] For Ling, valorizing ethnic literature's aesthetic "breaks" risks repeating the political instrumentalism of the content-based readings such formalist readings seek to redress, by simply relocating oppositional political value from the social content of the ethnic novel to its formal ruptures or generic breaks. For these critics, it is crucial to acknowledge that just as genres "are not laden with any intrinsic political freight," so too then "generic rupture does not automatically amount to political opposition."[24]

How then might we navigate not only the familiar divide between form and history that these critiques recall but also the dilemma specific to ethnic studies that they also bring forward – the problem of acknowledging cultural difference without entrenching it? One alternative can be found in James Snead's discussion of a particular kind of break called the "cut," in his early essay "On Repetition in Black Culture" (1981). At first glance, in its titular reference to a seemingly monolithic "black culture," Snead's essay seems to promise precisely the kind of cultural reification that critics like Dubey and Ling warn against. Snead seems to fulfill this promise as he goes on to cite Hegel's pronouncement that the African "is that which is without history and resolution, which is still fully caught up in the natural spirit, and which here must be mentioned as being on the threshold of world history" and then, stunningly, to declare that "Hegel was almost entirely correct in his reading of black culture." Yet what saves Snead's reading from the primitivism it seems to court – and, indeed, what works to vigorously challenge it – is his historicizing view. For he follows his unexpected endorsement of Hegel with the even more surprising comment that the nonprogressive, cyclical time Hegel associated with Africa "almost perfectly described the 'there' to which European culture was 'headed'."[25] How can this be so?

The answer lies in Snead's reading of Western modernism as, in one critic's words, "a century-long rapprochement between Western culture and its repressed African antecedents."[26] That is, rather than reflecting an essential truth about African culture, Hegel's comment reflects the way in which, for centuries, European culture has tended to repress life's inevitable cycles and repetitions by imposing "a character of progression and improvement" onto them, whereas black culture more often "highlights the observance of such repetition." Snead's primary example is the musical practice of the "cut," which describes an "abrupt, seemingly unmotivated break [...] with a series already in progress and a willed return to a prior series."[27] Snead traces the centrality of the cut across a variety of African and African American expressive forms, from African drumming to the music of James Brown, and from jazz improvisation to literary texts by Jean Toomer, Toni Morrison, and Ishmael Reed. But if this seems to return us to Hegel's view of black culture as irrepressibly "other," Snead upends this possibility with his concluding argument that this very same practice of the "cut" is also the signal feature of the Western literary modernism of James Joyce, William Faulkner, and T. S. Eliot. In doing so, he emphasizes the "cut" not as the expression of innate difference, but as an aesthetic practice, a formal device of narrative interruption that reveals the breaks and convergences – what Edward Said would call the "contrapuntal" relation – of European and African histories.[28]

Borders

The sign of an authentic voice is thus not self-identity but self-difference.
—Barbara Johnson, "Metaphor, Metonymy, and Voice in *Their Eyes Were Watching God*"

Snead's dialectical understanding of the "cut" as a form of racial "break" that emerges only through an already existing entanglement reminds us of the ways in which the specificity of the ethnic text – and its power – often arises not only from the "breaks" it marks out but also from the boundaries it puts into question.[29] Against the assertion of distinct ethnic traditions, much ethnic literary criticism has sought instead to challenge the boundaries separating the ethnic from the dominant, the minority from the mainstream. Indeed, many of ethnic literary criticism's most eloquent and powerful theorizations could be described as threshold concepts, from W.E.B. DuBois's notion of double-consciousness to Gloria Anzaldúa's concept of the borderlands to Homi Bhabha's model of colonial hybridity. Such scholarship recalls us to the way that race – like language – inhabits the border of the real and the imaginary, the objective and the subjective; to the ways that both race and language are externally imposed but internally lived and felt; structurally or institutionally defined, yet individually experienced; and as such, how the study of ethnic literature demands critical practices attentive to the porousness of those borders.

Although we saw an intimation of this hybridity in Gates's model of Signifyin(g), the notion would be taken up more directly by two subsequent and highly influential texts: Paul Gilroy's *The Black Atlantic* (1993) and Homi Bhabha's *The Location of Culture* (1994). For Gilroy, the borders that the ethnic text broaches are primarily national, and his work maps large-scale intellectual, political, and cultural flows between Europe, America, Africa, and the Caribbean, encapsulated in his organizing trope of "ships in motion" across the Atlantic.[30] For Bhabha, on the other hand, hybridity is located within the colonial text's internal antagonisms, where the boundaries between East and West, self and other become fluid and unstable. Despite these differences in scale, for both these critics "creolisation, metisage, mestizaje, and hybridity" are posed against binary logics and the notion of "an absolute break" in the histories of whites and blacks, colonizers and colonized.[31] Shifting from breaks to borders, the hybridity theory of Gilroy and Bhabha can also be seen as resituating the problematic of racial difference from a temporal to a spatial frame, replacing the multiple modernities underwriting the work of the previous section with an emphasis on anatomizing the contradictions and instabilities of what Bhabha calls "the enunciative present."[32]

While this spatializing impulse is obvious in Gilroy's call for "an explicitly transnational and intercultural perspective," we can also detect a shift toward a more synchronic mode of analysis in *The Black Atlantic*'s other major claim: that the experience of transatlantic slavery is central to both Western modernity and African diasporic experience. For in addition to contesting the national boundaries separating these histories, Gilroy's insistence that contemporary black culture is best understood through its "continued proximity to the unspeakable terrors of the slave past" can be seen as marking, if not inaugurating, what Stephen Best calls the "melancholic turn in recent African Americanist and African diasporic cultural criticism," or a critical preoccupation with memory, haunting, trauma, and melancholia that I would argue marks contemporary ethnic literary criticism more generally.[33] In such scholarship, the conventional idea that the past shapes the present is hypostasized into a conflation of past and present that dissolves not only narratives of progress or development but time itself, such that, in Best's words, "the past simply is our present."[34] Replacing the idea of linear time with Walter Benjamin's concept of time as a "constellation," *The Black Atlantic* and the work that followed in its wake opened literary criticism to both a geographically expanded archive and to new models of narrative form inspired by the recursive, repetitive, and stalled temporalities of trauma, melancholia, and affect.

The emphasis on the synchronic is equally clear in Bhabha's work, with its spatial metaphors of "interstitiality," "in-between spaces," and various "sites" and "terrains" of cultural contestation. Yet space for Bhabha is not static or reified, but a dynamic realm of social and linguistic struggle. Against the rigid binaries of a colonial framework opposing colonizer and colonized, the West and the rest, Bhabha draws on psychoanalytic and deconstructive theory to forward an alternate lexicon of colonial splitting, ambivalence, mimicry, and hybridity. Foregrounding the iterative and performative aspects of colonial discourse, Bhabha converts metaphors into metonymies, injecting a sense of process into historically sedimented concepts such as nation and culture. Thus the "historical certainty and settled nature" of the Western nation is rewritten as a "narration," and the "fixity" of the colonial stereotype is unmasked as a structure of anxious repetition on the model of the Freudian fetish. Revealing colonial discourse to be ambivalently riven from within by perpetual slippages of language and desire, Bhabha challenges earlier figurations of "the intentionality and unidirectionality of colonial power," disrupting its "closure and coherence."[35]

While *The Location of Culture*'s broadly interdisciplinary and cosmopolitan archive is one of its signature features, its primary model for colonial struggle is localized in the psyche of the colonial subject, where the negotiations of the self–other dynamic take center stage. Consequently, some of the most innovative work in hybridity theory comes from psychoanalytic critics focused on the subjective and affective consequences of racism's social divisions. One eloquent example is Anne Cheng's *The Melancholy of Race* (2001), which mobilizes Freud's formulation of melancholia as perpetually unresolved grief (in which the lost object is not relinquished through mourning but rather incorporated into the ego as a site of ambivalent identification) to describe the dynamics of dominant white culture's simultaneous "rejection of yet attachment to the racial other" as well as "the ramifications that such paradox holds for the racial other." While clearly taking up Bhabha's insights about the interpenetration of dominant and minority cultures, Cheng departs from Bhabha's more celebratory account of the subversive potential of this ambivalent situation to bring forward a sense of racial agency as "convoluted, ongoing, generative, and at times self-contradicting." Foregrounding the paralysis of the melancholic situation, Cheng shows how this dynamic of mutual incorporation and rejection structuring US race relations emerges formally in literary texts in such varied ways as: a discrepancy between form and content in the musical *Flower Drum Song*; a contradiction in characterization in the same text; the reversibility of subject positions in the play *M. Butterfly*; and a series of rapid character substitutions in Anna Deavere Smith's docudrama *Twilight: Los Angeles, 1992*.[36]

As the many Asian American examples in Cheng's study suggest, the concept of hybridity has had a particular resonance for Asian American literary criticism. As a racial group that is typically perceived as "exceptionally assimilable to U.S. national identity," Asian Americans are something like hybrid subjects par excellence, and so it comes as little surprise that two of the most innovative extensions of the hybridity thesis treat Asian American contexts.[37]

While recent decades have seen Asian American literary studies preoccupied with demonstrating the discursive construction of racial identity, Rachel Lee's *The Exquisite Corpse of Asian America* (2014) makes its intervention by retraining our attention on the biological body. Literalizing the metaphors of division and fragmentation that Bhabha, Cheng, and other psychoanalytic critics use to describe subjective experiences of racialization, Lee explores representations of bodily fragmentation in racialized contexts, from a Lois Ann Yamanaka poem about cutting to the cadaver exhibit *Body Worlds*, and from ethnographies of Third World "tissue economies" to Amitav Ghosh's science-fiction novel *The Calcutta Chromosome* (1995). In much the same way that Bhabha focuses on unsettling the "fixity" of colonial discourses, Lee shows how the seemingly inert materiality of the body in fact comprises "circulations of energy, affects, atoms, and liquidity." As with earlier theorizations of hybridity that reveal racial agency as indeterminate and multiform, Lee's concern is with the way in which these somatic networks model novel forms of agency that are neither centralized nor singular but resemble "scattered forms of discoordinated antagonisms." These forms of agency inspire such narrative innovations as the "peristaltic," repetitive aesthetic of Margaret Cho's comedy, which "imitates not forward progress but cyclic or helical stagings of opposite phenomena" or the "complicated character system and set of nested plots" of Ghosh's novel, which "allegorize the parasitic and commensal entanglements humans have with microorganisms." Extending hybridity to encompass new scales of biosociality and posthuman ecologies, Lee's study initiates a pathbreaking investigation into the narrative forms that reflect these emergent configurations.[38]

If "biology" names the wider frame into which Rachel Lee inserts ethnic and specifically Asian American writing, Yoon Sun Lee's *Modern Minority* (2013) aims to resituate Asian American literature not in relation to race or nation but within the broader context of a modern sense of time inhering in the concept of the "everyday." Recalling Gilroy's insistence that African diasporic cultures should be understood as resolutely located within Western modernity, Yoon Lee's study argues for "the minority status of Asian Americans as a concentration, intensification, or localization of the minorness that attends the modern capitalist everyday." A structure of feeling that emerges through capitalism's processes of "abstraction, equivalent exchange, and the commodification of labor," the everyday names a form of "minimal sociality: the side by side," which Lee argues finds expression as a "minimal narrativity – one thing after another." The modern everyday thus surfaces in Asian American writing as "an impulse away from strong narrative emplotment" in which principles of proximity and adjacency take precedence over causality or telos. Although the modern everyday is often "a realm of abstraction and diminishment through replication." Lee, like Bhabha, is concerned to foreground the "unstable, equivocal character" of this situation, showing how the everyday can at times "reverse itself, change its valence or even become a rallying point." Like Bhabha's accounts of a colonial discourse that undermines itself from within, Lee discovers the everyday as "both the crowning achievement of modernity and its strongest unspoken critique," though she emphasizes this as a dialectical, rather than a deconstructive, insight. As hybridity here takes on the shape of a mutual reconceptualization of modernity and Asian American narratives, the result is nothing less than a new and expansive set of terms for understanding ethnic literature's strategies and desires, its forms and its limits.[39]

Utopia

> In that case, the deepest subject [...] would not be utopia as such, but
> rather our own incapacity to conceive it in the first place.
>
> –Fredric Jameson, *Archaeologies of the Future*

It is perhaps both paradoxical and inevitable that, in providing us with bold new paradigms for reading the social and aesthetic complexities of the ethnic text, both *The Exquisite Corpse of Asian America* and *Modern Minority* also carry us to the limits of ethnic literary criticism. For although neither jettisons the framework of race – and indeed both derive some of their most creative insights by attending to the particularities of Asian American racial form – by inserting the ethnic text into the broader frames of biopolitics and capitalist modernity, both these critical works cannot help but raise the question of postracialism – and thus, for the ethnic literary critic, the question of utopia.

To be sure, neither of these ideas has had much currency in ethnic studies; on the one hand, postracialism has been roundly dismissed as another itera- tion of the neoliberal fallacy of colorblindness, while on the other, the "melancholic" turn in ethnic studies has meant that, despite its roots in the undeniably utopian energies of 1960s social movements, the scholarship of recent decades has more often focused on recovering the past than on what Robyn Wiegman calls "the utopian generation of a future tense."[40] Indeed, these tendencies are mutually constitutive, since it is precisely the persistent failure of multiculturalism to deliver on its utopian promises that generates the turn toward the redemptive possibilities of the past. In this sense, then, both the postracial and the utopian stand as markers for ethnic literary criticism's political and narrative limits.

Kenneth Warren's *What Was African American Literature?* (2011) draws our attention to this horizon in provocative ways. Urging a view of African American literature as a "historical" entity occasioned by the specific condi- tions of Jim Crow segregation rather than as "the ongoing expression of a distinct people," Warren argues that today's changed circumstances render the category of African American literature obsolete.[41] While the widespread disenfranchisement and legalized segregation of African Americans during the Jim Crow era could justify a politics based on African American elites representing the race as a whole, such a project can only be viewed as anachronistic in an era governed by new modalities of inequality. In particular, while Jim Crow marked an era of legalized racism, Warren suggests that today's inequalities are accompanied, and even fostered, by a rhetoric of official *anti*racism. In this context, preserving the notion of a distinct and transhistorical African American literature can only constitute a nostalgic identitarian fantasy.

As his critics have pointed out, Warren's account of our present racial regime is elliptical at best, and apart from the relatively modest call for a more precise periodization of African American literature, he doesn't offer a paradigm to replace the idea of a racially distinct literature born in the era of Jim Crow. Yet rather than see this as a failure on Warren's part, this lacuna in his argument (and the strong resistance to it) can be read as a symptom of his project's utopian – that is to say, transformative – aspirations.[42] For as Fredric Jameson reminds us, the value of utopian thinking lies not in the radical alternatives it provides us but in how it reveals "in local and determinate ways [...] our constitutional inability to imagine Utopia itself, and this, not owing to any individual failure of imagination but as the result of the systemic, cultural, and ideological closure of which we are all in one way or another prisoners."[43] In other words, Warren's critical project, like all utopian thinking, returns us to the limitations of our present, which in the case of ethnic literary studies is precisely the narrative of antiracism that enables and constrains it.

Posed against the limitations of such antiracism, the idea of the "post-racial" can now stand for a more genuine transformation of our racial regime than it has typically connoted. This more capacious vision of social transformation emerges more pointedly in Warren's study *So Black and So Blue: The Occasion of Ralph Ellison* (2003), which makes a similar argument for a more punctual African American literary history but – perhaps because it was published before the presidency of Barack Obama would inspire countless pronouncements of a "completed" civil rights project – in a more openly utopian register. In this work, Warren agues that rather than venerating Ellison's novel *Invisible Man* (1952) as a collection of timeless truths about African American experience, we would do better to see it as indelibly shaped by the legally segregated America in which it was written. The point is not to diminish Ellison's accomplishment but to lessen its authority as a model for contemporary forms of social engagement and literary practice alike and, more gener-ally, to loosen the grip of the past "on the levers that control the present and future."[44] In doing so, we might be reminded that Ellison's ultimate aim was not to celebrate racial invisibility but to eradicate the social conditions that give rise to it, and that, rather than count the longevity of Ellison's novel as a tally on the side of African American humanity, we should be working for a social order in which such tallying is unnecessary because that humanity is taken for granted. Measured against the "suc-cess" of a single writer, even one as deserving as Ellison, this deeper transformation, Warren writes, "would be a marvelous thing, indeed."[45]

Warren's text thus reminds us that, if guided by our most utopian desires, "the future of ethnic studies," as Anne Cheng writes, "may take a form very different from its original inception."[46] But rather than sounding the death knell of ethnic literary criticism, we should view the advent of unfamiliar, even "postracial," social orders as posing new opportunities for this field. Indeed, to the extent that, as Jameson tirelessly reminds us, the question of utopia is a narrative one fully as much as a political one, then it is precisely a narrative poetics of race that can help us illuminate our lately unfolding present, even as this changing social backdrop heralds as yet unimagined configurations of race and narrative poetics.

Notes

1. Paul de Man, *Allegories of Reading: Figural Language in Rousseau, Nietzsche, Rilke, and Proust* (New Haven, CT: Yale University Press, 1979), 5.
2. Cheryl A. Wall, "On Freedom and the Will to Adorn: Debating Aesthetics and/as Ideology in African American Literature," in *Aesthetics and Ideology*, ed. George Levine (New Brunswick, NJ: Rutgers University Press, 1994), 286; Ann duCille, *The Coupling Convention: Sex, Text, and Tradition in Black Women's Fiction.* (New York, NY: Oxford University Press, 1993), 6.
3. Henry Louis Gates Jr., "Criticism in de Jungle," in *Black Literature and Literary Theory* (New York, NY: Methuen, 1994), 6; duCille, *Coupling Convention*, 7.
4. For instance, Larry Neal writes that "the Black Arts Movement eschews 'protest' literature. It speaks directly to black people. Implicit in the concept of 'protest' literature [...] is an appeal to white morality." Among contemporary critics, Kimberly Benston and Evie Shockley have outlined some of the formal innovations of the Black Arts Movement. Larry Neal, "The Black Arts Movement," *The Drama Review: TDR*, "Black Theatre" 12, no. 4 (1968): 28–39, 30; Kimberly Benston, *Performing Blackness: Enactments of African-American Modernism* (New York, NY: Routledge, 2000); Evie Shockley, "The Black Arts Movement and Black Aesthetics," in *The Cambridge Companion to Modern American Poetry*, ed. Walter Kalaidjian (New York, NY: Cambridge University Press, 2015).
5. Timothy Yu, *Race and the Avant-Garde: Experimental and Asian American Poetry since 1965* (Stanford, CA: Stanford University Press, 2009), 7. Edward Said makes a similar point about ideological concerns taking shape through aesthetic means: "The main battle in imperialism is over land, of course; but when it came to who owned the land, who had the right to settle and work on it, who kept it going, who won it back, and who now plans its future – these issues were reflected, contested, and even for a time decided in narrative" (Edward Said, *Culture and Imperialism* [New York, NY: Knopf, 1993], xii). In a similar vein, Ulka Anjaria notes how in the writings of the All-India Progressive Writers' Association "the very meanings of ideas such as "justice, fairness and harmony" were developed, contested, and reclaimed within aesthetic and formal elements such as characterization, plot, and narrative time" (Ulka Anjaria, *Realism in the Twentieth Century Indian Novel: Colonial Difference and Literary Form* [New York, NY: Cambridge University Press, 2012], 4).
6. Barbara Christian, "The Race for Theory," *Cultural Critique*, "The Nature and Context of Minority Discourse," no. 6 (1987): 51–63, 52; Joyce A. Joyce, "'Who the Cap Fit': Unconsciousness and Unconscionableness in the Criticism of Houston A. Baker, Jr., and Henry Louis Gates, Jr." *New Literary History* 18, no. 2 (1987): 371–384, 382.

7. Fredric Jameson, *Postmodernism, or The Cultural Logic of Late Capitalism* (Durham, NC: Duke University Press, 1991), 250.

8. Sue J. Kim, "Introduction: Decolonizing Narrative Theory," *JNT: Journal of Narrative Theory* 42, no. 3 (2012): 233–247, 237.

9. Christian, 52; Henry Louis Gates Jr. *The Signifying Monkey: A Theory of African American Literary Criticism* (New York, NY: Oxford University Press, 1988), xix.

10. Gates, *Signifying Monkey*, xxiii.

11. See for instance Diana Fuss, *Essentially Speaking: Feminism, Nature, and Difference* (New York, NY: Routledge, 1989) and Kenneth Warren, *So Black and So Blue: Ralph Ellison and the Occasion of Criticism* (Chicago, IL: University of Chicago Press, 2003).

12. Paul Gilroy, *The Black Atlantic: Modernity and Double-Consciousness* (Cambridge, MA: Harvard University Press), 222. For a different kind of "rupture" foundational to US racialized experience, we might consider how Gloria Anzaldua's Chicana feminist classic *Borderlands/La Frontera* describes the US-Mexico border as a "1,950 mile long open wound." Gloria Anzaldúa, *Borderlands/La Frontera*, 2nd ed. (San Francisco, CA: Aunt Lute, 1999), 24.

13. As Fredric Jameson writes, "modernism must be seen as uniquely corresponding to an uneven moment of social development, or to what Ernst Bloch called the 'simultaneity of the nonsimultaneous,' the 'synchronicity of the non-synchronous.'" Though Jameson is here referring to European high modernism, scholars have extended this insight to the analysis of literary production emanating from capitalism's peripheries (Jameson, *Postmodernism*, 307). See S. N. Eisenstadt, "Multiple Modernities," *Daedalus* 129, no. 1 (2000): 1–29, and Benita Parry, "Aspects of Peripheral Modernisms," *Ariel* 40, no. 1 (2009): 27–55. Recently, Jed Esty and Colleen Lye have called for a consideration of "peripheral realisms" to supplement postcolonial studies' disproportionate attention to modernism (Jed Esty and Colleen Lye, "Peripheral Realisms Now," *Modern Language Quarterly* 73, no. 3 [2012]: 269–288).

14. Gilroy, *The Black Atlantic*, 197.

15. Lisa Lowe, *Immigrant Acts: On Asian American Cultural Politics* (Durham, NC: Duke University Press 1996), 6.

16. Ibid., 98–100.

17. Ibid., 127, 126.

18. DuCille, *Coupling Convention*, 3.

19. Claudia Tate, *Domestic Allegories of Political Desire: The Black Heroine's Text at the Turn of the Century* (New York, NY: Oxford University Press, 1992), 9, 15; Rachel C. Lee, *The Americas of Asian America: Gendered Fictions of Nation and Transnation* (Princeton, NJ: Princeton University Press, 1999), 64, 133.

20. Beth Piatote, *Domestic Subjects: Gender, Citizenship and the Law in Native American Literature* (New Haven, CT: Yale University Press, 2013), 12.

21. Madhu Dubey, "Contemporary African American Fiction and the Politics of Postmodernism,"special issue, *Novel: A Forum on Fiction"* 35, no. 2/3 (2002): 151–168, 153; Madhu Dubey, *Signs and Cities: Black Literary Postmodernism* (Chicago, IL: University of Chicago Press, 2003), 8.

22. Dubey, *Signs and Cities*, 8.

23. Jinqi Ling, *Narrating Nationalisms: Ideology and Form in Asian American Literature* (New York, NY: Oxford University Press, 1998), 9.
24. Dubey, "Contemporary African American Fiction and the Politics of Postmodernism," 158.
25. James A. Snead, "On Repetition in Black Culture," *Black American Literature Forum* 15, no. 4 (1981): 146–154, 148.
26. Jennifer L. Fleissner, *Women, Compulsion, Modernity: The Moment of American Literary Naturalism* (Chicago, IL: University of Chicago Press, 2004), 258.
27. Snead, "On Repetition in Black Culture," 149, 150.
28. Said, *Culture and Imperialism*, 62.
29. Lowe, *Immigrant Acts*, 172.
30. Gilroy, *The Black Atlantic*, 5, 4.
31. Ibid., 2.
32. Homi Bhabha, *The Location of Culture* (London: Routledge, 1994), 178.
33. Gilroy, *The Black Atlantic*, 15, 73; Stephen Best, "On Failing to Make the Past Present," *Modern Language Quarterly* 73, no. 3 (2012): 454–474, 456.
34. Best, "On Failing," 463.
35. Bhabha, *The Location of Culture*, 140, 66, 72.
36. Cheng, *The Melancholy of Race*, xi, 15, 42, 43, 117, 172.
37. Colleen Lye, "Introduction: In Dialogue with Asian American Studies," *Representations* 99, no. 1 (2007): 1–12, 4.
38. Rachel C. Lee, *The Exquisite Corpse of Asian America: Biopolitics, Biosociality, and Posthuman Ecologies* (New York, NY: New York University Press, 2014), 7, 24, 123, 29.
39. Yoon Sun Lee, *Modern Minority: Asian American Literature and Everyday Life* (New York, NY: Oxford University Press, 2013), 20, 4, 7, 4, 9.
40. Robyn Wiegman, "Feminism's Apocalyptic Futures," *New Literary History* 31 (2000): 805–825, 805.
41. Kenneth Warren, *What Was African American Literature?* (Cambridge, MA: Harvard University Press, 2011), 8.
42. For a sample of responses to Warren, and Warren's reply to them, see the "Theories and Methodologies" section of PMLA 128, no. 2 (2013): 386–408.
43. Fredric Jameson, *Archaeologies of the Future: The Desire Called Utopia and Other Science Fictions* (London: Verso, 2005), 289.
44. Warren, *So Black and Blue*, 7.
45. Ibid., 108.
46. Cheng, *The Melancholy of Race*, 24.

11

VALERIE ROHY

Queer Narrative Theory

In "Queering Narratology," Susan S. Lanser notes that two queer texts lie at the heart of narrative studies: Balzac's "Sarrasine," as read by Roland Barthes, and Proust's *À la recherche du temps perdu*, as read by Gérard Genette.[1] Conversely, questions of narrative lie at the heart of queer theory – namely, in Eve Kosofsky Sedgwick's use of René Girard to propose triangular, rivalrous relationships as a fundamental narrative structure in *Between Men* (1985), the book most frequently adduced as the foundation of LGBT literary studies.[2] Yet today, when some scholars locate queerness in opposition to narrative as such, it is clear that no single story can explain the relationship of queer theory with narrative theory over recent decades. Instead, we find a complex interlacement of attraction and repulsion spanning elements of genre, chronology, and emplotment. In a recent text, Lanser, with Robyn Warhol, asks "whether and how narrative might be turned to queer ends," and the question admits no simple answer.[3]

In fact, queer readers and writers have regarded narrative both as a normalizing system that will contain whatever homosexuality it fails to exclude and as a vital tool of visibility and self-expression that LGBT people must claim for themselves. Writing of lesbian narratives, Marilyn Farwell situates these opposing views historically in a progression from the quest for political betterment through narratives of coherent lesbian-feminist subjects to later queer and postmodernist readings focused not on identity but on textual effects, where the lesbian subject, redefined, becomes "a powerful disrupter of the narrative."[4] Lynne Huffer echoes this chronology, arguing that "a metanarrative has developed in which the fluid, destabilizing queer performance stakes out its difference from that which came before by setting up a stable, fixed feminist narrative as its nonqueer identitarian other."[5] For others such as Lee Edelman, queerness is categorically opposed to "narrative intelligibility" and "narrative teleology."[6] Clearly, relations between the two are conflicted: queerness is excluded from or denigrated by conventional narrative forms; LGBT people struggle to appropriate narrative for their own ends; perversity resides in the necessary but subordinate middle of the narrative arc; or queerness emblematizes the self-resistance inherent in narrative, much as the unsymbolizable Real, in Lacan's terms, supplies the constitutive antagonism of the symbolic order.[7]

Love and Death

In narrative terms, Mary Wilkins Freeman's 1891 story, "A New England Nun," is the markedly uneventful story of a woman who evades the only event that might register as such by refusing her sole opportunity to marry. When her fiancé returns from a long sojourn abroad, Louisa Ellis finds that she cannot forego the "peculiar features of her happy solitary life."[8] Freeman suggests that Louisa's choice is not ascesis but a queerly antisocial enjoyment, the "throbs of genuine triumph" afforded by her domestic life, where tasks are performed for "mere pleasure," not the reproductive ends that marriage would serve.[9] Of course, the pre-eminence of the marriage plot has been explored by feminist critics since the 1970s, when scholars such as Jean Kennard, Evelyn Hinz, and Rachel Blau DuPlessis, recognizing the ways in which narrative structures are ideologically freighted, unpacked the gendered implications of the marriage plot as the novel's paradigmatic form.[10] Not all marriage plots are alike: African American feminist scholars such as Ann duCille and Claudia Tate later showed how race inflects the meaning of the "coupling convention" in American literature.[11]

Such studies informed LGBT readers' approaches to marriage. Joseph Allen Boone's *Tradition Counter Tradition* explores the ways in which novels problematize, as well as promote, the institution of marriage and acknowledges the presence of homosexuality in such texts.[12] From works like this one derive readings that locate sexual perversity not outside the marriage plot, but imbricated within it – at least until the final act. Joseph Litvak argues that in Proust, the lack of "the teleological alibi of a subsuming marriage plot" means that elements normally vanquished by that ending persist: "narrative closure" is pitted against "childish pleasures."[13] This pattern extends to narratives in which something other than literal marriage constitutes the end of aberrant sexuality and the start of heteronormative, reproductive adulthood. In Nathaniel Hawthorne's "The May-Pole of Merry Mount" (1832), for example, childish pleasures must be outgrown, for "the future complexion of New England" is at stake; thus the young man and woman who are married amid the "perverted Wisdom" of the sensual May-Pole carnival finally return to their proper roles, "bringing up babes" in the "moral gloom" of the Puritan community.[14]

Until quite recently, the corollary to the marriage plot for visibly queer characters could best be described by the 1994 film *Four Weddings and a Funeral*, whose fatality, of course, befalls a gay man. It is not that straight characters do not at times meet tragic ends; it is the fact that queer characters so often do. Until recent years, a Manichean law of narrative closure seemed to require, along with the social compliance of the heterosexual, the destruction of the pervert. In his pathbreaking study of homosexuality in film, Vito Russo concludes with a "Necrology," enumerating the causes of death for gay characters in forty films of the twentieth century – including falling trees, the electric chair, cannibalism, and, inevitably, suicide.[15] In literature as well, the ends reserved for queer characters are typically less than sanguine – so much so that Patricia Highsmith's *The Price of Salt*, published in 1952, is widely considered the first lesbian novel to have a happy ending.[16] Even in the work of queer authors, queer characters fail to survive: consider Willa Cather's "Paul's Case," James Baldwin's *Giovanni's Room*, Oscar Wilde's *The Picture of Dorian Gray*, and Christopher Isherwood's *A Single Man*.

Whether marriage or fatality is the conclusion, queer characters often find themselves banished from the text. Reading *The Woman in White*, D. A. Miller suggests that "[w]hat the narrative must most importantly get straight is, from this perspective, as much certain sexual and gender deviances as the obscure tangles of plot in which they thrive."[17] Out of confusion comes clarity, and out of perversity, the restoration of the norm. In Nella Larsen's *Passing* (1929), beautiful Clare Kendry draws the obsessive interest of her friend Irene Redfield; Deborah E. McDowell notes that "Clare is both the embodiment and the object of the sexual feelings that Irene banishes."[18] As such, she must befall what may or may not be a "terrible accident," a "death by misadventure."[19] Some fifty years after Larsen, the trope endures; in *Dancer from the Dance*, Andrew Holleran depicts a fictional novelist whose friend suggests that writing a gay novel is a "nearly impossible" task, not merely because it would not appeal to straight readers, but also because "they would demand it be ultimately violent and/or tragic."[20] Citing Radclyffe Hall's *The Well of Loneliness*, Catharine Stimpson adds that when the lesbian character's ending is not death, it is usually "damnation."[21] Where their end is not fatal, that is, queer figures are relegated to punitive or pathological roles.

Beyond such less than happy endings, queerness has been subject to other forms of hostile narrativization, which suppress the "love that dare not speak its name"; queer readers find their collective past "hidden from history," untold in the story of human existence.[22] Thus, Terry Castle argues that lesbians are, even in the twentieth century, "elusive, vaporous, difficult to spot" because they have been "vaporized by the forces of heterosexual propriety."[23] Paul Monette, a tireless chronicler of the AIDS crisis, recalls his sense of "how tenuous our history was" – so tenuous that it is significant merely to say "*Someone was here*."[24] To narrative such writers turn to ease the hurts imposed by other narratives. Fed by the desire to articulate LGBT experience, the coming-out story, factual or fictional, became for a time queer authors' predominant form. In such accounts, an adult narrator typically recalls a character's first sense of difference, her discovery of same-sex attraction, and her struggle to connect with the gay community. As such, the coming-out narrative rivals the marriage plot in its linear form and evident teleology. Whether fiction or nonfiction, coming-out narratives claim an authenticity of experience in, for example, Frances Rummel's *Diana: A Strange Autobiography* (1939), Rita Mae Brown's *Rubyfruit Jungle* (1973), Edmund White's *A Boy's Own Story* (1982), Audre Lorde's *Zami* (1982), and Jeanette Winterson's *Oranges Are Not the Only Fruit* (1985).[25]

Transgender life writing shares this narrative urgency: Jack Halberstam writes trenchantly about the need for trans people to tell their own stories, lest their stories be, like those of Brandon Teena and Billy Tipton, distorted by others' "all-encompassing fantasy of moral order."[26] Jackie Kay's *Trumpet*, while a work of fiction, is structured by precisely this question: Who controls the narrative of a trans person's life? Who gets to define what is real? In the novel, various people who had known the late jazz musician Joss (once Josephine) Stone give their accounts of him, some derogatory and some compassionate. Though some regard his life as an elaborate deception, his wife, Millie, does not: "I didn't feel like I was living a lie. I felt like I was living a life."[27] Transgender autobiographies such as those by Christine Jorgensen, Aaron Raz Link, and Jennifer Finney Boylan labor to tell the truth of their authors' lives – a truth others cannot tell. In such texts, queer communities cultivate their own generic forms, seeing narrative as not only compatible with queerness but essential to it. Each story becomes part of LGBT history – a source of meaning and cultural identity but also, like all history, an illusory chronology that may favor progress over plurality.[28]

The making of a popular narrative, in short, may come at the cost of difference. The coming-out plot became so formulaic that queer readers began to doubt its vitality and critique its implicit norms, not least its insistence on a single model of maturity. Prominent authors such as White and Dorothy Allison have noted its ubiquity, and recent queer scholars have approached the genre with ambivalence.[29] Their concerns are not merely aesthetic, for prevalent genres cannot help but enforce expectations into which by no means all subjects will fit. Dean Spade explains the pressures that result in transgender people "strategically deploying medically-approved narratives in order to obtain body-alteration goals" – narratives that render their status pathological, depoliticize identity issues, and enforce binary notions of gender.[30] It is as if, to adapt Foucault's account of the nineteenth-century homosexual, the transgender subject must become "a personage, a past, a case history and a childhood" concordant with a medical "specification of individuals."[31] Similarly, Jay Prosser argues that transgender life writing is inevitably shaped by the conventions of autobiography as such, including conformity to a "destined patterns."[32] Insofar as autobiography produces a stabilization of subjectivity, the forms in which that subjectivity can be intelligible will be ideologically determined; thus queer readers opposed to identity politics and committed to indeterminacy might conclude, as does Brian Loftus, that "[t]he notion of a queer autobiography is a contradiction in terms."[33]

Story-Time

Autobiography, as we know, is a retroactive construction of a past self; it is a trick done with time. That truism takes on new meaning, Prosser suggests, in the context of transgender texts whose subject must, by transitioning, "become what, according to the subject's deepest conviction, s/he already truly was."[34] Other queer stories share this dislocation of narrative chronology. Kathryn Bond Stockton presents the queer child as a kind of ghostly effect, never present to herself, for she only exists in the retrospective imagination of the queer adult.[35] The same backward construction is present in psychoanalytic and sexological case studies, as Jana Funke explains: "What is at stake in the production of narrative coherence is the repression of sexual dissidence: a period of latency is overcome in favour of a single true sex, or a stable sexual identity, which is, furthermore, retrospectively projected onto the past."[36] Psychoanalytic theory occupies a crucial but unresolved place in relation to homosexuality and narrative time. Some queer readers see restrictive conventionality in Freud's stories about human sexual development, both normative and nonnormative. Where homosexuality is concerned, Paul Morrison charges Freud with an insistence on developmental teleology that precludes endless, unproductive pleasure in favor of reproductive conclusions. "Like the well-made narrative," Morrison writes, "normative sexuality is end-haunted, all for its end."[37] Others have noted in Freud's work the persistent cultural associations of queerness with atavism and anachronism; for gay and lesbian people, the charge of arrested development, of failing to move one's story along, is all too familiar. Moreover, today's conversations about the cause of homosexuality mimic earlier etiological narratives, both psychoanalytic and biomedical.[38] As retroactive narratives that revisit the past to explain the present, scientific etiologies formally engage with literary traditions – most obviously the detective novel, to which the psychoanalytic case study has been compared. But they are always stories of pathology, deviance, and disorder; what is normal never needs to be assigned a cause.

At the same time, psychoanalysis exemplifies a resistance to narrative. Freud depicts the infant's progression toward heterosexual adulthood as fraught with possible wrong turns: sexuality is always in process, always overdetermined, and always to some degree a failure. This is why Judith Butler suggests that all "sexuality may be said to exceed any definitive narrativization."[39] And while the goal of clinical analysis is often said to be the closure that would restore psychic order, the analyst's story may itself be neurotic, falling short of coherence. Reading the famous Dora case, Claire Kahane notes Freud's inability to finish his own story. She observes that while Freud has been understood in terms of "the case history as a genre," his studies frequently withhold conclusions. Indeed, she writes, Freud was "obsessively disconcerted by the fragmentary form of his narrative, which linked him to Dora."[40] And narrative failure brings us back to queerness, for although narrative completion is foreclosed when Dora abandons the analytic project, it is also foreclosed, as Freud belatedly admits, because he fails to grasp Dora's "deep-rooted homosexual love" for the woman identified in the case study as Frau K.[41]

Apart from its developmental narratives, psychoanalytic theory has also informed efforts to compare narrative form to the physiological sequence of sexual arousal and completion, a trope that queer and feminist scholars have resisted. Teresa de Lauretis charges Robert Scholes with sexism for his description of narrative in terms of "tumescence" and "delaying climax" – notions that are not only masculinist but also implicitly heterosexual, positing a "marriage" between reader and author and even the possibility of procreation.[42] Reading Scholes along with Peter Brooks, Judith Roof examines the heteronormative narrative theory that links the closure of "completed knowledge" to death and orgasm in literature and psychoanalysis.[43] By contrast, this model locates perversion in the pointless detours of a text's middle section, much as deviance and mistaken object choices supposedly precede the individual's final commitment to adulthood and reproduction in the developmental narrative of psychoanalysis.[44] As Miller's work demonstrates, it is not necessary to invoke psychoanalytic theory to locate homosexuality in the middle of the narrative arc, but for scholars like Roof, Freud's writing does not constitute a master theory; instead, it provides invaluable primary texts that echo ideological patterns found in literature. These patterns can be paradoxical. On the one hand, she writes, "homosexualities are seen as threatening to narrative closure and/or its attendant (re)productivity," but on the other, "[t]he point where homosexuality is recognizable is the point that catalyzes the return of the heterosexual and closure."[45] For Roof, queerness opposes narrative closure, not narrative as such; instead, by prolonging narrative and delaying closure, it plays a vital role in many stories.

Queer literary critics have also asked to what degree nonnormative narrative is cognate with nonnormative sexuality and gender experience. In arguably the first lesbian theory of narrative, in 1978, Barbara Smith cites Bertha Harris, who believes that "if in a woman writer's work a sentence refuses to do what it is supposed to do, if there are strong images of women, and if there is a refusal to be linear, the result is innately lesbian literature." Further, Smith argues, "form and language" have as much to do with lesbian literature as erotic relationships.[46] More recently, Eric Newman identifies gay male cruising as the thematic counterpart and structural model of an "episodic and wandering" narrative form in the work of Claude McKay, where cruising is key to "the formal innovations that mark him as a modernist prose stylist."[47] Still, we cannot assume that the nonlinear effects attributed to queerness always align with literary deviations from narrative conventions, as we see with the issue of narrative temporality. True, a teleological temporal order underlies the causal chain of consequential events considered fundamental to narrative. Meir Sternberg argues that chronology is essential to narrative sense making: "From early to late is [...] not only the order of nature but also the order of causality, hence of plot coherence."[48] But we would do well to question the equation of plot coherence with naturalness, as if narrative were not itself artificial, cultural, and ideological. Does nature determine the order that narrative then follows, or does narrative invent the temporality we then take as natural? After all, many stories do not proceed "from early to late." Considering prolepsis and analepsis in literature, Genette acknowledges that anachrony is neither "a rarity nor a modern invention. On the contrary, it is one of the traditional resources of literary narration"; the "perfect temporal correspondence" that would avoid anachrony, he continues, is "more hypothetical than real."[49] Yet a narrative cannot be atemporal, *beyond* time, even in the absence of linear chronology.

We have already seen autobiographies and case studies, whether queer or not, whose retroactivity defies movement "from early to late." Similarly, literary modernism offers myriad examples of nonlinear temporality, only some of which can be considered queer. Even for gay and lesbian authors, the meaning of formal innovation may not be sexual. In Gertrude Stein's *Autobiography of Alice B. Toklas*, Alice's first arrival in Paris occurs at least five times, leading her to remark in the fourth chapter, "Once more

I have come to Paris and now I am one of the *habitués* of the rue de Fleurus."[50] Is this narrative temporality an extension of Stein's coded language for lesbian desire, or is it merely a manifestation of her Cubist interest in repetition? Annamarie Jagose argues that even Virginia Woolf's *Mrs. Dalloway* upholds the logic of sexual sequence in which same-sex love must be superseded by marriage; in fact, heteronormative commitment is "secured by precisely those 'so queer and so masterful' modernist techniques of representation that would seem to eschew it."[51] In her own reading of *Mrs. Dalloway*, Kate Haffey takes an opposing view, positing a nascent connection between the active recent work on queer temporality and new queer narrative theories, informed by nonsequential and nonprogressive time.[52]

While the relation of "unnatural" narrative sequence and temporality to literary queerness is an area of ongoing interrogation, other salient work addresses the sexual implications of narratorial styles. Lanser discovers narrator-narratee female eros in early pornography and eighteenth-century courtship novels; even if the sex under discussion is heterosexual, the erotic *frisson* thus enabled is decidedly not.[53] Another approach centers on the limits of the omniscient narrator. Taking a cue from Sedgwick's notion of homosexuality as an epistemological problem and Miller's Foucaultian analysis of panoptic narration, Jagose traces the way Dickens presents the perverse Miss Wade as unknowable to the omniscient narrator of *Little Dorrit*.[54] She must be, for "what omniscience claims not to know – like what it claims to know – is a defense against the erosion of the distinction made between character and narrator" – that is, against a possible similarity or identification.[55] From a different angle, Michael Lucey traces the inflection of first-person narration to the articulation of same-sex desire in the works of Proust, Gide, and Colette.[56] And Kevin Ohi links Henry James's use of free-indirect discourse in *The Wings of the Dove* to narrative focalizations that mediate identification and desire, as well as the disavowed possibility of homosexuality.[57] Both the effects of narrative style and voice and queer theories of temporality will likely shape queer readings yet to come.

Beginning at the End

Two further, starkly dissimilar articulations of "queer" and "narrative" have emerged in the twenty-first century. We began with the marriage plot, which promotes the heterosexual bond as, in the words of "A New England Nun," the "inevitable conclusion of things."[58] Across a century of scholarship, it has been axiomatic that queerness is excluded from the marriage plot or included merely as a temporary obstruction. But gay and lesbian marriage plots are now possible. It is not only the United States Supreme Court ruling in *Obergefell v. Hodges* (2015) that extended the privilege of marriage to same-sex couples, but also the wider cultural transformations that have allowed at least some LGBT people to participate in dominant narratives of family, consumerism, patriotism, and so on – the movement toward assimilation that Lisa Duggan has named homonormativity.[59] The Supreme Court majority opinion, after all, rested upon two interlocking premises: marriage "safeguards children and families," and "marriage is a keystone of our social order."[60] But suppose one had less faith in our social order, with its cult of child-worship, less faith in humanist ideals and sociality. If so, one might reject the gay and lesbian assimilation by the marriage plot, a mechanism through which, when we think we are claiming narrative, narrative may be claiming us.

Indeed, one might posit a fundamental opposition between queerness and narrative as such. Reading *Three Essays on the Theory of Sexuality*, Leo Bersani notes Freud's "teleological perspective" on sexual development, but he suggests that teleology fails in the face of repetition: "The end of the story is already in the beginning of the story; the teleological movement goes into reverse at the very moment when it reaches its goal; and the narrative line of sexuality completes itself as a circle."[61] The adult subject, that is, strives to "domesticate, structure, and narrativize" sexual excitement but cannot succeed in that task. Thus, the unnarrativized remainder of sexuality, what cannot be ennobled by the purpose of reproduction, projectively becomes the burden queerness must bear, as Edelman argues. Edelman's work pits heteronormative "reproductive futurism" against a queerness associated with the future-negating death drive, the persistent repetition that, meaningless and objectless, threatens the symbolic order. As such, it is inherently opposed to narrative, including "the familiar familial narrativity of reproductive futurism" and extending to narratives of political progress.[62] In a dialogue with Lauren Berlant, he describes their project as an effort of "thinking about alternatives to narrative knowledge and knowledge as narrative."[63] Here it is not just that reproductive futurism *works through* narratives of deferred satisfaction that rob the present of its value, but that narrative *as such* constitutes such a deferral.

Echoing Huffer's account of the antagonism between "queer performance" and its "identitarian other," Wendy Moffatt, the author of an acclaimed recent biography of E. M. Forster, has criticized the "queer resistance to the narrative of actual gay lives."[64] Edelman might suggest that it is the proper role of queerness to resist "the narrative of actual gay lives," to deny the process through which narrative domesticates queerness into the fictional coherence of this reality. After all, it is narrative that turns queerness into LGBT identity, normalizing deviance into a difference that makes no difference and domesticating sexuality to fit the marriage plot.[65] But this does not imply that queer theory should, or could, discontinue its engagement with narrative form. Instead, it must continue with rigor as long as narrative has the power to define the actual and the natural, the meaningful and the inevitable.

Notes

1. Susan S. Lanser, "Queering Narratology," in *Ambiguous Discourse: Feminist Narratology and British Women Writers*, ed. Kathy Mezei (Chapel Hill, NC: University of North Carolina Press, 1996), 259.
2. Eve Kosofsky Sedgwick, *Between Men: English Literature and Male Homosocial Desire* (New York, NY: Columbia University Press, 1985). Her argument remains unusual: whereas other queer readers have seen same-sex desire in traditional novels as subordinate to the inevitable heterosexual end, Sedgwick sees heterosexual relationships – two men's pursuit of a structurally necessary woman – as a means to accomplish or sustain their same-sex relationships.
3. Robyn Warhol and Susan S. Lanser, "Introduction," in *Narrative Theory Unbound: Queer and Feminist Interventions*, ed. Warhol and Lanser (Columbus, OH: Ohio State University Press, 2015), 8.
4. Marilyn Farwell, *Heterosexual Plots and Lesbian Narratives* (New York, NY: New York University Press, 1996), 16.
5. Lynne Huffer, *Are the Lips a Grave?: A Queer Feminist on the Ethics of Sex* (New York, NY: Columbia University Press, 2013), 57.
6. Lee Edelman, *No Future: Queer Theory and the Death Drive* (Durham, NC: Duke University Press, 2004), 132–133.
7. Jacques Lacan, *The Seminar of Jacques Lacan: Book I*, ed. Jacques-Alain Miller, trans. John Forrester (New York, NY: W.W. Norton, 1991), 66–67.
8. Mary E. Wilkins Freeman, *A New England Nun and Other Stories* (New York, NY: Penguin, 2000), 27.
9. Freeman, *A New England Nun*, 27–28, 9.
10. See, for example, Jean Kennard, "Victims of Convention," *Pacific Coast Philology* 8 (1973): 23–27; Evelyn Hinz, "Hierogamy versus Wedlock: Types of Marriage Plots and Their Relationship to Genres of Prose Fiction," *PMLA: Publications of the Modern Language Association of America* 91, no. 5 (1976): 900–913; and Rachel Blau DuPlessis, *Writing beyond the Ending: Narrative Strategies of Twentieth-Century Women Writers* (Bloomington, IN: Indiana University Press, 1985).
11. See Claudia Tate, *Domestic Allegories of Political Desire: The Black Heroine's Text at the Turn of the Century* (New York, NY: Oxford University Press, 1992), and Ann duCille, *The Coupling Convention: Sex, Text, and Tradition in Black Women's Fiction* (New York, NY: Oxford University Press, 1993).
12. Joseph Boone, *Tradition Counter Tradition: Love and the Form of Fiction* (Chicago, IL: University of Chicago Press, 1987), 8.

13. Joseph Litvak, "Strange Gourmet," in *Novel Gazing: Queer Readings in Fiction*, ed. Eve Kosofsky Sedgwick (Durham, NC: Duke University Press, 1997), 89.

14. Nathaniel Hawthorne, "The May-Pole of Merry Mount," in *Young Goodman Brown and Other Tales*, ed. Brian Harding (New York, NY: Oxford University Press, 1998), 139, 137, 143.

15. Vito Russo, *The Celluloid Closet: Homosexuality in the Movies*, 2nd ed. (New York, NY: Harper and Row, 1987), 347–49.

16. Like any claim of priority, this was subject to later revision. *Diana: A Strange Autobiography*, published pseudonymously in 1939, has a clearly affirming conclusion. However, it was not originally known to be fiction, and its author was not identified as Frances Rummel until 2010. See Diana Fredericks, *Diana: A Strange Autobiography* (New York, NY: New York University Press, 1995), and "History Detectives: Diana," PBS.org, July 26, 2010. http://video.pbs.org/video/1918179946/.

17. D. A. Miller, *The Novel and the Police* (Berkeley CA: University of California Press, 1988), 165.

18. Deborah E. McDowell, "Introduction," in Nella Larsen, *Passing* (New Brunswick, NJ: Rutgers University Press, 1986), xxix.

19. Nella Larsen, *Quicksand and Passing*, ed. Deborah E. McDowell (New York, NY: Penguin, 1986): 239, 246n9. McDowell faults Larsen for following convention (xxx), citing Rachel Blau DuPlessis on the traditional death of the inappropriate character. See *Writing beyond the Ending: Narrative Strategies of Twentieth-Century Women Writers* (Bloomington, IN: Indiana University Press, 1985), 15.

20. Andrew Holleran, *Dancer from the Dance* (New York, NY: Plume, 1986), 16, 15.

21. Catharine Stimpson, "Zero Degree Deviancy: The Lesbian Novel in English," *Critical Inquiry* 8, no. 2 (1981): 224, 369. Stimpson states that lesbian novels tend to be "formally staid," as if to counterbalance their unconventional content (377), though she cites Bertha Harris's *Lover* as a notable exception.

22. See, for example, Martin Bauml Duberman, Martha Vicinus, and George Chauncey, Jr., ed. *Hidden from History: Reclaiming the Gay and Lesbian Past* (New York, NY: New American Library, 1989).

23. Terry Castle, *The Apparitional Lesbian: Female Homosexuality and Modern Culture* (New York, NY: Columbia University Press, 1993), 2, 7.

24. Paul Monette, *Last Watch of the Night* (Boston, MA: Mariner Books, 1995), 227, 214.

25. Similarly, Angus Gordon notes the coming-out story's "retrospective narrativization of adolescence"; see "Turning Back: Adolescence, Narrative, and Queer Theory," *GLQ: A Journal of Lesbian and Gay Studies* 5 (1999): 3. See also Esther Saxey, *Homoplot: The Coming-Out Story and Gay, Lesbian, and Bisexual Identity* (New York, NY: Peter Lang, 2008), 5.

26. Jack (Judith) Halberstam, *In a Queer Time and Place: Transgender Bodies, Subcultural Lives* (New York, NY: New York University Press, 2005), 74.

27. Jackie Kay, *Trumpet* (New York, NY: Vintage, 1998), 95. Halberstam discusses this novel in conjunction with Billy Tipton and Brandon Teena (*In a Queer Time and Place*, 56–59).

28. Dana Heller notes the "progress narrative" template in another setting, LGBT-related television; see "Visibility and Its Discontents: Queer

Television Studies," *GLQ: A Journal of Lesbian and Gay Studies* 17, no. 4 (2011): 674, 667.

29. Quoted in Jay Prosser, *Second Skins: The Body Narratives of Transsexuality* (New York, NY: Columbia University Press, 1998), 199.

30. Dean Spade, "Mutilating Gender," in *The Transgender Studies Reader*, ed. Susan Stryker and Stephen Whittle (New York, NY: Routledge, 2006), 316. On "transnormativity" and the "injunction to self-narrate," see also Kate Drabinski, "Incarnate Possibilities: Female to Male Transgender Narratives and the Making of Self," *Journal of Narrative Theory* 44 (2014): 304–329.

31. Michel Foucault, *The History of Sexuality, vol. 1: An Introduction*, trans. Robert Hurley (New York, NY: Vintage, 1990), 43.

32. Prosser, *Second Skins*, 116.

33. Brian Loftus, "Speaking Silence: The Strategies and Structures of Queer Autobiography," *College Literature* 24 (1997): 33. A similar argument appears in Francesca T. Royster's introduction to a journal issue on queer writers of color, "Introductory Notes: Performing Queer Lives," *Biography* 34, no. 3 (2011): v–xii, as well as Margaretta Jolly, "Coming Out of the Coming Out Story: Writing Queer Lives," *Sexualities: Studies in Culture and Society* 4 (2001): 474–496.

34. Prosser, *Second Skins*, 118.

35. Kathryn Bond Stockton, *The Queer Child, or Growing Sideways in the Twentieth Century* (Durham, NC: Duke University Press, 2009), 5.

36. Jana Funke, "The Case of Karl M.[artha] Baer: Narrating 'Uncertain' Sex," in *Sex, Gender and Time in Fiction and Culture*, ed. Ben Davies and Jana Funke (New York, NY: Palgrave Mcmillan, 2011), 138.

37. Paul Morrison, *The Explanation for Everything: Essays on Sexual Subjectivity*. (New York, NY: New York University Press, 2002), 59.

38. I discuss homosexual etiology at length in *Lost Causes: Narrative, Etiology, and Queer Theory* (New York, NY: Oxford University Press, 2015), 1–55 and *passim*.

39. Judith Butler, "Imitation and Gender Insubordination," in *The Lesbian and Gay Studies Reader*, ed. Henry Abelove, Michele Aina Barale, and David M. Halperin (New York, NY: Routledge, 1993), 315.

40. Claire Kahane, "Introduction: Part 2," in *In Dora's Case: Freud – Hysteria – Feminism*, 2nd ed., ed. Charles Bernheimer and Clare Kahane (New York, NY: Columbia University Press, 1990), 19, 25, 26. See also Steven Marcus, "Freud and Dora: Story, History, Case History," in the same volume (56–91).

41. Sigmund Freud, "The Aetiology of Hysteria" (1896), *The Standard Edition of the Complete Psychological Works of Sigmund Freud*, trans. and ed. James Strachey, 24 vols. (London: Hogarth, 1953–1974), 7: 105n2.

42. Teresa de Lauretis, *Alice Doesn't: Feminism, Semiotics, Cinema* (Bloomington, IN: Indiana University Press, 1984), 107, 108. The object of her critique can be found in Robert Scholes, *Fabulation and Metafiction* (Urbana, IL: University of Illinois Press, 1979), 26–27. On the gender bias in narrative, see also Susan Winnett, "Coming Unstrung: Men, Women, and Narratives of Pleasure," *PMLA* 105, no. 3 (1990): 506.

43. Roof locates the conjoining of "Oedipal pleasure" and readerly mastery in Roland Barthes's *The Pleasure of the Text*, trans. Richard Miller (New York, NY: Hill and Wang, 1975), 47. Unlike like Scholes and Brooks, Barthes does not figure narrative as a sexual encounter, but offers an implicitly queer account of narrative perversity. See Roof, *Come as You Are: Sexuality and Narrative* (New York, NY: Columbia University Press, 1996), xxiii–xxiv, 56–60.

44. An insightful application of these ideas to the fiction of Louisa May Alcott is Karin Quimby's "Middles: The Story of Jo: Literary Tomboys, Little Women, and the Sexual-Textual Politics of Narrative Desire," *GLQ: A Journal of Lesbian and Gay Studies* 10 (2003): 1–22.

45. Roof, *Come as You Are*, 85.

46. Barbara Smith, "Toward a Black Feminist Criticism," *Radical Teacher* 7 (1978): 23.

47. Eric Newman, "Ephemeral Utopias: Queer Cruising, Literary Form, and Diasporic Imagination in Claude McKay's *Home to Harlem* and *Banjo*," *Callaloo* 38 (2015): 169, 167.

48. Meir Sternberg, "Telling in Time (I): Chronology and Narrative Theory," in *Narrative Theory: Special Topics*, vol. 2, ed. Mieke Bal (New York, NY: Routledge, 2004), 95.

49. Gérard Genette, *Narrative Discourse: An Essay in Method*, trans. Jane E. Lewin (Ithaca, NY: Cornell University Press, 1980), 36.

50. Gertrude Stein, *The Autobiography of Alice B. Toklas* (New York, NY: Vintage, 1990), 69.

51. Annamarie Jagose, *Inconsequence: Lesbian Representation and the Logic of Sexual Sequence* (Ithaca, NY: Cornell University Press, 2002), 78. An earlier reading by Susan Stanford Friedman concludes that there is no stable opposition between the homosexual, pre-Oedipal, lyric mode and the heterosexual, narrative, Symbolic order. See Friedman, "Lyric Subversion of Narrative in Women's Writing: Virginia Woolf and the Tyranny of Plot," in *Reading Narrative: Form, Ethics, Ideology*, ed. James Phelan (Columbus, OH: Ohio State University Press, 1989), 179.

52. Kate Haffey, "Exquisite Moments and the Temporality of the Kiss in *Mrs. Dalloway* and *The Hours*," *Narrative* 18, no. 2 (2010): 137–162. Still, a general reluctance to align experimental narrative forms with queerness is suggested by the absence of narrative questions from two recent essays on "Queer Modernism" by Heather Love and Benjamin Kahan. See Heather Love, "Modernism at Night," *PMLA* 124 (2009): 744–748; and Benjamin Kahan, "Queer Modernism," in *A Handbook of Modernism Studies*, ed. Jean-Michel Rabaté (Malden, MA: John Wiley & Sons, 2013), 348–361.

53. Susan S. Lanser, "Novel (Sapphic) Subjects: The Sexual History of Form," *Novel: A Forum on Fiction* 42 (2009): 497–503.

54. Miller, *The Novel and the Police*, 16–18.

55. Jagose, *In Consequence*, 55.

56. Michael Lucey, *Never Say I: Sexuality and the First Person in Colette, Gide, and Proust* (Durham, NC: Duke University Press, 2006.

57. Kevin Ohi, *Henry James and the Queerness of Style* (Minneapolis, MN: University of Minnesota Press, 2011), 68–70.

58. Freeman, *A New England Nun*, 27.
59. Lisa Duggan, *The Twilight of Equality?: Neoliberalism, Cultural Politics, and the Attack on Democracy* (Boston, MA: Beacon, 2003), 50.
60. *Obergefell v. Hodges*, No. 14–556 (U.S. June 26, 2015), 14–16.
61. Leo Bersani, *The Freudian Body: Psychoanalysis and Art* (New York, NY: Columbia University Press, 1986), 35.
62. Edelman, *No Future*, 9, 17.
63. Lauren Berlant and Lee Edelman, *Sex, or The Unbearable* (Durham, NC: Duke University Press, 2013), 3.
64. Wendy Moffatt, "The Narrative Case for Queer Biography," in *Narrative Theory Unbound: Queer and Feminist Interventions*, ed. Robyn Warhol and Susan S. Lanser (Columbus, OH: Ohio State University Press, 2015), 213.
65. Eve Kosofsky Sedgwick, *The Weather in Proust* (Durham, NC: Duke University Press, 2011), 183.

12

GARRETT STEWART

Screenarration: The Plane and Place of the Image

If I had headed an article with such a title when I first began writing in earnest on film, some three decades ago, it might have heralded a commentary on motion pictures – narrative film in particular – in regard to the visual realm of contemporary culture, where the dance of image across the screen frame, in the shifting *planarity* of its indiscernible separate micro-frames on the strip, never exhausts the *place*, the locus or scope, of visuality's power in civic and commercial society. The title might thus have suggested a study in extrapolation from screen to communal mediation in a society of the spectacle, that sort of thing. Let's say a genre study, perhaps, where each mode of screen narrative has its dominant iconology: the Western its panoramic landscape shots, sci-fi its astral tableaux or pulsing event horizons, or, more to the point for the coming examples, the paranoid thriller its close-ups on the forensic ransacking of newsprint archives or, more recently, the rifling of laptop files. In codified narrative formats of this sort, culture pictures its visual archetypes back to itself in images of just such mass-recognition variety. And in twentieth-century culture's most popular armature of visual storytelling – namely, mainstream cinema – the work of screen narration is always to deploy the iconic in the service of the dramatic. The very point of intersection – when the general place of a received image repertoire coincides with, and is caught up in, that planar advance of images known as screen plot – offers the immanent definition of narration as a propulsive force in any reconfiguration of the visual given.

Times change, and time-based media with them. We have arrived at the point where popular screen practice is no longer confined to that moving of separate pictures cells, called photograms, on the film strip (twenty-four transparencies per second) by which viewers once identified the basis of "motion pictures" – as pictures in motion. Nor is cinema's screening even limited these days just to the picture cells (etymological origin of the phonetically blurred pix[c]els) in the optical data files of digital theatrical projection. Instead, such screening has gone radically off-site – both prosthetic and global in connectivity – across a whole scalar spectrum of screens flat and rounded, handheld to eye-glassed, with the reign of cortical implants pending. In this way, the ubiquitous *place* of the image is as much a technological as a cultural supplement to the layered race of its differential *planes* (and constitutive rectilinear bits) on any narrative screen. At that enacted point of interpenetration in my title – where screen imaging is acknowledged as coextensive with narrative execution at the lexical hinge of the portmanteau term *screenarration* – there are certain plots that engage directly, in their own shifting optic planes, with precisely this expanded place of the computerized image in culture.[1]

I don't just mean here the new prevalence of cell phones as criminal affordances in the modernized gangster picture, as well as in every other plot whose genre permits a contemporary upgrade. Nor do I mean to reference primarily those moments when the presentation of the main narration, as if in a kind of technological free-indirect discourse, is given over to full-frame text messaging – or to what we might call "instagraphy" rather than cinematography – in the momentary displacement of plot info by social media's own participant witnessing and transmission. Nor am I thinking in particular about entire narratives that pass in review as if downloaded from gamer screens or Skype sutures. I have in mind, rather, those more pervasive maneuvers, just short of a digital "aesthetic," by which certain genres gravitate, on the one hand, to an image system deflected and vexed by a portrayed voyeuristic access to subsidiary action on recessed and reframed screens – often in the form of surveillance cams replacing "omniscient" camerawork. On the other hand, there are films whose *screenarration* probes its own electronic substrate in disruptive moments not of remote imaging but of outright pixel breakup in default of narration's own representational authority.[2] The latest entry on the roster of a redoubtable thriller franchise (*Jason Bourne*, 2016; Paul Greengrass) should serve to illustrate that first tendency in its telescoped narrative presentation, with electronic frame-ups uploaded to the management of narrative discourse itself. By contrast, in exemplifying those episodes in which the picture plane all told is compromised in such a way that its constituent bit-mapped fragments are surfaced in disclosure and occlusion, a 2015 film called *Selfless* by another hyperkinetic stylist and cult director, Tarsem Singh, paints this tendency into an unusual new corner of inverted and self-reflexive irony – and, at just that climactic turn, false optical expectation.

Two perspectives we might call media-philological also converge here to help pinpoint the issues. What this further terminological leverage should serve to highlight is the fact that, increasingly, in the cultural dimensions of "recognition technology," the image is almost the least of it. Think how the faintly oxymoronic compression of "watch list" for terrorist alerts delineates the cusp between facial recognition and dataveillance, reminding us how the increasingly leveled distinction between these modes of algorithmic detection pervades the channels of forensic mediation and the routes of physical transit alike. The verb *surveil* thus oscillates between metaphoric and literal usage, and not least when it seems to underscore the delegated work of the narrative camera under certain spectatorial conditions. Here, as so often, the technological gets a jump on the etymological. *Monitor* is, of course, both a verb for *surveil* or *keep track* and a noun at first used to indicate a person standing watch over standardized procedures, as in a schoolroom, or say a prison (recalling the original French title of Michel Foucault's *Surveiller et Punir* – rather than the misleading English version, *Discipline and Punish*). Only in the 1930s did the noun form of *monitor* morph – to speak anachronistically – into its televisual application, and since then into its consolidated sense for any electronic screen. And it is only then that the circle is closed with the surveillance quotient there at the origin of the verb. It is as if, by a metahistorical back-formation, the long evolution from an embodied panoptic gaze to the first phase of automatization, in a detached and machinated cinematic image track, has mutated further from serial frames through the scan lines of video signal and on to digital bits in the new dispensation of a continuous tracking (both senses now: depictive and detective) associated at once with handheld cellular recording, stanchioned CCTV, aerial reconnaissance feeds, drone cross-hairs, and the rest – all in the widening circle from "reality TV" to an exponentially televisual (and more deeply computerized) reality. Into this global blanket of backlit digital mediation, anything called fictional narrative on screen must find a way to insert not just its own temporal operations but its tacit sociology, if not ethics, of ubiquitous *imageering*.

One way to sort out this long curve of medial evolution, and of narrative structure as its pressure point in screen rendering, is to recall the threefold history of communicative optics advanced in the "mediology" of Régis Debray, in which the *logosphere* of the divine Word, once followed by a *graphosphere* leading from print through the evolution of realist painting to cinematography, was succeeded, from broadcast TV forward, by the *videosphere* of remote telepresence.[3] This last is the domain of the free-floating image per se, rather than the word or picture, fixed or serial. Precipitated out from this increasingly permeating sphere of contemporary culture, now nearing its global saturation point, are those nodes of imaging in narrative film that question what we might call their own *epistemography*: their way of making graphically visible what they need us to know. The ambient videosphere thus extends, beyond Debray's own writing, to the electronic cloud of universal record and storage, where a high proportion of human gesture and motion – once, well over a century ago, analytically quantified by chronophotography in the run-up to cinema – is now channeled, unseen and instantaneous, into a banking of images freed from any necessary viewing. The 24/7 trace of civic motion is thus the typically unglimpsed backdrop for those salient moments of dedicated tracking whose video transmits in the thriller plot – when executed in real time, not "retrieved" but immediately delivered – are often in themselves weaponized in return.

In order to see how this cultural logic of the image might be emplaced and remotivated within explicitly narrative structures (with space here only for a couple of recent exemplary cases), there's use, first, for returning briefly to pre-cinematic narrative maneuvers in educing some basic principles of storytelling as kinetic representation in the marshaling of images. And as the great Russian director and theorist Sergei Eisenstein knew so well, there is no better textbook for this than the almost randomly chosen pages of Victorian novelist Charles Dickens, whose visual effects Eisenstein claimed were a primer for the montage of early Hollywood narrative in the innovations of D. W. Griffith.[4]

From Postfilmic to Pre-Cinematic

Dickens isn't just cinematic, I would insist, but filmic: with a prose cellular, serial, flickering in its phonetic and grammatical uptakes like the usually fused – but sometimes fertilely intermittent – photograms diverted into some optic skid, overlapping ligature, or step-time screen advance. Consider, from his 1848 *Dombey and Son*, a truncated melodramatic moment of male-on-female violence of the sort that was to become a staple in Griffith, dispatched by the Victorian stylist with the full arsenal of his "editorial" ingenuity in the shifting foci and force of phrase. In these closing silent exchanges of chapter 47, the narratological concept of focalization is operating at full tilt in the mode of shot-reverse-shot.[5] Close-up: vicariously venting his rage against his adulterous trophy wife by taking it out on his long-undervalued daughter, we see Dombey furiously strike the demeaned Florence to the floor. Reverse shot – with all reaction under traumatized negation: "She did not sink down at his feet; she did not shut out the sight of him with her trembling hands; she did not weep; she did not utter one word of reproach. But she looked at him, and a cry of desolation issued from her heart." Cued by this look, we cut to the countershot of a figurative self-homicide, the willful annihilation of man as father in the heroine's field of view – and thus the close-up facial emblem of her sudden orphaning, manifest in the father's returned gaze and its fatal look(s): "For as she looked, she saw him murdering that fond idea to which she had held in spite of him." A sentence later – the last of this penultimate paragraph – and sprung again from a reverse angle capturing now her own horrified stare and physical recoil: "She saw she had no father upon earth, and ran out, orphaned, from his house." Following upon that double sub-jectivity of self-recognition, syntactic and psychological both, and operating across the almost seesaw pivot of "she saw she" (his face the mirror held up to her rejected love), the grammatical subject disappears – when precipitating the chapter's final brief paragraph – into the virtual cinematic loop of a repeated, now fragmented, predicate: "Ran out of his house" (with the minimal shift of "from" to "of" serving only to mark the deep intractability of this iteration).[6]

Thus are triggered the jolts of precipitated instant replay, where "A moment" both fixates the iteration and then, in an instantaneous shift of focus ("Another moment"), is swollen, almost like a visual bruise, to imply a sequential "moment later." The loop effect begins with the elided human agency of that obliterated filial "subject" in "Ran out of his house." Over this optic hiccup in the prose of emphatic downbeat, grammar still hovers momentously: "A moment, and her hand was on the lock, the cry was on her lips, his face was there," and so on.[7] The barrage of comma-spliced impressions, grammatically compressed, now gives way to that condition "out of his house" that implies the euphemized fate of all "fallen women" (recurrent motif in this novel), who, when the destination is pluralized and abstracted like this, are, as the paragraph (and chapter) ends for Florence, "in the streets." In this way has the whole artificially protracted and iterative arc of this passage – this threshold moment of passing over – operated to widen by idiomatic reversal the normative inside/outside antithesis by a gap between "ran out" ("from" or "of" private shelter) and "was in" (of anon-ymous social space): a breach effected and traversed at the interface of reverse focus itself.

Here, then, is where stylistics has much to add to narratology, and not least an intermedial stylistics of Victorian fiction as a proto-cinematic form. All five narrative codes of Roland Barthes's classic study, *S/Z*, are, for instance, cooperating here: the *semic* (connotative) code of character (in this case, vulnerable and abject versus rigid and patriarchal) in a *proairetic* (action) code of violence organized on the model of the life/death dyad in the *symbolic* code of structuring antitheses (where ultimate binaries organize the arche-types of cultural assumption). Here too, in a resonant further distinction in Barthes, the "character" of the stiff, cruel businessman becomes the self-murdering "figure" of the phallic Father precisely when intersected by the *cultural* code of male patrilineage at its misogynistic worst – and thereby, in the enigmatic fate of the rejected daughter, engaging at just this point the *hermeneutic* code of "what next?" in the drive toward narrative resolution.[8] Such a taxonomy, however, given the generalized stratum of the action code on which it rests, is all but blind (or deaf) to any smaller-scale dynamism of the text but the jammings and backtracks of hermeneutic sequence in quest of narrative closure. Yet in any *narratographic* response to Dickens, of the sort I have elsewhere argued for in comparison precisely with screen reading, what happens next, certainly in a densely scripted moment like this, is first of all a microstylistic question: a matter of lexicon and syntax and the figuration that braids them.[9]

This urgency of Dickensian wording only thickens in effect as the daughter's exile opens the floodgates of metropolitan kinesis after the dilated moment of exit. Following upon that whiplash version of the close-ups in Griffith that Eisenstein ascribed to the tutelage, or at least precedent, of Dickens, we come upon what the Russian director also picked out in Dickens as the headlong urban syntax of the tracking shot, the cross-fade, and, in rarer cases, the superimposition of two vectors of action upon each other. With Florence swept up into the surge of London street traffic, prose develops so close a contiguity between her headlong course and the rushing river that an overlapping match emerges between the lateral flux of the streets and the polluted floodtide of the Thames. It is as if a parallel montage were engaged, across their shared and impulsive forward thrusts, to infiltrate each channel of description with the figurative energy – and mounting turmoil – of the other. With Florence "in the streets," that is, the "roar soon grew more loud, the passengers more numerous, the shops more busy" – rather than (more lexically crowded than) "busier" – "until she was carried onward in a *stream of life*." What seems at first a dead metaphor is charged into active figural life as an overt trope across the tidal pull from concrete to abstract ("marts," say, to "evil") on the way to the flipped switch of simile when we hear that all is "flowing, indifferently, past marts and mansions, prisons, churches, market-places, wealth, poverty, good, and evil, *like* the broad river side by side with it, awakened from its dreams of rushes, willows, and green moss, and rolling on, turbid and troubled, among the works and cares of men, to the deep sea."[10] In that parallel personification of the river, physically as well as emotionally synchronized with the girl's flight, one can almost sense a flashback overlap, a kind of superimposed memory fade, of a pastoral landscape traversed in bucolic ripples by the fledgling stream long before it surges forward through the town – with the double-tracked analogy in all this for Florence's defiled innocence. Yet nothing in the passage is more protocinematic, to my mind – and this by being more narrowly protofilmic in its differential seriality, more cellular and incremental – than what one can borrow from Eisenstein's own method to call the dialectical montage of syllabification itself in that nearly anagrammatic bond between "turbid and troubled." Here, so to speak, is the frame-advance of lexical accretion itself, propelled by individual differentials in the building gestalt of image – in particular, the overlap of disturbances psychic and material alike. It is as if "turbid" plus "troubled" – those disyllables literal and figurative by turns, the objectively glimpsed over against the suggestively personified – condense and replay, in manifest form, the full watery parallel with Florence's anguished and aimless exile, with all sense of future clouded, occluded, churned to the point of turbidity by present grief.

I linger over the folds and interstices of this remarkable but not anomalous narrative span in Dickens not just to suggest a serial commonality between the so-many-phonemes-per-second of complex narrative prose and the twenty-four frames per second of the flicker effects that underwrite, at the level of film's spooling material substrate, all those differential cross-cuts that volatize the projected strip as much as the ribbon of syntax – and thus permit the edited shifts of focus and suturing returns that make for immersive cinema. Not for this alone, but to suggest as well that the image as such, figurative or literal, inheres in the flux – sometimes as flux itself: stream, flow, flood, cascade – as both the momentum and the upshot of narrative, its means and its yield. And in cinema not least, dependent as the medium is on the generative difference between picturation and framed view, motored pictures and moving image: between, in short, the planing past of specular signals and the resulting on-screen spectacle.

In any such narratographic reception of style's molecular increments and overlaps, Dickens stands out only the more clearly than otherwise as one retrospective marker (and historical harbinger) of screen techniques – seen now, of course, in the rearview mirror of electronic display and its post-aesthetic uses. Parallel montage and tracking shots and superimpositions still, digitally edited, articulate the grammar of a postfilmic cinema, to be sure, but not with the same relation to imageering's material support.[11] And in certain telltale screen genres, these modes of editing, camera-movement, and their resulting focalization are off-loaded onto narrated instrumentalities of surveillance rather than being retained in the purview of narration's own form. I mentioned rifled laptop files, at the start, as one visual signature of the latest paranoid thrillers. More iconic yet is the inset monitor in the tracking of bodies in remote space – often in that mode of preemptive interception by facial-recognition technology that one might take to be the latest "enhanced" fate of the Dickens/Griffith close-up. In the process, one encounters a hermeneutic code reduced to the forensics of algorithmic correlation: "That's him: computer identification 95%."

Image Emplaced: The Planar Recess

The aesthetic dimension of this medial d/evolution has a unique and vanishing formal flashpoint. In the filmic (pre-digital) phase of screen narration, the deepest subliminal disclosure, the most extreme and fundamental "baring of the device" (in the Russian Formalist sense), occurs in moments like slow or accelerated motion or the freeze-frame.[12] The medium-specific reveal: "Oh, yes, right, all this motion picturing is only the shuttle or jam of photograms, a time-based medium rooted in the seized moment of the still, an illusion, a machination." Mutatis mutandis, once the platform of commercial "filming" and projection has gone over to its current digital basis, the comparable, though so far less frequent, moment of roughened – deepened – disclosure is perforce less specific: "Oh, yeah, this is only pixels *too*, like most everything else we look at." Medium specificity has become to this extent generic, cross-platform, a function of universal computerization in what has come to be termed "convergence culture."[13] But as commercial production converges more all the time with non-narrative technologies of civic control and military surveillance, something else has happened. In the widening blanket of global fiber optics and universal relay, with its nonmaterial picturing of the world in networked streams, the film that installs a disclosure of its digital constitution, especially if privacy is among its themes, has thus reflexively engaged not just with its basis but with its antithesis – with the instrumental rather than the narrative image, or in other words with the valences and protocols of visual "recognition" in and beyond the narrative screen plane. This is to say that the disruptive stutters or seizures of medium specificity in filmic cinema, "modernist" stock-in-trade of 1960s European auteurism and inherited by the New American Cinema of the 1970s – once having been shrunk (or broadened) to the glitches of digital ubiquity in postfilmic cinema – is lately extruded, as imageering per se, in that further dovetailing of screenarration, more thematic than directly constitutive, that one has grown accustomed to in the form of *surveillancinema*. The inset plane of monitored action reframes the entire narrative enterprise from within – opening out in the process, yet again, to the cultural place and valence of the image per se in its networked proliferation.

The difference between spy-cam remediation and full digital disclosure, even within a shared ethos of surveillant visuality, has perhaps never been clearer than in the two recent films of high-tech foul play to which we can turn in pursuit of an ingrained byplay between narrative drive and image generation. It is all but explicit in the end-title paratext of Greengrass's film. In the logjam of production credits and logos for *Jason Bourne* – if you have waited out the stupendous number of human and electronic contributions to that point, body doubles, pyrotechnicians, digital VFX (visual effects) studios, and the like – you reach the deliberately retro black-and-white flicker of single blank, backlit photograms in series reeling vertically past on the nostalgic strip for the K/M (Kennedy/Marshall) sign-off (Figure 12.1), not included in the remarketed DVD, as it happens. Digital glitz suspended – as it is in fact kept mostly invisible in this film's actual narrative, latent only on the underside of showy "production values" – the retro-gesture of this logo seems bent on advertising that this is just good old-fashioned moviemaking after all. Indeed, except for the obvious "narrative digitization" (computer cosmetics) that allows us to see a newly "shot" scene of Bourne's young self in a revelatory flashback with his father, the screen surface otherwise, though fractured continuously by the director's signature editing, is never in itself digitally shivered or pixelated all told, still less the intact, buffed, and entirely material body of the hero – except when spied upon and rescreened by surveillance relays, in all their instability, intermittence, and surface static. These secondary and manically reframed transmissions dominate the first half of the film, all "monitored" (literally and figuratively) from Langley – including the undecidable play between POV and dash-cam from the wheel of the CIA assassin's car in pursuit of Bourne, glimpsed at first alongside its aerial sat-cam view (Figure 12.2), and then rendered in frame-filling car chase mode.

That's phase 1. But by gradual declension to full-screen fleshed presence from there out, even with Bourne pilfering some of the latest demo equipment at a Las Vegas surveillance display (shades of Gene Hackman surveying the detective convention wares in Francis Ford Coppola's 1974

12.1 Celluloid cells in passing

12.2 Dash cam: "Eyes on" vs. overview

The Conversation), the espionage prosthetics take a turn into a predominantly *audio* cross-cutting. At which point it becomes enough that *we* are watching. And what we see, after the frantic, inexact service provided by directional GPS sensors and the compensatory linkage of shots through wired audio, is a climactic assassination attempt averted not by some cutting-edge video intervention but by the timely swerve of an old-fashioned theatrical spotlight (turned from intended on-stage victim to blind the sniper and foil his shot). Then, in the move toward an open-ended closure meant to keep the franchise on life support, after more on-camera (but "behind the scenes") bloodshed, the surveillance punch line arrives in the entirely old-fashioned comeuppance of an audio bug, where Bourne – remotely, and long gone from the scene – reveals to the manipulative female agent, supposedly devoted to reintegrating him into the Agency, that he knows she has promised to "put him down" otherwise.

So it is that, after frenetically mediated and recessional screens-within-screen in the tech-savvy first half, the visuals to follow are entirely straightforward in the full-frame fissurings and elisions of Greengrass's micro jump cuts, often swerving between vectors of action in continuous real space rather than just between remote planes of materialization in real time. The surveillance battery of part 1 (in effect weaponized by the rapid dispatch of armed "units") can redirect CCTV to track Bourne wherever he goes, and no crowd cover can avoid facial recognition and its "enhance" and zoom functions for long – including the wily recourse to social media (one new wrinkle in the surveillance arsenal) via randomly uploaded cell phone images (Figure 12.3) that may have inadvertently caught a glimpse of Bourne (Figure 12.4). Just this inflection of screen technique with state apparatus technics is, as it happens, a kind of thematic halfway house en route to the

12.3 "Isolate all social media posts!"

12.4 Bourne "enhanced"

global internet surveillance that the Apple-like privacy advocate and tech guru in the subplot is targeted by the CIA for resisting. But once all this familiar constitutional paranoia is set securely in place by the plot, we are free to watch Bourne turn it to his own advantage, as repeatedly happens in the surveillance genre, in order to address the very real threat of remote social control in a fantasy, instead, of embodied heroics. Here, as usual, tracking, sighting, and chasing down the bad guys – ultimately mano a mano, and in an underground Las Vegas sewer tunnel not fitted out with CCTV, thus slipping under a malign supervisory radar altogether – remains the overriding dramatic goal amid the sensationalist wonders, and corrupt wielders, of e-spionage gone wrong.

A non-narrative work of face-recognition technology, almost as frenetically edited as *Jason Bourne*, offers a stark contrast on just this score – developing, as it does, its borrowed "aesthetic" in a Conceptual art context rather than for yet another mainstream plot. In a 2016 exhibition called "Public, Private, Secret" at the International Center for Photography in Manhattan, a remarkable 2015 video by John Houck revisits the already vexed epistemology of Michelangelo Antonioni's classic voyeurism-turned-surveillance film, *Blow Up* (1966). In *Portrait Landscape*, named paradoxically for its conflation of art historical genres as well as for its digital transmediation, the artist has applied rapid-fire face-recognition software to excerpts from *Blow Up*. Activated here is an appropriated and maladjusted program that almost comically spots and brackets misrecognized human features in bushes, peeling walls, fabric folds, fences, and the like – singling them out in miniature square frames, sometimes almost at the search rate of twenty-four per second: a contrapuntal film within (and athwart) the film. As with Antonioni's narrative to this extent, Houck's repurposed apparatus suspects what it cannot more closely inspect. In its forensic irrelevance as "surveillance" software, then, and in this respect inverting the scopophilic drive of film narratives like *Bourne* as much as *Blow Up*, Houck's work inhabits an incompatible interface between algorithms and celluloid, function and fiction, in its nervous repurposing – with the optic frame dismantling its own cogency in a machine-gun-like blitz of misrecognition.

Image Regressed: The Planar Default

Mainstream film, too, as well as experimental video, can play between the facial recognitions inherent to software programs and those normal optics so often analyzed and refigured in screen narrative by way of mirrors magic or otherwise. So we turn from the frenetic editing of Greengrass to that of another director schooled in the vehement montage associated with music videos. This is Tarsem Singh, whose *Self/less* (2015) is a thinly veiled remake of John Frankenheimer's *Seconds* (1966), a classic noir gothic – punctuated by ironic mirror shots of subjective misrecognition – where, by a lucrative corporate scheme of human recycling, efficiently slain corpses of the already walking dead are provided as alibis for other defeated and escapist selves like them hoping to become "reborn" after staged accidental fatalities. Yet these new selves, in *Seconds*, live out their confected second life under constant eyes-on surveillance from an unacknowledged cohort of fellow anatomical reboots – until these latest misfits are repurposed in turn as surrogate corpses for new paying clients. In this vicious circle of displacement, the second chance not only requires somatic "seconds," leftovers, but renders even the new selves serially obsolescent.

In contrast, the apparent premise of *Self/less*, by which we are strung along for a good while, is that stem cell research has caught up with such a macabre gothic plot and, via the generic shift to sci-fi, turned it all too true. In service to the dying body now, rather than just the alienated psyche (as in *Seconds*), the electronic process of "shedding" (rather than "rebirth") names the technological metempsychosis by which the consciousness of the dying self can be expensively computer-transplanted into a younger, abler body – no one else's really this time, no worries, just cloned from a healthy specimen. That's what we're told, the client hero along with us. This cover story is sustained until the plot twist reveals that these proxy bodies do, nonetheless, turn out to be (as in *Seconds* after all) murder victims done in when needed in the corporate scheme of things. Yet the system isn't perfect. Even after electronic brain transplant, identity traces of the formerly incarnate subjects threaten to erupt into the newly implanted consciousness, causing psychotic breakdown (figured by visual disintegration) if medication isn't routinely administered.

The dashing evil genius behind the corporate scheme of Singh's plot – who, we discover, has had his own psyche nefariously transplanted in this way – is at the last minute cornered by the self-"shed" hero in the surveillance chamber of the megalomaniac's own laboratory. It is there, once before, that the hero himself had been trapped, while otherwise equally subject to off-site monitoring in the need to police his transformation and keep its secret. This primal mise en scène is a foursquare space enclosed by two-way mirrors whose bulletproof glass the corporate guru has earlier and high-handedly demonstrated by the futile ricochet of bullets. But the tables are now turned on Dr. Frankenstein. In this ironic staging of their final face-off, the slick reincarnated villain can persist in languorously threatening the hero only by narcissistically staring at his own mirror image while merely imagining his miced interlocutor in the space beyond. With the biotech entrepreneur's enraged antagonist looking back, unseen, through the irreversible glass interface, the protocols of suture in the shot/countershot pattern are deactivated on the spot. It is as if the riving slash of the title *Self/less* were finally marking the out-of-field blind spot of being-seen (the so-called Absent One of apparatus theory[14]) as inherent, by viewer participation, in such intercutting itself – rather than just a thematized negation of the autonomous subject under biotech innovation.

But we haven't seen anything yet. In snide conversation with his own image, behind which waits, invisibly, the potential nemesis of his whole criminal empire, the suavely suited mad scientist notices that his wavering sight must be distorting his features in the mirror – in some kind of psychosomatic mirage

(Figure 12.5). This is a fact silently conveyed to us, through his eyes, by way of the optic (presumably digital) warping of his mirrored face (stopping just short of pixel breakup): just the kind of computerized effect we've associated earlier in the film with unbidden flashbacks from a co-opted body's former psychic tenant, when the proper medication is wearing off. No problem, thinks the villain, with a confident smirk. A pill will normalize (Figure 12.6). Here, then, in a play of reverse shots alternating between already reborn subject and his undulating mirror double, the re-embodied mastermind is, we presume, only *seeing things*. Yet that presumption survives no longer than the villain himself. For what we take as the entirely subjective POV shot of the buckling mirror isn't subjective at all, but rather – as it gradually comes clear to us, by coming literally *through* to us – the objectively glimpsed result of a discovered flame-thrower wielded by the invisible hero and burning through the otherwise impenetrable reflective pane from its far side (Figure 12.7). The effect is almost black-comic. Non-virtual countershot at last: the immediate incineration of the no-longer-reflected villain. And no less ironic, of course, because this too is only a digital simulation begun with the wavering liquefaction of the mirror.

So it is that the mistaken plane of image, from within a misjudged subjective shot, ends up decimating the space of mere looking. The in-joke of this optical boomerang is a kind of cognitive double helix. Though interpreted as a biomedical glitch from the villain's literalized point of view, the shock for the supposedly knowing viewer – sharing that line of vision – amounts to a techno-rhetorical irony when we realize that the passively accepted digital morph of the villain's mirrored face has, in fact, in media-historical terms,

12.5 Apparent psychosomatic warping (at cheek and neck)

12.6 Stabilizing medication on hand

12.7 Mirror mirror: Melting interface

been reverse engineered so as to disclose its optical evidence as the simplest mechanical action of scorch and melt across a vulnerable material surface. He thinks his vision is playing tricks on him when, instead, the film has been – on ours. As a misread symptom of ocular and somatic disintegration, the mirror shot has routed through the deceptive (for us) free-indirect discourse of the victim's eyeline match. It has thereby generated less a visual pun on smoke and mirrors plural than all at once the symbolic, media-archaeological, and metanarrative site of a single incinerated plane – and resultant smoke – that marks the cremation of an already once-reanimated villain, ashes to ashes.

Symbolic, because the shot is found framing in its own field of view the culture of narcissism that fuels the entire corporate scheme. Media-archaeological, because, once again, the rectangle of narrative projection embeds and emblemizes the place of the image not only in a broader cultural surround but in an inferred rehearsal, rippling pixelations included, of its own technological evolution – so that the villain's last preening image of self-scrutiny bears overtones of an entire selfie culture as the fragile destiny of automatic optic record. And metanarrative, because the storytelling force of the sci-fi plot is rendered at just this moment indistinguishable from the layered medial provisions it evokes. Plot reverts here, that is, from a punitive retinal and ultimately psychic trauma to a performed gloss on the primary material friability of the single image surface. It is almost as if the mirror were a plane of throwback celluloid – cinema in retroactive resume – succumbing to the heat of its own manifestation as projected image. And in that "almost" in nearly everything. Screenarration achieves resolution – and only through dissolution in this case – by optic parable. Live by the remade body image, die by it. The cult of eternal youth has turned a latter-day cinema of reversible exhibitionism and surveillance, vanity and threatened constraint, back upon the question (here the trick) of the isolated image yet again – and has found a surprising new way to exact a price for the optics of auto-affection.

A telling crisis in screen fiction comes here, as so often, at the crossroads of story and the images as such that bear and ferry it: a crisis of narration per se. Protocinematic Dickensian narrativity, I've wanted to show by brief example, works to maximize the lexicon and syntax of its own prose medium, as medium, in the propellant flux of described flow (or vice versa). Such is Victorian prose storytelling in distilled and concentrated form. Classic films certainly take their lead from this steeping of story in its own means. And even in a postfilmic era, without a frame-by-frame intermittence to confess, still any cinema worth its salt – worth, that is, the underlying granulation and grit of its bit-mapped digital generation – tends to speak, these days, not only in but *of* image: taking up visual information's place beyond the narrative plane. In certain genres especially, serious filmmaking is likely to isolate the *status* of the ocular trace even in the rush of its successive installations. Cinema's mutable *plane* becomes in this way a mere placeholder for a universal dispersal of streamed image. As such, visual plotting is now burdened, as latent topic, with the algorithmic glut of its own digital material and its suspect *place* in a data-gathering computer ecology. And one ongoing problem for screen-arration is that this larger story has no closure.

Notes

1. It is this kind of fulcrum-like moment, where plot institutes its own medial investigation, that has guided my considerations in a trilogy on the evolution of screen narrative from filmic through digital to post-CCTV projection: *Between Film and Screen: Modernism's Photo Synthesis, Framed Time: Toward a Postfilmic Cinema*, and *Closed Circuits: Screening Narrative Surveillance* (Chicago, IL: University of Chicago Press, 2000, 2007, 2015).

2. Recent films that indulge themselves in such digitization at the surface of narration (as the exposed face of mimesis itself) – effects thus thrown into relief against the tacit backdrop of unmarked CGI (computer generated images) – include *Source Code* (Duncan Jones, 2011), *Transcendence* (Wally Pfister, 2014), and *Lucy* (Luc Besson, 2014), as well as others previously examined in *Framed Time* and *Closed Circuits* – and more recently in my essay "Digital Mayhem, Optical Decimation: The Technopoetics of Special Effects," *Journal of Popular Film and Television* 45 (2017): 4–15.

3. See Régis Debray, "The Three Ages of Looking," trans. Eric Rauth, *Critical Inquiry* 21, no. 3 (1995): 529–555.

4. An extended treatment of Eisenstein's sense of Dickens's cinematic idiom and its influence on Griffith in particular, as well as on the whole grammar of cinema, appears in the appendix to *Framed Time*, "Precinematics; or, Reading the Narratogram," rounding out a study launched in part by a shot/reverse-shot analysis of "sutured" dialogue in Henry James (35–38) as a further instance of cinematized prose, with all the specialized vocabulary of narratography and its cinematographic registers glossed under "Terms" at the end (283–286).

5. This is the concept put into wide circulation by Gérard Genette, explained as a "restriction" on omniscience running from zero to maximum degree, the latter as in an entirely subjective perspective. See Genette, *Narrative Discourse Revisited*, trans. Jane E. Lewin (Ithaca, NY: Cornell University Press, 1988), 74. In between the two extremes, in the particular optical rhetoric of cinema, is the point-of-view shot, as often exchanged between characters at the interface of shot and its answering, reverse-angle shot.

6. Charles Dickens, *Dombey and Son*, ed. Andrew Sanders (London: Penguin, 2002), 721.

7. Ibid.

8. I here summarize the codes threaded through the entire book-length analysis of Roland Barthes, *S/Z: An Essay*, trans. Richard Miller (New York, NY: Hill and Wang, 1974), as laid out first on pp. 18–20.

9. *Framed Time* (n. 1) is paired in this respect, in a cross-medial argument for narratographic reading, with *Novel Violence: A Narratography of Victorian Fiction* (Chicago, IL: University of Chicago Press, 2009).

10. Dickens, *Dombey and Son*, 723.

11. In parallel montage, narrative cuts between scenes of action are usually taken to be simultaneous; in tracking shots, the camera moves into or across a space to unfold its narrative action in continuous time; in superimpositions, as another means of advancing the narrative, one shot (often an entire setting) is briefly printed over another that thereby seems to dissipate (by "lap dissolve") into its successor.

12. This is the sense of "defamiliarization" (technique laid bare in its operations – one might also say denaturalized) developed in the 1920s work of formalist critic Viktor Shklovsky, especially in his important reading of Laurence Sterne's novel *Tristram Shandy*. See *Russian Formalist Criticism: Four Essays*, trans. Lee T. Lemon and Marian J. Reis (Lincoln: University of Nebraska Press, 1965), 25–57.

13. See, for instance, Henry Jenkins, *Convergence Culture: Where Old and New Media Collide* (New York: New York University Press, 2008).

14. In the logic of "suture," by which the viewer is seamed into the relay of shots between facing characters, the resulting optical position – now here, now there, and always invisible – is understood in theoretical terms as the "Absent One": the shifting anchor of the gaze for which the camera is a variable substitute.

13

JONATHAN CULLER

Narrative Theory and the Lyric

"Contemporary narrative theory is almost silent about poetry," writes Brian McHale, in an article entitled "Beginning to Think about Narrative in Poetry," and indeed much of what follows will try to show how narrative theory's failure to address lyric poetry except as a kind of narrative *manqué* helps identify what is specific to lyric.[1]

Thirty or forty years before McHale's comment, during the heyday of French feminist theory, there was an inclination to contrast poetry and narrative: narrative imposed order; it was gendered masculine, culturally authoritative, closed, paternal, oedipal, the figure of the law, whereas poetry, ordered by nonsemantic elements, was the repressed feminine, preoedipal, disruptive. Against "self-admiring, self-stimulating, self-congratulating phallocentrism," writes Hélène Cixous in "The Laugh of the Medusa,"

> at times it is in the fissure caused by an earthquake through that radical mutation of things brought about by a material upheaval, when every structure is thrown off balance and an ephemeral wildness sweeps order away, that the poet slips something by, for a brief span, of woman. [...] But only the poets – not the novelists, allies of representationalism. Because poetry involves gaining strength through the unconscious and because the unconscious, that other limitless country, is the place where the repressed managed to survive: women.[2]

Similar arguments, about the ordering force of narrative and the disruptive force of poetry, with its roots in the unconscious or the corporeal, can be found in other theorists of the period,[3] but these claims turn out not to deal with poetry as such. For Julia Kristeva, for instance, the prose of Lautréamont, Joyce, and Bataille is nearly as potent an instance of "la révolution du langage poétique" as the poetry of Mallarmé; and Cixous's own *écriture féminine* does not consist of poems but, as she describes it, "fictions, essays, theater." The traditional novel, Jean-Paul Sartre declares, "is told from the point of view of wisdom and experience, listened to from the point of view of order. Order triumphs, order is everywhere," but novelists have devised many disruptive techniques, and there is no need to make poetry the name of the disruptive force.[4] Even critics who had appealed to the initial distinction between narrative and poetry retreated from the simple opposition, noting that women writers deploy disruptive techniques in narrative prose and that women poets need narrative in their long poems.[5]

Ever since lyric was deemed one of the three major genres in the late eighteenth century, the opposition between lyric and narrative fiction on the one hand and drama on the other has been treated as fundamental to literary studies, but there have been few attempts by narratologists, or critics primarily interested in narrative, to define the contrast between lyric and narrative. Although discussions of narrative structure and technique may adduce examples from epic poetry, narrative theory has generally restricted its focus to prose fiction, which, of course, offers a very broad array of examples.[6] Often, poetry is not even on the radar.

Perhaps the clearest and most efficient account of the difference between lyric and narrative, which can serve as a point of departure for this discussion, is by the American narratologist James Phelan. In a brief section of *Narrative as Rhetoric*, usefully entitled "Distinguishing Lyric from Narrative," Phelan suggests that since the material of lyric and narrative can easily overlap, we look to differentiate them according to the attitudes readers are asked to adopt, the set of conventions we bring to the reading of lyric and narrative. Citing Frost's "Nothing Gold Can Stay" and "Stopping by Woods" as examples, he notes that if a character in a narrative were to speak the words of "Nothing Gold Can Stay" ("Nature's first green is gold, / Her hardest hue to hold") in arguing for the evanescence of beauty, these words would contribute to the characterization of the speaker and we would judge them as we judge other utterances by that character. Such "judgments would be internal to the narrative itself, part of its construction."[7] When the poem is read as a lyric, however, "the speaker's character is not a functional part of the poem; instead, it fades back into the image of the implied author. [...] With the conflation of the nondramatized speaker and the implied author, our attention is directed away from any mimetic representation of that speaker and toward the poem's thematic point about beauty."[8] We attribute both the claims about beauty and the powers of expression exhibited in the poem's use of rhyme, rhythm, and diction to the implied author (the alliteration of "hardest hue to hold" is not sign of the pretentiousness of a speaker/character but an authorial effect). In the case of a lyric, our judgment, when it comes, takes the form of an evaluation: whether the author has produced a successful, engaging poem and whether it makes a plausible point. In short, Phelan concludes, "a crucial difference between narrative and lyric is that in narrative internal judgments of characters (and narrators) are required, whereas in lyric such judgments are suspended until we take the step of evaluation."[9]

In a poem such as "Stopping by Woods," on the other hand, we have a first-person speaker in a situation (watching the woods fill up with snow), expressing a desire to stop traveling and give himself up to the woods ("The woods are lovely, dark and deep"). The lines are presented as the ruminations of a character, but, Phelan writes,

> The poem nevertheless remains lyric because of the way characterization and judgment work. Speaker and author are not identical, as we can see by reflecting that we intuitively assign the rhymes of the poem to Frost rather than to the speaker. [...] Yet the mimetic aspect of the speaker's character is highly restricted – the main trait is desire for surcease. This restricted characterization allows readers to project themselves into the poem, to experience vicariously the speaker's desire and choice.[10]

We are not asked to judge this character and his dispositions, as we would be in a narrative that put into a similar situation a character who reflects on the appropriate course of action. Once again, our judgments are not part of the structure of the literary work but evaluations external to the poem: judgments about whether it is successful, whether it offers a truth about the human condition, and so on. Offered the possibility of projecting ourselves into the character, we do not, I submit, unless led astray by dubious methodological models, develop hypotheses about the speaker's motivations or consider whether Frost is sympathetic or unsympathetic toward him, as we would if he were a character in a narrative. But if the lyric were to go a step further in fleshing out a speaker in such a way that we did speculate on his or her motives and about the author's attitude toward this speaker – as happens, for instance, in Browning's "My Last Duchess" – then we would find ourselves in a special genre on the borderline of lyric, the dramatic monologue. As Phelan observes, "It is also possible for the speaker to be more individualized than Frost's speaker, but it seems to me that once we move to a situation where the primary work of the poem is the creation of the character of a speaker (the dramatic monologue), we leave the territory of the lyric."[11]

This analysis raises a number of compelling points and is particularly striking in focusing, for the differentiation of lyric from narrative, not on the presence or absence of action or plot or of non-semantic structuring devices, but on conventions bearing on judgment and thematization. Narrative is generally mediated by a character of sorts, either a character-narrator or a character through whom action is focalized in more impersonal narration, and readers are invited to evaluate the character's actions and words and reflect on the authorial attitude toward that character.[12] We are dealing, we say, with a fictional world invented by the author but presented as if it were real by a narrator, overt or implicit. In lyric, by contrast, the author or implied author is responsible for the words of the poem and its claims about the world, except in the marginal case of the dramatic monologue, which explicitly presents a character and, sometimes, partial mimesis of a character's speech.[13] And while in narrative fiction readers may be invited to view situations from the point of view of a character or narrator, or to treat the narrator's understanding with skepticism, in lyric we are invited to speak the poem and put ourselves in the position of ritualistically articulating the language provided by the poet. (In narrative fiction, even if we are reading a story out loud, we do not see ourselves as occupying the position of speaker; at best we might imitate the speech of a character.) This is related to the central contrast: lyric foregrounds the present of discourse, whereas narrative emphasizes the past of story. These are broad generalizations, but they do put us on track of distinctions between lyric and narrative that have not been emphasized in narrative theory or in the theoretical treatment of poetry.

The attempt to treat lyric within a framework of narrative theory takes two forms, which I shall describe in order to indicate how their limitations suggest areas for future work. First, a recent research project led by scholars at the University of Hamburg has undertaken to promote studying lyric poetry, English and German, in the framework of narrative theory, and has provoked interesting discussion. The basic claim is that narrative theory is more sophisticated and more highly developed than theories of the lyric and that therefore a narratological approach to lyric should yield insights.[14] Defining narration as "the representation of chains of happenings in a medium by a mediating agent," they distinguish two fundamental constituents of narrative: temporal sequentiality and mediation.[15] This lowers the bar somewhat, since it is more common to say that narrative requires more than temporal sequentiality: a plot, notoriously, requires a relationship among events that is more than purely sequential.[16]

Early narratologists described general patterns of plot that make some sort of transformation fundamental to narrative: a state of equilibrium is disturbed and then some sort of resolution is reached, or a protagonist's desire meets resistance and either triumphs or fails.[17] To explain how readers identify plots when reading a novel, theorists cite cultural models or stereotypes. Roland Barthes identifies a *proairetic* code, the code of actions, whereby readers draw upon their cultural knowledge to identify a sequence as a kidnapping or falling in love – general headings under which we make sense of particular actions.[18] Cognitive narratologists now speak of *frames* (knowledge of objects or stereotyped situations) and *scripts* (cultural knowledge about stereotyped sequences of actions), but there is no systematic inventory of such models. In the case of lyric poetry, where actions may be very sketchily described, readers may especially rely on conventional lyric *topoi* and models of action to guide their attempts to grasp what is happening. But in both cases, narrative theory offers few guides and people working on the poetics of the lyric can propose their own classification of plots. Jack Stillinger, for instance, identifies five types of plots in British Romantic poetry: conflict between two forces (perhaps mental forces) and their resolution; journeys or quests; confrontation between imagination and reality, with consequent disillusionment; a violation and its consequences; and conflict between two time periods or strata or territories.[19] These are more specific versions of the general structures mentioned earlier: a disruption of equilibrium or a desire that encounters resistance.

The German narratologists, in their determination to apply a narrative framework to lyric poetry in general, focus particularly on poems that seem not to have plots. For instance, Marvell's "To His Coy Mistress," whose structure is usually said to resemble an argument (roughly: If we had time, I could woo you forever, but time presses, so let us seize the day), is said to consist of three versions of a love story: the narrator places several possible versions of their love story before the beloved. "The incidents in the happenings," write Hühn and Kiefer, "consist of the speaker's yearning love for the woman, his insistent pleas to let him fulfill his love for her, and her rejection of those pleas for what are clearly moral reasons, even though she shares his love (or, rather, the speaker assumes that she does or expects her to do so)."[20] What seems to have happened here is that the analysts have provided a backstory for the poem, imagining a reciprocated love and a moral objection, and ignored what the poem actually does (not a good sign): it does not report happenings but describes what the speaker and the lady *could* do if the situation were different, evokes the pressure of time and what might happen if they do not consummate their love, and finally urges that they do so. There are no reported, narrated events, only hypothetical ones. There seems little to be gained from calling each stanza a "story" of their love and much to be lost, as attention is deflected from the unfolding of the argument in the present tense and the shift from witty hyperbole to urgent plea.

Writing of Keats's "Ode on Melancholy," Hühn declares, "Since stories can in principle only be told after the event, retrospectively, and from the end, the speaker here, by *trying to* tell his story prospectively, before the event, places himself in a precarious position."[21] But of course what the speaker "tells" in this poem is not really a story: it is a series of injunctions: "No, no, go not to Lethe," but "glut thy sorrow on a morning rose," and so on.

But when the melancholy fit shall fall
   Sudden from heaven like a weeping cloud,
That fosters the droop-headed flowers all,
   And hides the green hill in an April shroud;
Then glut thy sorrow on a morning rose,
   Or on the rainbow of the salt sand-wave,
     Or on the wealth of globed peonies;
Or if thy mistress some rich anger shows,
   Emprison her soft hand, and let her rave,
     And feed deep, deep upon her peerless eyes.

These are stipulations about what to do when a melancholy fit comes on or if your mistress becomes angry – not singular actions of a story but acts to be repeated whenever the occasion arises. To say that the narrator puts himself in a precarious position by not making this a proper story is to mistake what is going on and to make conventional narrative the template. If he had said, "When I felt melancholy last week I glutted my sorrow on a morning rose and gazed deep into my mistress's eyes," this would be a story working to construct a character (a pretentious character!), but the ode's propositions are instructions for conduct and implicit assertions of value, not the illustration of character (a point made by Phelan).

Many lyrics do recount stories, but these narratologists seek to extend to all lyrics a narratological model by making sequentiality the determinant of narrative. So a story may consist of actions ascribed to a protagonist, the usual view, or of mental events, as in "Stopping by Woods," where a speaker first thinks about the owner of the woods, then about his horse, then about the temptation of the woods, and finally about his obligations. But further, since words necessarily appear in sequence, there is sequentiality in every poem, and a story may consist of "presentation events," at the level of discourse: addressing the beloved counts as a happening, and complaining of her disdain as another. Blake's "The Clod and the Pebble" illustrates the inclination to find narrative at every level.

"Love seeketh not itself to please,
Nor for itself hath any care,
But for another gives its ease,
And builds a Heaven in Hell's despair."

So sung a little Clod of Clay
Trodden with the cattle's feet,
But a Pebble of the brook
Warbled out these metres meet:

"Love seeketh only self to please,
To bind another to its delight,
Joys in another's loss of ease,
And builds a Hell in Heaven's despite."

Hühn and Kiefer describe this as a complex narrative, with two so-called stories told by the two character-narrators, the clod and the pebble ("in both cases the sequence of events [the plot] comprises the process from intention to action to factual result"), and then an external narrator who presents the two narratives in sequence, creating a narrative about narratives.[22] But it is hard to see that there is any gain in calling either the characterizations of love by each singer or the poem as a whole a narrative. It juxtaposes two present-tense claims about the nature of love, treating each as an event but inviting readers to reflect on them and on the propensity of those differently situated to have different views.

The superior sophistication of narrative theory evoked by these scholars lies in its dealing with mediation – the identification of narrative point of view and focalization – so here is where their efforts have focused. Identifying four "agents" of mediation, Hühn and his collaborators distinguish "(1) the empirical author/producer of a text, (2) the abstract author/composing subject [i.e., the authorial function posited by readers of a text, often called the *implied author*], (3) the speaker/narrator, and (4) a protagonist or character in the happenings."[23] These are seen as a fixed structure of mediating instances, "embedded in one another," and identifying these figures in any poem becomes central to this mode of analysis.[24]

The virtue of these attempts to apply narrative analysis to lyrics that scarcely seem narrative is that they help identify what is specific to lyric. It's not, Hühn stresses, a matter of leveling but of highlighting the differences. First, in lyric there is "the preference for generalized mental stories lacking concrete circumstantiality (thereby facilitating identification)."[25] The "events" of lyric are most often thoughts, feelings, memories. Second, there is a preference for tenses and moods that are not common in narrative fiction: present tense, the imperative, the second person, hypothetical scenarios.[26] In fact, these analyses suggest – although these theorists do not develop the point – that, in addition to the present tense of definition (as in "The Clod and the Pebble": love *does* this), there is very frequent modalization in lyric positing of events, as in "To His Coy Mistress" or the "Ode on Melancholy": what we find are not recounted happenings but possible events posited in various modes – I *could* do this, this *might* happen, *let us* do this. Third, lyric texts, Hühn and Sommer write, "can be reconstructed as reduced forms in which the range of instances of mediation varies."[27] For instance,

Werner Wolf notes, "if the utterance of the lyric persona is performative and refers to a present (inner or outer experience), a major narratological distinction, which is crucial for narrative fiction, [...] becomes meaningless for a large group of lyric texts: the distinction between extradiegetic and intradiegetic [i.e., is the speaker outside the story or within the story as participant or protagonist]" because all you have is discourse reflecting the present experience of the implied author or lyric speaker.[28] More generally, lyrics restrict the mediating structures because they often efface narrators and mediating characters, leaving us just with the author or implied author.

This analysis is valuable, but the approach treats narrative as the norm, as if it were natural and inevitable for there to be a narrator separate from the author, for example, and implies that lyric's apparent disregard of this foundational principle is something of an illusion: lyric texts, write Hühn and Sommer, "*seemingly* efface the narrator's level and create the *impression* of performative immediacy of speaking. As a result, the speaker's voice is *felt to* emanate from simultaneously occurring experience and speech."[29] Romantic poems, they write, "can be re-described as the *manipulated* collapse of the agents/instances and levels of protagonist, speaker, and author, as well as the *contrived* congruence of voice and focalization, creating the effect of unmediated subjectivity."[30] In reality, the idea seems to be, there must be a narrator, and the impression of immediacy is an illusion constructed by the concealment of a narrator. But when we start from what readers actually encounter – sentences announcing that "Nature's first green is gold" – one can certainly wonder whether the narratological distinctions themselves are not the dubious contrivances.

Hühn also notes that whereas narrative theory, separating narrator from author, makes it clear that the possibility of unreliable narration is easily available, "readers of poems with dramatized speakers apparently are not normally inclined to question the veracity of the statements."[31] It seems that they lack the sophisticated understanding of readers of novels. Are the analysts hoping to correct their naiveté, to make us suspicious readers of lyrics?

Although the fundamental problem is that narrative is taken as the norm and lyric as a variation, a specific difficulty is the presupposition that for every narrative there must be a narrator.[32] And it is unclear whether for these theorists lyric can actually be allowed sometimes to dispense with the narrator or whether this is just one of many illusions produced by the lack of theoretical sophistication of approaches to the lyric. The insights into the distinctiveness of lyric come at a price of treating it as a product of deviations from the fundamental structures of fictional discourse. Moreover, the inclination to treat all forms of sequentiality as narrative distracts from the need to analyze the ways in which lyrics actually make use of incident and event.

The second approach to lyric through narrative theory is implicit rather than explicit and consequently subtler and more consequential. Anglo-American New Criticism, resisting the treatment of the lyric as the discourse of the poet, to whose life and thought one should turn for an elucidation of its meaning, succeeded in substituting a *persona* for the poet and effectively replacing the old conception of lyric – the intense, affective expression of the poet – with the idea of lyric as representation of the speech of a fictional speaker or persona. The classic New Critical textbook *Sound and Sense* tells students, "To aid us in understanding a poem we may ask ourselves a number of questions about it. Two of the most important are *Who is the speaker?* and *What is the occasion?*" After reminding students that "[p]oems, like short stories, novels, and plays, belong to the world of fiction" and advising them to "assume always that the speaker is someone other than the poet," the textbook concludes that "[w]e may well think of every poem, therefore, as [. . .] the utterance not of the person who wrote it but of a fictional character in a particular situation that may be inferred."[33] The dramatic monologue, where an identifiable speaker addresses an audience, is made to incarnate the very idea of lyric poetry. Avoiding biographical criticism and the intentional fallacy, New Criticism, almost without realizing it, gave itself a model based on narrative fiction, where students are to focus on identifying the narrator, and reconstructing the situation and perspective of this fictional speaker, who is deemed to present everything to us, as fictional narrators do.[34]

Of course, many great poems in the English tradition are dramatic monologues, and it is possible to read other lyrics in this way, but this model deflects attention from what is most singular, most mind-blowing even, in those lyrics, and puts readers on a prosaic, novelizing track: While looking for a speaker who can be treated as a character in a novel, reconstructing his or her situation and motives, readers neglect the verse, which is produced by the poet, not a fictional speaker. They speculate about a fictional speaker, who does not speak in verse, instead of concentrating on the moment of speaking the verse themselves. This model gives students a clear task, but it is extraordinarily limited and limiting. It leads to neglect of the most salient features of many lyrics, which are not to be found in ordinary speech acts – from rhythm and sound patterning to intertextual relations.

There are perhaps three important points to be made here. First, many poems of the lyric tradition do not have "speakers" – do not record the speech of some person. This is especially obvious in poems whose verbal acrobatics prevents them from being taken as someone speaking – as in, for instance, most of the poems of Gerard Manley Hopkins (such as "Inversnaid"):

> This darksome burn, horseback brown,
> His rollrock highroad roaring down,
> In coop and in comb the fleece of his foam
> Flutes and low to the lake falls home.
>
> A windpuff-bonnet of fáwn-fróth
> Turns and twindles over the broth
> Of a pool so pitchblack, féll-frówning,
> It rounds and rounds Despair to drowning.

What we have here is poetic discourse from a remarkable poet, not the speech of a fictional speaker.[35] Even Hopkins's poems that contain a first-person pronoun are scarcely imaginable as the speech of a fictional character, but only as the splendid construction of a poet. (They give us not a voice but *voicing*: spectacular oral effects.) Similarly, Dylan Thomas's "Do Not Go Gentle into That Good Night" does contain a reference to "my father," but this villanelle is a poem to be ritualistically recited, certainly not read as the speech of a fictional speaker. Second, for many poems, imagining a speaker distracts us from the poem and engages us in a speculative and trivializing process. Are we supposed to imagine that some fictional person says, "So much depends upon a red wheelbarrow"? Who would this be? A gardener? Surely not. A gushing aesthete?[36] The poem does not create a character making an assertion in a fictional world but makes a statement about our world. Frost's "Nothing Gold Can Stay," cited earlier, is another poem where asking who is speaking, or why, or in what situation contributes nothing to our understanding of the poem or its artistry. It is the work of a poet. Imagining a speaker emphasizes the fictional dimension of the poem, neglecting those ritualistic and musical elements that make the poem compel our attention in the first place.

Above all, the adoption of the fictional model of attributing the poem to a speaker-narrator ends up ignoring lyric's capacity to articulate propositions about *our* world. Philip Larkin's most famous poem, "This Be the Verse," begins:

> They fuck you up, your mum and dad.
> They may not mean to, but they do.
> They fill you with the faults they had
> And add some extra, just for you.

The model of narrative fiction makes little allowance for such poems, which appear throughout the history of the genre, from Pindar to this day; they claim to cast values in a new light, to disclose aspects of the world and praise what should be noted and remembered, but they claim especially to offer thought in memorable form, truths to be absorbed and repeated by readers. This one clearly presents a proposition about our world, not a fictional world. It would, of course, be possible to ask who is speaking, in what circumstances, and to what end. We could imagine, for example, a misanthropic drunk in a bar who is complaining about his parents and the world in general and telling everyone what they should do about it. (The poem concludes, "Get out as early as you can, / And don't have any kids yourself.")

But to treat the poem in this way is to trivialize it: to relativize its claims by making them the assertions of an individual whom you would probably go out of your way to avoid, and thus depriving them of any authority; an authority that they implicitly claim by virtue of their carefully constructed nature (the rhythms and rhymes that make the poem more than a rant). If you work to reconstruct a fictional speaker, you will doubtless be puzzled by the contrast between the colloquial "they fuck you up, your mum and dad" and the poetic discourse of "Man hands on misery to man / It deepens as a coastal shelf" and have trouble imagining the character of the speaker – but of course this is the work of a poet, not a fictional character. To treat this poem as the discourse of a fictional speaker is to set aside as marginal everything that distinguishes this language from the rant of a drunk in a bar: everything that belongs to what I call the *ritualistic* dimension of lyric (on which more shortly) and makes this language that you want to repeat, to reread, to recite.

One theorist of narrative who has avoided treating lyric by a reductive narrative model is Käte Hamburger. Claiming to offer an analysis based on linguistic features, *The Logic of Literature* distinguishes two logical possibilities: a linguistic sequence can be the statement of a real subject about an object or it can be a function that creates fictive subjects and thus mimetic forms. The latter function does not belong to the statement-system of language: the author uses language to create a fictional representation of reality, in the form of fictional characters who may speak. Mimesis of enunciation is thus distinguished from real enunciation, and lyric, the subject of a short chapter, belongs to real enunciation or statement, non-mimetic and non-fictive. Our experience of a novel, she argues, is very different from our experience of a poem, which is the statement of a subject and not the representation of a fictional utterance or statement.[37]

Hamburger quickly explains that this is not a return to the romantic notion of the lyric as expression of the feeling of the poet: the statement-subject is not a personal "I" but a linguistic function. The statement-subject (*Aussagesubjekt*) is a subject of enunciation and not a person. (The statements of the lyric subject may or may not correspond to the experience of the author: that relationship is in principle indeterminate.) "What distinguishes the experience of lyric poetry from that of a novel or a drama is that we do *not* experience a poem's statements as semblance, as fiction or illusion."[38] The force of her argument is thus to distinguish the mediating function of fictional assertions, which posit a fictional narrator and fictional world, from lyric assertions that we receive directly, as statements of a lyric subject, and for which the implied author takes responsibility.

Hamburger's insistence that lyric is not a fictional mode, that lyrics do not project a fictional world but make reality statements about this world, seems an excellent basis for a theory of the lyric, but we need to go on to specify that of course lyrics often do contain fictional elements: rudimentary plots, often in the form of anecdotes, and characters.[39] The crucial question becomes what is the best framework for thinking about the role of fictional elements. We need a model that acknowledges the tension in lyric between the fictional (story and character) on the one hand and, on the other, what we might call song or, better, the ritualistic, while recognizing the ultimate dominance of song or the ritualistic as distinctive of lyric.

This distinction between the fictional elements and the ritualistic elements I take from Roland Greene's *Post-Petrarchism*. Discussing lyric sequences – series of related poems in which some sort of broad narrative is tantalizingly offered, as in Shakespeare's Sonnets or Petrarch's Canzoniere – Greene argues that "lyric discourse is defined by the dialectical play of ritual and fictional phenomena, correlative modes of apprehension that are nearly always available in every lyric, though particular specimens, collections, and schools may try to protect one at the expense of the other."[40] The ritual element is, first, everything that can be construed as directions for performance: lyrics are poems made to be uttered by readers, who may come ritualistically to occupy the place of the lyric *I*. From a fictional perspective, the poem is voiced not by a reader but a character, and it evokes past events rather than a performance in the lyric *now*. The tension between fictional/representational elements and the *ritualistic* comes out clearly in sonnet sequences, where readers struggle to identify a character and a plot but keep encountering rhymes, repetitions, elements of address, prominent sound patterning, and so on. From the ritualistic perspective, the reader voices the poem and the poem itself is the event. The fictional is what we produce when we attempt to imagine a persona or speaker and a world or situation of utterance and past events that are evoked in the act of lyric enunciation but characteristically subordinated in various ways to a present of enunciation.[41]

Attention to narrative in lyric should explore the characteristic ways in which lyrics can incorporate narrative elements. In a basic lyric structure, a past incident is narrated but then pulled into the time of the lyric *now* by reflection on its significance, as in Wordsworth's "I wandered lonely as a cloud." As so often, there is little narrative specification (nothing about time, place, etc.): just I wandered and saw a host of daffodils. And now, the poem concludes, "when on my couch I lie / In vacant or in pensive mood, / They flash upon that inward eye / Which is the bliss of solitude." An alternative is the structure of the ballad, which provides a sketchy plot, interrupted by a refrain that pulls us out of narrative time into the present of lyric enunciation, before reverting to rudimentary narrative.

Lyrics focused on the narration of past events are relatively rare. Those entirely narrated in the past tense are uncommon prior to the twentieth century: In the *Norton Anthology of Poetry* only 123 of 1,266 poems are in the past tense, and 21 of those are ballads; only two of Shakespeare's 154 sonnets remain in the past throughout, for instance. There is usually some present-tense conclusion. Poems that remain in the past either become allegorical, as in "I heard a fly buzz when I died," or, as in many twentieth-century poems, presume that the reader can *imagine* the present significance of the incident, as in Theodore Roethke's well-known "My Papa's Waltz," which concludes, without present comment:

> You beat time on my head
> With a palm caked hard by dirt,
> Then waltzed me off to bed
> Still clinging to your shirt.

There is considerable scope for the study of the functioning of narrative elements in lyric, but it is crucial for any theory of the lyric to foreground those features of the lyric that distinguish it from narrative fiction, which now so dominates the field of literary studies. Whence a default model of lyric as non-mimetic and non-fictional, though it can incorporate fictional and representational elements in its fundamentally ritualistic structures. We begin with the presumption that this is discourse about our world, not a fictional world, though filled with strange imaginings that we treat as figurative. The ritualistic takes many forms, from varied types of repetition, sound patterning, metrical structures, rhymes, and refrain, to apostrophes that stress the *now* of lyric enunciation, as the poem seeks to be not the representation of past events, but itself an event in our world.

Notes

1. Brian McHale, "Beginning to Think about Narrative in Poetry," *Narrative* 17 (2009): 11. There are notable exceptions, such as Rick Altman's *Theory of Narrative* (New York, NY: Columbia University Press, 2008), which makes the *Chanson de Roland* a primary example, but it does not deal with this long poem as verse. I am grateful to James Phelan and Matthew Garrett for helpful comments on a draft of this essay.
2. Hélène Cixous, "The Laugh of the Medusa," *Signs* 1 (1976): 879–880.
3. Thus, for instance, Julia Kristeva writes, "Indeed, with the bourgeoisie, poetry arrays itself against order at its most fundamental." It becomes "a permanent struggle to demonstrate the drives' breaking of paths [*frayage de la pulsion*] within the very order of language" (*La Révolution du langage poétique* [Paris: Seuil, 1974], 78).
4. Jean-Paul Sartre, "Qu'est-ce que la littérature?" *Situations II* (Paris: Gallimard, 1948), 181.
5. Susan Stanford Friedman concludes, "the transgressive and revolutionary potential of women's poetry does not lie in the fixed rejection of narrative [...] or in a negative association of narrative with the social" ("Craving Stories: Narrative and Lyric in Contemporary Theory and Women's Long Poems," in *Feminist Measures: Soundings in Poetry and Theory*, ed. Lynn Keller and Cristanne Miller [Ann Arbor: University of Michigan Press, 1994], 38). Friedman argues against the feminist critique of narrative as inherently masculinist that she had earlier offered in "Lyric Subversion of Narrative in Women's Writing: Virginia Woolf and the Tyranny of Plot," in *Reading Narrative: Form, Ethics, Ideology*, ed. James Phelan (Columbus: Ohio State University Press, 1989), 162–185.
6. A notable exception is Claire Kinney's *Strategies of Poetic Narrative* (Cambridge: Cambridge University Press, 1992), which focuses on narrative techniques in *Troilus and Criseyde*, book VI of *The Faerie Queene*, *Paradise Lost*, and "The Waste Land."
7. James Phelan, *Narrative as Rhetoric: Technique, Audiences, Ethics, Ideology* (Columbus: Ohio State University Press, 1996), 32. Further references to this text are given parenthetically. In a later work, Phelan develops the contrast between narrativity and lyricality, the conventions of judgment involved, and possibilities of hybrid forms: *Experiencing Fiction: Judgments, Progressions, and the Rhetorical Theory of Narrative* (Columbus: Ohio State University Press, 2007).
8. Phelan, *Narrative as Rhetoric*, 32–35.
9. Ibid., 33
10. Ibid., 34.
11. Ibid., 201n6.
12. I set aside, as beyond the scope of this essay, the question of whether communicational theories of narrative, which assume that every narrative necessarily has a narrator, can give a convincing account of what is called "third-person narration" or whether so-called "optional narrator theory," which asks not "who speaks?" but "how is it written?" is not a superior option. In addition to Ann Banfield's pioneering *Unspeakable Sentences: Narration and Representation in the Language of Fiction* (London: Routledge and Kegan Paul, 1982), see Käte Hamburger, *The Logic of Literature* (Bloomington:

Indiana University Press, 1973); Sylvie Patron, *La Mort du narrateur* (Paris: Lambert-Lucas, 2015); and Richard Walsh, *The Rhetoric of Fictionality: Narrative Theory and the Idea of Fiction* (Columbus: Ohio State University Press, 2007).

13. Note, though, that even in Browning's "My Last Duchess," while we take it that the choice of words reveals the Duke's character and attitudes, we do not credit him with speaking extraordinarily skillful pentameter couplets. We attribute the verse, the subtle rhymes, and so on to an author, even if we judge the Duke to be skillfully sending a warning to the next duchess.

14. Peter Hühn, "Plotting the Lyric: Forms of Narration in Poetry," in *Theory into Poetry: New Approaches to the Lyric*, ed. Eva Müller-Zettelmann and Margarete Rubik (Amsterdam: Rodopi, 2005), 147.

15. Peter Hühn and Roy Sommer, "Narration in Poetry and Drama," in *The Living Handbook of Narratology*, ed. Hühn et al. (www.lhn.uni-hamburg.de/article/narration-poetry-and-drama).

16. Jean-Michel Adam reflects a broader consensus, citing four different types of "basic non-narrative sequentiality" ("Conditions et degrés de narrativation du poème," *Degrés: Revue de synthèse à orientation sémiologique* 111 [2002]: 4. This issue of *Degrés* is entitled *Poésie et narrativité*).

17. Cf. Vladimir Propp, *Morphology of the Folktale*, 2nd ed., trans. Laurence Scott, ed. Louis A. Wagner (Austin: University of Texas Press, 1968); Claude Bremond, *La Logique du récit* (Paris: Seuil, 1973); A. J. Greimas, *Sémantique structurale* (Paris: Larousse, 1966).

18. Roland Barthes, *S/Z: An Essay*, trans. Richard Miller, (New York, NY: Hill and Wang, 1974).

19. Jack Stillinger, "The Plots of Romantic Poetry," *College Literature* 12 (1985): 95–112.

20. Peter Hühn and Jens Kiefer, *The Narratological Analysis of Lyric Poetry: Studies in English Poetry from the 16th to the 20th Century* (Berlin: de Gruyter, 2005), 46.

21. Peter Hühn, "Reading Poetry as Narrative: Towards Narratological Analysis of Lyric Poems," in *Investigations into Narrative Structures*, ed. Christian Todenhagen and Wolfgang Thiele (Frankfurt: Peter Lang, 2002), 24.

22. Hühn and Kiefer, *The Narratological Analysis of Lyric*, 15.

23. Ibid., 8.

24. Claudia Hillebrandt offers a critique of this schema, proposes one that omits the abstract author, and offers some further distinctions, including the possibility of a lyric text without a speaker but only with an author who produces the text ("Author and Narrator in Lyric Poetry," in *Author and Narrator. Transdisciplinary Contributions to a Narratological Debate*, ed. Dorothee Birke and Tilmann Köppe [Berlin: De Gruyter, 2015], 219–227).

25. Hühn and Sommer, "Narration in Poetry and Drama." Monika Fludernik, the most eminent German theorist of narrative, dissents, noting that the lack of specification of time, place, and agents means that "[m]uch that *appears* to be narrative in poetry does not actually qualify as such because it does not concern specific fictional personae but posits a hypothetical or allegorical scenario" (*Towards a "Natural" Narratology* [New York, NY: Routledge, 1996], 354).

26. Peter Hühn, "Transgeneric Narratology: Application to Lyric Poetry," in *The Dynamics of Narrative form: Studies in Anglo-American Narratology*, ed. John Pier (Berlin: de Gruyter, 2004), 152. Suzanne Fleischman emphasizes that "All genres that choose the present as the basic tense for reporting information work in some way against the narrative norm; they are consciously or unconsciously anti-narrative" (*Tense and Narrativity: From Medieval Performance to Modern Fiction* [Austin: University of Texas Press, 1990], 11).

27. Hühn and Sommer, "Narration in Poetry and Drama."

28. Werner Wolf, "Aesthetic Illusion in Lyric Poetry?" *Poetica* 30 (1998): 273.

29. Hühn and Sommer, "Narration in Poetry and Drama" (my italics). Sylvie Patron maintains that while one can speak of the effacement of the author, it is wrong to speak of the "effacement of the narrator," since that presupposes that there necessarily is one, which can occasionally be erased (*La Mort du narrateur*, 126).

30. Hühn and Sommer, "Narration in Poetry and Drama."

31. Hühn, "Transgeneric Narratology," 148.

32. There has been some resistance to this narratological claim, as I mention earlier, but it remains the model drawn on by the German narratologists developing a narratological approach to lyric.

33. *Perrine's Sound and Sense*, 14th ed. (New York, NY: Cengage, 2013), 27.

34. An excellent early essay that develops such points is Ralph Rader's "The Dramatic Monologue and Related Lyric Forms," *Critical Inquiry* 3, no. 1 (1976): 131–151.

35. The most influential articulation of the opposite position is by Barbara Herrnstein Smith, in *Poetic Closure: A Study of How Poems End* (Chicago, IL: University of Chicago Press, 1968) and *On the Margins of Discourse* (Chicago, IL: University of Chicago Press, 1978).

36. Hugh Kenner writes, "Try to imagine an occasion for this sentence to be said: 'So much depends upon a red wheelbarrow glazed with rainwater beside the white chickens.' Try it over, in any voice you like: it is impossible. [. . .] And to go on with the dialogue? To whom might the sentence be spoken, for what purpose? [. . .] Not only is what the sentence says banal, if you heard someone say it you'd wince. But hammered on the typewriter into a *thing made*, and this without displacing a single word except typographically, the sixteen words exist in a different zone altogether, a zone remote from the world of sayers and sayings." He adds, "Yet you do say, you do go through the motions of saying. But art lifts the saying out of the zone of things said" (*A Homemade World* [New York, NY: Knopf, 1975], 59–60).

37. Käte Hamburger, *The Logic of Literature* (Bloomington: Indiana University Press, 1973), 233–235.

38. Ibid., 271.

39. Of course characters may resemble the author; for Hamburger that relationship is in principle indeterminate, so it is convenient to speak of such elements as fictional.

40. Roland Greene, *Post-Petrarchism: Origins and Innovations of the Western Lyric Sequence* (Princeton, NJ: Princeton University Press, 1991), 5.

41. Though I adopt Greene's distinction, which seems to me very useful, it remains true that lyrics in general are not fictional and make assertions about our world, not a fictional world. See Jonathan Culler, *Theory of the Lyric* (Cambridge, MA: Harvard University Press, 2015), ch. 5, "Lyric Structures," and *passim*.

14

MARK CURRIE

Contemporary Formalisms

When T. J. Clark declared in 1999 that "Modernism is our antiquity," he captured a strange truncation of history that has taken a number of forms in the twenty-first century.[1] One example is the vocabulary that emerged in the theory of narrative at about the same time, which named structuralism as the "classical" phase of narratology and announced a broad postclassical period in which the founding assumptions of narrative semiology were developed, challenged, or rejected by contemporary critics and theorists. I would like to begin my essay by exploring the idea that it was, in particular, what Thomas Pavel called "the moratorium on referential issues" that marked the difference between the classical and postclassical phases, and therefore that narratology (and perhaps narrative theory in general) has abandoned the rigorously formalist foundations of its structuralist heritage.[2] I would like to propose instead that the theory of narrative, and contemporary narratology in particular, remains inherently formalist in orientation, but that the understanding of formalism has changed.

Not many histories of contemporary narrative theory would advance such a straightforward plot, and yet the shape of this story is discernible in a number of influential accounts. Perhaps for obvious reasons, narrative theorists are unusually alert to the plot types that operate in their self-understandings and self-historicizations. Monika Fludernik, for example, identifies two competing plots in the history of narratology, the first of which she names "The Rise and Fall of Narratology" and the second, "The Rise and Rise of Narratology."[3] In the first story, narratology begins in groundbreaking methodologies proposed by Roland Barthes and Tzvetan Todorov, climaxes ecstatically in the work of Gérard Genette, and then plunges into decline and death; in the second, now dominant account, it begins in a corner of literary studies, diversifies, and spreads in a joyous gallimaufry of applications. For David Herman, the success of contemporary narratology, of its diversity and diversification, is often bound up exactly with overturning the moratorium on referential issues that, according to critics like Pavel, Lubomír Dolezel, and Marie-Laure Ryan, involved the use of tools "from model-theoretic or possible-worlds semantics to characterize the world-creating properties of narrative discourse."[4] Governed by the structuralist moratorium on referentiality, narratology is doomed, but when that ban is overturned, critics can return to questions about the worlds created by stories, by the events that take place in those worlds and the beings who inhabit them. It was critical for narrative theory that people, places, and events should be allowed back into the conversation, and obvious that any moratorium on these aspects of narrative would be limiting. In Herman's case, one move in particular reopens the door to what he calls the who, what, when, and why of narrative content: to complicate the idea that, because narrative texts are made of language, linguistics is the global science of literary analysis. For Herman, the key to narrative is the idea that a reader or listener constructs a mental model of the world to which he or she is asked to relocate, and for this reason, the interpretation of narrative is always a cognitive process. To establish cognitive science as the master discipline of narrative study is not simply to displace linguistics as the global science, but to recognize the centrality of linguistics in the mind sciences: that linguistics was always a resource for, if not one of, the mind sciences. For Herman, this synthesis was what lay ahead for narratology:

> Both narratology and linguistics will contribute to rethinking narrative as a strategy for making mental representations of the world. This sort of redrawing of the architecture of inquiry is, I contend, no trivial pursuit. For one thing, it suggests that narrative theorists should combine several methods of linguistic analysis to study aspects of narrative understanding. For another, it alters and enlargens the horizons of linguistic research itself, recasting language as a crucial interface between narrative and cognition.[5]

In this triangulation of language, narrative, and cognition, the top-down relation of linguistics to narratology that Roman Jakobson and others proposed in the 1960s becomes more conversational, and a larger range of linguistic perspectives are admitted to a domain limited by its adherence to Saussurean linguistics in particular.[6] For my purposes, the important thing about this expansion of the linguistic model is that, while the formal orientations of linguistics were preserved in narratology, the bracketing of referential issues that characterized some structuralist narrative theory was superseded.

If this analysis were to be developed in full, it would have to show that the moratorium on referential issues was never supported by any straightforward premise in Saussurean semiology. It is not easy to demonstrate that a critique of reference is part of Saussure's *Course in General Linguistics*, and harder still to find any basis for it in the structuralism of Claude Lévi-Strauss, Roland Barthes, Émile Benveniste, Roman Jakobson, or Louis Hjelmslev. If the critique of reference is in fact absent, then it might also seem bizarre that literary criticism in general, and narratology in particular, should have mistaken the relational character of structuralist linguistics for an edict that excluded the who, what, when, and why of narrative from analytical attention. The explanation of this influential fallacy, this unsupportable argument that structuralism somehow denied that language could refer to the world, may lie in the complex conditions and controversies that surrounded the emergence of deconstruction in the late 1960s and 1970s in the United States. That intellectual storm focused particularly on Jacques Derrida and Paul de Man, whose work was perceived as a challenge to some of the basic precepts of literary criticism: that a literary text is a communication, and that a text might refer to the world. There was a special uncertainty about deconstruction's relation to formalism: were these interventions to be understood as a kind of radical formalism? Was Derrida's grammatology a radicalization of the New Criticism's emphasis on texts? Two factors in particular contributed to this uncertainty. The first was a rich and established formalist tradition in American criticism that included New Critical approaches to poetry, rhetorical approaches to fiction, point-of-view analysis, and various forms of new Aristotelianism. In the early and mid-twentieth century, these established formalisms were engaged in an ongoing polemic with the proponents of literary history, and indeed of historicism more generally. The second factor was that literary structuralism in general, and structuralist narratology in particular, had not figured in this spat between formalism and historicism and had no real foothold in intellectual life in the United States in 1966, when Derrida's work began to emerge. Thus narrative semiology was the target neither of historicist polemics against formalism nor of rival formalist positions. Structuralist narratology became a focus of attention in the mid-1970s, largely thanks to the lustrous mediations of Jonathan Culler.

The simple story of a suspension and resumption of referential issues in narrative theory and criticism obscures this history of a belated engagement with structuralism and an established and different formalist tradition in the United States. Any description of contemporary formalisms in narrative theory must also attend to marked differences of national context, the explanations of which are historical, institutional, and cultural. Despite strong internationalist movements in contemporary narrative theory, these national differences make it difficult to describe any shared enterprise between, for example, the work of narrative semiotics and discourse analysis in Europe and the kind of narrative criticism that flourishes in Great Britain, or even to posit a recognizable Anglo-American alliance of the kind that was visible for most of the twentieth century. The new formalisms in narrative theory and criticism are not properly described as new in Scandinavia or Tel Aviv, where the influence of the linguistic model in narrative studies has been more or less unbroken, and, equally, the kinds of formalism that have emerged with the new narratologies in the United States have a particular history of combat with historicism only partly shared by European narratology. Great Britain, on the other hand, is notable for a kind of nonparticipation in the new narratological projects, despite a long history of engagement with theoretical transformations since the 1980s, and indigenous traditions of formal narrative study, such as literary stylistics. To reduce this complexity, it is useful to distinguish broad trends that adopt different attitudes to the authority of linguistic models in narrative theory, both within postclassical narratology, and alongside it. My description of contemporary formalisms will proceed by exploring the legacy of deconstruction in narrative theory today, since deconstruction was, and is, the principal rebellion against the tidy formalist categories of linguistic science, while itself remaining (as I will suggest) a variety of formalism.

Narrative theory may have a modernist antiquity and a classical phase in structuralism, but it also has an actual antiquity, in which its core questions of mimesis, rhetoric, and form were defined. In this section I want to consider the legacy of deconstruction in contemporary formalisms in relation to these two antiquities, one recent, the other distant. One way to see deconstruction's intervention in critical and social theory was as a refusal of key methodological decisions that were established in structuralism in the 1960s, chief among which was the idea that structuralist analysis was synchronic. Many of narrative theory's most formalist orientations founded themselves in this notion that analysis should show that signs operated in a large structure of differential relations in a language system that could be frozen in time. Narrative structure could also be described in this way, not as a temporal unfolding, but as a synchronic structure that could be apprehended by analysis as a simultaneity. Although synchronicity may be best understood as itself a temporal concept, methodologically it often banished temporality, even historicity, from analysis. The work that introduced Derrida in the United States between 1966 and 1980 was primarily a demonstration that philosophy could speak back to this methodological orientation by insisting upon temporal aspects of language and literature that might disrupt the settled structures postulated by the linguistic model.[7] Russell Daylight, in his analysis of Derrida's readings of Saussure, argues that this intervention had little to do with Saussure's own considerations of time in the *Course in General Linguistics*, and everything to do instead with the way that synchronicity had come to inform structuralist criticism:

> Derrida's reading of Saussure is not always attentive to the text of the *Course*, nor does it always appear to be in good faith. But Derrida's object of criticism was not primarily the text of 1916, but the structuralism of 1966: the structuralism of Lévi-Strauss, Lacan, Barthes, Benveniste, and Martinet; the phonology of Jakobson and the glossematics of Hjelmslev. This was a structuralism that was not rigorously Saussurean; perhaps even less so than Derrida's radical reappraisal.[8]

Daylight's argument suggests that the Saussurean model was not, in fact, blind to time, and therefore that it was the insistence in Derrida on the temporality of language that characterized his reappraisal and his intervention. This attack on structuralism's purportedly synchronic orientation was part of a more general emphasis, clearly visible in the mediations of structuralism in the 1970s and 80s, on the thematics of movement, deferral, and instability in deconstruction's account of signification (which was perhaps the more credible version of what deconstruction meant for formalist criticism). We might say, with Daylight, that structuralist method underwent significant revisions and developments in the course of its evolution that corrected some of the more drastic readings of Saussure, reinterpreting the linguistic model to allow for the readmission of banished content. I would argue, with the benefit of hindsight, that the synchronic method of structuralist criticism is the more relevant topic for an understanding of deconstruction and its relation to postclassical and poststructuralist movements in narrative theory than any moratorium on referential issues: temporality, not the referent, was banished by formalist orientations.

The question of time is clearly central to narrative theory; it is less clear that it is a profoundly formalist concern. If, as Monika Fludernik observes, the classical phase of narratology reaches its height in the work of Gérard Genette, we must recognize that there was already, in structuralism, a major contribution to the understanding of narrative time. Genette's categories of *order, duration,* and *frequency* offered to narratology a tense structure under which to analyze variations in temporal structure. The category of *anachrony*, with its subdivisions of *prolepsis* and *analepsis*, developed in Genette's readings of Proust, are an example of an enduring legacy for the analysis of narrative order. Genette's framework produces new, defining problems for contemporary narrative theory rather than offering tidy solutions to old ones, sometimes in conflict with Aristotelian approaches. The work of Meir Sternberg is an interesting case for its critique of Genette's legacy in the name of Aristotelian concepts. Sternberg belongs to the school of narratologists based in Tel Aviv, a group that combines rhetorical and functional approaches and has also directed narratology away from some of its Genettian heritage.[9] For Sternberg, Aristotle is the source of the most basic problems about narrative time, and the *Poetics* "offers in some ways a lure, in others a mirror, in yet others a contrast to present day theorizing about narrative."[10] According to Sternberg, Aristotle's trinity of curiosity, suspense, and surprise outlines the basic dynamics of narrative; and the neglect of surprise in contemporary narratology drives his enquiry into questions of chronology and teleology. Surprise, for Sternberg, is one of the few narrative concepts that "absolutely live by temporal manoeuvring":

> Methodologically, it provides a standard whereby to distinguish true from false claims for dechronologizing and, even more elusive, true claims for dechronologizing from false claims against narration by chronology. Theoretically, surprise leads us straight to the heart of narrative dynamics, uniquely interrelating the communicative with the mimetic process.[11]

Surprise thus stages the question of chronology in narrative, the point at which narrative often dechronologizes events in the order of presentation. It raises questions that Genette's account of anachrony avoids, about the possibility of a mimetic relationsnip between narrative order and life, and also about the communicative process that engages a reader in the decoding of a narrative sequence, a process governed by the dynamics of curiosity, suspense, and surprise. In Genette, for example, prolepsis is a kind of excursion into the future of events not yet narrated, to tell something out of turn; but for Sternberg, the subtraction of anticipation from the dynamic between narrative communication and mimesis limits our understanding:

> What in reason justifies the monopoly on anticipation given to "prolepsis" by overt statement, such as a narrator's foretelling or a hero's foreboding of death, at the expense of established (if tacit) convention to the same effect, such as our foreknowledge of the unhappy end in tragedy; or at the expense of straight chronological development, inevitably generating and often polarizing expectations about the future towards which it marches?[12]

There is something exemplary in this question, illustrating as it does a certain dissatisfaction with the separation of a linguistic object from the dynamics of reading, or from the complexities of anticipation and expectation in readerly engagement. Sternberg sees Genette's description as stabilizing the narrative object against such dynamics. It might also be argued that it creates a new problem in proposing an equivalence between the proleptic excursion into the future of a narration and the anticipation or expectation of events to come: It crosses between linguistic structure (narrative order) and psychological anticipation (readerly experience) in a way that blurs the definition of prolepsis. The crossing perhaps helps us understand a turn toward dynamic interaction that reintroduces some disorder into the structuralist narratologist's tidy schemes.

Sternberg's preference for surprise over anachrony was based in a new contract between the communicative and the mimetic process, though he also insists that the doctrine of mimesis, which distinguishes between the time structure of the telling and the supposedly objective time sequence to which it refers, obscures the true nature of discursive teleology "as a two-sided affair transacted between author and audience, telling and reading."[13] The complexities of this analysis cannot be explored here in full, but it is clear that Sternberg wishes to elevate certain aspects of Aristotle's approach (the concept of surprise) while modifying, demoting, or abandoning others (the bracketing of the audience in mimeticism).

A similar return to narrative theory's more ancient antiquity is at work in Paul Ricoeur's *Time and Narrative* (1983–1985), a work that both clarified and complicated our understanding of the relationship between the Aristotelian and structuralist orientations in narrative theory, particularly on the topic of time.[14] Ricoeur's work was crucial for grasping both referentiality and temporality, and for rethinking mimesis as an interactive and dynamic process. For Ricoeur, mimesis is to be understood as a circle in which the configuration of plot (Aristotle's *muthos*) is but one part, the middle part, of a three-staged process by which narrative representations reflect and reshape the world of action. In the first place (the *prefiguration* of what Ricoeur calls $Mimesis_1$), a reader brings to a narrative a certain pre-understanding of the world, a certain experience and conceptualization of time that makes narrative comprehension possible; in the second stage (the *configuration* of $Mimesis_2$), events are given the shape of a plot, arranged, ordered, told; and in the third stage (the *refiguration* of $Mimesis_3$), we emerge from the narrative with a modified understanding of the world. These three parts of mimesis form a circle because the refigured understanding produced when we grasp a plot becomes part of a more general understanding of life and human action, an understanding that in turn modifies the preunderstanding that we bring to narrative in the first place. Importantly, this account of mimesis departs significantly from the classical formulation of imitation as a similarity between life and art, since similarity between a plot and lived temporal experience would produce no circulation whatever between life and art. In Ricoeur, it often seems that the circle turns at all only because of the difference between the temporal properties of narrative and of life, between the modification of art by life and of life by art. There is, in other words, a relation of fundamental dissimilarity at the heart of

Ricoeur's new mimesis that marks the difference between two zones: a narrative universe, in which the present is not present and the future has already happened; and the time of life, in which the present is ineluctable and the future is open, contingent, and unknowable.

In Ricoeur's work, there is a feeling that the reading of a narrative is not the easy consumption of a successful simulation, but a kind of struggle produced in this relation of dissimilarity, by the mismatch between narrative time and lived temporal becoming. The narrative present, for Ricoeur, is a quasi-present, which is to say that it is somebody else's present experienced vicariously by a reader *as if* it were unfolding before the eye. It is a present that has the form of the past, in the sense that it is rendered in the past tense, in the factive mood that applies to that which has already taken place, but decoded as a kind of presence. We might say that the past tense is not actually the relevant fact here about written narrative, since a narrative can be written in the present tense, and that it is the written nature of the written narrative, its very inscription, that announces the already-complete character of the narrative present (rather than the tense that refers to it in the past). According to the logic of Ricoeur's mimesis, we would then expect the form of written narrative, perhaps even the fact of writing itself, to inflect our experience of time in life: for the present-present to be modified by the past-present that we experience in narrative, or for the already-complete future of narrative to alter our conceptualizations of the open and opaque future.

Three aspects of Ricoeur's work come very close to deconstruction: first, the sense of struggle to reconcile fundamental dissimilarities, the temporal disjunction, between narrative time and lived experience; second, a mismatch between time and tense that Ricoeur takes to be always a part of that struggle, and the consequent recourse to the category of writing, rather than the tense of the verb, to determine temporal reference; third, a more general entanglement between the form of narrative time and the idea of lived experience, the idea that life might be modified by narrative, or that the present might be structured, in life as it is in narrative, by retrospection. These blurrings and entanglements, taken in conjunction with the new mimesis as a perpetual circulation, specify the distance between Ricoeur and the early formalist taxonomies, and the extent to which time, reference, and temporal reference have reestablished themselves in contemporary narrative theory. But they also bespeak a certain difficulty for any criticism with formalist tendencies: namely, that the analysis of temporal reference might not be anchored in textual cues or grammatical features of the text of the kind that established the linguistic model as the global science in narratology. One of the legacies of deconstruction (as we shall see in the next section) might be this emerging methodological position, for which the analysis of narrative form, far from being merely an extension of the grammatical analysis of a sentence as Barthes had described it,[15] might have to lift anchor from the formal properties of narrative sentences, or accept that the descriptive categories of the linguistic model might not capture these interactive and dynamic aspects of narrative comprehension.

The counterintuitive idea that some contemporary formalisms do not anchor themselves in formal, linguistic, or structural observation helps clarify the meaning and orientation of formalism in much of today's narratology. I have suggested that the postclassical phase of narratology departs from the classical linguistic phase in two ways: first, by admitting to the arena the dynamic engagement between textual cues and the activity of reading; second, by establishing the mind sciences as the model that not only informs but also is altered by postclassical narratology. In both cases, let us say for Sternberg and for Herman, the idea of the analytical model has been considerably expanded beyond Saussurean linguistics, and exactitude has been compromised. In Sternberg and in Ricoeur, we can see formalist method reaching back to its more distant antiquity in Aristotle and the concept of mimesis, and the need for a new mimesis capable of moving beyond what Derrida called the "order of truth": "the precedence of the imitated, that governs the philosophical or critical interpretation of 'literature', if not the operation of literary writing."[16] The question of time in particular brings into the foreground a certain disjunction between the textual surface of narrative and the complex temporal structures of reference that a fictional narrative can deploy. I would like to end, therefore, by offering two examples of these tendencies that adopt quite different approaches to the question of time. The first, from David Herman, represents a postclassical expansion of the linguistic model; the second, from Martin Hägglund, develops a recognizably Derridean model.

In *Story Logic*, Herman's discussion of temporality begins by setting out some of the achievements of classical narratology in the description of temporal structure, principally Genette's categories of order, duration, and frequency. Herman argues that these categories, which did so much to capture the ways in which "narratives cue recipients to build *temporally organized* models of the situations, events and entities told about over the course of a story," are less useful when it comes to inexactitude in narrative time:

> [I]nexactness with respect to the ordering of events in the storyworld constitutes a narrative strategy not easily described in classical terms. Inexactness of ordering prompts readers to model a world in which the temporal position of certain events remains indeterminate. Equally uncertain are the temporal and causal relations pertaining *between* indeterminately ordered events.[17]

Some narratives, Herman suggests, deliberately exploit such indefiniteness, and produce a "baroque temporal syntax that puts questions of before and after into question." Herman calls this "fuzzy temporality," a category that does not figure in classical frameworks, though many of our most complex stories are marked by it. Genette was not unaware of such ambiguous structures in his discussion of anachrony in Proust, but he tended to view them as instances of "timelessness," events that "somewhat disturb our reassuring ideas of retrospection and anticipation."[18] For Herman, there are reasons not to conflate the temporally indeterminate or the unplaceable with the timeless, since our not knowing is not to be confused with the achronic, or that which lies outside time. These are, for Herman, purposeful forms of vagueness, and our uncertainty is therefore produced as part of the work's aesthetic project, just as other forms of not knowing are controlled and produced by textual cues and absences. Sometimes, Herman argues, the aesthetic project supported by this kind of vagueness is a self-multiplication: a "kind of narrative that exploits indefiniteness to pluralize and delinearize itself, to multiply the ways in which the events being recounted can be chained together to produce 'the' narrative itself," and for the description of these multiple time frames, "narratologists might be warranted in using the term polychrony rather than achrony."[19] Herman illustrates this with a story by Anna Seghers, "Der Ausflug der toten Mädchen" (1943), which "purposely resists linearity by multiplying ways in which narrative events can be ordered."[20] Herman discusses in detail the textual cues that both allow readers to plot and prevent readers from plotting past events on a timeline, and in this duality an important methodological departure appears. Herman argues that polychrony is encoded in the textual surface of the discourse but that there is also "a more general way of characterizing the story's fuzzy temporal ordering": it prompts readers to make causal inferences about events at the same time that it "brings the scope and validity of those same inferences into question."[21] This contradiction belongs to the work, and yet it also describes a relation between textual cues and the readerly inferences they prompt but that are not themselves observable in linguistic form. On the one hand, writers exploit lexical and grammatical features; on the other hand, these features trigger complex acts of interpretation – in this case between contradictory preference rules available to the reader:

> The first rule: Use a bivalent temporal system to read later events as effects of earlier events and earlier events as causes of later ones. The second rule: Use a multivalent temporal system to read some events as indeterminate, that is, as occupying an inherently vague position on the chain of cause and effect undergirding the story, such that an event might precede its cause.[22]

Preference rules, and these more general questions of linguistic cues, prompts, and readerly inferences of causation, derive from functionalist rather than structuralist approaches. Herman characterizes the difference as follows:

> [F]unctional grammar reverses the direction of traditional grammatical explanations: instead of moving from an analysis of the forms of a language to an expression of what they mean, functionalist approaches proceed from an account of language as a system of meanings to an analysis of the forms by which those meanings can be realized.[23]

The linguistic model therefore ceases to describe a structural system and instead works backwards from concepts of meaning to forms that might produce, prompt certain kinds of inference in narrative comprehension. Although the critic must speculate about those inferences, Herman's approach nevertheless produces a formalism different from the kind that describes only what can be observed on the textual surface. It is on this basis that postclassical narratology has, mainly under Herman's direction, developed the notion of the mental model of a world in narrative comprehension, and has altered not only the narratological method but the classical theory of mimesis that underpins it. As a result, the value of inexactitude, which seemed alien to the literary structuralist, becomes part of the account of those mental representations in a way that runs parallel with the critique of stability developed in poststructuralist responses to structuralism. Vagueness supports an inversion of cause and effect that, in Herman's multivalent temporal system, recalls the logic of so many deconstructionist readings.

My second example affiliates itself openly with the Derridean critique of linguistic science and, at the same time, offers an account of time that pitches itself confidently against the possibility of timelessness. If David Herman's expansion of the linguistic model redraws the line between the formal and semantic properties of language, Martin Hägglund's approach to narrative roots itself in the concept that most directly defines Derrida's critique of synchronicity, namely the *trace*. Hägglund develops and clarifies both the logic and the philosophical implications of the trace. Derrida's readings of Saussure focus on the explicit phonocentrism (the sound-basis) of the analytical system and the idea of synchronicity by which it attempts to render time as structure. The concept of the trace addresses both of these concerns, being an account both of the sign as a written mark and of time as succession. In Derrida's writings on the trace, and its cognate terms, *arche-writing* and *différance*, we find language and time together, in categories that understand presence as a kind of impossible stasis and an unattainable self-identity. The presence of meaning is grounded in *temporal* presence, and it is thus understood as an indivisible presence, and not, as Derrida would say, constituted by retentions of the past and protentions of the future. The trace is a synthesis of these orientations toward what has been and what is to come that installs temporal succession in the very heart of the present, and therefore represents a temporalization of the sign, which exists always in a sequence that comes to mean only by bearing the traces of those that come before and after. Hägglund ably spells out the relationship between the trace, the issue of inscription (or writing), and the nature of temporal succession:

> Derrida defines the trace as the becoming-space of time and the becoming-time of space, which he abbreviates as spacing (*espacement*). This structure should not itself be understood as a *temporal* process, where time becomes space and space becomes time, but rather designates a *logical* co-implication of time and space. This logical co-implication is already implicit in the basic formulation of the problem of succession, namely, that the moment comes into being *at the same time* as it ceases to be. Given that every temporal moment immediately ceases to be, it must be inscribed as a trace in order to be at all.[24]

The trace, in other words, is spacing, or the making spatial of time, and it is the temporalization of space, since the trace is what enables the past to remain for the future, and for this, its present moment must be inscribed. Hägglund links time and writing, offering a formal argument that connects the logical co-implication of time and space to the question of meaning. The supervenience of time and space works as a methodological critique of synchronicity, but it also describes the metaphysics at work in writing. The question of inscription at the heart of the trace is, in other words, a formal logic that applies to any inscription, or any written sentence, and it is also a philosophical logic that describes a metaphysics of time that unsettles not only questions of meaning, but of identity more generally. As a reader of narrative, Hägglund prefers to focus on the second of these issues, in what we might refer to as a thematic (rather than formalist) approach. He identifies in the criticism on Virginia Woolf, for example, a tendency to focus on "moments of being," an aesthetic ambition that runs through all of her work to escape from the ephemeral into the timeless. Hägglund shows, on the contrary, that Woolf's interest in the moment is anything but an ambition toward timelessness, but rather a passion for the "radical temporality of life": the moment can only be given *as* a moment by passing away, and it is the passing away of the moment that induces the passion for it. Similarly, Proust's commentators have consistently argued that the *Recherche* "culminates in the revelation of a timeless being," which offends once more against the synthesis of the trace structure and the logical co-implication of time and space. Against the canonical reading,

Hägglund presents a "chronolibidinal" counterargument that seeks to show that all forms of timelessness should be understood as unbreachable attachments to temporal life. These are thematic readings in the sense that they do not root themselves in linguistic structures, or proceed through the observation of formal or structural properties of narrative; but they also represent the extent to which a Derridean model can work in the service of a distinctly referential aesthetic and methodology, one that operates according to a formal philosophical logic but that also wants to account for Woolf's ability to depict moments of time in their unique texture, or describe Marcel's ecstatic experience of involuntary memory in a philosophical language.

I claimed above that narrative theory and narratology might be inherently formalist in orientation, and also that the topic of time is a profoundly formalist concern. The examples offered here – Sternberg's invocations of, and disputes with, Aristotle; Ricoeur's reconstruction of the problem of mimesis; Herman's synthesis of structuralist and functionalist models; and Hägglund's applications of Derrida's trace structure to novelistic aesthetics – illustrate a number of things about contemporary formalisms. They show the tension between the different horizons of the modernist antiquity proposed by T. J. Clark and the ancient antiquity of Aristotelian poetics. There is clear evidence of diversification, on the story model that Fludernik proposed as "the rise and rise of narratology," to the point that we may question the continuing utility of the category of formalism itself. We can note a kind of convergence between once-opposed schools and orientations, partly brought about by an ongoing expansion of the linguistic model in narratology to embrace and include semantic and referential aspects of narrative. We can also recognize new projects, such as the description of narrative temporality, which forge new relations between formal and thematic engagements with time. The diversification and the synthesis might be so broad as to justify the conclusion that contemporary narrative theory has completed the project, begun in the 1960s by deconstruction, of drumming the concept of form, and its methodologies, out of what Ricoeur called the kingdom of the *as if*.

Notes

1. T. J. Clark, *Farewell to an Idea: Episodes from a History of Modernism* (New Haven, CT: Yale University Press, 1999), 3.
2. Thomas Pavel, *Fictional Worlds* (Cambridge, MA: Harvard University Press, 1986), 10.
3. Monika Fludernik, "Histories of Narrative Theory II: From Structuralism to the Present," in *A Companion to Narrative Theory*, ed. James Phelan and Peter Rabinowitz (Oxford: Blackwell, 2005), 36–7.

4. David Herman, *Story Logic: Problems and Possibilities of Narrative* (Lincoln: University of Nebraska Press, 2002), 4.
5. Herman, *Story Logic*, 5.
6. See Roman Jakobson, "Closing Statement: Linguistics and Poetics" in *Style in Language*, ed. Thomas Albert Sebeok (Cambridge, MA: MIT Press, 1960), 35.
7. See Jacques Derrida, "Structure, Sign, and Play in the Discourse of the Human Sciences," in *The Structuralist Controversy: The Languages of Criticism and the Sciences of Man*, ed. Richard Macksey and Eugenio Donato (Baltimore, MD: Johns Hopkins University Press, 1972).
8. Russell Daylight, *What if Derrida Was Wrong about Saussure?* (Edinburgh: Edinburgh University Press, 2012), 185.
9. See Eyal Segal, "The 'Tel Aviv School': A Rhetorical-Functional Approach to Narrative," in *Current Trends in Narratology*, ed. Greta Olson (New York, NY: Walter Gruyter, 2011), 297–311.
10. Meir Sternberg, "Telling in Time II: Chronology, Teleology, Narrativity," *Poetics Today* 13 (1992): 474.
11. Ibid., 507.
12. Ibid., 495.
13. Ibid., 513.
14. Paul Ricoeur, *Time and Narrative*, 3 vols., trans. Kathleen McLaughlin and David Pellauer (Chicago, IL: University of Chicago Press, 1984–1988).
15. Roland Barthes, "Introduction to the Structural Analysis of Narratives," *Image-Music-Text*, trans. Stephen Heath (New York, NY: Noonday-Farrar, Straus and Giroux, 1977), 83.
16. Jacques Derrida, "The Double Session," in *Dissemination*, trans. Barbara Johnson (Chicago, IL: University of Chicago Press, 1981), 192.
17. Herman, *Story Logic*, 218.
18. Gérard Genette, *Narrative Discourse: An Essay in Method*, trans. Jane E. Lewin (Ithaca, NY: Cornell University Press, 1980), 83.
19. Herman, *Story Logic*, 219.
20. Ibid., 221.
21. Ibid., 225.
22. Ibid.
23. Ibid., 126.
24. Martin Hägglund, *Dying for Time: Proust, Woolf, Nabokov* (Cambridge, MA: Harvard University Press, 2012), 15.

15

PATRICK JAGODA

Digital Games and Narrative

Introduction: Convergences of Games and Narrative

Digital games offer an opportunity for complicating and expanding the domain of literary studies in general and narrative theory in particular. Games can be studied as simulations with mechanics, rules, and objectives, but also as narratives that enter into conversations with both print and electronic media. The questions that resonate throughout the following pages are these: First, how do digital games approach, incorporate, and transform narrative? Second, what can narrative theorists contribute to the growing field of digital game studies that has seen much of its strongest work since the 1990s undertaken through methods emerging from art history, media theory, software studies, and platform studies? Finally, what might game studies contribute reciprocally to narrative theory in the twenty-first century?

Medium-specific analysis continues to be an important approach in game studies, especially as a corrective in the late 1990s and early 2000s by "ludologists" who were responding to an insufficiently discriminating incorporation of games by "narratologists."[1] At the same time, there is much to gain from comparative analyses between media and forms.[2] As Marie-Laure Ryan observes, "different media often incorporate common tracks or semiotic systems."[3] Rather than positing a strict definition of narrative games, or suggesting that English, Comparative Literature, or Rhetoric departments are the *proper* disciplinary landing spots for the future study of games, this chapter explores different ways that digital games enter into fruitful exchanges with narrative texts and could profit from continued study by literary critics.

Although I focus on narrative, it is worth foregrounding a broader convergence that is made visible by works that emerge at the boundaries or create new overlapping zones of the literary and the ludic. Digital games often resemble literary texts and come into conversation with them in a variety of ways. They do so, for instance, through both visual and verbal puns; metaphor, metonymy, and synecdoche; systemic interrelations of parts that create totalities that exceed the sum of the parts; imagistic condensations; multiple avatar perspectives or character viewpoints; interpellation of readers and players; affective modalities; visualizations of textual descriptions; different varieties of difficulty; and, as the focus of this chapter demonstrates, narrative forms, techniques, and media. In the early twenty-first century, games and literary texts also increasingly share distribution technologies, production and consumption mechanisms, forms of cultural knowledge, grant and research-support organizations, and professional and scholarly communities.

It is not insignificant that the works that I explore in this chapter are largely marketed and disseminated *as games*, and that they respond to specific genres and affordances that belong to the history of analog, computer, and video games. Nevertheless, I propose that we embrace the richness of the dual, though converging, lineage of narratives and games – much as Katherine Hayles has long done with her capacious sense of "electronic literature" that includes both literary and computational dimensions.[4] With a diversity of intersections between games and narrative, it is nonetheless important to think with greater care about ways that digital games expand and complicate how we think about storytelling. Certainly, numerous digital games, from *Tetris* (1984) to *The Marriage* (2007), do not include narratives and are primarily procedural, rule-based, and objective-oriented. Similarly, many analog games – card games like bridge or strategy board games like chess – do not depend on fictional scenarios or navigable worlds. Indeed, game studies scholar Gonzalo Frasca insists upon a firm distinction between "representation" and "simulation." For him, the difference between reading a novel and playing a simulation game is immense. Even within the realm of games themselves, "the feeling of playing soccer cannot be compared to the one of watching a match."[5]

The conceptual difference between representation and simulation – and by extension narrative and games – still serves as a useful heuristic. This chapter, however, contends that in a significant number of games these aspects are concurrent and compatible. Increasingly, digital games blur with categories such as interactive narratives or fictions. Many twenty-first-century videogames, such as *Bioshock* (2007), *Heavy Rain* (2010), *The Walking Dead* (2012), and *Life Is Strange* (2015), are concerned, first and foremost, with world creation, decision making, and storytelling. There are surely differences worth emphasizing between games and narrative texts, as when Hayles paraphrases Markku Eskelinen to observe that "with games the user interprets in order to configure, whereas in works whose primary interest is narrative, the user configures in order to interpret."[6] With a larger volume of artistically, literarily, and narratively inclined games, however, it is growing more difficult to determine, in certain cases, whether configuration or interpretation carries greater weight. Certainly, the habits and cultures of readers and players, writers and designers are not identical, but neither are these subject positions always separate. In light of the proliferation of narrative games and the diversity of ways in which players now encounter them, it is important to complicate the antinomy between narrative and games.

Game studies has already produced important work on topics such as the history of videogame software and platforms, the ethics of computer games, videogame violence, avant-garde and art games, the dynamics of gaming culture and eSports, and much more. Even as a number of careful analyses exist, scholars have more often tended toward a theoretically driven or culturally focused approach that treats particular games in a hasty and instrumental fashion. Attending more closely to narrative in games offers a way to understand how they work along aesthetic and formal, but also cultural and technological, lines. A narrative engagement with digital games is something that literary scholars are particularly capable of adding to the ever-expanding study of games.

There is no single or primary way in which digital games, since their emergence in the 1960s, have come into conversation with narrative. For this reason, I resist introducing yet another new umbrella term or theorizing the convergence of narrative and games *in general*. In mapping some of these convergences (an ongoing and large-scale project toward which this chapter can only gesture), it is important to consider comparative possibilities of content and form, genre and media, consumption and dissemination. In the four sections that follow, I offer a series of brief analytical categories and concepts that are organized around exemplary cases and genres of narrative games. These categories invite bidirectional analyses of narrative and games, and emphasize their convergences. In the first section, I consider text adventure games and interactive fiction, which are the closest analogs to text-based, print narratives and are arguably the narrative games to receive the most attention from literary critics to date. Despite similarities with print literary narratives, these texts encourage play that mediates between their technical platforms and their narrative affordances. In the second section, as ludology has demonstrated, narrative analysis of games demands medium specificity. I suggest one way that this approach might work through the type of spatial storytelling that supersedes textual narrative exposition in most games. In the third section, although medium specificity is important, narrative games also appear increasingly in a transmedia environment that promotes movement across media. As such, I analyze different ways that narrative games engage in adaptation across media. In the fourth and final section, I move from questions of form and design to the role of the player in narrative games. Here, I examine emergent stories that players improvise in games, as well as stories that players create for others through the use of software. All four of these sections explore ways in which narrative theory might help us better understand videogames and similar narrative-oriented media. In conclusion, I speculate regarding the opposite possibility that digital games might help us better understand – indeed, more actively *play with* – the print narrative texts that remain at the core of literary criticism. Overall, this chapter contends that the frequency and diversity of narrative in games serves as evidence of this convergence as a generative intellectual domain for ongoing scholarship.[7]

Textual Play: Adventure Games and Interactive Fiction

The history of digital games includes numerous works that privilege text-based narrative exposition. Two notable categories of such games are "text adventure games" and "interactive fiction." The differences between these categories are not completely agreed upon among critics and are often minimal, depending for instance on the distinction between the emphasis on puzzle solving in text adventures versus the focus on storytelling in interactive fiction. Both genres receive frequent comparisons to earlier *Choose Your Own Adventure* novels on the one hand and contemporary videogames on the other. I begin with these genres because they are largely undecidable limit cases that bring electronic literature and videogame studies into conversation and bidirectional analysis.

Text-based narrative game genres reached their height of popularity in the 1970s and 1980s. In most cases, they require players to type in instructions (usually verb-noun combinations) and to solve spatial-, verbal-, and object-oriented puzzles in order to reveal textual passages of a larger narrative. Text-only games such as *Colossal Cave Adventure* (1976), *Zork* (1977), and *Trinity* (1986), as well as adventure games with visual graphics such as *Mystery House* (1980), have already received critical attention in electronic literary circles. The same is true of multiplayer text adventure games, MUDs or Multi-User Dungeons such as *MUD1* (1978) and *AberMUD* (1987), which had much in common with single-player text adventures. In many cases, the multiplayer games adapted the rules of the narrative and role-playing tabletop game series *Dungeons & Dragons* (1974) for online play. Other text-based MUDs, such as *TinyMUD* (1989), deemphasized combat in favor of social interactions, role-playing, and world building.[8]

A critical appraisal of text adventures and interactive narratives has already benefited from applications of classical narrative theory.[9] It is also important, however, to emphasize the way that such texts allow for play that oscillates between their technical platforms on the one hand and their narratives on the other. Emily Short's interactive fiction work *Galatea* (2000) offers an exemplary case. In this work, Short creates a digital update of the Greek myth about the sculptor Pygmalion, who falls in love with his statue of Galatea, which Aphrodite then brings to life.[10] In *Galatea*, the player encounters a textual interface that describes a statue of Galatea that sits on a pedestal: "Unlit, except for the single spotlight; unfurnished, except for the defining swath of black velvet. And a placard on a little stand. On the pedestal is Galatea." Beyond this description is a command line into which the player can type in a statement in order to explore the space, converse with Galatea, and move forward in the narrative. As multiple engagements with *Galatea* demonstrate, the work is multilinear, leading to numerous and mutually exclusive endings. As Short herself has written of the form, "What I wanted to do was give the player the impression that the universe was completely open-ended, and that, rather than fumbling among a large number of options to find the one that I had chosen to implement, he could meaningfully do just about anything and get some kind of result."[11]

In order to come to terms with a game that feels "completely open-ended" in terms of narrative and world, but in fact is not, one must consider how *Galatea*'s technical platform relates to its formal narrative dimensions. Short created *Galatea* using the Inform programming language that has been used in a variety of interactive fiction works, ranging from Graham Nelson's *Curses* (1993) to Star C. Foster and Daniel Ravipinto's *Slouching towards Bedlam* (2003). Notably, games created in Inform depart from earlier text adventures in which a player usually types in a combination of a verb and a noun to describe an action ("open mailbox"). By contrast, *Galatea* is built primarily on a structure of relations between objects. Possible relations include the containment relation ("the letter is in the mailbox"), carrying relation ("the woman carried the letter"), adjacency relation ("the mailbox is south of the house"), and visibility relation ("the woman can see the mailbox").[12] Although *Galatea* enables a number of interaction types, the player frequently types in a sentence that includes a verb, an indirect object, and a direct object in the form of "ask Galatea about death." The player's action brings two objects ("Galatea" and "death") into relation in order to unlock new pieces of narrative. Short is savvy in the way she creates a resonance between the technical affordances of the Inform programming language (especially the way it privileges relations between objects) with the narrative form (a dialogue between the player and Galatea). Furthermore, the work may feel infinite in its scope because of a combination of its modular organization of nonlinear narrative units

(Galatea's answers to player questions) and a lack of feedback about whether the player has exhausted all possible endings.

Galatea is truly a narrative game insofar as it interpellates a person as both a narrative reader and a game player. On the one hand, if we provisionally treat narrative, following Ryan's account, as a text that must offer a sequence of events and "create a world and populate it with characters and objects" that "undergo changes of state" and enable "the reconstruction of an interpretive network," then *Galatea* qualifies.[13] The narrative is made up of a sequence of statements by the eponymous statue, the narration of past events, and the evocation of a broader world of characters and objects that change over time. Unlike the majority of prose narrative, this piece of interactive fiction can additionally be described as a "nonlinear" or more specifically a "multilinear" narrative.

Simultaneously, we can characterize *Galatea* as a game. Katie Salen and Eric Zimmerman offer a composite definition of a game as "a system in which players engage in an artificial conflict, defined by rules, that results in a quantifiable outcome."[14] In *Galatea*, "players" enter a "system" created by Emily Short in the Inform language, engage in an "artificial conflict" represented by Galatea's resistance to particular lines of questioning, follow a series of "rules" that takes the form of grammatical protocols about how to interact with Galatea, and pursue a "quantifiable outcome" in the form of varied endings to the interaction. Rather than deciding between these two possible classifications, a thorough analysis of a work such as *Galatea* depends on attending to the particular simultaneity of and convergences between narrative and game form.

Medium Specificity: Spatial Storytelling in Games

Medium specificity in game studies, which reached a critical threshold with the articulation of ludology as well as specific frameworks such as Ian Bogost's "procedural rhetoric," usefully informs the ways in which critics can analyze narrative in games.[15] One of the central medium-specific qualities of "digital environments," an umbrella concept developed by Janet Murray in 1997, is their spatial character. Computer programs, as Murray observes, can "represent navigable space." Moreover, "Linear media such as books and films can portray space, either by verbal description or image, but only digital environments can present space that we can move through."[16] The category of space becomes crucial to understanding videogames in general and narrative games in particular.

As new media scholar Henry Jenkins points out, when games incorporate narrative, they do not convey stories in the same way as novels, films, or television series. Digital games tend to replace linearity with nonlinear spatial organization. For this reason Jenkins contends that game designers might best be understood not as "storytellers" but as "narrative architects."[17] Spatial navigation proves primary in a variety of game genres, including the sequence of life events in the modern board of the *Game of Life* (1960), the linguistically represented cave space of the PC text adventure *Colossal Cave Adventure* (1976), the graphical castle environment of the Atari 2600 videogame *Adventure* (1980), and the massive three-dimensional realms of the open-world videogame *The Elder Scrolls V: Skyrim* (2013). Drawing from a range of examples, Jenkins offers a useful four-part taxonomy of modes of environmental storytelling:

> Environmental storytelling creates the preconditions for an immersive narrative experience in at least one of four ways: spatial stories can evoke pre-existing narrative associations; they can provide a staging ground where narrative events are enacted; they may embed narrative information within their mise-en-scene; or they provide resources for emergent narratives.[18]

Environmental or spatial stories expressed through games provide the medium-specific interface and tools for evoking, enacting, embedding, or enabling emergent narrative.

In order to elaborate these modes of narrative, it is useful to turn to the case of the videogame *Gone Home* (2013). Though this game does not exhaust the ways in which games convey spatial stories, it offers a variety of instructive examples. Notably, narrative is the central pleasure of *Gone Home* rather than a decorative or supplementary element that motivates gameplay. In 1995, the playable character of twenty-one-year-old Kaitlin Greenbriar returns from a one-year study-abroad trip in Europe. Upon arrival in the middle of the night at her family's new home in Arbor Hill, Oregon, Kaitlin finds the house evacuated of its usual residents: her mother, Janice; father, Terry; and sister, Sam. *Gone Home* invites the player to navigate a three-dimensional world from a first-person perspective. From the beginning, the game activates the familiar spatial experience and movement dynamics of first-person shooter games such as the *BioShock* series (the three founders of the Fullbright Company that designed the game previously worked on *BioShock 2: Minerva's Den*). Even as *Gone Home*'s interface implies a first-person shooter game genre and a horror narrative genre, the gameplay includes no shooting or combat. The player can only walk around the house, explore, pick up objects, read letters, listen to and watch media, and attempt to understand the ordinary secrets kept by Kaitlin's family. In other words, the primary work of the game involves making sense of the narratives contained within the house. The game's climax encourages one to read the "primary" narrative as the history of Sam and her lesbian relationship with Lonnie that led her to leave home.[19]

Across its approximately two-hour duration, *Gone Home* occasions all four of the forms of spatial storytelling that Jenkins elaborates. First, the game *evokes* narrative by borrowing from widely recognized genre conventions, especially of horror and the ghost story. Even prior to introducing its key narrative events, the game creates an atmosphere and invokes a genre that introduces narrative assumptions. Although the game uses familiar tropes such as a spooky, abandoned house on a dark and stormy night, it ultimately stages a reversal of expectation by emphasizing, for example, a narrative of Sam discovering her sexuality. Second, *Gone Home* offers a space in which the player *enacts* narrative events by exploring objects and spaces throughout the house. In some cases, this involves "broadly defined goals or conflicts." For instance, the player finds that a number of doors in the house are locked and require keys (e.g., the key to the front door that is hidden underneath a decorative Christmas duck) and passwords (e.g., the code to open Sam's locker) to yield further narrative discoveries. These challenges in the game require the player to explore the space and discover what Jenkins calls "micronarratives" that are organized around the small cast of absent characters. Third, the game *embeds* fragmented pieces of a linear story that the player must collect and reconstruct. In this case, the "game world becomes a kind of information space, a memory palace." The house is filled with letters, postcards, posters, VHS tapes, and tape cassettes that offer clues about the past and present of Kaitlin's family. In particular, the player searches for twenty-three entries of Sam's journal that together reveal what happened to her. Fourth, and finally, *Gone Home* presents a nonlinear space in which a story *emerges* in a variety of ways. As Jenkins contends, "emergent narratives are not pre-structures or pre-programmed."[20] Though the objects in *Gone Home*'s open world are finite, the emotional impact of the narrative varies depending on the sequence and manner in which the player encounters these objects. Moreover, the game invites players to tell different narratives of exploration with voiceovers for spectators to watch, for instance via YouTube.

Overall, these four modes of storytelling depart from the narrative techniques available to a novel or film, insofar as the game depends on player decisions and thereby introduces greater variability into the experience. Even so, game spaces invite experiences of and contributions to the narrative world. A growing number of independent videogames – including *Dear Esther* (2012), *The Stanley Parable* (2013), *Moirai* (2013), *The Beginner's Guide* (2015), *Everybody's Gone to the Rapture* (2015), and *Firewatch* (2016) – rely almost exclusively on the types of spatial storytelling that

Jenkins outlined over a decade ago. However, it is equally important to consider how such techniques inform even contemporary works that might primarily be characterized as action-adventure games such as *Uncharted 4: A Thief's End* (2016) or puzzle-platformer games such as *Inside* (2016).

Transmedia Analysis: Narrative Adaptation in Videogames

Spatial storytelling is increasingly situated within a multimedia and transmedia ecology. There are many ways of thinking about movement among and across media within narrative theory, one of which is adaptation. For example, a variety of games adapt literary texts into interactive formats. Such games include Frogwares's *Sherlock Holmes* puzzle-oriented game series (released between 2002 and 2012), Inevitable Entertainment's action-adventure *The Hobbit* (2003), and Charlie Hoey's platform game *The Great Gatsby* (2010). Videogame adaptations of films are also plentiful, including arcade games such as *Terminator 2: Judgment Day* (1991) and console games such as *GoldenEye 007* (1997). In tracking specific adaptation choices, critics might think more about the way that different modes of adaptation – for instance, film theorist Dudley Andrew's categories of "borrowing, intersection, and fidelity of transformation" – operate in videogames.[21] Games, after all, often share codes and techniques (such as narrative) with other media, while also introducing unique features such as navigable spatial worlds, hypermediated interfaces, and action-based mechanics. While many games seek fidelity to a popular narrative or at least evoke identifiable features of its world, others occasion more complex encounters or translations of texts from other media.

A notable example of a game that engages in adaptation without considerable narrative fidelity is Jonathan Blow's *Braid* (2008). This platforming game borrows elements of the *Super Mario Bros.* videogame series and introduces an innovation that allows the player to reverse time and manipulate it in unique ways in each world. *Braid* was inspired by two literary print texts: Italo Calvino's *Invisible Cities* (1972) and Alan Lightman's *Einstein's Dreams* (1992). Although the game is not a direct adaptation at the level of narrative, the influence of these experimental texts persists at representational, structural, and even procedural levels. In *Einstein's Dreams*, Lightman composes a series of vignette-length thought experiments about how alternative temporal logics might impact human life. In one such scenario, he writes, "There is a place where time stands still. [...] As a traveler approaches this place from any direction, he moves more and more slowly. [...] From this place, time travels outwards in concentric circles – at rest at the center, slowly picking up speed at greater diameters."[22] This passage enters *Braid* neither through quotation nor literal graphical reproduction, but instead through an elaboration at the level of the game mechanic. In the fifth world, the protagonist, Tim, has the ability to drop a ring that slows objects, including Tim's own movements, based on their proximity to the ring's center. Though the details of Lightman's vignette do not appear in *Braid* at a representational level, Blow turns the world of the thought experiment into an action-oriented scenario that allows the player to experiment with alternative physics and the temporality suggested by the original passage. This game mechanic, in turn, inflects the larger narrative of the game.

Although *Braid* does not depend on print as centrally as *Einstein's Dreams*, the game reflects on the convergence between the media of print books and videogames that undergirds the adaptation. At the entryway to each world, the player passes across lecterns that hold thick tomes and trigger blocks of text. Though the game marks its debt to print culture through graphical representations of books, it does not simulate a printed page in the manner of classical hypertext fiction or e-books. The text simply appears superimposed over the game screen, marking its digital status while constantly keeping its game space in view. The placement of the lecterns follows left to right. However, the player also has the option of reading these texts in a right-to-left order that produces a different though still-viable narrative – one of the many temporal reversals that the game invites. Here, *Braid* estranges Western reading practices, encouraging a textual engagement proper to languages such as Hebrew and Arabic as well as Japanese writing (including cultural forms such as manga that have intersected with videogame culture).[23] Instead of simply surpassing print or distancing itself from it, *Braid* uses adaptation to enter into a conversation between digital games and earlier literary narrative traditions.

Improvisational Play: Emergent Storytelling and Player-Generated Narratives

In the previous three sections, I have discussed game narrative primarily from the perspective of designers who create story spaces for players to experience and explore. Although I mentioned textual play in *Galatea* and player-centric narrative in passing during the discussion of *Gone Home*, the possibilities for this form of narrative play are far more extensive than what is made available in those games. Two different ways of thinking about player-driven narrative include emergent stories that unfold in digital game environments and stories composed by players through the use of game software.

First of all, many games, whether or not they foreground narrative, leave space for emergent storytelling. These include open-world games, such as the *Grand Theft Auto* (1997) and *Fallout* (1997) single-player series. Other games, including massively multiplayer role-playing games such as *Everquest* (1999) and *Guild Wars 2* (2012), invite social interactions between human players that are particularly generative of emergent narrative. While players may tell or role-play stories within the virtual space of such games, narratives may also extend outside of the game space. This form of emergent storytelling unfolds, for instance, both inside and outside of thatgamecompany's critically acclaimed game *Journey* (2012). In *Journey*, the player guides a robed avatar through a desert and up a mountain. After a short time, the player discovers that the game is networked and includes one other player at a time. That other player's movements are visible, but communication with them is not possible via either text or speech. During gameplay, *Journey*'s language-exclusion constraint invites the enactment of narrative and communication through avatar positions, actions, and gestures. Outside of the game, players have translated their narratives into language, posting them to blogs such as *Journey Stories*. This Tumblr blog is described as "[a] space to collect the stories of companionship, sadness, and joy experienced while playing the videogame Journey." The blog has yielded elaborate stories, poems, theories, and readings of the game's diegesis, as well as various forms of fan art, including images, sculptures, musical performances, comic strips, and tattoos. In effect, these blogs become a space for documenting and processing emergent narratives.[24]

Second, in addition to emergent narratives, there are also games that more explicitly invite players to create their own stories. One such piece is Jason Rohrer's story-building game *Sleep Is Death (Geisterfahrer)* (2010). Instead of offering a pre-authored play mode, this game relies entirely on the interactions between two players, who create a story together. Some players have even posted recordings of their narrative play-throughs to YouTube for spectators to view. In *Sleep Is Death*, each player manipulates objects – language and graphics – in order to create an emergent narrative through cooperative play. In this case, the primary constraint is time. Each player has only thirty seconds to alter objects or type in text (that is, to make a "move") before the other player responds. *Sleep Is Death* draws its interactive constraint from games, including turn-based analog card and board games that often set strict rules for engagement and videogames that frequently set time limits for finishing levels. While the game sets these temporal constraints, players are free to set their own formal and genre constraints and to compose any narrative they want within those parameters.

Though *Sleep Is Death* is a fairly obscure platform created by an art game designer, the larger videogame industry has also been impacted by player-centric storytelling, especially in conjunction with the growing prominence of networked game consoles. As videogames such as the popular PlayStation puzzle-platformer *LittleBigPlanet* franchise (2008) have demonstrated, the creation and sharing of user-generated content is often more compelling than playing through a designed game. In the primary mode of this game, players guide the protagonist, Sackboy, through platforming challenges and other mini-games. Arguably, the popularity of the series has had more to do with the opportunity for players to create their own levels of the game and short films, which they can then upload to the PlayStation Network and share with the game's community. In August 2012, players of the game had created and submitted 7 million levels.

Since that time, popular games such as *Super Mario Maker* (2015) have continued to invite players to create their own levels within familiar game worlds. Some of these levels even employ spatial storytelling techniques. For example, the level "Will You Save Your Son?" (created by player Geofferu Heromoto) borrows game assets from *Super Mario World* (1990) to stage a short story about Mario setting off to rescue his son. The level uses the elements and visual grammar of a *Super Mario* level to express linguistic information (e.g., coins ordered as letters that spell out words), stage micro-narratives (e.g., a scene in which the player must sacrifice the companion dinosaur, Yoshi, to progress), and enable narrative choices (e.g., the choice of a door marked "Yes" or "No" that constitutes a response to a question about whether the player regrets sacrificing Yoshi). In addition to creating the level and making it playable to other users of *Super Mario Maker*, Heromoto has posted a play-through of the level, which he performs and narrates, on YouTube, turning the game into a short narrative film. In all of these ways, game-based narrative has increasingly become a participatory form that concerns players as much as designers.

Conclusion: Reading Games, Playing Narratives

This chapter suggests ways in which the fields of game studies and narrative theory, with their distinct but increasingly overlapping traditions, might enter into a more vibrant ongoing conversation. Though I have primarily considered what literary critics can bring to game studies, there is also much that game studies, as a more mature field than it was in the 1990s, can now reciprocally contribute to narrative theory. As the preceding examples suggest, games can be read and interpreted through literary critical techniques. The reverse of this point is also true: narrative texts can often be played.

Certainly, the concept of play does not originate in game studies and circulates throughout literary criticism in the latter half of the twentieth century. Notably, in the late 1960s, play both organized Jacques Ehrmann's structuralist volume of Yale French Studies on *Game, Play, Literature* and appeared as a key term in Jacques Derrida's "Structure, Sign, and Play in the Discourses of the Human Sciences."[25] Even so, videogames bring varied forms of play into sharper relief, while also introducing concepts such as rules, puzzles, and procedures more centrally into a literary critical vocabulary.

As games explore the possibilities and limits of language, at both the level of interface and code, so print and electronic literary texts participate in what Noah Wardrip-Fruin describes as "the expression of ideas through processes."[26] Indeed, recent literary criticism has used both analog and digital games to analyze novels and other non-gamic texts.[27] Furthermore, numerous narrative texts respond, at a formal level, to games and ludic intertexts.[28] Transmedia novels such as Mark Danielewski's *House of Leaves* (2000), Sean Stewart and Jordan Weisman's *Cathy's Book* (2006), and Steven Hall's *The Raw Shark Texts* (2007) have all been taken up by communities that play alternate reality games. *House of Leaves*, for instance, likens its own structure to that of a riddle that may offer "answers" or only "torment."[29] The online forum for the novel has generated thousands of posts from readers who have delved into the novel's mysteries together and sought to solve its riddles, much as gamer communities share tips, observations, and walkthroughs.[30] If *House of Leaves* suggests a transmedia game, the novel *Cathy's Book* comes much closer to actually constituting such a game. The book contains a pouch that includes illustrations, postcards, napkins, and other artifacts that allow a deeper engagement with the story's central mysteries. The narrative directs readers to web pages, social networking sites, and phone numbers. One site, for instance, contains a puzzle linked to a birthdate. While most dates lead to random messages, entering the birthday of the protagonist Cathy, which must be discovered within the book's text, yields new narrative information that must be organized by the reader. *Raw Shark Tales* initiates even more complex games. The novel requires two forms of decoding: close reading and a capacity to decipher difficult ciphers. As Hayles observes, the novel simultaneously emphasizes "the decoding process of making letters into words, words into narratives" as well as decoding challenges that incorporate, for instance, Morse code letters encrypted through QWERTY keyboard codes.[31] Though all of these texts are marketed and largely read *as novels*, to fully appreciate them requires skills more commonly developed through gameplay.

Traditional works of literature could also profit from the terms and techniques of game studies. Although I can only be gestural here, such convergences between narrative and games invite thick comparative analyses. What, we might ask, would it mean to read a literary romance by Thomas Malory alongside a platform game such as *Super Mario Bros.*? What would it mean to read encyclopedic novels such as James Joyce's *Ulysses* (1922) as world-building exercises that share properties with a virtual world such as *World of Warcraft* (2004)? And then, how might we read the influence of naturalism in Theodor Dreiser's novel *Sister Carrie* (1900) on the economic realism of *Cart Life* (2011) or the everydayness of games such as *Life Is Strange* (2015)? Finally, how can formally experimental games such as Mary Flanagan's *[domestic]* (2003) return us to modernist novels such as the work of Marcel Proust or Virginia Woolf? These juxtapositions are meant to be suggestive of many others.

Admittedly, such comparisons between literary texts and narratives games must be approached with care. Literary texts, especially those that appear prior to postmodernism, often demand precise distinctions among concepts such as genre, mode, and style. These concepts, however, may be co-present and particularly difficult to parse out within an early twenty-first-century videogame. For example, *Braid* draws from and redeploys everything from chivalric romance to postmodern fragmentation to electronic literature lexia to platformer videogames. As such, the game's historicity becomes slippery. Even the more proximate genealogies of modernism and postmodernism become inadequate to comprehending the game. It blurs, for instance, the line between modernist parody and postmodern pastiche in its repetition, with a difference, of the famous *Super Mario Bros.* line that grows more surreal with each redeployment: "Thank you Mario! But our princess is in another castle!" In this case, neither parody nor pastiche prove adequate, signaling instead to an extended reading of the repetition through a media archaeology that draws from and complicates the history of literature, the development of videogames, and the expansion of technoscience through the twentieth century.

Along with the categorical hybridity and undecidability of so many of the games described in this chapter, I mean for the preceding questions to invite critics to further explore convergences between digital games and narrative texts. Particularly at a historical moment in which creative production is informed increasingly by transmedia techniques, the capacity to read at the intersections between these categories promises to yield fresh methods, habits, and relations of reading and play.

Notes

1. It is important to acknowledge the historical tensions between "narratology" and "ludology" that characterized the games studies turf wars of the late 1990s and early 2000s. During these years, scholars such as Espen Aarseth, Markku Eskelinen, Gonzalo Frasca, and Jesper Juul argued, in different ways, for a field of "ludology": a formalist discipline that takes game mechanics and rules as its core elements of study. Though multiple game types informed this discussion, critics directed most of their critical energy to digital games or videogames. In effect, ludology insisted on the medium specificity of games, as distinct from print or screen-based narrative. Ludology responded in part to visible early new media studies research, from scholars such as Janet Murray and Brenda Laurel, who treated digital games as an extension of drama and narrative. For all of the utility of these debates to a discrete field of game studies, they sometimes resulted in polemics that prematurely dismissed rich intersections between the literary and the ludic and, more specifically, narrative and game form.

2. See, for instance, N. Katherine Hayles and Jessica Pressman, *Comparative Textual Media: Transforming the Humanities in the Postprint Era* (Minneapolis: University of Minnesota Press, 2013).

3. Marie-Laure Ryan, "Introduction," in *Narrative across Media: The Languages of Storytelling* (Lincoln: University of Nebraska Press, 2004), 34.

4. N. Katherine Hayles, *Electronic Literature: New Horizons for the Literary* (Notre Dame, IN: University of Notre Dame Press, 2008).

5. Gonzalo Frasca, "Simulation versus Narrative: Introduction to Ludology," in *The Video Game Theory Reader*, ed. Mark J. P. Wolf and Bernard Perron (New York, NY: Routledge, 2003), 222 and 224. It is worth noting that at the time that Frasca made the argument about gameplay experience versus observation, the world of eSports and videogame spectatorship on platforms such as Twitch and YouTube was not as developed as it is today. Although it is outside of the bounds of this chapter, the significant growth of videogame viewing audiences may further complicate Frasca's early twenty-first-century opposition between simulation and representation.

6. N. Katherine Hayles, *Electronic Literature*, 8.

7. I lay out the growing diversity of the category of "game" within twenty-first-century videogame culture, including in narrative games, in Patrick Jagoda, "Videogame Criticism and Games in the Twenty-First Century," *American Literary History* 29 (2017): 205–218.

8. Gregory Lastowka and Dan Hunter, "The Laws of the Virtual Worlds," *California Law Review* 92 (2004): 18–21.

9. For analysis of text adventure games that enter into conversation with classical narrative theory, see Janet Murray, *Hamlet on the Holodeck* (New York, NY: Free Press, 1997), and a summary of such applications in Britta Neitzel, "Narrativity of Computer Games," in *Handbook of Computer Game Studies*, ed. Joost Raessens and Jeffrey H. Goldstein (Cambridge, MA: MIT Press, 2005). Earlier analyses of hypertext fiction are also important here, especially insofar as they examine the effects of nonlinear and multilinear hypertexts on classical frameworks, including Aristotle's theory. Exemplary here is the chapter "Reconfiguring Narrative," in

George P. Landow, *Hypertext: The Convergence of Contemporary Critical Theory and Technology* (Baltimore, MD: Johns Hopkins University Press, 1992).

10. Emily Short's interactive fiction is one of a larger collection of adaptations of the myth of Pygmalion and Galatea into plays (George Bernard Shaw's *Pygmalion*), musicals (Alan Jay Lerner and Frederick Loewe's *My Fair Lady*), novels (Richard Powers's *Galatea 2.2*), and other forms.

11. Emily Short, "Multilinear IF," in Emily Short's Interactive Storytelling blog, https://emshort.wordpress.com/how-to-play/writing-if/my-articles/multilinear-if-older/.

12. Inform, "Writing with Inform," in "Chapter 13: Relations," http://inform7.com/learn/man/WI_13_1.html

13. Marie-Laure Ryan, *Narrative across Media*, 8–9.

14. Katie Salen and Eric Zimmerman, *Rules of Play: Game Design Fundamentals* (Cambridge, MA: MIT Press, 2003), 80.

15. Ian Bogost, *Persuasive Games: The Expressive Power of Videogames* (Cambridge, MA: MIT Press, 2007).

16. Janet Murray, *Hamlet on the Holodeck*, 79.

17. Henry Jenkins, "Game Design as Narrative Architecture," in *First Person: New Media as Story, Performance, and Game*, ed. Noah Wardrip-Fruin and Pat Harrigan (Cambridge, MA: MIT Press, 2003), 121.

18. Ibid., 123.

19. Gone Home still offers a largely legible queer narrative. For an exploration of the ways that queer games complicate narrative in more radical ways, see Whitney Pow, "Reaching Toward Home: Software Interface As Queer Orientation in the Video Game Curtain," The Velvet Light Trap 81 (2018): 43–56.

20. Ibid., 124, 125, 126, and 128.

21. Dudley Andrew, *Concepts in Film Theory* (Oxford: Oxford University Press, 1984), 98.

22. Alan P. Lightman, *Einstein's Dreams* (New York, NY: Pantheon Books, 1993), 53–54.

23. For a more detailed analysis of *Braid*, including its relationship to novelistic intertexts, see Patrick Jagoda, "Fabulously Procedural: *Braid*, Historical Processing, and the Videogame Sensorium," *American Literature* 85 (2013): 745–779.

24. For an extended analysis of *Journey*, including its narrative structure, see Patrick Jagoda, *Network Aesthetics* (Chicago, IL: University of Chicago Press, 2016), 166–77.

25. See Jacques Ehrmann, *Game, Play, Literature* (New Haven, CT: Yale University Press, 1968), and Jacques Derrida, "Structure, Sign, and Play in the Discourse of the Human Sciences," in *Writing and Difference*, trans. Alan Bass (Chicago, IL: University of Chicago Press, 1978). For a reading of the role of play as it stretches across literary criticism and game studies, see David Golumbia, "Games without Play," *New Literary History* 40 (2009): 179–204.

26. Noah Wardrip-Fruin, *Expressive Processing* (Cambridge, MA: MIT Press, 2009), 417.

27. See, for instance, Mark Seltzer, "Parlor Games: The Apriorization of the Media," *Critical Inquiry* 52, no. 1 (2009): 100–133, and G. S. Jackson, "A Game Theory of Evangelical Fiction," *Critical Inquiry* 39, no. 3 (2013): 451–485.

28. Numerous literary texts also have a representational relationship to games. The texts here are too numerous to summarize, but they would include texts about card games (Stephen Crane's 1900 short story "A Poker Game"), chess (Vladimir Nabokov's 1930 novel, *The Luzhin Defense*), military simulations (Orson Scott Card's 1985 novel, *Ender's Game*), massively multiplayer online game worlds (Ernest Cline's 2011 novel, *Ready Player One*), and live-action role-playing games (e.g., Jenny Davidson's 2013 novel, *The Magic Circle*).

29. Mark Z. Danielewski, *House of Leaves* (New York, NY: Pantheon, 2000), 33.

30. Mark Z. Danielewski, http://forums.markzdanielewski.com/forum/house-of-leaves.

31. N. Katherine Hayles, *How We Think: Digital Media and Contemporary Technogenesis* (Chicago, IL: University of Chicago Press, 2012), 209.

16

MARGARET COHEN

Narrative Theory and Novel Theory

The novel is a latecomer to the pantheon of literary genres. Long narratives in prose have existed since antiquity. However, recognition of these works as belonging to a form – the novel (*le roman, il romanzo, der Roman*, and so on) – and the recognition of this form as worthy of serious aesthetic attention date to Western modernity. When Aristotle opened his foundational treatise on poetics, he distinguished tragedy, comedy, drama, epic, and dithyrambic poetry as mimetic genres. It was not until Georg Lukács's *The Theory of the Novel* (written 1914–1915, published 1920) that the novel received a "theory" of its own.

Lukács's work launched the paradigm of novel theory we still use today. At the same time, it was the culmination of agitation over three centuries on the part of writers and readers that the novel should be taken seriously. From the first modern long prose narratives, novelists and their publics advocated the form's ability to entertain, to instruct, and to illuminate the human condition, ranging from universal passions to preoccupations of the present everyday. This advocacy for the form was contained in prefaces and introductions, and confirmed by readers in reviews and treatises. One of the earliest examples of such promotion is the preface to the Spanish *Don Quixote*, Part 1 (1605). Through the persona of a friend of the author, Miguel Cervantes praised the novel for striking a note of ease against obviously mannered genres. In contrast to overworked literature, the novel should be admired for its "expressive, decorous and well-ordered words [set down] in a straightforward way."[1] French aristocrat Madame de Lafayette's *The Princesse de Clèves* (1678) is often considered the first psychological novel. When her contemporary, the neoclassical aesthetician Pierre-Daniel Huet, wrote a treatise on novels, he lauded its "plausibility of action joined with true feelings; characters taken from nature, and a narration [*marche*] drawn with art, where the art is not overly felt."[2] Almost a century later (1766–1767), German author Christoph Martin Wieland vaunted the criterion of plausibility in keeping with social norms as a merit of his foundational novel of the education (*Bildungsroman*) subgenre. In opening *The History of Agathon*, readers learned that "[t]he truth [...] of a work of this kind [...] must depend entirely upon it's [sic] consistency with the general customs of the world."[3] Jane Austen fused these diverse attributes – everyday yet elegant language, plausibility, psychology, and a poetics at once artful and discreet – in her narrator's pitch in *Northanger Abbey* (1803). In response to a female character who somewhat embarrassedly admits that her reading is "only" of novels, the narrator ripostes: "only," that is to say, "some work in which the greatest powers of the mind are displayed, in which the most thorough knowledge of human nature, the happiest delineation of its varieties, the liveliest effusions of wit and humour are conveyed to the world in the best chosen language."[4] In his 1842 "Avant-propos" to the novels forming *The Human Comedy*, French novelist Honoré de Balzac amplified Austen's understated claim to put novelists in charge of an entire body of knowledge about human nature and manners.[5]

A theory of the novel, however, must offer more than the description of salient features. Georg Lukács found his model for how to conceptualize the novel's cultural significance in the cultural importance ascribed to the epic in German idealism. What Lukács called his "historico-philosophical" approach, in particular, derived inspiration from G. W. F. Hegel's *Lectures on Aesthetics*, where Hegel gave the epic a role defining the "entire world-outlook and objective manifestation of a national spirit presented in its self-objectifying shape as an actual event."[6] Lukács took as his point of departure the novel's salient focus on individuals and their interiority, which he linked to the difference between the cultural moment when the epic thrived and modern society. The epic was an expression of what Lukács called "integrated civilisations": societies whose values were intrinsic, created by theology and the tight-knit structures of community.[7] To these societies, Lukács contrasted the disintegration of modernity, deriving above all from secularization, whose impact he expressed in a variety of ways. He wrote, for example: "The novel is the epic of an age in which the extensive totality of life is no longer directly given [...] yet which still thinks in terms of totality." "The novel is the epic of a world that has been abandoned by God." "[T]he novel form is, like no other, an expression of this [the modern's] transcendental homelessness."[8]

As these famous sentences show, Lukács represented the novel's modernity as an expression of existential structures rather than as a delineation of social and historical transformation. In keeping with such a focus on ontology, the aspect of narrative most important to Lukács was the character of the protagonist, a problematic individual who in some way did not fit with his society. For Lukács, a paradigmatic type of novel was the novel of formation, the *Bildungsroman*, where the youthful protagonist through his or her adventures developed (or failed to develop) a harmonious relationship with the surrounding society. Nonetheless, Lukács's attention to the *Bildungsroman* was not prescriptive. He saw the defining features of the novel, in contrast to the epic, as an emphasis on formal "structuration" (to use a term that Roland Barthes would highlight in *S/Z*), whatever the specific poetics. The reason for such tightly drawn form was that the novel created in the domain of poetics compensation for a civilization where totality and a unity of values had been obscured. Lukács wrote, "The epic gives form to a totality of life that is rounded from within; the novel seeks, by giving form, to uncover and construct the concealed totality of life."[9] Such thorough formal organization was compatible with openness to the future: "the novel, in contrast to other genres [...] appears as something in the process of becoming."[10]

The Theory of the Novel made its pronouncements in an abstract, authoritative voice, substantiated with only a few examples. It is as if "it is the Novel itself that tells us the history of its own development, very much as, in Hegel's *Phenomenology*, it is the Spirit who narrates its own voyage," observed Paul de Man.[11] Such abstraction makes *The Theory of the Novel* dense, but its style should be understood as heavy lifting. With abstraction, Lukács makes a bid to raise the novel above its own immersion in detail and particularity, as well as above its entertainment value, to the level of an abstract object suited to philosophy.

At the same time, abstraction requires, of course, reduction. Lukács's creation of the novel as amenable to "theory" opened the way for alternative paradigms when critics addressed the novel's diversity of practice beyond the *Bildungsroman* and historical realism. Writing primarily during the Stalinist era, Russian literary critic M. M. Bakhtin offered what has proved to be the most fruitful revision of Lukács, seeking to make sense of a more expansive canon. As Bakhtin's translator and editor, Michael Holquist, remarked, Bakhtin embedded the novel within a long history of prose forms, reaching back to the "very earliest classical texts [...] Hellenistic and Roman texts [...] medieval romances [...] as well as elements from the oral tradition of folklore."[12] Further, Bakhtin admitted into his purview of the novel all novels called such, rather than only those novels that speak with elevated social and philosophical purpose, from the *Satyricon* of Petronius to gothic and popular novels.

For Bakhtin as for Lukács, the novel offers an alternative to a theological worldview. Lukács expressed this alternative as the loss of a sacred harmony with the cosmos, writing in almost tragic terms about modernity's homeless individual. Bakhtin, in contrast, prized the novel's work of desacralization through parody and laughter, finding its genesis in anthropological practices overturning hierarchy, such as the Catholic carnival. For Bakhtin, the novel's principal agent of desacralization was language, unruly and transformative, in contact with the open-ended present. This contact zone where literature met life oriented Bakhtin toward a novel's diverse poetics of expression, in contrast to the more character-centric analysis of Lukács. Because one defining feature of the novel for Bakhtin was its construction in "a zone of contact with the incomplete events of a particular present, the novel often crosses the boundary of what we call fictional literature."[13] Not only, Bakhtin suggested, did the novel incorporate other everyday and nonliterary genres, but once the novel was on the scene, the hierarchy of genres itself was threatened in a process Bakhtin designated as novelization. Bakhtin was a proponent of a multivocal notion of the novel as the formal gathering place of the many diverse genres and voices of a culture, which he also termed throughout his writings as "dialogism."

While Lukács formulated the seminal notion of the protagonist as in some way exceeding or failing to fill his or her social place, Bakhtin viewed the novelistic character as entangled in a cluster of the novel's formal features, which he called the chronotope. For Bakhtin, the chronotope most obviously united a setting and a way of organizing time. As Bakhtin expounds on this notion, it also becomes clear that setting and time shape a particular plot and a cast of characters. A good example of the saturation of the chronotope with diverse aspects of a novel's poetics is the chronotope of the road, which enables chance as a principle of plot construction, as well as "the collapse of *social distances*."[14] The road thus is an important setting in novels that depict "the *sociohistorical heterogeneity* of one's own country."[15] Bakhtin speculated that chronotopes might indeed be so central to a novel's organization that they could be identified with discrete subgenres. While the chronotope of the road characterized picaresque novels, Bakhtin considered whether the gothic novel might be encompassed by the chronotope of the *castle* associated with "the time of the historical past."[16] Among the aspects of narrative that castle time encouraged were the incorporation of other types of historical records, including "the ancestral portrait" and "the family archives," as well as "legends and tradition."[17] The historical present, in contrast, was the defining time of the space of the salon or parlor emerging in nineteenth-century realism. In these spaces, novels wove together "historical and socio-public events [...] with the personal and even deeply private side of life."[18]

Bakhtin's theory of the novel is remarkable for incorporating realism into a much more heterogeneous array of long prose fictions than notable subsequent conceptualizations of the Western novel in the wake of Lukács. The first critic in this lineage was Lukács himself, after his shift to a Marxian paradigm of modern capitalist society. In *The Historical Novel*

(1937), Lukács addressed the novel's interest in discordance at the level of the collective, concentrating on the lineage of historical realism. Lukács suggested that the novel was a form grasping the contradictions fissuring society, and hence driving history. For Lukács, "[t]he great novels of world literature, in particular those of the nineteenth century, portray not so much the collapse of a society as its process of disintegration."[19] In this view, the struggles of characters in novels conveyed the struggles of competing historical groups. The ideal protagonist to take the reader through this disintegration was no longer the problematic individual, but rather the "middle way" hero, who was able, in his or her very lack of distinction, to traverse different social factions at war with each other, whether in a novel by Manzoni, Hugo, Stendhal, or Cooper. The novel's historicity for Lukács in this new iteration was its ability to isolate the conflicts driving collective history expressed through individual characters. Thus, he wrote of "*historical faithfulness*" in Scott that it derived from showing how "historical necessity asserts itself [...] through the passionate actions of individuals," even "against their individual psychology".[20] Similarly, Lukács remarked how authors like Scott and Balzac delineated these contradictions, even when their recognition conflicted with their conscious ideology.

The appreciation of the novel as expressing collective processes of modernization through individual psychology would dominate theories of the novel in the remainder of the twentieth century. These theories accordingly prized historical realism, with its interpenetration of character and social milieu, to cite a term used by Erich Auerbach in his *Mimesis* (1953). This collection of essays does not present itself as a theory of the novel explicitly but rather delineates some of the great Western poetic techniques of realism, from *The Odyssey* to Woolf's *To the Lighthouse*. Yet Auerbach in practice offers us a value-laden genealogy of mimesis, culminating in the classics of the nineteenth century. Auerbach's view of the novel's cultural import is evident if we contrast his comments on Petronius with those on Balzac. Auerbach writes, "[B]ehind the bustle which Petronius sets before us, we sense nothing which might help us understand the action in terms of its economic and political context; and the historical movement [...] is here only a surface movement." Balzac, in contrast, portrays characters in a way that "reflects all of French history from the Revolution to the Restoration."[21] Auerbach will develop this with an emphasis on the "harmony" (Auerbach's word) between characters and their milieu, a term he translates from sociology to literature. For Auerbach, Balzac is also deeply historical, and thus realist, because "the source of his invention is not free imagination but real life, as it is presents itself everywhere."[22]

In the Anglo-American tradition, Ian Watt consolidated the notion that realism was the destiny of the novel, in *The Rise of the Novel: Studies in Defoe, Richardson and Fielding* (1957). Recognizing that the term "realism" was not coined until the middle of the nineteenth century (moreover in France, apropos of visual art), Watt nonetheless identified a literary strain of English "realism" crystallizing earlier with the advent of modern bourgeois society. For Watt, defining features of such novels were plots that were invented rather than taken from past historical precedents. These plots were often inspired by recent events, marked by the "individualisation" of characters and "the detailed presentation of their environment."[23] Detail was thus extremely important to Watt's account, which situated the novel in the context of the rise of science, a culture of quantification, and the takeoff of capitalism – in short, features of modernity isolated by German sociologist Max Weber, as well as by a Marxian lineage. The expansion of the reading public, including middle-class women as readers, also was a hallmark of the conditions fostering the form. In the particularized individuals of novels, Watt suggested, readers recognized social types. Specific details on setting, place, and characters conveyed the writer's aim to "make the words bring his object home to us in all its concrete particularity."[24] Unlike Bakhtin, who celebrated the diversity of the novel as a uniquely unruly form, Watt laid to the side novels that did not hew to realist norms, notably the French novel during the late seventeenth and eighteenth centuries.

Watt's interest in the concomitant rise of capitalism and the development of the realist novel was refined by American critics attending to the discourses dominating capitalist culture in the early modern period. Michael McKeon's *The Origins of the English Novel, 1600–1740* (1987) notably enriched Watt's history by showing how the novel's techniques are embedded in discourses of science, politics, travel, and philosophy.[25] While Watt suggested that the novel emerged as a form to shape the uncertainty attending the wane of religious hegemony in the West, McKeon pointed out the instability of values and epistemologies at such a moment, noting, for example, both naïve empiricism and extreme skepticism as responses to the demise of Christian doctrine. The qualities associated with virtue, too, became similarly unstable in this period of radical social change, when it no longer was synonymous with nobility. In its vivid empirical detail as well as in the actions of its eccentric characters, the novel was trafficking in questions of truth and questions of virtue, in McKeon's memorable phrase. Its plots, moreover, exhibited the instabilities of these defining aspects of societal identity up for grabs at the time.

The specific formulation of the relation between virtue and truth was less important than the novel's preoccupation with defining it. Thus, McKeon contrasted the positions of Defoe, for whom virtue was no longer given by status and honor, but rather achieved through work and agency, and Swift, who viewed inherited rank as a guarantee if not an absolute certainty of value. Moreover, McKeon noted that this concern with stabilizing epistemology and ethics was fundamentally bourgeois. McKeon's analysis thus in some ways rearticulated the notion offered by Lukács that the novel's purview is social dislocation and discomfort – although he aligns what Lukács called "transcendental homelessness" with specific historical developments rather than with the pervading expression of modern consciousness.

The effort to align virtue and truth described by McKeon is one example of how Marxian thought has valued the novel's power to provide imaginary solutions to social contradictions, whether they drive history or alleviate its blockage. Fredric Jameson drew on a compensatory notion of art to explain the importance of the novel in *The Political Unconscious* (1981), when he added romance to the pre-history of the form. Modeling his notion of romance on the paradigm of Northrop Frye, Jameson described it as an expression of "Utopian longings" and "a renewed meditation on the Utopian community."[26] With a Nietzschean slant to his Marxism, Jameson applied Frye's notion of romance to the novel beyond a Judeo-Christian notion of good and evil. "The novel," Jameson wrote, "is then not so much an organic unity as a symbolic act that must reunite or harmonize heterogeneous narrative paradigms which have their own specific and contradictory ideological meaning."[27] In Jameson's account, the content of the harmonization varied according to the historical moment. With the advent of bourgeois hegemony, "new positivities (theology, psychology, the dramatic metaphor) substitute for the older magical content." With the exhaustion of positivism at the end of the nineteenth century, modernist novels reformulate utopian longing as an "*absence* at the heart of the secular world."[28] Jameson primarily focused on character, plot, and setting in his analysis of the novel's workings; however, he added his own version of Bakhtin's more entangled chronotope by invoking the Heideggerian notion of *Stimmung*, a kind of mood revealed in details, landscapes, and entities that brings forth the "world" of the novel, and imbues it with imaginative force. Jameson elaborates on the rich permeation of *Stimmung* throughout all aspects of narrative poetics in *Antinomies of Realism* (2013). His preferred reference points are predominantly from the nineteenth and twentieth centuries, including realist and modernist artistic movements as well as novels. The concept is, however, transportable to other historical and literary contexts, if we recognize that codes differ for expressing embodiment, affect, and temporality at historical moments distant from the realist/modernist lineage.[29]

The novels in all these paradigms are busy: entertaining, revealing, compelling, obfuscating our horizons or expanding them. It is hard to resist the novel's activity, given that it makes meaning through the syntax of prose, conjuring subjects and actions before our eyes – even in fantastical or surrealistic form. However, Anne-Lise François suggests in *Open Secrets* (2008) that at least some novels find a way to still this incessant business and reconnect with a tradition of contemplation.[30] This slim book would not appear in a search for "novel theory," and indeed, François includes in her study just two novels – Madame de Lafayette's *The Princesse de Clèves* and Jane Austen's *Mansfield Park* – along with poetry. Moreover, these novels showcase protagonists who are heroines despite themselves, pressed by others into worldly transactions. Following the withdrawal of such heroines from society, François proposes the notion of what she calls "recessive action." François thereby suggests the possibility for reading the novel, or at least some novels, as opening a space for contemplation and repose. She does not politicize this space, associating it rather with values of lightness, grace, reticence, and even economy of form. At the same time, such resistance is in keeping with Marxian theories about the potential for aesthetic activity to resist capitalist ideology, meshing with avant-garde notions of art. For François, then, too, the novel preserves romance, or perhaps what Bakhtin would call the "idyll," which he considers an important strand of prose fiction dating from antiquity.

The Marxian notion of the novel as a site for vital imaginative work indeed runs throughout theories of the novel, notably in the later twentieth century. One of the most important cultural roles given to the novel is by Benedict Anderson, who proposed that it had the power to join within a single imaginative space and time individuals and communities that could not interact in real life. The novel effected such cohesion through its plots and also through its readers who compared reactions to popular works, Anderson argued in *Imagined Communities* (1983). He accorded the modern novel, along with the newspaper, a formative role in unifying far-flung individuals as members of a modern nation-state, an abstract idea capable of soliciting emotions. For Anderson, the novel's impact inhered in narrative poetics, which created for the reader a sense of simultaneity among diverse social groups, events, and types of spaces that nonetheless were joined, in fiction, as in fact, as belonging to a single national state. In Anderson's influential account, novels hence promoted the emergence of modern citizenship, first in Europe and subsequently across the globe, whether it was Lafayette's *The Princesse de Clèves* (1678), written in France as it was being unified by the absolutist monarchy, or José Rizal's *Noli Me Tangere* (1887), by the "Father of Filipino Nationalism."[31]

The novel's ability both to expose social contradictions and to reconcile them has intrigued feminist novel theorists, who note the importance both of female heroism and female reading publics in the development of this form. They also note that the novel's focus on private life suited it as a genre to delineate the realm where women's existence was circumscribed in ascendant middle-class culture. In *Desire and Domestic Fiction* (1987), Nancy Armstrong suggested that courtship-plot heroines found across the history of British fiction exhibited a new, middle-class form of moral authority with historical power. Armstrong's point of departure in *Desire and Domestic Fiction* was the insights of Michel Foucault and late 1960s feminism that sexual relations were a domain of what Foucault called micro-politics, or, to cite the feminist slogan, "the personal is political." In Armstrong's formulation, "'Foucault [. . .] makes it possible to consider sexual relations as the site for changing power relations between classes and cultures as well as between genders and generations."[32] The lower-class female heroines of novels from *Pamela* to *Jane Eyre* seduced through their virtue and thereby created a new social contract between the emergent bourgeoisie and the aristocracy. This social contract was a relation of power, but virtuous heroines, like novels, exercised soft power as opposed to repressive power, which both their charm and the novel's entertaining presentation helped conceal. In place of the crude economic contract proposed by Mr. B to Pamela, for example, Pamela converts Mr. B to sentimentality, just as she turns sex into endless writing, in her artful letters. The novel thus does away "with [overtly] political categories," the better to circulate and implant them.[33] However, the power of the sexual contract to renew the social contract does not prove able to deal with the conflicts between bourgeois and working-class values emerging in the nineteenth century. Thus, Armstrong's theory of the novel, like those previously discussed, predominantly focuses on the novel as an expression of bourgeois hegemony.

When inquiring about the novel's appeal to female readerships, feminist theorists have emphasized the ability of the form to nurture utopian longings for women trapped in domestic ideology or duties, as well as to subvert patriarchy from within. These insights have been formulated more often apropos of individual writers such as Jane Austen as analyzed by Claudia Johnson or Georges Sand by Naomi Schor than offered within the framework of an overarching novel theory.[34] Thus, Naomi Schor contrasted Sand and Balzac as writers of idealism and realism, offering a feminist reading of the utopian longings at issue in Sand's ambition to portray the world as it should be rather than the world as it was.

Anchored in the debates of feminism, Janice Radway refreshed the familiar canon of the realist/modernist lineage in recognizing that popular romance novels might also contain substance, using sociological tools and psychoanalytic theory in *Reading the Romance* (1984).[35] Interviewing readers frequenting a midwestern bookstore that excelled in choosing successful romance novels, Radway suggested that her (female) group of readers were nurtured by their reading, even as they educated themselves about a range of historical and social moments through factoids giving context to romance action. Radway located such nurturing in the plot dynamic, where spunky, intelligent young women were able at once to overcome challenges and enjoy submission to powerful yet protective romantic male leads. Such protection, Radway suggested, was lacking in these women's lives, where their social identities were defined by their family roles as constant, selfless caregivers. In their time away from such duties, Radway's subjects used the adventures of romance heroines to cultivate in their imagination a form of self-care.

Radway's study of popular novels gives meaning to formulaic literature that does not meet our criteria for enduring works of art. The pleasures of romance novels are exhausted with a single reading, they do not pose fundamental questions about human existence, and they are crafted with effective but not in any way remarkable or innovative poetics. Even as Radway's work is a model for how to reclaim a neglected province of the novel, her explanation for the psychological appeal of romance novels does not translate to the form of the novel more generally. This shift from a theory of the novel to theories of different kinds of novels has characterized the later twentieth century and continues into our present. With enhanced sensitivity to social diversity and to global literature, critics find increasingly problematic the project to write *the* or even *a* theory of *the* novel. It has become apparent that Lukács and his lineage have only been able to theorize "the" novel by restricting their canon to a small subset of novels fashioned across the advent of Western modernity – most, moreover, adhering to a realist aesthetic.

It also has become apparent that such theories discard many words and sentences on the pages of the novel to come up with useful yet at the same time reductive abstractions, such as the novel's power to harmonize class conflict through the courtship plot. Along with sociology and ethnography, cultural history has the power to enrich our theories of the novel, enabling us to understand the coherence of hitherto illegible genres and aesthetics. In "Narratology in the Archive of Literature," I have sketched some principles for this archaeology, inspired by a range of influential novel critics who seek to recover the literary historical importance of forgotten works, genres, and poetics in the history of the Western novel: an importance not derived from literature's interest as a historical curiosity but rather from its expressive aesthetic. This recovery does not apply of course to the novel alone; however, novel studies abounds in opportunities for such criticism, given the profusion of works in this genre and their sheer length. Even the most concise novels are loose, baggy monsters in contrast to the economy of drama and the self-designating highly crafted language of poetry. Profusion of detail in novels has been explained by Roland Barthes as "the reality effect," a term he coined for details that do not have an immediate use in the plot, and thus show that the imaginary world of the novel extends beyond the covers of the book.[36] However, details may also have meaning within systems, discourses, and paradigms that the critic doesn't have the conceptual matrices to understand. One way to expand the purview of the novel is to scrutinize works for meaningful patterns that are hidden in plain view. To recognize overlooked patterns also often requires that we delve into the cultural context of the time. The discourses relevant to the actions of novels at the time when they were written, as well as the literature and response they provoked, can offer insights that expand their significance.[37]

One signature of novel theory today is hence that it unfolds at the conjuncture of historical specificity, formal analysis, and abstraction. This conjuncture of history, poetics, and theory is particularly salient when critics attend to novels written outside the "core" (to use the world-systems theory term) of Western modernity, where the modern novel emerged, and which has been the focus of this article. Fredric Jameson contrasted the unique work of the Western novel intertwining individual and society with alternate possibilities in his controversial article "Third-World Literature in the Era of Multinational Capitalism." While not writing about the novel specifically, narratives figure prominently for Jameson in advancing the proposal that literature from "third-world" countries should be read allegorically. Jameson chose the notion of allegory because this form of signification separated different levels of meaning from one another, rather than unifying them. Jameson proposed that it was thus more accurate to emphasize the distinctions and difficulties in passage across different levels of society in contexts where political access for individual subjects was in some way problematic. "[F]ar from dramatizing the identity of the political and the individual or psychic, the allegorical structure tends essentially to separate these levels in some absolute way. We cannot feel its force unless we are convinced of the radical split between politics and the libidinal," which aesthetic products confirm rather than overcome.[38] No sooner had Jameson advanced his thesis than its broad-brush generalities came under scrutiny, starting with a polemical article by Aijaz Ahmad in *Social Text*, followed by Jameson's response in the same issue.[39] Is non-European literature to be reduced to the "other" of Western literature? The West, moreover, is itself a homogenizing category, effacing, for that matter, differences among specific national and regional or transnational contexts. Is allegory an appropriate Western category to impose on plural non-Western contexts? Jameson's thesis, additionally, is anchored in the homologies between text and historical conjuncture, without entering into details about the complex institutions for the publication and consumption of literature, including those that trouble a First World/Third World divide. Whatever one's investment in this debate, Jameson's article energized an examination of non-Western novel traditions whose specificity is lost when characterized by theories of the novel focused on Western modernity and the European bourgeoisie. It also energized an examination of how cultural institutions of literary production, translation, and consumption cut across divides among the First, Second, and Third World, drawing on theories such Pierre Bourdieu's model of the field of cultural production in his *The Rules of Art*.[40]

The Jameson debate, like so many other novel theories surveyed in this chapter, shows the ongoing inextricability of the novel from modernity and modernization. Franco Moretti expressed this entanglement succinctly in his "Conjectures on World Literature," where he proposed that "the modern novel arises [across the globe] [...] as a compromise between a western formal influence (usually French or English) and local materials," notably local forms.[41] Or, as Moretti wrote in "The Novel: History and Theory," "the great theories of the novel have been theories of modernity."[42] Perhaps comparatist collaboration on long fictions in prose in diverse traditions will finally generate alternative points of departure for theories of the novel that do not rely on modernity to give the form cultural importance.

Such a liberation of the novel from its role as an agent of modernity can already be gleaned from the theory of Mikhail Bakhtin, who remains remarkable for his interest in drawing together the novels of the nineteenth century with a long tradition of prose fictions reaching back to classical antiquity, including Menippean satire and Hellenic romance. For Bakhtin, the novel destabilizes hierarchies with its openness into the present and its incorporation of the variety of genres and discourses. Bakhtin wrote of the novel, "[h]owever forcefully the real and the represented world resist fusion, however immutable the presence of that categorical boundary line between them, they are nonetheless indissolubly tied up with each other and find themselves in continual mutual interaction [...] similar to the uninterrupted exchange of matter between living organisms and the environment that surrounds them."[43] Because of such openness, the novel is for Bakhtin an agent of change and renewal – *renewal*, tellingly, not modernity or modernization, which, of course, may be one of its expressions. However, modernization can be as fossilized or noxious as the hierarchies this concept has been summoned to destroy. Thus, Bakhtin considered the novel as a guardian of hope and humanity imbued with potential, rather than anchored in specific histories. He found such appeal epitomized in the novels of his beloved Rabelais: "All historical limits are [...] destroyed and swept away by laughter," and "[t]he field remains open to human nature."[44]

Notes

1. Miguel Cervantes, *Don Quixote*, trans. John Rutherford (London: Penguin Books, 2000), 16.
2. Pierre-Daniel Huet, *Traité de l'origine des romans* (Paris: N.L.M. Desessarts, 1799), 140; my translation.
3. C. M. Wieland, *The History of Agathon*, 4 vols. (London: T. Cadell, 1773), 1: xviii.
4. Jane Austen, *Northanger Abbey* (London: Penguin, 2003), 36–37.
5. Honoré de Balzac, "Avant-propos" (1842), in *Œuvres complètes de H. de Balzac* (Paris: A. Houssiaux, 1855), 1: 17–32, https://fr.wikisource.org/wiki/Avant-Propos_de_La_Com%C3%A9die_humaine.
6. Georg Wilhelm Friedrich Hegel's Aesthetics, Lectures on Fine Art, trans. T. M. Knox (Oxford: Oxford University Press, 1975), II: 1044.
7. Georg Lukács, *The Theory of the Novel*, trans. Anna Bostock (Cambridge, MA: MIT Press, 1971), 29ff.
8. Ibid., 56, 88, 41.
9. Ibid., 60.
10. Ibid., 72–73.
11. Paul de Man, "Georg Lukács's *Theory of the Novel*," *Modern Language Notes* 81 (1966): 528.
12. Michael Holquist, "Introduction," M. M. Bakhtin, *The Dialogic Imagination: Four Essays*, trans. Caryl Emerson and Holquist, ed. Holquist (Austin: University of Texas Press, 1981), xxix.
13. M. M. Bakhtin, "Epic and Novel," in *The Dialogic Imagination*, 33.
14. M. M. Bakhtin, "Forms of Time and of the Chronotope in the Novel," in *The Dialogic Imagination*, 243.
15. Ibid., 245.
16. Ibid., 246.
17. Ibid.
18. Ibid., 247.
19. Georg Lukács, *The Historical Novel*, trans. Hannah Mitchell and Stanley Mitchell (Lincoln: University of Nebraska Press, 1962), 144.
20. Ibid., 59.
21. Erich Auerbach, *Mimesis: The Representation of Reality in Western Literature*, trans. Willard. R. Trask (Princeton, NJ: Princeton University Press, 2003), 32.
22. Ibid., 480.
23. Ian Watt, *The Rise of the Novel: Studies in Defoe, Richardson, and Fielding*, new ed. (Berkeley: University of California Press, 2001), 18.

24. Ibid., 29.
25. Michael McKeon, *The Origins of the English Novel, 1600–1740* (Baltimore, MD: Johns Hopkins University Press, 1987).
26. Fredric Jameson, *The Political Unconscious: Narrative as a Socially Symbolic Act* (Ithaca, NY: Cornell University Press, 1981), 105.
27. Ibid., 144.
28. Ibid., 134.
29. Fredric Jameson, *The Antinomies of Realism* (London: Verso, 2013).
30. Anne-Lise François, *Open Secrets: The Literature of Uncounted Experience* (Stanford, CA: Stanford University Press, 2008).
31. Benedict Anderson, *Imagined Communities: Reflections on the Origins and Spread of Nationalism*, rev. ed. (London: Verso, 2006), 26.
32. Nancy Armstrong, *Desire and Domestic Fiction: A Political History of the Novel* (New York, NY: Oxford University Press, 1987), 10.
33. Ibid., 121.
34. See, for example, Claudia L. Johnson, *Jane Austen: Women, Politics, and the Novel* (Chicago, IL: University of Chicago Press, 1981), and Naomi Schor, *George Sand and Idealism* (New York, NY: Columbia University Press, 1993).
35. Janice A. Radway, *Reading the Romance: Women, Patriarchy, and Popular Literature*, rev. ed. (Chapel Hill: University of North Carolina Press, 1991).
36. Roland Barthes, "The Reality Effect," in *The Rustle of Language*, trans. Richard Howard. (Berkeley: University of California Press, 1989), 141–148.
37. See Margaret Cohen, "Narratology in the Archive of Literature," *Representations* 108, no. 1 (2009): 51–75.
38. Fredric Jameson, "Third-World Literature in the Era of Multinational Capitalism," *Social Text* 15 (1986): 79.
39. See Aijaz Ahmad, "Jameson's Rhetoric of Otherness and the 'National Allegory,'" and Fredric Jameson, "A Brief Response," *Social Text* 17 (1987): 3–25 and 26–27.
40. See Pierre Bourdieu, *The Rules of Art*, trans. Susan Emanuel (Stanford, CA: Stanford University Press, 1995).
41. Franco Moretti, "Conjectures on World Literature," in *Distant Reading* (London: Verso, 2013), 50. The notion that the novel transforms local materials with the advent of modernity could, moreover, be used to explain the ways in which older literary forms, such as the epic and romance, were important foils in conceptualizing the cultural work of the novel in the West, from the first emergence of novel theory.
42. Moretti, "The Novel: History and Theory," in *Distant Reading*, 176.
43. Bakhtin, "Forms of Time and of the Chronotope in the Novel," in *The Dialogic Imagination*, 254.
44. Ibid., 240.

FURTHER READING

Narrative has no beginning or end, and it often seems that the same is true for writing about narrative. The best guides to further reading are the endnotes to the essays in this volume, where the reader will find a great diversity of material. In general, texts referenced in the endnotes have not been included in this bibliography, which focuses mostly on books. The reader should take this list as a supplement to the volume as a whole rather than a shortcut to the major writings in narrative theory, though the items listed under "Introductions and Guides" and "Anthologies and Reference Works" give excellent primers (sometimes addressing subjects, such as music and law, that are not included in this volume). These entries are suggestive rather than comprehensive; for ease of use, they are limited to a very few select items. For further references, see the Chronology to this volume.

Introductions and Guides

Abbott, H. Porter. *The Cambridge Introduction to Narrative*. Second ed. Cambridge: Cambridge University Press, 2008.

Bal, Mieke. *Narratology: Introduction to the Theory of Narrative*. Second ed. Toronto: University of Toronto Press, 1997.

Fludernik, Monika. *An Introduction to Narratology*. New York, NY: Routledge, 2009.

Herman, Luc and Bart Vervaeck. *Handbook of Narrative Analysis*. Lincoln: University of Nebraska Press, 2005.

Puckett, Kent. *Narrative Theory: A Critical Introduction*. Cambridge: Cambridge University Press, 2016.

Rimmon-Kenan, Shlomith. *Narrative Fiction: Contemporary Poetics*. London: Routledge, 1989.

Scholes, Robert, James Phelan, and Robert Kellogg. *The Nature of Narrative: Fortieth Anniversary Edition, Revised and Expanded*. New York, NY: Oxford University Press, 2006.

Recent Anthologies and Reference Works

Greene, Roland, ed. *The Princeton Encyclopedia of Poetry and Poetics*. Fourth ed. Princeton, NJ: Princeton University Press, 2012.

Herman, David. *The Cambridge Companion to Narrative*. Cambridge: Cambridge
University Press, 2007.
Herman, David, Manfred Jahn, and Marie-Laure Ryan. *Routledge
Encyclopedia of Narrative Theory*. London: Routledge, 2005.
Herman, David, James Phelan, Peter J. Rabinowitz, Brian Richardson, and Robyn
R. Warhol. *Narrative Theory: Core Concepts and Critical Debates*. Columbus:
Ohio State University Press, 2012.
Phelan, James and Peter J. Rabinowitz. *A Companion to Narrative Theory*.
Oxford: Blackwell, 2005.
Warhol, Robyn and Susan S. Lanser. *Narrative Theory Unbound: Queer and
Feminist Interventions*. Columbus: Ohio State University Press, 2015.

Any journal devoted to the study of culture deals in one way or another with
narrative. Following are those titles that often publish articles contributing to
the field of narrative theory: *Critical Inquiry* (University of Chicago Press), *Film
Quarterly* (University of California Press), *Journal of Narrative Theory* (Eastern
Michigan University), *Narrative* (official journal of the International Society for
the Study of Narrative, Ohio State University Press), *Novel: A Forum on
Fiction* (Duke University Press), *Poetics Today* (Duke University Press), and
Screen (Oxford University Press).

Book Series

All of the major university and academic presses publish significant work in
narrative theory. Ohio State University Press hosts the influential series Theory
and Interpretation of Narrative – edited by James Phelan, Peter J. Rabinowitz,
and Robyn Warhol – which has published major titles since 1989. University of
Nebraska Press has published many important monographs in its Frontiers of
Narrative series, edited by Jesse E. Matz.

Narrative Theory's *Longue Durée*

Of the books that take the long historical view of narrative theory, and of
theory and criticism more generally, the following stand out: Peter Brooks,
Reading for the Plot: Design and Intention in Narrative (Cambridge, MA:
Harvard University Press, 1992); Andrew Cole, *The Birth of Theory*
(Chicago, IL: University of Chicago Press, 2014); Sarah Kofman, *Nietzsche
and Metaphor*, trans. Duncan Large (Stanford, CA: Stanford University Press,
1993); Amélie Rorty, ed. *Essays on Aristotle's* Poetics (Princeton, NJ: Princeton
University Press, 1992); and Raymond Williams, *Marxism and Literature*
(Oxford: Oxford University Press, 1978).

Questions of Scale

Narrative scale is dealt with, as a matter of course, in all work on narrative. Studies that foreground the problem of scale, from diverse critical perspectives, include the following: Theodor Adorno, *In Search of Wagner*, trans. Rodney Livingstone (London: Verso, 2005); Matthew Garrett, *Episodic Poetics: Politics and Literary Form after the Constitution* (New York, NY: Oxford University Press, 2014); André Jolles, *Simple Forms*, trans. Peter J. Schwartz (London: Verso, 2017); Franco Moretti, *Modern Epic: The World System from Goethe to García Márquez*, trans. Quintin Hoare (London: Verso, 1996), and *The Way of the World: The Bildungsroman in European Culture*, trans. Albert Sbragia (new ed., London: Verso, 2000); James Phelan, *Reading People, Reading Plots: Character, Progression, and the Interpretation of Narrative* (Columbus: Ohio State University Press, 1989); and Alex Woloch, *The One vs. the Many: Minor Characters and the Space of the Protagonist in the Novel* (Princeton, NJ: Princeton University Press, 2003).

Shklovsky's Theory of Narrative

For the overall scope of Soviet and Russian literary theory, see *A History of Russian Literary Theory and Criticism*, ed. Evgeny Dobrenko and Galin Tihanov (Pittsburgh, PA: University of Pittsburgh Press, 2011). Although they are cited elsewhere in the present volume, it bears repeating that the two best general English-language guides to Russian Formalism remain Victor Erlich, *Russian Formalism* (The Hague: Mouton, 1955), and Fredric Jameson, *The Prison-House of Language: A Critical Account of Structuralism and Russian Formalism* (Princeton, NJ: Princeton University Press, 1972). For further reflection on plot in line with the discussion of Shklovsky's work in the present volume, see Shklovsky, *Energy of Delusion: A Book on Plot*, trans. Shushan Avagyan (Champaign, IL: Dalkey Archive Press, 2007).

Adventures in Structuralism

For a good map of the basic terrain see Jonathan Culler, *Structuralist Poetics: Structuralism, Linguistics, and the Study of Literature* (Ithaca, NY: Cornell University Press, 1975), and *On Deconstruction: Theory and Criticism after Structuralism* (Ithaca, NY: Cornell University Press, 1982). The best history is François Dosse, *History of Structuralism*, 2 vols., trans. Deborah Glassman (Minneapolis: University of Minnesota Press, 1997). The best short studies of Barthes are D. A. Miller, *Bringing Out Roland Barthes* (Berkeley: University of California Press, 1992), and Jonathan Culler, *Roland Barthes: A Very Short Introduction* (Oxford: Oxford University Press, 2002). Genette has yet to receive his due; the reader is advised to examine his works beyond *Narrative Discourse*, starting with *The Architext: An Introduction*, trans. Jane E. Lewin (Berkeley: University of California Press, 1992); *Paratexts: Thresholds of Interpretation*, trans. Jane E. Lewin (Cambridge: Cambridge University Press, 1997);

and *Palimpsests: Literature in the Second Degree*, trans. Channa Newman and Claude Doubinsky (Lincoln: University of Nebraska Press, 1997).

Feminist Foundations

For readers seeking a deeper engagement with the feminist theories of narrative that seek to challenge or supersede the sexual binary, the following books are a useful starting place: Marianne Hirsch, *The Mother/Daughter Plot: Narrative, Psychoanalysis, Feminism* (Bloomington: Indiana University Press, 1989); Molly Hite, *The Other Side of the Story: Structures and Strategies of Contemporary Feminist Narratives* (Ithaca, NY: Cornell University Press, 1989); Barbara Johnson, *The Feminist Difference: Literature, Psychoanalysis, Race, and Gender* (Cambridge, MA: Harvard University Press, 1998); Susan Sniader Lanser, *Fictions of Authority: Women Writers and Narrative Voice* (Ithaca, NY: Cornell University Press, 1992); Elizabeth A. Meese, *(Sem)erotics: Theorizing Lesbian: Writing* (New York, NY: New York University Press, 1992); and Trinh T. Minh-ha, *Woman, Native, Other: Writing Postcoloniality and Feminism* (Bloomington: Indiana University Press, 1989).

Philosophies of History

For a few perspectives on the basic issues from diverse positions, the reader may consult: Marc Bloch, *The Historian's Craft*, trans. Peter Putnam (New York, NY: Alfred A. Knopf, 1953); Joan Copjec, *Read My Desire: Lacan against the Historicists* (Cambridge, MA: MIT Press, 1994); Georg G. Iggers, *Historiography in the Twentieth Century: From Scientific Objective to the Postmodern Challenge* (Middletown, CT: Wesleyan University Press, 2005); Reinhart Koselleck, *Futures Past: On the Semantics of Historical Time*, trans. Keith Tribe (Cambridge, MA: MIT Press, 1990); Georg Lukács, *History and Class Consciousness: Studies in Marxist Dialectics*, trans. Rodney Livingstone (Cambridge, MA: MIT Press, 1971); and Enzo Traverso, *Left-Wing Melancholia: Marxism, History, and Memory* (New York, NY: Columbia University Press, 2016).

Character

Two extraordinary recent works have set the course for the theory of character into the foreseeable future: John Frow, *Character and Person* (Oxford: Oxford University Press, 2014), and Alex Woloch, *The One vs. the Many: Minor Characters and the Space of the Protagonist in the Novel* (Princeton, NJ: Princeton University Press, 2003). Readers should also consult James Phelan, *Reading People, Reading Plots: Character, Progression, and the Interpretation of Narrative* (Chicago, IL: University of Chicago Press, 1989); Saidiya V. Hartman, *Scenes of Subjection: Terror, Slavery, and Self-Making in Nineteenth-Century America* (New York, NY: Oxford University Press, 1997);

and, for a theory of character and film, Karla Oeler, *A Grammar of Murder: Violent Scenes and Film Form* (Chicago, IL: University of Chicago Press, 2009).

Time

Two important, recent works at the edge of the essay in this volume are David Wittenberg, *Time Travel: The Popular Philosophy of Narrative* (New York, NY: Fordham University Press, 2013), and Mark Currie, *The Unexpected: Narrative Temporality and the Philosophy of Surprise* (Edinburgh: University of Edinburgh Press, 2013).

Pleasure

The foundational (and anti-foundational) text is Sigmund Freud, *Beyond the Pleasure Principle*, trans. James Strachey (New York, NY: W.W. Norton, 1961). See also Julia Kristeva, *Desire in Language: A Semiotic Approach to Literature and Art*, trans. Thomas Gora and Alice A. Jardine, ed. Leon S. Roudiez (New York, NY: Columbia University Press, 1982); Caroline Levine and Mario Ortiz-Robles, ed., *Narrative Middles: Navigating the Nineteenth-Century Novel* (Columbus: Ohio State University Press, 2011); and D. A. Miller, *Narrative and Its Discontents: Problems of Closure in the Traditional Novel* (Princeton, NJ: Princeton University Press, 1981).

Race and Narrative Poetics

Beyond the comprehensive references in this volume's essay, and for extensions of the argument in different directions, see: Marcial González, *Chicano Novels and the Politics of Form: Race, Class, and Reification* (Ann Arbor: University of Michigan Press, 2008); Saidiya V. Hartman, *Scenes of Subjection: Terror, Slavery, and Self-Making in Nineteenth-Century America* (New York, NY: Oxford University Press, 1997); Fred Moten, *In the Break: The Aesthetics of the Black Radical Tradition* (Minneapolis: University of Minnesota Press, 2003); José Esteban Muñoz, *Cruising Utopia: The Then and There of Queer Futurity* (New York: New York University Press, 2009); and Amy C. Tang, *Repetition and Race: Asian American Literature after Multiculturalism* (New York, NY: Oxford University Press, 2016).

Queer Narrative Theory

Studies that extend the work of this chapter include: Christopher Looby, "John Marcher's Queer Timing." *Henry James Review* 33 (2012): 265–271; Barry McCrea, *In the Company of Strangers: Family and Narrative in Dickens, Conan Doyle, Joyce, and Proust* (New York, NY: Columbia University Press, 2011); Nancy K. Miller, ed., *The Poetics of Gender* (New York, NY: Columbia University Press, 1986); Valerie Rohy, *Lost Causes: Narrative, Etiology, and Queer*

Theory (New York, NY: Oxford University Press, 2015); Matthew Tinkcom, *Working Like a Homosexual: Camp, Capital, Cinema* (Durham, NC: Duke University Press, 2002); Mikko Tuhkahnen, "Binding the Self: Baldwin, Freud, and the Narrative of Subjectivity." *GLQ: A Journal of Lesbian and Gay Studies* 7 (2001): 553–591; and Patricia White, *Uninvited: Classical Hollywood Cinema and Lesbian Representability* (Bloomington: Indiana University Press, 1999).

Screenarration

Among the many contributions to the study of narrative and film that resonate with this volume's essay, readers may especially consult: David Bordwell, *Narration in the Fiction Film* (Cambridge, MA: Harvard University Press, 1985) and Sergei Eisenstein, *Film Form*, trans. and ed. Jay Leyda (New York, NY: Harcourt, 1978). For more close looking consonant with the present volume's essay, see D. A. Miller, *Hidden Hitchcock* (Chicago, IL: University of Chicago Press, 2016), and Garrett Stewart, *Closed Circuits: Screening Narrative Surveillance* (Chicago, IL: University of Chicago Press, 2015).

Narrative Theory and the Lyric

Jonathan Culler's *Theory of the Lyric* (Cambridge, MA: Harvard University Press, 2015) may be the preeminent study for some time, and its argument may be read in productive tension with that of *The Lyric Theory Reader*, ed. Virginia Jackson and Yopie Prins (Baltimore, MD: Johns Hopkins University Press, 2013), and Virginia Jackson, *Dickinson's Misery: A Theory of Lyric Reading* (Princeton, NJ: Princeton University Press, 2005). See also Monique Morgan, *Narrative Means, Lyric Ends: Temporality in the Nineteenth-Century British Long Poem* (Columbus: Ohio State University Press, 2009).

Contemporary Formalisms

For a recent précis of the cognitive approach to narrative, and to culture more generally, see Lisa Zunshine, *Introduction to Cognitive Cultural Studies* (Baltimore, MD: Johns Hopkins University Press, 2010). For further considerations on deconstruction and narrative, see, among others, Daniel Punday, *Narrative after Deconstruction* (Albany, NY: SUNY Press, 2002).

Narrative Theory and Digital Games

Readers may wish to return to N. Katherine Hayles, *Electronic Literature: New Horizons for the Literary* (Notre Dame, IN: University of Notre Dame Press, 2008); Patrick Jagoda, *Network Aesthetics* (Chicago, IL: University of Chicago Press, 2016); and Mark J. P. Wolf and Bernard Perron, ed., *The Video Game Theory Reader* (New York, NY: Routledge, 2003).

Narrative Theory and Novel Theory

Readers will find guidance through the dense field of novel theory in collections such as *Theory of the Novel: A Historical Approach*, ed. Michael McKeon (Baltimore, MD: Johns Hopkins University Press, 2000); *The Novel: An Anthology of Criticism and Theory 1900–2000*, ed. Dorothy Hale (New York, NY: Wiley-Blackwell, 2005); and, crucially, *The Novel*, 2 vols., ed. Franco Moretti (Princeton, NJ: Princeton University Press, 2007).

INDEX

1,001 Nights, 52–53

Aarseth, Espen, 245n1
Abbott, H. Porter, 120
AberMUD (game), 234
Absent One (film theory), 195, 200n14
acrobatics, 54–55
actant (Greimas), 108. *See also* character
action, narrative, 30–31
Adam, Jean-Michel, 215n16
Adventure (game), 237
aesthetics, 8
affect, 146, 150n45
African American literature, 153, 154–155,
    157–159, 161, 164–165
Ahmad, Aijaz, 258–259
AIDS narrative, 172
Algee-Hewitt, Mark, 42n1
Alghieri, Dante, 19, 107
All-India Progressive Writers Association,
    166n5
allegory, 258–259
Allison, Dorothy, 172
Altman, Rick, 214n1
anachrony (Genette), 41, 69, 120, 175,
    221–223, 225–227
Anderson, Benedict, 255
Anderson, Perry, 98n1, 98n7, 100n32
Andrew, Dudley, 239
Anjaria, Ulka, 166n5
Ankersmit, Frank, 98n7
Anzaldúa, Gloria, 160, 167n12
arche-writing (Derrida), 227
Arendt, Hannah, 19
Aretino, Pietro, 135
aristocracy, 251–255, 256

Aristotle
    Aristotelian criticism, 220, 221, 223, 229,
        245n9
    on character, 107–108
    on content and form, 7, 100n28
    on mimesis, 225, 248
    on plot, 31, 33, 98n6, 120, 223
    on time, 222, 223
    on tragedy, 17–19
Armstrong, Nancy, 256
Asian American literature, 156–157, 158,
    161–163, 164
Atlas, James, 136
Auerbach, Erich, 252
Augustine, Saint, 24
Austen, Jane, 24, 249, 255
autobiography, 172–173

Baker, Houston A., Jr., 154
Bakhtin, Mikhail, 99n12, 100–101n33,
    131n29, 250–251, 254, 255, 259–260
Bal, Mieke, 121, 122, 124, 131n29
Baldwin, James, 171
ballad, 213
Balzac, Honoré de, 34, 63, 64, 169, 249,
    252, 256
Banfield, Ann, 214n12
Banville, John, 107
Baraka, Amiri, 156
Barthes, Roland, 61–67
    formation of narrative theory and, 21,
        29, 217
    narrative scale and, 31–35
    on history-writing, 90–95
    on narrative codes, 63–67, 187, 199n8, 204
    on narrative grammar, 50, 51, 225

Cambridge Companions to ...

AUTHORS

TOPICS

Printed in August 2022
by Rotomail Italia S.p.A., Vignate (MI) - Italy